OFF THE BENCH

TUN DATO' SERI ABDUL HAMID OMAR

OFF THE BENCH

Mrs Jenny:

Our Best Wishes and to your good health.

19-4-99

Pelanduk Publications

Published by,
Pelanduk Publications (M) Sdn Bhd
24 Jalan 20/16A 46300 Petaling Jaya
Selangor Darul Ehsan, Malaysia.

Address all correspondence to
Pelanduk Publications (M) Sdn Bhd
P.O. Box 8265, 46785 Kelana Jaya
Selangor Darul Ehsan, Malaysia.

Perpustakaan Negara Malaysia Cataloguing-in-Publication Data

Off the bench / Tun Dato' Seri Abdul Hamid Omar;
co-edited by S. Augustine Paul.
Includes index.
ISBN 967-978-545-9
1. Common law—Malaysia. 2. Construction industry—Law and legislation—Malaysia. 3. Freedom of the press—Malaysia.
4. Justice of the peace—Malaysia. I. Paul, S. Augustine. II. Title.
340.09595

Printed by Tien Wah Press (M) Sdn. Bhd.

PREFACE

OFF THE BENCH is a collection of some of the lectures, speeches and keynote addresses which I delivered both at formal and informal gatherings spanning a period of over a decade when not on the Bench. During that time I was serving as the Chief Justice of the High Court of Malaya (1984-1988) and as Lord President of the Supreme Court of Malaysia (1988-1994). The collection covers topics such as the Common Law, Construction Law, Industrial Relations, Freedom of the Press, The Role of Justices of Peace, International Humanitarian Law and a host of others.

As may be observed, these writings encompass a wide spectrum of subjects relevant to events and occasions ranging from proceedings at opening and closing of conferences, seminars and workshops; at various institutions of higher learning and at judicial conferences. They were also delivered to voluntary organizations like the Malaysian Press Institute, at Rotary Club functions, Red Crescent Society meetings and many others.

I believe that the publication is but an insignificant attempt on my part to provide readers with reading materials for their leisure time. What is important, however, is that with the publication of this book the speeches will be in a permanent form and will be accessible to the reading public. Above all I had them published for the sake of posterity.

I am indebted to Mr Augustine Paul who has, despite his busy schedule as the Chairman of the Special Commissioners of Income Tax, found time to assist me in the editing of this book. I am also thankful to the editorial staff of Pelanduk Publications for having published the book at such short notice. I am also grateful to Mr Faisal Kutty, my Secretary for over a decade, for the painstaking efforts he had taken to keep copies of all my writings in good order. I also appreciate the invaluable assistance rendered by Misses Evelyn Devadason, Esther Jeyaraj, Toong Jo-Ann and Toong Jo-Lin.

Tun Dato' Seri Abdul Hamid Omar

For my wife Azian,
my children and
all my grandchildren.

Yang Amat Berbahagia·Toh Puan Seri Azian bte Aiyub Ghazali.

CONTENTS

LIST OF STATUTES

TABLE OF CASES

INTERNATIONAL HUMANITARIAN LAW AND THE GENEVA CONVENTIONS: THE MALAYSIAN EXPERIENCE*

As this subject is not sufficiently well known, a great majority of people do not really understand what it means and, speaking for myself, I too know little of this branch of international law. I have only shown interest in it after I joined the Malaysian Red Crescent Society. Even then I am far from being an expert in this field. Whatever knowledge I have acquired on the subject is very basic and elementary. For the purposes of this talk I shall be making frequent references to a book entitled *The Principles of International Humanitarian Law*.

The International Humanitarian Law covers a very wide field and it is therefore quite impossible for me to speak on the subject in very great detail. I would thus confine my talk to certain areas of the law which I think would be of interest to you.

I shall begin by addressing you on the following matters which I have framed in the form of questions:–

(1) What is International Humanitarian Law? How is it defined? What are its origins, scope and fundamental principles?

(2) Is Malaysia a party (signatory) to the Geneva Conventions? Have any of their provisions ever been invoked in Malaysia? If so, under what circumstances did Malaysia experience them?

What is International Humanitarian Law?

Basically it is "that considerable *portion of international law* which owes its inspiration to a feeling for *humanity* and which is centred on the protection of the individual". (Jean Pictet at page 9). (Emphasis is mine).

The expression "Humanitarian Law" appears to have been designated by a combination of two ideas of a different character. They are legal and moral. The latter is in fact a transposition into international law of a consideration of a moral order more especially humanitarian.

**At The Forum For Police Officers And The Malaysian Red Crescent Society, Sarawak Branch On 21st October 1984 At Kuching, Sarawak.*

Looking at it more closely it can be seen that International Humanitarian Law can be broadly divided into two branches. They are:

(1) The law of war which constitutes all international legal provisions, written or customary, ensuring respect for the individual and his well-being; and

(2) Human Rights.

In International Humanitarian Law what are of considerable significance are the four Geneva Conventions concluded in 1949 for the protection of victims of war.

In the sphere of human rights the Proclamation of the Universal Declaration of Human Rights was made in 1948 and the European Convention of Human Rights came into existence in 1950. As you will gather from my address there is a distinction that can be drawn between the two i.e. the Geneva Conventions and the Human Rights Conventions.

It must be made clear that it is generally accepted that Humanitarian Law is no longer a mere branch of international law but is a province in its own right with a wide measure of autonomy. Having considered the definition of International Humanitarian Law I shall now deal with its specific aspects.

The Law of War

As I mentioned earlier this is one of the branches of International Humanitarian Law. The Law of War is the law that is designed to regulate hostilities and attenuate their hardships in so far as military necessity permits. This law may be subdivided into two categories: (1) The Law of The Hague (the law of war properly so-called); and (2) The Law of Geneva (humanitarian law properly so-called).

Tonight I shall deal in slightly greater detail with the latter i.e. The Law of Geneva. Be that as it may, it seems appropriate that I should also explain very briefly what is meant by The Law of The Hague (the law of war). The Law of The Hague is the law that determines the rights and duties of belligerents in the conduct of operations and limits the choice of the means of doing harm. These provisions were the result of The Hague Conventions of 1899, revised in 1907. The Hague Regulations also cover Conventions such as the St. Petersburg Declaration of 1868, prohibiting the use of certain projectiles in times of war and the Geneva Protocol of 1925 condemning asphyxiating, poisonous or other gases and bacteriological methods.

You will note that it is within the province of the Law of The Hague (the law of war) to ensure maximum protection for the civilian population against the dangers of indiscriminate warfare.

To add to my brief account on the Law of The Hague, may I also state that there are two fundamental principles of this law:

(1) Belligerents (aggressors or hostile parties) shall not inflict harm on their adversaries (enemies) out of proportion with the object of warfare, which is to destroy or weaken the military strength of the enemy; and

(2) Belligerents have limited choice in the means of inflicting damage on the enemy.

I shall now deal with the second category.

The Law of Geneva (Humanitarian Law properly so-called)

I shall examine this category of International Humanitarian Law in some detail. As you will obviously know this has everything to do with the Red Cross Movement. The object of the Law of Geneva is to safeguard (i) military personnel placed *hors de combat*, as well as (ii) persons not taking part in hostilities. To elaborate I can do no better than refer to the work of Jean Pictet where it is stated - "Since 1949, the Law of Geneva has been put in concrete form by the four Conventions of that name. This monumental legal work of over four hundred articles is at the same time the most recent codification and also the most complete of the standards giving protection to the individual in the case of armed conflict. Offering a more specifically humanitarian character, a primary element of civilization and peace, the Law of Geneva incarnates the very ideal of the Red Cross. It was moreover the International Committee in Geneva which gave it its initial impulse and origin. It is therefore sometimes called the 'Law of the Red Cross'."

You would have noticed, therefore, that it was the International Committee in Geneva which gave this category of law its initial impulse and origin. For this reason it is appropriate that at this point I relate to you very briefly the origin of this law. Before I do so I would stress that the International Humanitarian Law is undoubtedly of great concern to all of us as its aim is protecting man against the consequences of war. Pictet defines the scope of this law in the following words:

> "to alleviate the sufferings of all the victims of armed conflicts who are in the power of their enemy, whether wounded, sick, shipwrecked, prisoners of war or civilians."

For the first time in 1949, the Geneva Conventions covered individuals who did not belong to the fighting forces and who were neither wounded, sick, shipwrecked nor captives. The purpose of the new provisions was, to some extent, to prevent civilians from becoming the direct victims of war.

Pictet has pointed out the distinction between the Movement of Geneva and that of The Hague. He said that:

> "The Geneva texts have been drawn up solely for the benefit of the individual. Generally they do not accord rights between States. The case is otherwise for the laws of war, whose object is to regulate operations which are partly based on military necessity. Within Humanitarian Law (properly speaking) certain medico-legal circles distinguish an addition of an 'international medical law' covering the provisions which aim at ensuring medical relief which apply to the wounded, sick and medical personnel."

If one looks at the development of this category of the Humanitarian Law it will be noticed that until the middle of the 19th century agreements to protect the victims of war were of a merely temporary character, binding only upon the contracting parties thereto, and based on strict reciprocity. Basically they constitute purely military agreements, usually effective only for the duration of a particular conflict. The birth of Humanitarian Law, associated with the emergence of the Red Cross Movement, changed this state of affairs. From then on, States were bound by the universal treaty, applicable at all times and in all circumstances.

The origin of the International Humanitarian Law

I now turn to the origin of the International Humanitarian Law. In this regard I may fairly assume that those involved in the Red Cross or Red Crescent Movement will be sufficiently familiar with this part of the history of Red Cross.

Henry Dunant, a Swiss, in the year 1859, was traveling across the war-ravaged plains of Lombardy. He arrived in the vicinity of Solferino just after a terrible battle, and was horrified to see thousands of wounded soldiers abandoned without care, facing certain death. The idea of the Red Cross was born from that dreadful sight. After organizing relief activities on the spot, improvising them with the means at hand, Dunant undertook to tell the world what he had seen, by writing *A Memory of Solferino*.

In this story he proposed a remedy to the deficiencies of army medical services by training voluntary relief workers in peacetime and securing for them a "neutral" status, even on the battlefield. Four citizens of Geneva, Gustave Moynier, General Guillaume Henri Dufour, Dr. Louis Appiaa and Dr. Theodore Maunoir joined Dunant in setting up the "International Standing Committee for Aid to Wounded Soldiers", which subsequently became the International Committee of the Red Cross (ICRC). By dint of enthusiasm and perseverance, they succeeded in 1864 in persuading the Swiss Government to convene an international conference, in which the representatives of twelve States participated and the tangible result of which was the signing in that same year of the "Geneva Convention for the Amelioration of the Condition of the Wounded in Armies in the Field".

From then on, wounded and sick soldiers were to be rescued and cared for, with no adverse discrimination based upon the side to which they belonged. Medical personnel, equipment and installations were to be respected. They were to be identified by a distinctive emblem - a red cross on a white background. The first Geneva Convention, signed in 1864, marked the beginning of International Humanitarian Law. In 1899, at The Hague, another Convention was signed, adapting the principles of the Geneva Convention to warfare at sea. In 1906, the provisions of the 1864 Convention were improved and supplemented. In 1907, the Fourth Hague Convention defined the categories of combatants entitled to the status of prisoner of war when captured, and to a specified treatment during the whole period of their captivity. These three Conventions were reaffirmed and further developed in 1929. In 1949, the four Geneva Conventions which are at present in force were adopted. The Diplomatic Conference of 1949 was of vital importance for more than one reason. It not only adopted the "Geneva Convention Relative to the Protection of Civilian Persons in Time of War", but also carried out a revision of the three earlier Conventions, the texts of which were brought into harmony. The four 1949 Geneva Conventions I mentioned earlier containing some 400 articles, constitute a legal achievement of historic importance which for almost 35 years now has afforded protection for the countless victims of armed conflicts. You will therefore observe that since 1949, the Law of Geneva has been put on solid foundation by the four Geneva Conventions. Pictet describes the Geneva Conventions very appropriately as the law with humanitarian characters, the primary elements of civilization and peace, which incarnates the very ideals of the Red Cross.

I have so far dealt with the Law of The Hague (the law of war) and the Geneva Conventions both of which constitute one branch of the Humanitarian Law, the other being Human Rights.

Legislation on Human Rights

Now, before I proceed to deal with a brief analysis of the fundamental provisions of the Geneva Conventions, permit me to say a word on the object of legislation on Human Rights. Its object is to guarantee at all times the enjoyment of fundamental rights and liberties for all persons and to protect them from social evils.

I had mentioned earlier that a distinction is to be drawn between Human Rights and Humanitarian Law properly so-called. That which essentially distinguishes this field from the previous one is the fact that it finds its application in times of peace as well as in times of war. Here, the promoting institution on the universal level is not the Red Cross but the United Nations Organization, itself the successor of the League of Nations. Also contributing, in their geographical framework, are such movements as the Council of Europe and the organization of American States.

Under this wide heading, one can also add not only the codification of Human Rights laws, but also amongst others, the laws condemning slavery, the white-slave traffic and the drug traffic, the Convention relative to the status of refugees and, to a certain extent, labour legislation. (See Pictet - page 12).

As most of you probably know the Proclamation of the Universal Declaration of Human Rights, as a standard of achievement for all nations, was made on December 10, 1948 in the General Assembly of the United Nations whereupon all member countries were urged to publicise the text of the Declaration and to cause it to be disseminated, displayed, read and expounded.

Human Rights and the Malaysian Constitution

As we all know we have a chapter in our Constitution enshrining various articles relating to fundamental rights and liberties, for example, the right of everyone to life, liberty and security of person - (Article 5); that no one shall be held in slavery or servitude - (Article 6); that all are equal before the law and entitled to the equal protection of the law - (Article 8); that no one shall be banished or exiled - (Article 9); that everyone has the right to freedom of speech and expression - (Article 10); that everyone has the right to profess and practise his religion - (Article 11) and that no person shall be deprived of property save in accordance with law - (Article 13).

These provisions are to be found in Part Two of our Constitution. However, though not strictly pertinent to the subject of my talk tonight, I feel that while speaking of fundamental rights and liberties it is important that we should bear in mind that while the Constitution protects and guarantees the liberties of the people provisions governing social security are equally important. Lord Denning on one occasion said:

> "Presently freedom must be matched, of course, with social security, by which I mean the peace and good order of the community in which we live.

> The freedom of the just man is worth little to him if he can be preyed upon by the murderer or thief. Every society must have the means to protect itself from marauders. It must have powers to arrest, to search, and to imprison those who break the laws. So long as those powers are properly exercised, they are themselves the safeguards of freedom. The moral of it all is that a true balance must be kept between personal freedom on the one hand and social security on the other."

Basically the question is the manner of maintaining a proper balance between individual liberty and legal control. My view is that even those who prize their freedom most highly should be prepared to accept such restrictions, both being necessary and just.

I shall now deal with the fundamental principles of Humanitarian Law followed by the Geneva Conventions and the Malaysian exprience.

Fundamental Principles

Speaking of the fundamental principles of Humanitarian Law, you will see that they ensued as a result of a compromise between two opposing notions, the principle of humanity and the principle of necessity.

Bearing in mind these sources of Humanitarian Law, it is to be observed that humanity always requires action for man's good. On the other hand, the principle of necessity propounds that the maintenance of public order legitimates the use of force: the state of war justifies resort to violence. The fundamental concept of Humanitarian Law therefore is that respect for the individual and his well-being shall as far as possible be compatible with public order and in times of war, with military exigencies.

I shall now explore further the fundamental principles of the Law of Geneva, i.e. the Humanitarian Law properly so called. As I mentioned earlier, this law is to ensure that persons placed *hors de combat* shall be respected, protected and treated humanely. Under this category there emerged certain principles considered as proper for the victims of conflict. They are neutrality, normality and protection which shall be dealt with now.

(a) Neutrality

Under this head it is a fundamental principle that humanitarian assistance is never an interference in a conflict. Three aspects arise from its application. They are

(i) in exchange for the immunity granted to it, medical personnel should refrain from any hostile act;

(ii) medical personnel are given protection as healers and

(iii) no one shall be molested or convicted for having given treatment to the wounded or sick.

(b) **Normality**

The fundamental principle under this heading is that protected persons must be able to lead as normal a life as possible. Its rationale is that captivity is not a punishment but only a means of keeping an adversary from being in a position to do harm.

(c) **Protection**

Under this principle a State must ensure the protection, both national and international, of persons who have fallen into its power. This principle is to be applied in three ways as follows:

(i) the prisoner is not in the power of the troops who have captured him but of the State on which these depend;

(ii) the enemy State is responsible for the condition and upkeep of persons of whom it has guard and, in occupied territory, for the maintenance of order and public services;

(iii) the victims of conflict shall be provided with an international protector once they no longer have a natural protector.

Earlier I addressed you on the distinction between the Law of Geneva and Human Rights. Now I shall state briefly the principles that are common to both.

(a) **Inviolability**

The individual has the right of respect for his life and integrity, both physical and moral, and of the attributes inseparable from his personality. The areas of its application are:

(i) a man who has fallen in combat is inviolable and an enemy who surrenders shall have his life spared;

(ii) torture, degrading and inhuman punishment are forbidden;

(iii) everyone is entitled to recognition as a person before the law;

(iv) everyone has the right of respect for his honour, his family rights, his convictions and habits;

(v) anyone who is suffering shall be sheltered and receive the care which his condition requires;

(vi) everyone has the right to exchange news with his family and receive relief parcels; and

(vii) no one may be arbitrarily deprived of his own property.

(b) Non-discrimination

Individuals shall be treated without any distinction based on race, sex, nationality, language, social standing, wealth, political, philosophical or religious opinions or on any other criteria. Its scope of application is that differences in treatment should, however, be made for the benefit of individuals in order to counter inequalities resulting from their personal situation, their needs or their distress.

(c) Security

The third common principle is security. Everyone has the right to security of person. Its areas of application are:

(i) no one can be held responsible for an act he has not committed;

(ii) reprisals, collective punishment, the taking of hostages and deportations shall be prohibited;

(iii) each person shall benefit from legal guarantees recognised by civilized peoples; and

(iv) no one can abrogate the rights which the humanitarian Conventions accord him.

In view of time constraint, I have merely stated the main points without elaborating on them. However, I feel that they would suffice for the time being.

(d) Additional Protocols I and II

I wish, however, to draw your attention to two additional principles described as Protocols I and II. They were adopted by the Diplomatic Conference in 1977. Protocol I relates to Protection of Victims of International Armed Conflicts and Protocol II relates to the Protection of Victims of Non-International Conflicts. Malaysia has indicated agreement to Protocol II. There are 102 articles in Protocol I and 28 articles in Protocol II. It would take some time if I were to explain all these. Therefore I propose not to deal with them.

Malaysia and the Geneva Conventions

I return to the Geneva Conventions. Malaysia is a signatory to the Geneva Conventions. Indeed in 1961 a Bill entitled the Geneva Conventions was tabled in Parliament. It was stated therein that it is "An act to enable effect to be given to certain International Conventions done at Geneva on the Twelfth day of August, Nineteen Hundred and Forty-Nine, and for purposes connected therewith". The Explanatory Statement states that the "Bill is designed to adopt the four Conventions signed at Geneva on 12th August, 1949, dealing respectively with wounded and sick members of the armed forces in the field, with wounded, sick and shipwrecked members of the armed forces at sea, with treatment of prisoners of war, and with protection of civilian persons in time of war. These conventions are set out in the four Schedules".

The Geneva Conventions as contained in and by reason of the Geneva Conventions Act 1962 have now become part of our law. And Malaysia is a party to it. The question that arises now is whether the Geneva Conventions or any part of them have ever been invoked in Malaysia. The answer is yes.

You will recollect that some time in September 1964 there was an Indonesian invasion of Malaysia. This was during the Indonesian confrontation when members of an armed force of their paratroopers wearing camouflage uniform under the command of the Indonesian Air Force were dropped in Johore by parachutes. They carried firearms, ammunitions, hand grenades, food rations and other military equipments. Of the main party thirty-four out of the forty-eight were Indonesian soldiers and fourteen were Malaysian Chinese. Twelve of the fourteen were charged in court and they claimed trial. In one of these cases, *Lee Hoo Boon* v *Public Prosecutor* (1966) 2 MLJ 167 the accused was charged and convicted on charges of consorting with armed Indonesians and for being in possession of arms and ammunition in contravention of sections 57(1) (a), (b) and 58(1) of the Internal Security Act, 1960. In the appeal by the accused to the Federal Court one of the grounds of appeal considered by the Court, in fact the only one which gave the Court some concern, was whether the accused, a Malaysian national, was a prisoner of war and thereby entitled to the benefit of the Geneva Conventions under the Geneva Conventions Act 1962. Thomson, L.P. sitting with Harley, Ag. C.J. (Borneo) and Raja Azlan Shah, J. (as he then was) had this to say at p.169,

> "In our view the Geneva Conventions are to be read in the light of that statement which after all is a statement of a principle of international law by a

recognised authority and read in that light the present appellant is not entitled to the protection of the Conventions even if he did become a member of the Indonesian Armed Forces because he was a traitorous subject of the Ruler of the State of Johore and was engaged in assisting the Republic of Indonesia in armed conflict with this country of which Johore is part."

Thomson, L.P. referred to the argument that on the evidence the accused was a member of the Indonesian military forces and in reply to that his Lordship said,

> "He had associated himself with them. He had been trained by them. He formed part of an organised company with them. He was wearing Indonesian uniform. He was carrying weapons. Then it was also argued that the relationship between this country and the Republic of Indonesia if it did not amount to actual war in the conventional Grotian sense amounted to a state of hostilities as envisaged by the Geneva Conventions of 1949 relating to prisoners of war. Therefore in the circumstances the appellant was entitled to the benefit of these Conventions to which this country is a party and which have become part of our municipal law by reason of the Geneva Conventions Act, 1962."

The Court found that he was not entitled to the protection. The judgment was founded on the basis that the accused was a Johore national. In this connection Thomson, L.P. said:

> "There is, however, one other relevant fact and that is that on the appellant's own admission he was born in the State of Johore. There is no other evidence having any bearing on his national status and from the admitted fact that he was born in the State of Johore then in the absence of anything to the contrary it must be presumed that whatever the position as regards citizenship he is at all material times a Johore national."

As for the Geneva Conventions the court pronounced to this effect.

> "With regard to the Conventions I would observe that they are a treaty or, at any rate, an international agreement analogous to a treaty and treaties are not to be interpreted in the same way as ordinary contracts. What I have in mind is better said by Professor Keith in *Wheaton's Elements of International Law* (6th Ed.) at page 522:-
>
> > 'The general principle is that treaties, being compacts (sic) between nations, are not to be subjected to the minute interpretation which in private law may result in defeating through technical construction the real purpose of the negotiators.'
>
> Bearing that in mind we are entitled to conclude that the parties to the Geneva Conventions had in mind the general principles of international law and of the law of nations and on the particular point with which we are concerned here I would read a passage by Dr. Lauterpacht from *Oppenheim's In-*

ternational Law (7th Ed.). He discusses in Chapter VI the armed forces of the belligerents in general and their privileges in particular and he concludes with the following passage (p.268):

> 'The privileges of members of armed forces cannot be claimed by members of the armed forces of a belligerent who go over to the forces of the enemy and are afterwards captured by the former. They may be, and always are, treated as criminals. The same applies to traitorous subjects of a belligerent who, without having been members of his armed forces, (that is their own armed forces) fight in the armed forces of the enemy. Even if they appear under the protection of a flag of truce, deserters and traitors may be seized and punished'."

In two other cases *Ooi Hee Koi v Public Prosecutor* and *Ooi Wan Yui* v *Public Prosecutor*, (1966) 2 MLJ 183 the two accused were also convicted under the Internal Security Act 1960 for consorting with armed Indonesians and for being in possession of firearms and ammunition. They claimed to be prisoners of war and the question was whether they had the benefit of the protection. The Federal Court in a differently constituted panel from the case I referred to earlier adverted to the facts which were almost similar to the facts attended to in *Lee Hoo Boon's* case in that they were members of the Armed Forces of forty-seven paratroopers, under the command of Lieutenant Sutikno of the Indonesian Air Force, who in the early hours of September 2, 1964, were dropped from a Hercules plane belonging to the Indonesian Air Force over the Labis area of Johore. All members of this invasion force were in camouflage uniform and carried firearms, ammunitions, hand grenades, etc. Here, too, the question of protection under the Geneva Conventions was considered by the Court and in its judgment it stated that the appellants' claim to be prisoners of war made it necessary to refer to the definition of that term in Article 4 of the Third Schedule to the Geneva Conventions Act, 1962, the relevant portion of which reads:

> "Prisoners of war, in the sense of the present Convention, are persons belonging to one of the following categories, who have fallen into the power of the enemy:
>
> > (1) Members of the armed forces of a Party to the conflict as well as members of militias or volunteer corps forming part of such armed forces."

The Court went on to say that this category includes members of volunteer corps forming part of the armed forces of a party to the conflict. The Court observed that the evidence of the prosecution left no room for doubt that the appellants were in fact members of the Indonesian armed forces commanded by

Lieutenant Sutikno, whether as volunteers or as conscripts. And that being the case, the appellants ought *prima facie* to be regarded as prisoners of war unless there were circumstances which disentitled them to treatment as such. The Court then referred to the judgment of Thomson, L.P. and after citing certain passages of that judgment pronounced that with respect it did not agree with that judgment. The Court had this to say:

> "Lee Hoo Boon did not automatically become a citizen of the Federation of Malaya merely by reason of his being born in the State of Johore: see articles 14(1) (a), 16, 18(1) of the Constitution of the Federation of Malaya. Not being 'Malay' as defined in the Johore Nationality Enáctment, 1952, his birth within the State of Johore did not *per se* clothe him with the status of a national of that State: see sections 2, 4(c) & (f) and (5) of the Enactment. We do not think that any fact may be presumed when the onus of proving such fact lies on the prosecution."

It would seem to me that the Court was proceeding upon the basis that only 'traitorous subjects' are disentitled to the benefits of the Geneva Conventions. The Court expressed the view that in the case of *Ooi Wan Yui*, one of the accused, there was uncontroverted evidence that he was born in China and there was not an iota of evidence to prove that he owed allegiance to His Majesty the Yang Di-Pertuan Agong. Furthermore he was alleged by the prosecution, supported by evidence, to be a member of the Indonesian armed forces. It is interesting to note that the Court held that the onus did not rest on him to prove that he was not a subject of or by reason of his past residence owe allegiance to His Majesty the Yang Di-Pertuan Agong. The Court also expressed the view that long residence alone is insufficient to found allegiance.

In the final analysis it was the Court's finding that the prosecution failed to prove that the accused was a person who owed allegiance and consequently he should have been held a prisoner of war and was entitled to the same treatment accorded to Lieutenant Sutikno and the Indonesians under his command.

As for the second accused Ooi Hee Koi who held a blue identity card and classified as Warganegara Persekutuan but born in China the Court posed this question:

> "Is the question of Ooi's allegiance resolved by the mere production of his identity card?"

The Court answered it in the negative stating that proof of birth rested on the prosecution and there being no such proof the second accused therefore stood on the same footing as the first accused.

The matter was resolved by the Privy Council in *P.P.* v *Oie Hee Koi & Associated Appeals* (1968) 1 MLJ 148.

In all these cases the accused were Malaysian Chinese born or settled in Malaysia but whose nationality had not been proved. They were all captured during the Indonesian confrontation campaign against Malaysia having landed and infiltrated into Malaysian territory. They were armed and accompanied by Indonesian military personnel. All were tried and convicted under the Internal Security Act. On appeal to the Federal Court all appeals except the two *Oie Hee Koi* and *Ooi Wan Yui* were dismissed. At the hearing before the Privy Council, ".... the accused argued (a) that the provisions of the Geneva Convention were also applicable to Malaysian nationals or persons owing allegiance; and (b) that any contrary customary international law denying the status of prisoners of war to such individuals had been abrogated by the Geneva Convention." The Privy Council held (Lord Guest and Sir Garfield Barwick dissenting) that:

(1) the Geneva Convention does not extend the protection given to prisoners of war to nationals of the detaining power. The same principle applies to persons who, though not nationals of, owe a duty of allegiance to the detaining power;

(2) the Geneva Convention had not changed or abrogated customary international law on this question;

(3) no question of mistrial exists where the accused did not raise a doubt whether they were entitled to treatment as protected prisoners of war and where no claim had been made to provide any basis for the court to apply; no burden lay on the prosecution, but the onus was on the accused to prove that they were so entitled.

Lord Hodson (delivering the majority judgment) referred to the Geneva Convention relative to the treatment of prisoners of war (3rd Schedule, Geneva Convention Act 1962) and the definition of a protecting power and then proceeded to observe that the Act does not indicate directly whether or not a protected prisoner of war includes nationals of or persons owing allegiance to the captor State. His Lordship further observed as follows:

> "Reference to the protecting power does indicate indirectly that the prisoner of war whose interest is to be protected is a national of some state other than the captor state, or a member of the forces of a party to the conflict but this leaves open the question whether prisoner of war status can be claimed by persons in the latter category who are nationals of or owe allegiance to the captor state."

A thorough examination was made of Article 4 of the Convention to ascertain the extent of the protection. In doing so it was observed that:

"Article 4 of the Convention is general in its terms and on its face is capable of including the nationals of the detaining power who are captured by that power."

The Privy Council also observed that the trials of the accused were conducted on the assumption that there was an armed conflict between Malaysia and Indonesia bringing the Convention into operation. Further there was an assumption that both Malaysia and Indonesia are parties to the Convention. Upon these premises the Privy Council concluded that whether any individual accused was entitled, under the Act of 1962, to be treated as a protected prisoner of war, would depend upon the following:

"(1) Whether, as a matter of fact he was a member of the armed forces of Indonesia or of a volunteer corps forming part of such armed forces and if so

(2) Whether, as a matter of law, the Convention, and consequently the Act, applies to persons of Malaysian nationality or owing allegiance to Malaysia

(3) Whether, as a matter of fact, he was a national of Malaysia or a person owing allegiance to Malaysia."

The Privy Council dealt at length with the issues and in the course of the judgment approved that passage on page 268 of volume 2 of the 7th edition of *Oppenheim's International Law*, as was cited by Thomas, L.P. in his judgment which I have referred to earlier. A number of authorities were also analysed and it was the view of the majority that:

"A study of the Convention relative to the treatment of prisoners of war leads to a strong inference that it is an agreement between states primarily for the protection of the members of the national forces of each against the other.

Each of these articles appears to rest upon the assumption that a 'prisoner of war' is not a 'national of the detaining power'. Moreover the reference to the duty of allegiance might fairly suggest the further inference that a person who owes this duty to a detaining power is not entitled to prisoner of war treatment. If the matter rested on inference from these articles alone, the argument might not be conclusive, but as has been shown, the inference so to be drawn coincides, as regards nationals of the detaining power, with commonly accepted international law."

To conclude I would refer briefly to the case of *Osman & Anor* v *Public Prosecutor* (1968) 2 MLJ 137. The accused persons, tried in Singapore (then part of Malaysia), were convicted of the murder of three civilians by planting explosives in a building called MacDonald House in Orchard Road, Singapore. Their appeals to the Federal Court were dismissed. The matter went up to the Privy

Council. The question of right to status as prisoner of war was considered and the Privy Council held, dismissing the appeal, that under the law it was clear that the appellants, if they were members of the Indonesian armed forces, were not entitled to be treated on capture as prisoners of war under the Geneva Convention when they had landed to commit sabotage and had been dressed in civilian clothes both when they placed the explosives and lit them and when they were arrested. The appeal was heard on the basis that the Convention applied to Singapore and that at the time there was a state of armed conflict between Indonesia and Malaysia. The Federal Court held that there could not be the least doubt that the explosion at MacDonald House was not only an act of sabotage but one totally unconnected with the necessities of war and therefore the accused were not prisoners of war. The Privy Council considered the question in great detail and had regard to certain regulations in the Laws and Customs of War on Land of 1907, Article 4 of the Geneva Convention as to categories of persons entitled to treatment as prisoners of war and came to the conclusion that it does not suffice in every case to establish membership of an armed force to become entitled on capture to treatment of a prisoner of war and that the donning of civilian clothes by soldiers to commit sabotage would deprive them of the status of privileged belligerents.

That in a nutshell is a brief dissertation of International Humanitarian law and the Geneva conventions viewed from the Malaysian experience.

THE PROBLEMS IN THE ADMINISTRATION OF JUSTICE IN THE SUBORDINATE COURTS*

Today I shall speak to you on the topic entitled "The Problems in the Administration of Justice in the Subordinate Courts". The scope of the subject is very wide and I do not think I am exaggerating when I say that there are many problems. A lot of time would be taken up if I am to deal with each and every one of the problems in great detail. In view of the time constraint, I propose only to highlight some of these problems and then allow you to discuss them with a view to exploring ways and means of effectively solving them. I hope to convey to you some of my views on certain matters and put forward my suggestions, and when I do so you should not hesitate to analyse them and make your own comments and suggestions.

These problems could be either common or specific. Common problems are the perennial ones such as delays in the disposal of cases, omission or failure to write judgments, delays in the writing of grounds of judgment and so forth. Specific problems are those which concern the conduct or behaviour of a President or Magistrate in connection with a particular incident or those which relate to a failure or omission to perform or give effect to a certain judicial function. Common problems are invariably recurrent and require vigilant and effective action. Specific problems on the other hand are those which, first of all, have to be looked into before any further action could be taken in the matter. Before I highlight some of the problems in the administration of justice in the subordinate courts it seems appropriate that I should remind you of some of the fundamental principles pertinent to the administration of justice.

Fundamental principles pertinent to the administration of justice

When we speak of administration of justice we are referring to the exercise of judicial and legal functions in the courts. The authority to administer justice is derived from the Federal Constitution where it is provided that the judicial power of the Federation shall be vested in the two High Courts (Malaya and Borneo) of co-ordinate jurisdiction and status and in such inferior courts as may be provided by federal law. The inferior courts, commonly and usually re-

---

**At The Conference Of Presidents, Sessions Courts And Magistrates On 19th April, 1985 At Merlin Hotel, Bukit Fraser.*

ferred to as the subordinate courts, are the Sessions Courts and the Magistrates' Courts (the Penghulus' Courts have now ceased to function). They are established under the Subordinate Courts Act 1948 which is a federal law. It provides for matters such as the establishment of these courts and the legal limits within which they operate. In other words these courts exercise their function to dispense justice within the limits provided by law. What appears clear is that the administration of justice in these courts is not only a part of the country's judicial and legal system but is also as important as the administration of justice in the superior courts.

Fundamentally, therefore, these courts are equally responsible to see that the independence of the iudiciary is maintained. I am sure you do appreciate that this concept is crucial to the administration of justice. This concept has to be fully understood if we are to appreciate what is really demanded of us in order to execute our judicial functions to administer and dispense justice in accordance with the rule of law. I must add, however, that independence of the judiciary would mean nothing if those who carry out judicial functions do not possess the necessary integrity to uphold the concept. It is only when there is integrity that you can dispense justice without fear or favour.

Courts to administer justice impartially

Primarily it is the duty of the courts to administer justice impartially between citizen and citizen and between citizen and state according to law. In this respect there is no real distinction between the functions to be performed by Presidents, Magistrates and Judges of the High Court. Their functions are basically the same and therefore the proper approach is expected from Judges, Presidents and Magistrates alike to uphold the rule of law.

Closely related to the duty to administer justice impartially is the duty of each and every President and Magistrate to conduct himself in a manner consistent with the dignity and standing of his office. This is necessary if these judicial officers are to perform their judicial functions effectively and achieve the hallmarks of an independent judge. Some members of the public and lawyers have expressed concern about the increasing threats to the independence of the judiciary at all levels. This is understandable in view of what I have said earlier. To digress, may I say that lawyers are also involved in the administration of justice and conceivably they cannot play their role unless the courts before whom they practice are independent, competent and conscientious in the application of the law. The importance of an independent judiciary is critical as the community's interest would clearly depend not only on whether a Judge,

President or Magistrate can play and maintain the role of an impartial umpire but also by his conduct demonstrate the dignity and standing of his office.

As for conduct generally of judicial officers I would like to say that it is important that Presidents and Magistrates do not act in a manner that is likely to tarnish or lower the image of the Judiciary. There have been complaints in the past of certain Presidents and Magistrates making remarks in open court which were uncalled for. To my mind Presidents and Magistrates ought to refrain from making such remarks for by doing so it is not only they who lose the respect that they ought to command but also such conduct would tarnish the image of the judiciary.

Free from bias

In relation to the role of an impartial umpire I would like to point out a very significant element of that role, that is to say, that in order to do justice between the parties, it is necessary that a President or Magistrate when hearing a case should ensure that he is free from bias. An allegation of bias may emanate from or is likely to be levelled at a President or Magistrate by a party in a civil suit or an accused in a criminal case. An allegation of bias may result from the conduct of a President or Magistrate or may emerge from certain utterances he may have made in court or outside. These are the kind of problems that are described as specific problems. The conduct of a President or Magistrate which gives rise to an allegation that he is biased may well have been on account of his close association or intimate relation with a particular lawyer. I am not saying that a close association *per se* gives rise to a suspicion of bias but such a suspicion may in certain circumstances be justified especially in cases where a Magistrate not only maintains a very close association or intimate relationship with a particular lawyer who happens to appear before him frequently but also whose conduct is likely to arouse suspicion that that lawyer would be likely to receive special favour from the President or Magistrate. It is in a situation such as this that the party whose opponent is represented by a lawyer who is an intimate friend of the President or Magistrate may feel that he may not get a fair hearing and could not expect to get justice done in that court. A doubt of that sort raised in the mind of a party, however small it may be, where circumstances warrant, cannot be said to be insignificant or misconceived and cannot consequently be viewed lightly. In my opinion it is serious when viewed in the light of the well settled maxim that justice must not only be done but must manifestly be seen to be done. The question that consequently arises is thus: How should a President or Magistrate conduct himself? For myself I should think that every Magistrate who is entrusted with the responsibility of the administration of justice must appreciate the need to conduct himself in a manner that would not provide room or give rise to suspicion that justice cannot be meted out by him. The solution indeed lies with him. It is for the Magistrate to constantly remind himself of the need to uphold a certain standard of conduct as a judicial officer so as not to create the kind of situation that I described earlier. Be that as it may, what I have said does not mean that a Magistrate should be hostile to or be unfriendly with lawyers. I personally feel that it is necessary for courts to maintain a close rapport with members of the Bar generally for they too, as officers of the court, have a responsible role to play in the proper administration of justice.

Lawyers as officers of the court

I repeat that lawyers have a role to play in the administration of justice. In this respect they are expected, as officers of the court, to assist the court. If we are to succeed in our efforts to dispose of cases speedily and efficiently, lawyers ought to assist the courts to attain this objective. However, lawyers have on many instances sought postponement of cases on various grounds. In many cases the reasons advanced are flimsy and frivolous. This practice has contributed much to the delay in the disposal of cases. Indeed the problem has come to such a stage that I think we should consider rejecting requests for postponements made on grounds that a lawyer is required to appear in the High Court or Supreme Court or attend Parliament or State Assembly sittings and so forth. Clearly, if a lawyer is unable to appear in a case on those grounds, it is only proper that the case be handled by someone else who is able to do so. This is necessary in view of the increasing volume of cases which now come before the courts. As I have observed, this is one of the causes of the backlog of cases. There have also been many instances where postponements have been sought at the last minute. The adjournment of a case at that stage may result in the wastage of the days that have been set aside for the hearing of that particular case and it will not be possible for the courts to fix other cases at the last hour. Clearly, therefore, this is one of the areas where lawyers could co-operate and assist the court. If indeed there are valid reasons for a postponement, then lawyers should make it a point to see that an application is made as early as possible. Speaking of requests for postponements may I remind you of the direction, given by one of my predecessors, which I think should constantly be borne in mind by Presidents and Magistrates. I shall highlight some of the important issues with regard to postponements which should always be remembered:

(1) As there are many cases which are postponed in the subordinate courts, the habit of some Presidents and Magistrates of granting postponements

on flimsy and frivolous grounds at the instance of the prosecution, defence counsel or the court itself should be stopped.

(2) In some civil cases, counsel for the plaintiff or defendant are known to indulge in postponement of cases with the connivance of the court. This is a degrading practice.

(3) Postponement of a case already fixed for hearing should be an exception rather than the rule. Only in exceptional cases should an application for postponement at a short notice be granted. This is especially so in criminal cases where witnesses and accused persons have to attend court and a postponement at the last moment will cause great inconvenience to members of the public and result in a wastage of judicial time and public funds.

(4) If the prosecution or the defence are not ready to proceed with the case on the date fixed after reasonable adjournments have been granted, an accused person should not be allowed to suffer from the dilatoriness of the prosecutors or defence counsel by being left with the charge hanging over his head indefinitely.

(5) Where the prosecution or the defence are unable to proceed on account of difficulty in securing a witness or for some other reasonable cause but are able to satisfy the court that they will proceed within a reasonable time, a final adjournment may be granted.

(6) What are considered as reasonable grounds for granting an adjournment? How many adjournments are considered reasonable? The granting or refusal of requests for adjournments is a matter of the court's discretion. These are some of the guidelines to be followed in exercising that discretion:

   (a) If the ground advanced in an application for adjournment is reasonably foreseeable, no postponement should be granted.

   (b) Conversely, if the reason is not reasonably foreseeable, it should not be refused.

   (c) An exhaustive catalogue of all possible instances where adjournments should or should not be granted cannot possibly be given.

   (d) Examples where adjournments should be refused include cases where the prosecuting officer does not have the investigating papers or the investigating officer has failed to complete investigation without excuse or has failed to subpoena witnesses or is not free because of other engagements.

(e) Adjournments should however be granted where the prosecuting officer or defence counsel or any material witness is suddenly taken ill or where there is difficulty in tracing a witness.

(7) On the question of the number of adjournments that should be granted, the rule is that once a case is fixed for trial it should only be adjourned for a good cause:

(a) The court should be reluctant to grant a second adjournment particularly in criminal cases where the accused person is not on bail.

(b) Once the court has commenced a trial it should be carried on from day to day until the case is finally disposed of unless some unforseen circumstances occur during the trial whereby the granting of an adjournment becomes essential.

(c) The court must be firm in exercising its discretion in granting adjournments.

(d) Once a date of hearing has been fixed and the parties informed a maximum of three adjournments only should be allowed except where the accused is not on bail in which case it should be disposed of as early as possible. If the prosecution is not ready, the accused should be discharged.

(e) If the defence is not ready, the case must proceed as fixed with or without defence counsel.

(f) In civil cases if the plaintiff is not ready, the case should be dismissed or struck out; if the defendant is not ready, the plaintiff must proceed with his case and obtain judgment.

(8) More importantly, the court should bear in mind that it should not be the cause of the postponement especially in cases where the grounds advanced are flimsy and frivolous. The court's main duty is to hear and dispose of cases without delay. A President or Magistrate should not postpone a case simply because he or she wants to have a staff meeting or attend to some administrative or personal matter.

Part-heard cases

I direct your attention to this matter with a view to creating a greater awareness on the need to observe Practice Directions and other guidelines given from time to time to assist you in adopting the right approach in hearing a case. They are aimed at improving efficiency in the performance of your judicial functions.

You will appreciate the seriousness of the problem if we allow too many part-heard cases to remain pending. Administratively the difficulty created is that if a Magistrate who has started hearing a particular case is transferred to a new post as, say, a Deputy Public Prosecutor before the case is completed, he cannot continue to hear the part-heard case unless he is re-gazetted as a President or Magistrate as the case may be. Even if this is done, it does not seem to be a proper way to solve the problem. It should therefore be a practice that once a hearing is commenced, it should proceed until it is disposed of. A similar problem would also arise when a President or Magistrate with part-heard cases resigns from the service. In that event the part-heard cases would inevitably have to be tried *de novo*.

Apart from the administrative problem that I have highlighted, you will find that once a case is postponed to another date for continued hearing, especially if it is to be continued after a lapse of many months, the facts of the case may no longer be fresh and may have been forgotten. In that event it is inevitable that the Magistrate has to review the whole of the evidence recorded in order to refresh his memory. Even then, there would be a problem for invariably he would have lost much of the impressions that he had formed of a particular witness. This is crucial to the making of a decision, especially in cases where the outcome rests primarily on facts and credibility of witnesses. Viewed in that light, therefore, it is best to complete the hearing of a case once started and give judgment on the matter without delay. This is more so in criminal cases where there is always the likelihood of the accused being remanded in prison to await the outcome of a case even in bailable offences where the accused is unable to secure a bailor. A delay in the disposal of a case would mean that by the time the case is completed an accused would have served a considerable period of time in prison. It is basically for this reason, that in practice, courts give priority to criminal cases. The practice, however, should not be over-stretched as this would delay the disposal of civil cases.

Writing judgments and supplying grounds

One of the more serious problems in the administration of justice is the failure of Presidents and Magistrates to write judgments and supply grounds thereof. I am conscious of the fact that we are short of Magistrates and indeed they have to cope with a lot of work. However, writing judgments and supplying grounds of judgment where a party has appealed is part of the judicial function. If judgment is reserved in a particular case, delay in giving judgment would conceivably deny justice to either or both the parties. In a criminal case the delay may mean that an accused may have to spend more time than necessary in prison if he should eventually be acquitted. Similarly, where an accused has been convicted and given a custodial sentence and has appealed, the delay in writing the grounds of judgment would also mean that the accused would have to spend more time than necessary in prison if he should eventually be set free by the appellate court.

Generally speaking, the delay in delivering judgments or in supplying grounds of judgment would not only reflect the inefficiency on the part of the courts but would also tarnish the image of the judiciary. It is therefore the responsibility of each and every President and Magistrate to eradicate any unfavourable image that may be projected as a result of such delays.

Now, may I remind you that in an appeal an appellate court is primarily interested to know the main reasons for a decision. In a majority of cases it is quite unnecessary for a President or Magistrate to write lengthy judgments. Suffice, to my mind, if he should state the grounds shortly and very briefly. Reasons for a decision could even be recorded in the form of notes of finding in the note-book itself. In the event of an appeal, they could be supplied as grounds of decision. They should be sufficient for the appellate court to be informed of the reasons for a particular decision. Similarly, in criminal cases the reasons could be reduced to writing before recording a conviction and passing sentence. I am of the view that it is not too difficult to do it at that stage because in arriving at a finding of guilt or otherwise, a President or a Magistrate would already have formed in his mind the grounds for such a finding. What is required of him to do is only the need to reduce them into writing. It is only in complicated cases that more time may be needed. My view, therefore, is that the practice of making notes of the reasons for a decision would greatly reduce the delay in the supply of grounds and judgments. It is to be observed that the decisions in most of these cases rest essentially on questions of fact. The same applies to civil cases, for example, running down cases. The findings are invariably based on questions of fact. At this point may I relate to you the experience I had in dealing with running down cases. Some years back I experimented by fixing 25 running down cases in a week for hearing and I did this for two consecutive months. The total number of cases fixed for these two months was 185. At the end of the two months 153 cases were disposed of. The breakdown is as follows: 50 per cent were settled; 35 per cent were tried either on liability or quantum and 15 per cent were postponed for good reasons. The point I am trying to make is this: in cases where I thought parties might appeal, I recorded my findings before giving judgment by stating very briefly the reasons for such findings and the reasons for damages awarded. In the event of an appeal what was needed was to supply the notes together with my recorded reasons for the decision.

More Magistrates and support staff and courtrooms

If we are to really speed up with the disposal of cases and cope with the increase of cases, there should also be a corresponding increase in the establishment. This is partly an answer to our problems. It is, however, not a complete answer as there is also the question of shortage of court premises for the cases to be heard. There is also the problem of support staff to be addressed. New premises are needed to provide more courtrooms as well as to replace some of the premises which are no longer suitable for court proceedings to be held. This matter should urgently be looked into by the Ministry of Justice to enable us to efficiently and speedily dispose of cases. It is to be observed that if the number of Magistrates are increased it would also be necessary to correspondingly increase the number of supporting staff, for example, registrars of Sessions Court, interpreters, court clerks and so forth.

High Court's revisionary and supervisory jurisdiction

I now move on to refer briefly to certain sections in the Courts of Judicature Act 1964 (Act 91), in particular, sections 31 to 36 and also section 54 of the Subordinate Courts Act 1948 (Act 92).

My reason for drawing your attention to them is to emphasize that they are there for certain specific purposes. By invoking these provisions quite a lot of cases that have been dealt with by the subordinate courts could finally be disposed of by the High Court in the exercise of its revisionary jurisdiction.

The exercise of judicial functions generally by the subordinate courts should also be subject to general supervision by the High Court—an exercise of its general supervisory jurisdiction. If the functions are effectively carried out many of the problems in the subordinate courts could be expeditiously overcome. Indeed they should be attended to as and when the problems arise.

Remarks and interruptions

Finally, may I say this. I made a brief reference when dealing with the general conduct of Presidents and Magistrates in the course of a proceeding, that they should refrain from making uncalled for remarks which could be hurtful to those who appear before them. In certain instances the remarks made by Presidents and Magistrates could even be on a matter which is controversial. From the nature of our office we cannot reply to criticisms made in response to such remarks. What I am trying to say is that we cannot afford to enter into a public controversy. That being the case we must rely on our conduct itself to be its own vindication. No doubt we are exposed to criticisms. Nonetheless nothing should deter us from doing what the occasion requires provided it is pertinent to the matter in hand.

Conclusion

To conclude I reiterate that as judges you are entrusted, on behalf of the community, with a very heavy responsibility—to weigh the conflicting interests; to weigh on the one hand the respect due to the profession and on the other hand to ensure that the ultimate interest of the community in seeking justice is guaranteed.

A President or Magistrate should not therefore talk too much. May I in this regard refer to the case cited by Lord Denning in his book *The Due Process of Law* at page 58 about a judge who talked too much in order to prove the point. That case in *Jones* v *National Coal Board* (1957) 2 QB 55 where the widow of a coal miner killed after the roof of a coal mine had fallen on him claimed damages. The case was tried by Hallet J. who dismissed the claim. She appealed. One of the grounds of appeal was that the judge's interruptions had made it impossible for her counsel to put her case properly. The Board under cross-appeal also raised as one of the grounds the fact that the judge's interruptions prevented the Board from having a fair trial. Speaking for the whole Court, Denning, LJ (as he then was) had this to say:

> "No one can doubt that the judge, in intervening as he did, was actuated by the best motives. He was anxious to understand the details of this complicated case, and asked questions to get them clear in his mind. He was anxious that the witnesses should not be harassed unduly in cross-examination and intervened to protect them when he thought necessary. He was anxious to investigate all the various criticisms that had been made against the board, and to see whether they were well founded or not. Hence, he took them up himself with the witnesses from time to time. He was anxious that the case should not be dragged on too long, and intimated clearly when he thought that a point had been sufficiently explored. All those are worthy motives on which judges daily intervene in the conduct of cases, and have done for centuries.
>
> Nevertheless, we are quite clear that the interventions, taken together, were far more than they should have been. In the system of trial which we have evolved in this country, the judge sits to hear and determine the issues raised by the parties, not to conduct an investigation or examination on behalf of society at large, as happens, we believe in some foreign countries. Even in England, however, a judge is not a mere umpire to answer the question 'How's that?' His object, above all, is to find out the truth, and to do justice according to law; and in daily pursuit of it the advocate plays an honourable and necessary role. Was it not Lord Eldon LC who said in a notable passage that 'truth is best discovered by powerful statements on both

sides of the question'?: see *Ex parte Lloyd* (1822) Mont 70 at 72n, And Lord Greene MR who explained that justice is best done by a judge who holds the balance between the contending parties without himself taking part in their disputations? If a judge, said Lord Greene, should himself conduct the examination of witnesses, 'he, so to speak, descends into the arena and is liable to have his vision clouded by the dust of conflict': see *Yuill* v *Yuill* (1945) P15 at 20, (1945) 1 All ER 183, 61 TLR 176.

Yes, he must keep his vision unclouded. It is all very well to paint justice blind, but she does better without a bandage around her eyes. She should be blind indeed to favour or prejudice, but clear to see which way lies the truth: and the less dust there is about the better. Let the advocates one after the other put the weights into the scales—the 'nicely calculated less or more'—but the judge at the end decides which way the balance tilts, be it ever so slightly. So firmly is all this established in our law that the judge is not allowed in a civil dispute to call a witness whom he thinks might throw some light on the facts. He must rest content with the witnesses called by the parties: see *In re Enoch & Zaretzky, Bock & Co.* (1910) 1 KB 327. So also it is for the advocate, each in his turn, to examine the witnesses, and not for the judge to take it on himself lest by so doing he appear to favour one side or the other: see *R* v *Cain,* (1936) 25 CrAppRep 204; *R* v *Bateman* (1946) 31 CrAppRep 106 and *Harris* v *Harris* (1952), *Times*, 9 April; *Judgments of the Court of Appeal, 1952,* No.148 by Birket LJ especially. And it is for the advocate to state his case as fairly and strongly as he can, without undue interruption, lest the sequence of his argument be lost: see *R* v *Clewer* (1953) 37 CrAppRep 37. The judge's part in all this is to harken to the evidence, only himself asking questions of witnesses when it is necessary to clear up any point that has been overlooked or left obscure; to see that the advocates behave themselves seemly and keep to the rules laid down by law; to exclude irrelevancies and discourage repetition; to make sure by wise intervention that he follows the points that the advocates are making and can assess their worth; and at the end to make up his mind where the truth lies. If he goes beyond this, he drops the mantle of a judge and assumes the robe of an advocate; and the change does not become him well. Lord Chancellor Bacon spoke right when he said that: 'Patience and gravity of hearing is an essential part of justice; and an over-speaking judge is no well-tuned cymbal'.

Such are our standards. They are set so high that we cannot hope to attain them all the time. In the very pursuit of justice, our keenness may outrun our sureness, and we may trip and fall. That is what has happened here. A judge of acute perception, acknowledged learning, and actuated by the best of motives, has nevertheless himself intervened so much in the conduct of the case that one of the parties—nay, each of them—has come away complaining that he was not able properly to put his case; and these complaints are, we think, justified."

ADMINISTRATION OF JUSTICE IN MALAYSIA: THE MALAYSIAN JUDICIAL SYSTEM*

In order to appreciate the present judicial system and the administration of justice in Malaysia, one needs to trace the origin and history of the Malaysian Bench. As will be seen, the growth and development of the Malaysian judiciary were directly consequent to the political changes which took place in the country. The history of judicial development is therefore reflective of the political changes and will constitute the first half of the discussion. The second half will be devoted to a discussion of the present day system, the hierarchy of the courts and their powers and jurisdiction. This paper will conclude with an attempt to postulate future changes in the Malaysian judiciary consequent to the creation of the Supreme Court of Malaysia.

The history of the Malaysian judicial system is closely interrelated to the history of British intervention in the Malay Peninsula. It is proposed to divide our study of the Malaysian Judicial System into four distinct periods, viz.:

(1) British Colonial Rule: 1786-1941 (Pre-war period);

(2) Japanese Occupation (World War II): 1942-1945;

(3) British Colonial Rule: 1946-1956 (Post-war period);

(4) Independence and thereafter: 1957-1980s.

A. History of Judicial Development

1. British Colonial Rule: 1786-1941

Varying degrees of British involvement can be seen in the differing governmental structures in Malaya; the Straits Settlements, the Federated Malay States and the Unfederated Malay States which constituted the three stages of British intervention. Whilst the first were settled colonies, the latter two were mere protectorates.

---

*At The Asian Chief Justices' Conference In Penang From 19-22nd August, 1985.

a. Straits Settlements (S.S.)

The first stage in British intervention began when the East India Company which had created outposts in Penang (1786), Malacca (1824) and Singapore (1819) transferred them to the British Crown. Collectively known as the Straits Settlements, they came directly under the responsibility of the British Colonial Office in 1876.

The judicial system in the Crown Colony first evolved when the First Charter of Justice of 1807 established the Courts of Judicature in Penang. By the Second Charter of Justice of 1826, the united Courts of Judicature were established for the three settlements of Penang, Malacca and Singapore. These Charters of Justice were significant for they heralded the reception of English common law and equity into the Malay Peninsula. As stated by Malkin R in *In the Goods of Abdullah* (1835) 2 Ky.Ecc. 8 at pp.9-10:

> "I refer to the case of *Rodyk* v *Williamson*........ in which I expressed my opinion that I was bound by the uniform course of authority to hold that the introduction of the King's Charter into these Settlements had introduced the existing law of England, except in some cases where it was modified by express provisions, and had abrogated any law previously existing."

It is important to note that the Court of Judicature was to administer in the Straits Settlements the principles of common law and equity which were then in force in England "as far as local circumstances will admit". In *Yeap Cheah Neo* v *Ong Cheng Neo* (1875) LR 6 PC 381, Sir Montague Smith on behalf of the Judicial Committee of the Privy Council said at p.394:[1]

> "In applying this general principle [the applicability of English law to the Straits Settlement], it has been held that statutes relat-

1. The application of United kingdom common law, rules of equity and certain statutes in Peninsular Malaysia is now governed by section 3 of the Civil Law Act, 1956 (Revised–1972). For easy reference, the provision is spelt out:

   Section 3(1)
   "Save so far as other provision has been made or may hereafter be made by any written law in force in Malaysia the Court shall—

   a. in West Malaysia or any part thereof apply the common law of England and the rules of equity as administered in England on the 7th day of April, 1956; (continued next page.)

> ing to matters and exigencies peculiar to the local condition of England, and which are not adapted to the circumstances of a colony, do not become a part of its law, although the general law of England may be introduced into it."

A distinct feature of early day British administration of justice was the lack of separation between the Judiciary and the Executive. Prior to 1867, the Courts consisted not only of professional judges called "Recorders", but also of lay judges. The latter comprised the Governor who was the chief executive authority of the State and members of the Executive Council. It was only when the Straits Settlements came under the control of the British Colonial Office that the Judiciary became separate from the Executive. In 1868, when the Supreme Court of the Straits Settlements was established, the "Recorders" of the former Courts of Judicature became the sole judges.

In 1873, the Supreme Court was reorganized under four Judges: the Chief Justice, Judge of Penang, Senior Puisne Judge and Junior Puisne Judge. A Criminal Court known as the Court of Quarter Sessions was also established and was presided in Singapore by the Senior Puisne Judge, and in Penang by the Junior Puisne Judge. A Court of Appeal was also established. This was the position in the Straits Settlements until the invasion by Japan of British Malaya.

b. Federated Malay States (F.M.S.)

The F.M.S. which comprised Perak, Selangor, Negri Sembilan and Pahang came into being in 1895. Between 1874 and 1887, each of the four States came under British protection when their rulers, in exchange for British recognition of their claim as rulers of the respective Malay States, agreed to accept British resi-

b. in Sabah, apply the common law of England and the rules of equity, together with statutes of general application, as administered or in force in England on the 1st day of December, 1951;

c. in Sarawak, apply the common law of England and the rules of equity, together with statutes of general application, as administered or in force in England on the 12th day of December, 1949, subject however to subsection (3)(ii):

Provided always that the said common law, rules of equity and statutes of general application shall be applied so far only as the circumstances of the States of Malaysia and their respective inhabitants permit and subject to such qualifications as local circumstances render necessary."

dents whose advice had to be asked and acted upon on all questions other than those touching Malay religion and custom.

Prior to 1895, each of the States had its own State Judiciary for the administration of justice. The then existing judicial institutions consisted of the Magistrates' Courts, the Court of Senior Magistrate and lastly, the final Court of Appeal, the Sultan-in-Council. However, the actual decision maker in the State Council was the British Resident. There was no separation of the Judiciary from the Executive.

When the Federation was formed in 1895, a common judiciary was introduced when a common form of legislation was passed in each of the four States to establish a common Court of Appeal called the Court of the Judicial Commissioner. It was the highest court in the F.M.S. However, in 1905, it was superseded by the Supreme Court of the F.M.S.

The Supreme Court consisted of a Court of Appeal and a Court of the Judicial Commissioner. Whilst the former replaced the 1895 Court of Judicial Commissioner, the latter replaced the Senior Magistrate's Court. Strangely enough, this Supreme Court was not a Federal Court and was established in each State by State legislation and had jurisdiction only as regards the State concerned. However, in 1918, a Federal Supreme Court was created for the F.M.S. by Federal legislation. The F.M.S. remained in existence until the Japanese invasion in December 1941.

c. The Unfederated Malay States (U.F.M.S.)

The U.F.M.S. consisted of Kedah, Perlis, Kelantan, Trengganu and Johore. The first four States came under British protection beginning from 1909 when the Siamese transferred to the British their rights of suzerainty, protection, administration and control over the States. A British Adviser was appointed for each State under a series of agreements. Johore accepted a British Adviser in 1914. Like that of the F.M.S. advice of the British advisors had to be asked and acted upon by the rulers of the U.F.M.S. on all questions other than those touching Malay religion and custom.

With respect to the administration of justice, each State had its own State Judiciary. Each also had its own Supreme Court although the Constitution of the Courts varied from State to

State. The U.F.M.S. remained outside the Federation until the end of World War II.

2. Japanese Occupation (World War II): 1942-1945

The Japanese Occupation of British Malaya commenced in December, 1941. Nothing much is known either of the judicial system or the administration of justice in the Malay Peninsula during this period. However, it appears that there were two courts functioning during that time; the Military or Special Courts and the Civil Courts.

The Special Court was set up to try civilians charged with offences under the Japanese Maintenance of Public Peace and Order Law. It was presided by a Japanese judge. With respect to the Civil Courts, their jurisdiction was confined to civil and criminal cases only. In this respect, it appears that the pre-existing laws of the S.S., the F.M.S. and the U.F.M.S. continued in force until changed or repealed by the Japanese Military Administration. The Civil Courts were presided by local judicial officers. In 1943, pursuant to the Judicial Organization Ordinance, a Supreme Court, High Court, District and Magistrates' Courts, Penghulu's Court and Kathis' Courts were established during the Japanese Occupation.

Speaking of the Japanese Occupation, an interesting question for consideration is whether the occupation was, in law, an occupation or conquest. The Japanese were in occupation of Malaya from the middle of February, 1942 to September, 1945. Nevertheless, the question remains whether the occupation was in fact a mere occupation or a conquest of Malaya by the Japanese. I do not propose to provide the answer but would refer to two articles appearing in Volume 12 of the 1946 Malayan Law Journal.[2]

3. British Colonial Rule: (1946-1956) (post-war period)

a. British Military Administration (B.M.A.)

The surrender of the Japanese forces in 1945 saw, once again, the reinstatement of British Colonial rule in the Malay Peninsula. From September, 1945 to April, 1946, the Peninsula was placed under the British Military Administration. During that

2. See note, "Powers and duties of an Enemy Occupant" (1946) 12 MLJ i;, Note, "British law and Police Officers during Japanese Occupation" (1946) 12 MLJ lxv-lxix; Note, "Occupation or Conquest?" (1946) 12 MLJ xvii.

period, the B.M.A. set up a system of courts called the Superior Courts (B.M.A.) and the District Courts (B.M.A.). The administration of justice during this period was in the hands of British Military officers.

As can be seen, the British Military Administration was a transitional phase prior to the introduction of civilian rule. Towards this end, the British Military Courts played a crucial role in converting chaos, which was prevalent during the Japanese Occupation, to orderly government. The jurisdiction of the courts and the objectives of their creation may be seen in *In re Lam Weng Chak* (1946) 12 MLJ xxxiii.[3]

In that case, the accused was charged with four counts of having voluntarily caused hurt for the purpose of extorting confessions in March 1942, under section 330 of the Penal Code (F.M.S.). At the hearing of the case, a preliminary objection was raised over the jurisdiction of the Ipoh Superior Court (B.M.A.) to take cognizance of offences alleged to have been committed in Malaya during the Japanese Occupation.

In support of the above objection, counsel for the accused pointed out that Proclamation No. 3 which established Military Courts and conferred on them jurisdiction 'over persons charged with offences committed either before or after the establishment of such control'[4], was promulgated by the General Officer Commanding Military Forces Malaya pursuant to Proclamation No. 1. The latter, promulgated by Lord Mountbatten, the Supreme Allied Commander South East Asia Command, provided that the Malay Peninsula (the Straits Settlements and the Malay States) were placed under Military Administration 'by reason of military necessity and for the suppression of disorder and the maintenance of public safety'.[5] It was argued that in so far as Proclamation No. 1 did not expressly provide for any retrospective effect of subsequent proclamation made under it, Proclamation No. 3 was therefore ultra vires and the Ipoh Superior Court was not competent to try the accused.

This submission was rejected by the President, Lt-Col J.G. Adams, who held that the immediate effect of Proclamation No. 1 was to restore the law as it was before the Japanese occupied

3. See note, "Jurisdiction of Military Courts" (1942) 12 MLJ xxxii.
4. Ibid., xxxiii.
5. Id.

Malaya in 1942 such as those of the S.S., the F.M.S. and the U.F.M.S. In his view time never ran against the Crown and the courts, being set up by reason of military necessity for the administration of those laws that existed before the existence of the Japanese Occupation, should have exactly the same jurisdiction as the criminal courts then in existence had before the Japanese Occupation. He summed up by saying that the courts were set up to administer the law that existed prior to the Japanese Occupation and therefore had jurisdiction to try all offences against the Penal Code of the F.M.S. whenever they were committed.

b. The Malayan Union

The B.M.A. was a brief interlude and was replaced by the British Malayan Union in 1946. The establishment of the Malayan Union which comprised the F.M.S., U.F.M.S. and the S.S. witnessed the unification of the three separate judicial systems mentioned earlier. Under section 85 of the Malayan Union Order in Council, 1946, the Malayan Union Ordinance 3/46 was enacted whereby a Supreme Court (a Court of Record) was established, comprising the High Court having jurisdiction throughout the Malay Peninsula with power to exercise original and appellate civil and criminal jurisdiction, and the Court of Appeal which shall exercise appellate civil and criminal jurisdiction.[6] The Ordinance also dealt with the establishment, constitution and powers of subordinate civil and criminal courts.

The lower courts consisted of the District Courts and Magistrates' Courts. Authority was vested in the Governor to constitute by order in each State and Settlement so many courts as he thought fit and to assign local limits of jurisdiction to them. Where he deemed necessary, the Governor may extend the jurisdiction of a court beyond the boundary of such State or Settlement.

c. Federation of Malaya (1948)

The Malayan Union proved unpopular and amidst intense Malay opposition was superseded by the Federation of Malaya on 1st February, 1948. Under the Federation of Malaya Agreement,

6. It should be noted that by 1946, Singapore had become a separate Crown Colony and was given a separate Supreme Court. However, in practice, judges of the Supreme Court, Malayan Union, could preside as judges of the Supreme Court, Singapore, and vice versa.

1948 each State and Settlement was to retain its own individuality but all were to be united under a strong central government. The demise of the Malayan Union saw the restructuring of the courts particularly at the subordinate level. The Courts Ordinance 1948 established, in place of the Malayan Union Subordinate Courts, a new structure of inferior courts comprising the Sessions Courts, Magistrates' Courts and Penghulus' Courts. This structure is continued up to the present day. With respect to the Superior Courts, the Federation of Malaya Agreement continued the pre-existing structure, i.e. the Malayan Union Supreme Court which consisted of the Court of Appeal and a High Court under a Chief Justice. The 1948 Agreement further provided that the Chief Justice and Judges of the Supreme Court of the Malayan Union were to be the first Chief Justice and Judges of the Supreme Court of the Federation of Malaya.

4. Independence — Federal Constitution 1957

On 31st August, 1957 the Federation of Malaya became an independent sovereign country. However, the Supreme Court of pre-independence was continued. The Supreme Court therefore still consisted of a High Court and a Court of Appeal. The establishment, jurisdiction and powers of all courts, excluding Muslim courts, are matters within the legislative powers of the Federation. Article 121 of the Federal Constitution[7] provided that "The Judicial power of the Federation shall be vested in a Supreme Court and such inferior courts as may be provided by federal law" and, by Article 122(1)[8], "The Supreme Court shall consist of a Chief Justice and other Judges".

The Supreme Court of independent Malaya not only retained its previous powers but its jurisdiction was considerably enlarged. Under the Federation of Malaya Agreement, 1948, the Court of Justice was not competent to question the validity of an Ordinance[9] and no Court of Justice, including the Supreme Court itself, had any power to interpret the Federation Agreement[10]. As can be seen the power to interpret the consitution was vested in an

7. The Federal Constitution as at 31st August, 1957.
8. Id.
9. Federation of Malaya Agreement 1948, Clause 66.
10. Federation of Malaya Agreement 1948, Clause 153.

ad hoc Interpretation Tribunal. In contrast, under the 1957 Constitution the Supreme Court was not only given the original, appellate and revisional jurisdiction as may be provided by federal law but also, to the exclusion of any other court, the jurisdiction to determine any dispute between States or even between Federation and any State[11]. In this connection, however, it is to be observed that certain disputes relating to land and those arising under Articles 83 to 87 had to be referred to the Land Tribunal.

The Supreme Court's special jurisdiction to interpret the Constitution was provided by Article 129 which read: "Without prejudice to any appellate or revisional jurisdiction of the Supreme Court, where in any proceedings before another court a question arises as to the effect of any provision of this Constitution, the Supreme Court may, on the application of either party to the proceedings, determine that question and either dispose of the case or remit it to the other court to be disposed of in accordance with the determination."[12]

Its advisory jurisdiction as provided by Article 130 reads:

> "The Yang di-Pertuan Agong may refer to the Federal Court for its opinion any question as to the effect of any provision of this Constitution which has arisen or appears to him likely to arise, and the Federal Court shall pronounce in open court its opinion on any question so referred to it."

Another major change introduced by the Federal Constitution is the appointment of the Chief Justice and judges of the Supreme Court. Under the Federation of Malaya Agreement, 1948, the appointment of judges was made by the High Commissioner for and on behalf of His Majesty and the Ruler,[13] whereas under the 1957 Constitution the Chief Justice and other judges of the Supreme Court were appointed by His Majesty the Yang di-Pertuan Agong.[14]

a. Tenure of office and independence of the judiciary

The Reid Commission Report contained a recommendation on the tenure of office of a judge. Basically the object was to ensure

11. Federal Constitution 1957, Article 128(1) and (128(2).
12. Article 129 has since been repealed and the power to interpret the Constitution is now enshrined in Article 128 of the Federal Constitution.
13. Federation of Malaya Agreement 1948, Clause 77(4).
14. Federal Constitution 1957, Article 122B.

the independence of the judges. This recommendation was to the effect that:

> "Since under the new Constitution the powers of Her Majesty's Government and the High Commissioner will disappear, it has been necessary to insert the provisions, usual in democratic Constitutions, for the maintenance of the independence of the Supreme Court. Under our proposals (Article 116) a judge cannot be removed except by an order of the Yang di-Pertuan Agong in pursuance of an address passed by a majority of two-thirds of each House of Parliament; and before any such motion is moved there must be proved misconduct or infirmity of mind or body. Subject to this provision, the age of retirement has been at 65."

With a view to ensuring further the independence of the courts, a provision was also made for the remuneration of judges of the Supreme Court to be charged to the Consolidated Fund.[15] There was also enshrined in the Constitution a provision to the effect that the remuneration and other terms of office (including pension rights) of the judges of the Supreme Court shall not be altered to their disadvantage after their appointment.[16] One other provision which is significant is contained in Article 127 which provides that:

> "The conduct of a judge of the Federal Court or High Court shall not be discussed in either House of Parliament except on a substantive motion of which notice has been given by not less than one quarter of the total number of members of that House, and shall not be discussed in the Legislative Assembly of any State."

As for the subordinate courts their position remained the same and their powers are derived from federal law enacted by virtue of Article 121 of the Federal Constitution.

5. Malaysia (1963)

The subsequent development in our judicial system came about in 1963 when Malaysia was formed on 16th September, 1963 with Sabah, Sarawak and Singapore as the three new component States of the Federation of Malaysia.

15. Federal Constitution 1957, Article 125(6).
16. Federal Constitution 1957, Article 125(7).

Consequent to the formation of Malaysia, Part IX of the Constitution was amended to effect the restructuring of the courts primarily at the Superior level. The amendment made provision for the judicial power of the Federation to be vested in three High Courts of co-ordinate jurisdiction and status. They are the High Court of Malaya, the High Court of Borneo and the High Court of Singapore. The amendment also made provision for the establishment of a Federal Court consisting a President of the Court to be styled Lord President, the Chief Justices of the High Courts and other Federal Court Judges.[17] The Federal Court was also vested with original, appellate and advisory jurisdiction. Article 121 of the Federal Constitution provides:

> "(2) The following jurisdiction shall be vested in a court which shall be known as the Federal Court and shall have its principal registry in Kuala Lumpur, that is to say, -
>
> (a) exclusive jurisdiction to determine appeals from decisions of a High Court or a judge thereof (except decisions of a High Court given by a registrar or other officer of the court and appealable under the federal law to a judge of the Court); and
>
> (b) such original or consultative jurisdiction as is specified in Articles 128 and 130,"

Its original jurisdiction as set out in Article 128 reads:

> "(1) The Federal Court shall, to the exclusion of any other court, have jurisdiction to determine -
>
> (a) any question whether a law made by Parliament or by the Legislature of a State is invalid on the ground that it makes provision with respect to a matter with respect to which Parliament or, as the case may be, the Legislature of the State has no power to make laws; and
>
> (b) disputes on any other question between States or between the Federation and any State.
>
> (2) Without prejudice to any appellate jurisdiction of the Federal Court, where in any proceedings before another court a question arises as to the effect of any provision of this Constitution, the Federal Court shall have jurisdiction (subject to any rules of court regulating the exercise of that jurisdiction) to determine the ques-

17. Federal Constitution 1957, Article 122.

tion and remit the case to the other court to be disposed of in accordance with the determination.

(3) The jurisdiction of the Federal Court to determine appeals from a High Court or a judge thereof shall be such as may be provided by federal law."

Article 130 sets out the advisory jurisdiction of the Federal Court the provisions of which are similar to Article 130 of the Federal Constitution, 1957. They remain so until the present day.

As may be observed, from Malaysia Day, 16th September, 1963, the Supreme Court was replaced and was substituted by a Federal Court. But the Federal Court, unlike the Supreme Court, was not a Court of Record and no longer consisted of a Court of Appeal and a High Court. It stood on its own in the structure of the court system. It is also to be observed that the word "power" is used in Article 121 to describe the authority vested in the three High Courts of co-ordinate jurisdiction and status. As for the subordinate courts, there was, however, no change in their structure.

On 9th August, 1965, Singapore broke away from Malaysia leaving therefore the two existing High Courts, namely that of Borneo and Peninsular Malaysia, till today.

6. East Malaysia

An account of the judicial system and the administration of justice in Malaysia, it is submitted, is incomplete without mentioning briefly the position in East Malaysia.

North Borneo (now Sabah) and Sarawak became British protected States as early as 1888 by virtue of an agreement made between the local rulers and the British North Borneo (Chartered) Company. Like their counterparts in the Malay Peninsula, the Company was to administer justice with due regard to native customs and laws and was not to interfere with the religion of the inhabitants.

With respect to the administration of justice, North Borneo was divided into sessional and magisterial divisions. The former was executively administered by the British Residents, and the latter by District Officers. The Chief Court comprised of the Governor, the Judicial Commissioner and other judges temporarily appointed by the Governor. As for Sarawak, its momentous legal history began with the proclamation of James Brooke as the first Rajah and Governor of Sarawak. His main task was to establish law and order in the country. From 1870 onwards he established a number of courts comprising the Debtors' Courts, Chinese Courts, Courts of Requests, Bankruptcy Courts, Native Courts and Supreme Courts. The present day High Court in East Malaysia can trace its origin from this early set up.

In 1922, the Courts were reorganized by the Courts Order, 1922. In that year, five courts were constituted viz., the Supreme Court which exercised original and appellate jurisdiction, Resident's Courts, District Courts, Magistrates' Courts and Native Courts. The administration of justice continued to be carried out by these Courts until 1946 when Sarawak (so also Sabah) was ceded to the British Crown. In 1947 two Circuit Courts were constituted which, for the first time, were presided by legally qualified people.

In 1951 a major change took place in the Borneo States. By the Sarawak, North Borneo and Brunei (Courts) Order in Council, 1951, a Combined Judiciary was established for the three States in Borneo. The Order in Council established one superior court of record styled the Supreme Court of Sarawak, North Borneo and Brunei consisting of the High Court of Sarawak, North Borneo and Brunei and the Court of Appeal of Sarawak, North Borneo and Brunei. However, this Combined Judiciary disappeared when North Borneo (Sabah) and Sarawak joined the Federation of Malaya to form Malaysia in 1963. The jurisdiction of the High Court in Sarawak and Sabah was retained whilst the appellate jurisdiction of the Court of Appeal was assumed by the Federal Court of Malaysia. With effect from 1st January, 1985 this appellate jurisdiction is now vested in the Supreme Court of Malaysia.

7. Appeals to the Privy Council

It is of interest to note that the pre-independence right of appeal to the Privy Council commenced as early as the establishment of the Straits Settlements, the Federated Malay States and the Unfederated Malay States. Penang, for instance, acquired that right in 1807 by virtue of the First Charter of Justice. Malacca and Singapore were next conferred such right in 1827 by the Second Charter of Justice.[18] The F.M.S. acquired such a right when, in 1906, the F.M.S. Appeals Order in Council was passed which provided for

18. The first reported Privy Council appeal from the Straits Settlements was the case of *Yeap Cheah Neo* v *Ong Cheng Neo* (1875) LR 6PC 381.

appeals from the Court of Appeal of the F.M.S. to be made to the Privy Council. As for the U.F.M.S., no such right existed as the same was not provided for in their respective Courts Enactments. Johore, however, acquired such a right when provision for appeals to the Privy Council was incorporated in her Courts Enactment passed in 1920. However, since each of the component parts of the Malay Peninsula had its own Supreme Court from whose decision an appeal would lie to the Privy Council, there was no uniformity in legislation governing such a right. Uniformity was only achieved in 1948 when Clause 83 of the Federation of Malaya Agreement provided specifically for appeals to be made to His Majesty in Council from the Malayan Supreme Court.

Upon independence on 31st August, 1957, the right to appeal from the Supreme Court to the Privy Council was retained and embodied in Article 131 of the Malayan Federal Constitution. When Malaysia was formed on 16th September, 1963, the Malaysian Federal Constitution by Article 131 continued to preserve that right. At the same time, the Malaysia Act, 1963, substituted the words 'Federal Court' for the words 'Supreme Court'. Article 131 neatly circumvented the anomaly of appeals coming from an independent country with its own sovereign to another country with a separate sovereign by providing that in law the appeals were addressed not direct to the Privy Council but to His Majesty the Yang di-Pertuan Agong who referred them for advice to the Privy Council and who, in turn, advised His Majesty accordingly. Pursuant to Clause (1) of Article 131, the Courts of Judicature Act 7 of 1964 was enacted to make provision for the reference of appeals to the Privy Council.

It is undoubtedly clear that the Malaysian Parliament may at any time restrict or abolish altogether the right of appeal to the Privy Council. Such a move was successfully initiated in October, 1975 when P.U.(A) 320/75 made the decision of the Federal Court in criminal cases tried under the Essential (Security Cases) Regulations, 1975 non-appealable to the Privy Council. However, a more serious curtailment was seen in January, 1978 when appeals to the Privy Council in criminal and constitutional matters were abolished altogether by amendments made to S.74 of Act 7 of 1964. Malaysia ultimately witnessed the abolition of appeals to the Privy Council when Act A566/83 (P.U.(B) 589/84) repealed Article 131 of the Malaysian Federal Constitution with effect from 1st January, 1985. This significant decision not only saw the demise of the Federal Court but also the birth of the Supreme Court of Malaysia which is now the final court of appeal in constitutional, civil and criminal matters. This historic event has thus made appeals to the Privy Council history in Malaysia.

A material feature of the newly-created Supreme Court which needs to be mentioned is that, unlike the Supreme Court which existed under the 1948 Federation of Malaya Agreement and the 1957 Malayan Federal Constitution, the Supreme Court of 1st January, 1985 is not a Court of Record. It does not consist of a Court of Appeal and a High Court but is solely an entity standing on its own.

B. The Malayan Judicial System —- Powers And Jurisdiction

As may be discerned from the aforesaid discussion, the Malaysian judiciary, except for Islamic courts, is entirely a federal organization. At the apex of the organization is the Supreme Court which is now the highest court and final appellate body in the country. Next in status and jurisdiction comes the High Court followed by the subordinate courts which, in descending order, comprise of the Sessions Court and the Magistrate's Court. The Federal Constitution and the Courts of Judicature Act, 1964 (Revised–1972), make provisions for the constitution, powers and jurisdiction of the Supreme and High Courts whilst the powers and jurisdiction of the subordinate courts are spelt out in the Subordinate Courts Act, 1948.

1. Superior Courts

Before embarking on a discussion of the powers and jurisdiction of the Supreme Court and High Courts, it is necessary to mention in brief the appointment of judges in general. By Article 122B of the Federal Constitution, the Lord President, the Chief Justices of the High Court of Malaya and Borneo, the other judges of the Supreme Court and judges of the High Court are all appointed by the Yang di-Pertuan Agong, acting on the advice of the Prime Minister, after consulting the Conference of Rulers.

The Constitution stipulates that before tendering his advice on the appointment of a judge other than the Lord President, the Prime Minister shall consult the Lord President. Before tendering his advice on the appointment of the Chief Justice of a High Court, the Prime Minister shall consult the Chief Justices of the two High Courts and, if the appointment is to the High Court in Borneo, he shall also consult the Chief Minister of Sabah and Sarawak.

Lastly, before tendering his advice on the appointment of a judge other than the Lord President or a Chief Justice, the Prime Minister shall consult, if the appointment is to the Supreme Court, the two Chief Justices and, if the appointment is to one of the High Courts, the Chief Justice of that Court.

a. Supreme Court

The Supreme Court consists of the Lord President, the Chief Justices of the High Court in Malaya and Borneo, and seven Supreme Court Judges.[19] If the interests of justice so require, the Lord President may also nominate a High Court Judge to sit as a judge of the Supreme Court. Proceedings before the court are usually heard and disposed of by a panel of three judges nominated by the Lord President.[20] Sometimes, in certain special cases, it sits in a panel of five. In the absence of the Lord President the senior member of the Court shall preside.

The Supreme Court is vested with original, appellate and advisory jurisdiction. Article 121(2) of the Federal Constitution provides that the Supreme Court shall have -

(a) exclusive jurisdiction to determine appeals from decisions of a High Court or a judge thereof (except decisions of a High Court given by a registrar or other officer of the court and appealable under federal law to a judge of the High Court);

(b) such original or consultative jurisdiction as is specified in Articles 128 and 130; and

(c) such other jurisdiction as may be conferred by or under federal law.

With respect to its appellate jurisdiction, the Supreme Court shall hear appeals in criminal matters from a decision of the High Court made in the exercise of its original criminal jurisdiction.[21] With respect to the decisions of the High Court made

19. Federal Constitution 1957, Article 122(1). See also P.U.(A) 144/1982.

20. Courts of Judicature Act, 1964 s.38 (hereafter referred to as 'The 1964 Act').

21. The 1964 Act, s.50.

in the exercise of its appellate criminal jurisdiction, the Supreme Court shall only hear references on any question of law of public interest which has arisen in the course of an appeal from the subordinate court and the determination of which by the High Court has affected the event of the appeal.[22] However, in civil matters, the Supreme Court has jurisdiction to hear and determine appeals from any judgment or order of the High Court whether made in the exercise of its original or appellate jurisdiction.[23]

The original and advisory jurisdiction of the Supreme Court as provided by Articles 128 and 130 respectively have earlier been spelt out and will not be repeated here. However, it must be pointed out that in the exercise of its original jurisdiction under Article 128(1)(b) in respect of a dispute between the States or between the Federation and any State, the Supreme Court shall not pronounce any judgment other than a declaratory judgment.[24] Under Article 128(2), the Supreme Court also has jurisdiction to determine constitutional questions referred to it by the High Court.

An account of the Supreme Court also necessitates a brief mention of the functions and duties of the Lord President. To a certain extent, they have already been stated in the opening paragraphs. As head of the Supreme Court, it is the Lord President who determines the dates and places for sittings of the court. The Supreme Court not only sits regularly in Kuala Lumpur but also travels on circuit to the major state capitals. The Lord President may from time to time give such directions with respect to business in the Supreme Court Registry as he considers necessary.[25]

By virtue of his position, the Lord President after consultation with the Prime Minister, can initiate the machinery for the removal of a judge of the Supreme Court from office on ground of misbehaviour or of inability from infirmity of body or mind or any other cause, properly to discharge the functions of his office. The Lord President may make representations to the Yang di-Pertuan Agong who shall appoint a tribunal consisting of

22. The 1964 Act, s.66.
23. The 1964 Act, s.67.
24. The 1964 Act, s.46.
25. Rules of the Supreme Court 1980, r.138.

five judges to be presided by the Lord President himself to report and make recommendations on the matter. Pending the report, His Majesty may on the recommendation of the Prime Minister after consulting the Lord President, suspend a judge of the Supreme Court from the exercise of his functions.[26]

The Lord President's duty and function may also be seen with reference to the Judicial and Legal Service Commission established under Article 138 of the Federal Constitution. The Commission's jurisdiction extends to all members of the judicial and legal service and it has the power to appoint, confirm, promote, transfer and discipline officers of the service. It is noteworthy that members of the Commission who are either judges of the Supreme or High Courts are appointed by the Yang di-Pertuan Agong on the recommendation of the Lord President. The Lord President is also the Chairman of the Rules Committee established under Section 17 of the Courts of Judicature Act, 1964.

b. High Court

Since 9th August, 1965, Malaysia has had two High Courts of co-ordinate jurisdiction and status; namely, the High Court in Malaya which has its principal registry in Kuala Lumpur, and the High Court in Borneo which has its principal registry in Kuching, Sarawak. Each consists of a Chief Justice and so many judges of the High Court as may be prescribed by Article 122A of the Federal Constitution

Proceedings before the High Court are usually heard and disposed of by a judge sitting alone except in certain cases.[27] For instance, when hearing land references, i.e. appeals in respect of compulsory acquisition of land, a High Court Judge sits with two assessors. Likewise, he sits with two assessors when trying offences under the Kidnapping Act, 1961, and with a jury when trying capital cases.

The powers and jurisdiction of the High Court are rather extensive. Subject to the original, appellate and advisory jurisdiction of the Supreme Court, the judicial power of the Federation is vested in the two High Courts which have equal and co-ordinate jurisdiction, and also in the subordinate courts as may be

26. Federal Constitution 1957, Article 125.
27. The 1964 Act, s.18.

provided by federal law.[28]

The High Court is vested with original and appellate jurisdiction in criminal and civil matters.[29] Its original jurisdiction with respect to both is unlimited as cases outside the jurisdiction of the subordinate courts are brought before it. In addition to its appellate jurisdiction, the High Court also exercises powers of revision in respect of criminal proceedings in the subordinate courts,[30] and may call for records of civil proceedings so as to satisfy itself of the correctness, legality or propriety of any decision recorded or passed by the subordinate courts.[31] The High Court has general supervisory and revisionary jurisdiction over all subordinate courts.[32]

As mentioned earlier, appeals against the decisions of the High Court in criminal matters made in the exercise of its original jurisdiction, and in civil matters made in the exercise of both its original and appellate jurisdiction, lie to the Supreme Court. Whilst no civil appeal from the subordinate courts shall lie to the High Court where the amount in dispute or value of the subject-matter is five thousand ringgit (RM5,000) or less except on a question of law,[33] no civil appeal from the High Court shall lie to the Supreme Court when the amount or value of the subject-matter at the trial is less than one hundred thousand ringgit (RM100,000), except with leave of the Supreme Court or a judge of the High Court.[34]

As is obvious, an account of the High Court is incomplete without some mention of the functions and duties of the two Chief Justices. By virtue of Article 122A of the Federal Constitution, the Chief Justice, Malaya, and the Chief Justice, Borneo, are the respective heads of the High Court in Malaya and the High Court in Borneo. Furthermore, by virtue of the High Court's general supervisory and revisionary jurisdiction over all

28. Federation Constitution 1957, Article 121(1).
29. The 1964 Act, ss.22, 23, 26 and 27.
30. The 1964 Act, s.31.
31. The 1964 Act, s.32.
32. The 1964 Act, s.35; s.325 Criminal Procedure Code (F.M.S. Cap.6).
33. The 1964 Act, s.28(1).
34. The 1964 Act, s.68(1)(a). The old monetary limit of ten thousand ringgit (RM10,000) was substituted for one hundred thousand ringgit (RM100,000) by Act A606 with effect from 1st January, 1985. The amendment was introduced consequent to the creation of the Supreme Court of Malaysia.

subordinate courts, it follows that the Chief Justices are also heads of the subordinate courts in their respective territories.

As head of the High Court, it is the Chief Justice who determines the dates and places for sittings of the Court.[35] Directions as to the distribution of business among judges of the High Court, whether of a particular or general nature, are also given by the Chief Justice.[36] The Chief Justice may also issue directions with respect to the distribution of business in the various departments of the High Court Registry.[37] With respect to the subordinate courts, it is also the Chief Justice who is empowered to determine the places where Sessions[38] and Magistrates' Courts[39] shall ordinarily be held.

Perhaps, the powers of the Chief Justice may be best appreciated in the area of appointments and/or dismissal of judges, and that of officers in the Judicial and Legal Service. As previously noted, the Prime Minister shall, before tendering his advice on the appointment of a judge to one of the High Courts, consult the Chief Justice of that Court. Likewise, a judge of a High Court may be suspended by the Yang di-Pertuan Agong from the exercise of his functions only after consultation with the Chief Justice of that Court. As for judicial officers, Presidents of Sessions Court and First Class Magistrates for the Federal Territory are appointed by the Yang di-Pertuan Agong on the recommendation of the Chief Justice.[40] First Class Magistrates for States other than the Federal Territory are appointed by the State Authority on the Chief Justice's recommendation.[41] On the question of dismissal or termination of service of these officers, the matter shall be referred to the Judicial and Legal Service Commission of which the two Chief Justices are members.

It is apparent from the above that the Chief Justice has administrative jurisdiction over judicial officers. The nature of the

35. The 1964 Act, s.19.
36. The 1964 Act, s.20.
37. Rules of the High Court, 1980, O.60 r.1.
38. Subordinate Courts Act, 1948, s.59 (hereafter referred to as 'The 1948 Act').
39. The 1948 Act, s.76.
40. The 1948 Act, s.59.
41. The 1948 Act, s.78. See also s.106 which empowers the Chief Justice with the concurrence of the Yang di Pertuan Agong to appoint so many subordinate officers (eg., process servers) as the Chief Justice deems necessary for the due administration of justice.

jurisdiction was described by the Lord President in *Cheah Yoke Thong* v *Public Prosecutor* (1984) 2 MLJ 119 at p.121 as follows:

> "The Magistrate is not appointed by the Attorney-General but appointed by the Ruler of the State (or in the case of the Federal Territory by the Yang di-Pertuan Agong) on the advice of the Chief Justice to whom the Magistrate is responsible and under whose administrative control he is placed. (See sections 78 and 79 of the Subordinate Court Act). His transfer from one judicial post to another judicial post is completely under the authority of the Chief Justice, and as regards his transfer from a judicial post to a legal post under the aegis of the Attorney-General, this is a matter of consultation and agreement between the Chief Justice and the Attorney-General. Similarly, as regards his promotion and advancement in the service, the confidential report on the Magistrate for this purpose is written by a judge of the State where the Magistrate is currently or previously posted and this report is subject to the comments or recommendations by the Chief Justice for the ultimate consideration of the Judicial and Legal Service Commission."

The Chief Justices, as earlier stated, are, by virtue of their office, members of the Supreme Court. The Chief Justice of the High Court in Malaya, by virtue of his seniority in the Supreme Court i.e. "having precedence next after the Lord President", is vested with the powers and shall perform the functions of the Lord President whenever the latter, during any period of time, is unable to perform his duties owing to illness or absence from Malaysia.[42] In this instance the Chief Justice, Malaya, shall be the Acting Lord President.

It should be mentioned also that the Chief Justices are empowered under the Legal Profession Act, 1976 to suspend an advocate and solicitor from practice, and to appoint, on the application of the Bar Council, a Disciplinary Committee to conduct formal inquiry into any complaint made against an advocate and solicitor.[43] Like the Lord President, the Chief Justices are also members of the Rules Committee and it is pertinent to note that no rule shall be made relating to any High Court without the consent thereto of the Chief Justice of that High Court.

42. Federal Constitution 1957, Article 131A. See also The 1964 Act, s.9(1).
43. The Legal Profession Act, 1976 ss.88A and 99.

2. Inferior or Subordinate Courts

The subordinate courts for the administration of civil and criminal law as established by the Subordinate Courts Act, 1948 comprise of the Sessions and Magistrates' Courts. In West Malaysia, the Penghulu's Court is also an inferior court but will not be discussed here as it hardly ever tries cases owing to its minimal jurisdiction.

a. Sessions Court

A Sessions Court consists of a President who is legally qualified and a member of the Judicial and Legal Service of the Federation. It hears and determines any civil or criminal cause or matter arising within the local limits of its jurisdiction

In criminal matters, the Sessions Court has jurisdiction to try all offences other than those punishable with death and may pass any sentence allowed by law other than the sentence of death.[44] In civil matters, subject to certain exceptions, it has jurisdiction to try civil suits where the amount or value of the subject-matter does not exceed twenty-five thousand ringgit (RM25,000)[45]. Appeals from the criminal and civil decisions of the Sessions Court lie to the High Court.

It is of interest to note that the President of a Sessions Court may call for the civil records of a Magistrate's Court within his local limits of jurisdiction for the purpose of satisfying himself as to the correctness, legality or propriety of any decision recorded or passed, and as to the regularity of any proceeding of that court. However, since the President does not have any revisionary or supervisory jurisdiction and therefore cannot interfere with the decision so recorded, in the event he considers them illegal or improper, he shall forward the records with his remarks, if any, to the High Court.[46] As stated earlier, only the High Court has general supervisory and revisionary jurisdiction over all subordinate courts.

b. Magistrates' Courts

A Magistrate's court consists of a Magistrate sitting alone. There are two classes of Magistrates whose jurisdiction differs: first

44. The 1948 Act, ss.63 and 64.
45. The 1948 Act, s.65.
46. The 1948 Act, s.54.

class Magistrates and second class Magistrates. The first class Magistrate is often a legally qualified person appointed by the Yang di-Pertuan Agong or the State Authority on the recommendation of the Chief Justice. The second class Magistrate is usually an administrative officer who performs magisterial functions and is appointed by the Yang di-Pertuan Agong or the State Authority. A Magistrate's court has jurisdiction to hear and determine any civil or criminal matter arising within the local limits of its assigned jurisdiction.

Briefly, in criminal matters, a first class Magistrate has jurisdiction to try offences for which the maximum term of imprisonment does not exceed ten (10) years' imprisonment or which are punishable with fine only.[47] He may, however, pass any sentence allowed by law not exceeding —

(a) five (5) years' imprisonment;

(b) a fine of ten thousand ringgit (RM10,000);

(c) whipping up to twelve (12) strokes; or

(d) any combination of the above sentences.

The criminal jurisdiction of a second class Magistrate on the other hand is very much reduced; a second class Magistrate has jurisdiction to try offences for which the maximum term of imprisonment does not exceed twelve (12) months' imprisonment or which are punishable with fine only.[48] In West Malaysia, he may pass any sentence allowed by law not exceeding -

(a) three (3) months' imprisonment;

(b) a fine of two hundred and fifty ringgit (RM250); or

(c) any combination of the above,

and in Sabah and Sarawak, he may pass any sentence allowed by law not exceeding -

(a) six (6) months' imprisonment;

(b) a fine of one thousand ringgit (RM1,000); or

(c) any combination of the aforementioned.

47. The 1948 Act, s.85.
48. The 1948 Act, s.88.

With respect to civil matters, a first class Magistrate may try suits where the amount in dispute or value of the subject-matter does not exceed ten thousand ringgit (RM10,000). A second class Magistrate on the other hand may try civil suits where the plaintiff seeks to recover a debt or liquidated demand in money not exceeding two hundred and fifty ringgit (RM250) in West Malaysia and five hundred ringgit (RM500) in Sabah and Sarawak.

Appeals from the decisions of a Magistrate in criminal and civil matters lie to the High Court.

C. Is There A Need For Reform?

The creation of the Supreme Court brought about a drastic amendment to Section 68 of the Courts of Judicature Act, 1964.[49] The section now provides that no appeal shall be brought to the Supreme Court when the amount or value of the subject-matter at the trial is less than one hundred thousand ringgit (RM100,000), except with the leave of the Supreme Court or a judge of the High Court. The old monetary limit was ten thousand ringgit (RM10,000). One may venture to question the direct effect of the said amendment. In my view, this drastic amendment does not appear to be satisfactory for it deprives a litigant of his automatic right of appeal to the Supreme Court which he would have had under the old provision when the value of the subject-matter was above RM10,000. As the amendment stands, he now requires leave of the Court to appeal.

As may be appreciated, Section 68 has posed considerable difficulties in its implementation owing primarily to the ambiguity of its operative words 'amount or value of the subject matter at the trial'. In a substantial number of cases, the value of the subject matter is usually less than RM100,000. The problem is compounded when leave to appeal is refused by the High Court and/or the Supreme Court. In other words, there would certainly be a total denial or deprivation of a right of appeal against a decision of the High Court. In this regard it means that there is virtually a one tier system.

In view of the above, one may consider the soundness of having a Court of Appeal to replace the Federal Court with the jurisdiction to hear appeals as provided for under the unamended provision of Section

49. Amendment effected by Act A606/84 with effect from 1st January, 1985.

68, viz. the retention of the monetary limit of RM10,000. Thus, if the value of the subject matter is less than RM100,000, an appeal would lie to the Supreme Court only with leave. This therefore means that the Supreme Court would take the place of the Privy Council. However, the idea of a three tier system is not new and has in fact been rejected by the relevant authority. The rejection being a policy decision of the government, it appears unlikely that this proposal will be entertained. What then is the alternative?

A practical solution to the problem, I believe, could be achieved by the enlargement of the jurisdiction of the Sessions Court in both criminal and civil matters. Section 65 of the Subordinate Courts Act, 1948 may be amended to confer jurisdiction on Sessions Court to hear cases (except certain specific cases as mentioned in the Act), where the amount in dispute or the value of the subject-matter does not exceed RM100,000 instead of the monetary limit of RM25,000 as presently provided. In the light of this, other relevant provisions as contained in sections 69, 70 and 71 will have to be reviewed.[50]

By reason of the enlargement in jurisdiction, a litigant, where the amount in dispute or the value of the subject-matter is less than RM100,000 and therefore within the jurisdiction of the Sessions Court, may file his claim in the Sessions Court. By doing so, he automatically has a right of appeal to the High Court for under Section 28 of Act 7 of 1964, the High Court has jurisdiction to hear appeals from a Subordinate Court where the amount in dispute or the value of the subject-matter exceeds five thousand ringgit. And with leave either from the High Court or the Supreme Court as required under the present law, the litigant may go further and appeal to the Supreme Court from a decision of the High Court. From this it is submitted that one may discern a three tier system.

The administration of justice in Malaysia may also be adequately served by a Small Claims Court which, as its name suggests, would deal basically with small claims. Under Article 121 of the Federal Constitution, a federal law may be passed to constitute such court an inferior court and therefore part of the Judicial System.

The need for a small claims court is obvious. Owing to the depreciation in money value, small claims of litigants may be such that recourse to the ordinary court of law with its attendant legal representation may

50. Section 69 deals with the exceptions to the jurisdiction of the Sessions Court; section 70 talks about its jurisdiction to hear matters pertaining to the recovery of immovable property and section 71, covers its jurisdiction to adjudicate on title to immovable property with the consent of the parties.

prove extremely costly. For example, the fees to counsel for legal representation alone may far exceed the amount in dispute or value of the subject matter of the claim. It is suggested that a Small Claims Court be established with jurisdiction to try civil cases where the amount in dispute or value of the subject matter does not exceed, say for instance, three thousand ringgit (RM3,000). The Court should be manned by experienced officers, not necessarily legally qualified, and legal representation, by the nature of the claim, may not be necessary. In this way, not only would the costs of litigation be minimal, there would also be a speedy disposal of cases. The proposed establishment of the Small Claims Court is now under active consideration by a Committee appointed to submit all necessary recommendations.

BIBLIOGRAPHY

STATUTES

Civil Law Act, 1956 (Revised–1972)
Courts of Judicature Act, 1964
Federation of Malaya Agreement, 1948
Federal Constitution 1957
Legal Profession Act, 1976
Subordinate Courts Act, 1948

ARTICLES

Note,*Jurisdiction of Military Courts* (1946) 12 MLJ xcxxii.

Lee, H.H. *A Short Legal History of Sarawak* (1977) 2 MLJ lviii.

Sim, E.E. *An Account of the Japanese Occupation of the Settlement of Penang, Straits Settlement (1941-1945) with Special Reference to Administration in the Judicial Department (1981)* 2 MLJ clxix.

Yusof, M.A. *Post-War Political Changes, Constitutional Developments Towards Independence and Changing Conceptions of Judicial Review in Malaysia* (1982) JMCL 19-40.

BOOKS

Hashim, M.S. *An Introduction to the Constitution of Malaysia* Kuala Lumpur: Government Printers, 1972.

Hashim, M.S., H.P. Lee and **F.A. Trinidade** (ed.). *The Constitution of Malaysia—1st Development: 1957-1977* Kuala Lumpur: Oxford University Press, 1978.

Sheridan, L.A. and **H.E. Groves.** *The Constitution of Malaysia* 3rd ed., Singapore: Malayan Law Journal (Pte.) Ltd, 1979.

Chew Aiman, *The Development of the Malaysian Judiciary* (unpublished Doctor of Philosophy Thesis).

ACKNOWLEDGEMENT

I express my thanks to Miss Soo Ai Lin, LLB (Hons.) (Mal.), LLM (Monash), Senior Assistant Registrar, Supreme Court, Malaysia, for the valuable assistance rendered in putting up this paper.

POSTSCRIPT

Courts of Judicature (Amendment) Bill 1986
Subordinate Courts (Amendment) Bill 1986

In Part C of my paper entitled "Is there a need for reform?", mention was made of the difficulties posed by and the resultant problems created by the operation of Section 68(1)(a) of the Courts of Judicature Act, 1964. As also stated, the prescribed ceiling of one hundred thousand ringgit (RM100,000) has rendered most civil appeals from the High Court non-appealable to the Supreme Court unless prior leave to appeal was obtained either from the High Court or the Supreme Court. Implicit in the suggestion put forward for an enhanced civil jurisdiction of the Sessions Court is an attempt to introduce into the existing structure a three-tier system in the Malaysian administration of justice.

I am pleased to say that the aforesaid suggestion will soon see the light of day and its objective attained. At the time of writing this postscript, the Courts of Judicature (Amendment) Bill 1986 and the Subordinate Courts (Amendment) Bill 1986, which seek to amend Section 68(1)(a) and enhance the civil jurisdiction of the Sessions Courts respectively, have been tabled before the Malaysian Parliament. They have since gone through the First Reading at the Dewan Rakyat. The Bill has, however, been deferred for consideration by Parliament at its sitting in March, 1987.

By section 3 of the Subordinate Courts (Amendment) Bill 1986, section 65 of the Subordinate Courts Act, 1948 is proposed to be amended by substituting the words "twenty-five" by the words "one hundred" appearing therein. The new section 65 which refers to the civil jurisdiction of a Sessions Court will therefore read:

> "... a Sessions Court shall have jurisdiction to try all actions and suits of a civil nature where the amount in dispute or value of the subject-matter does not exceed one hundred thousand ringgit."

In line with this enhanced jurisdiction, by section 2 of the Bill, the designation of "President of Sessions Court" will be substituted with "Sessions Court Judge."

The proposed amendment to Section 68(1)(a) of the Courts of Judicature Act, 1964 by section 4 of the Courts of Judicature (Amendment) Bill 1986, reads as follows:

> 68.(1) No appeal shall be brought to the Supreme Court in any of the following cases:
>
> (a) when the amount or value of the subject matter of the claim (exclusive of interest) is less than one hundred thousand ringgit, with the leave of the Supreme Court or a judge of the High Court.

It is to be observed that the words "amount or value'of the subject matter at the trial" in the unamended section 68(1)(a) which had caused considerable difficulties in interpretation, have been deleted in the proposed amendment.

AMENDMENTS TO THE COMPANIES ACT: IMPACT AND IMPLICATIONS*

I am very honoured to be present here this morning to deliver the Opening Address at the Seminar on Amendments to the Companies Act: Their Impact and Implications.

I am of the view that the real impact and implications of some of these amendments could only be fully appreciated as and when they come up for judicial determination in a court of law.

Speaking of law, many are ignorant of it. Judges are no exception so the story goes. I am reminded of the story of Lord Mansfield, appointed Chief Justice of the King's Bench in 1756, who was a man noted for his impartiality, which his sterner critics put down to his ignorance of the higher principles of the law. When confronted with the leading advocates of the day his Lordship sometimes allowed his heart to rule his tongue. To Sergeant Davy who was arguing a knotty point before him he was rash enough to comment without any justification, "If this be law, sir, I must burn all my books," which allowed Sergeant Davy to retort, "your Lordship had better read them first."

Be that as it may, I have always held the view that well-informed public discussions on laws enacted by Parliament are essential in a parliamentary democracy such as ours. Such discussions result in a greater understanding of new legislations; they could serve to disentangle the mysteries and complexities of the laws: they do provide a forum for the users of law to identify inherent weaknesses in the law, and more importantly, they help to create a better understanding between law makers and those for whom the laws are made.

The law being so mysterious and complex, it is sometimes said that it is an ass. The question that arises is this: is it in law or in fact? In a matter that came up before a judge in a Chicago Court the judge ruled that certain evidence presented before him was inadmissible. This greatly annoyed the attorney concerned, who insisted that there was nothing wrong with it. "I know, your Honour, that it is proper evidence," he complained. "Here I have been practising at the bar for forty years, and now I want to know if I am a fool?" "That," replied the judge quietly, "is a question of fact, and not one of law, and so I won't pass upon it, but will let the jury decide."

**At The Seminar Organized By The School Of Law And School Of Accountancy Of ITM On 1st October, 1985.*

But some may say that law is life itself, at any rate, like life itself. As the legal authority, J.A.R. Cairns, put it most precisely in his book *The Loom of the Law*:

> "Like life itself, it is packed with paradoxes, incongruities, absurdities; laughter jostles the heels of despair, sunshine peeps through clouds and shadows, yet everything seems just as it ought to be. The loom has been built piece by piece through long generations. It is a vast complex machine of infinite parts, and it bears the impress of manifold limitations. Every living soul is within the reach of its machinery, and you and I may be of its weaving tomorrow."

George Bernard Shaw's splendid definition of law reads:

> "We expect it to be ideal and almost inspired," he said, "whereas it is only an imperfect, rough-and-ready device of mankind to keep people from sending each other to the devil."

I would like to add that specialised and technical laws such as those affecting corporations and the securities industry are more often infringed because of lack of understanding of the laws rather than through wilful disobedience. These laws prescribe a new commercial morality which has to be strictly adhered to for the commercial system to work efficiently. Sometimes they need to adhere to rules which are seemingly innocuous. Take, for example, the laws regulating insider dealing. It is essential for the proper working of the securities market that all investors should have equal access to information and that insiders in companies whose securities are traded in the market should not exploit confidential information for their own advantage or for the advantage of their relatives or friends. There seems to be a clear prohibition in law against disclosure of such information. Yet, many company officers and employees continue to give friendly "tips" to friends and family. They fail to see the seriousness of such divulgences. They see their act as being harmless because there is no visible or obvious consequences to their act.

It would therefore take education, as much as law and enforcement, to make people understand the seriousness of such acts and their cumulative effect on the securities market. Seminars like this would help to ensure that knowledge of the purpose of this type of law extends to all persons involved in the securities market. It is extremely gratifying to see institutions of higher education organizing public seminars and conferences to discuss new laws. I am happy to see that the organizers of the seminar have sought the support of legal and accounting professionals to achieve their objectives.. From the impressive list of professionals delivering papers and acting as discussants, I am confident that the participants present here would all enjoy a very lively and lucid discussion of the new amendments to the Companies Act 1965.

Changes to company legislation are slow in coming and far in between. The Companies Act was passed in 1965 and as far as I can recollect, there has only been one other amendment to the Act. Even the present amendments went through a gestation period of almost ten years. This is how it has to be because commercial men, more than others, need certainty in the laws that affect them. It would not serve the interests of commerce to have frequent changes made to the law. It is very unsettling. The recent amendments, while not altering the basic jurisprudence of common law company legislations, have brought about some very significant and innovative changes to many parts of the Act. Some of the provisions introduced have been long looked forward to by Malaysian companies. The new law on merger-accounting is the first of its kind in this region. I am sure that these provisions would be very beneficial to companies effecting mergers. Other amendments like the new disclosure provisions may involve additional financial burden to companies. The extensive disclosure provisions would also require a greater degree of frankness from shareholders as to their shareholdings in public companies. Substantial shareholders may no longer be able to conceal their ownership of shares. These and other regulations may take a long time getting used to but in the end they would ensure a greater efficiency and orderliness in the market.

Before ending my short address, I would like to take this opportunity to congratulate the School of Law and the School of Accountancy of ITM for organizing this timely seminar. I hope that you have a successful deliberation.

THE LABOUR LAWS OF MALAYSIA : THEIR PRACTICE, SAFEGUARDS AND SHORTCOMINGS*

It is a privilege to be invited by the Pudu Rotary Club to deliver the Opening Address and to declare open the Seminar on The Labour Laws of Malaysia. A few weeks ago, to be exact on 1st October, 1985, I declared open a Seminar on Amendments to the Companies Act. It would thus seem that I am fast becoming a regular customer in delivering opening addresses.

Speaking of a regular customer, I am reminded of a story where a circuit judge, before passing sentence on a burglar previously convicted five times, cautioned him that it is time that he be checked on his career of crime. The judge then asked him,

> "How many years imprisonment did you get on the last occasion?"
>
> "Seven, my Lord."
>
> "Seven!" remarked the Judge. "Then this time I shall give you a maximum of fifteen."
>
> "Maximum?" replied the burglar. "Do I not as a regular customer get a bit of discount?"

Seriously speaking, I am confident that this Seminar will be a great success. It would undoubtedly provide an opportunity for both speakers and participants to air their views on matters pertinent to the theme of the Seminar, to put across whatever doubts that may be entertained, to highlight the shortcomings and, maybe, to offer constructive suggestions as to how the shortcomings may be remedied.

Speaking of success, a great deal also depends upon the relevancy and liveliness of the topics to be discussed. Like all discussions, however, they could be very tedious and devoid of any pleasure.

Speaking of being tedious, the story goes that a Lord Justice in London delivered a ruling after hearing a tedious argument from a verbose barrister as follows:

**At The Seminar Organized By The Pudu Rotary Club Held In Putra World Trade Centre On 2nd November, 1985.*

"Counsel for the appellant has raised six points in support of this appeal. On the first point, there is nothing and the same applies to all the others. Five times nothing is nothing. The appeal is dismissed."

Another Lord Justice was presiding over a case in which a leading lawyer argued a long and dreary political dispute (present dispute excepted). The lawyer was still addressing the Court when adjournment time came and consequently asked his Lordship when it would be his pleasure to hear the remainder of the argument. His Lordship replied,

"I am bound to hear you out, Sir, and it will be soon. But take it from me, the pleasure has long been out of the question."

I have noticed that the topics to be discussed are covered by the papers to be presented at this Seminar and are indeed very appropriate to the theme, namely, *The Practice, Safeguards and Shortcomings of the Labour Laws of Malaysia*. The topics on the Role of the Government in Industrial Relations, that of employers in promoting such relations and the Role of Industrial Relations in Public Service are very topical and would undoubtedly generate a lot of interest. Incidentally it is common knowledge that members of the Public Service Unions form one of the largest work forces in this country. By and large, Public Service employees have been able to work harmoniously with the Government. But recent developments like members of Public Service Unions speaking of picketing and intending to hold a general strike seem to have given rise to some anxiety. The question therefore is, can it be that somewhere along the line, communications between the Government and the Public Service Unions have broken down? In this regard the paper on "Industrial Relations In Public Service" is appropriate and timely. Issues such as how industrial relations are to be co-ordinated and carried out at the Public Service level, the rules and regulations that govern the conduct of such industrial relations and the mode of solving industrial problems in the public service are matters of public importance.

The paper on "The Role of Government In Industrial Relations" would, I am sure, highlight issues such as whether the country enjoys industrial peace and harmony or, on the contrary, is beset by industrial strife and discord. In this regard a matter of concern is the attitude of the Government towards industrial relations. All these, I am sure, would stimulate active discussion.

I do not propose to speculate but I believe some of the participants may express the view that the Government is impervious and deaf to the welfare and wishes of the country's work force and they account for industrial unrest, while some may take the opposite view and contend that the Government has given in too much to the demands of Trade Unions.

For myself I would say that by and large, this country is relatively free from industrial strife and unrest. This fact speaks well of the Government, the Unions, the employers and employees and is a matter to be proud of. It also bears testimony to the mature and responsible attitude of the Government towards industrial relations; an attitude that favours the creation of a proper balance between the needs and welfare of the workers and the business well-being of the employers. Be that as it may, a further question necessarily emerging is whether there can be industrial peace or harmony, despite such an attitude on the part of the Government, unless there is support and co-operation from employers and employees. The question begs an answer. In the circumstances, therefore, it is of utmost importance to bear in mind that all parties concerned — the Government, the employers and employees — have very vital roles to play in the stability and well-being of a nation.

On that note, I declare this Seminar open.

APPLICATION FOR A SPEECH*

During the last few days when I was in Penang presiding over the Supreme Court Sitting an application was made to me. In response to the application made by Mr. Ronald Khoo accompanied by an affidavit in support affirming that my wife and I and my colleagues and their wives have been invited to the Bar Council Dinner at no charge, I came back. I have been chosen to pay for the dinner with a speech. On that strong ground I gave the O.I.T. No order as to costs was made.

Since we are given free meals, the least I can do is to convey to the hosts our sincere thanks and appreciation for the kind gesture. And I am sure they would continue to invite us in the future.

The order in terms was for me only to give a short speech. Indeed it will be so. The food has been very good and I have eaten too much. With a heavy stomach I suffer from an empty head to give a long speech. The reason why this is so may also be due to the fact that we are so used to speaking while towering on a Bench so high up that we are quite hopeless on the floor so low down. Be that as it may, this should not be so because language and words are the tools of our trade.

Speaking of tools of trade, I am reminded of a defendant who was charged with burglary and for being in possession of a burglar's implements such as screw-driver, jack, hammer, etc. He explained to the judge that they were the tools of his trade. "That precisely is what the prosecution is alleging," said the judge.

At this point may I seriously say that we are pleased to be present with all of you at this social gathering. We enjoyed the dinner. I should not therefore spoil it with a serious speech. I must, however, stress that the opportunity to be together with lawyers, judges, judicial and legal officers is most welcome. It should help to build up a spirit of goodwill and friendship among us. This is essential to foster a closer rapport between the Bench, the Bar and other members of the legal service.

At this point, may I also say that I had in the past expressed the hope that there would be a speeding-up of trials. I had done this to remind all parties

---

**At The Bar Council Dinner In Ming Court Hotel, Kuala Lumpur On 14th March, 1986.*

concerned that we do have a serious problem of backlog of cases in our courts. To ensure success in our efforts to dispose of them, positive action taken by the courts alone is not enough. It is necessary that lawyers co-operate. There is a need for total commitment by all parties concerned to solve the problem. Basically this is the reason why I have time and again stressed my disapproval of unnecessary applications for postponements.

I have promised to be short and less serious for the reason that this is a social gathering. Speaking of social gatherings, the story goes that at one of them the Lord Chief Justice, present company excepted, was asked if he had tried gin and ginger. "No," replied the Lord Chief Justice, "but I have tried a lot of chaps who have."

After listening for some time to a case between two neighbours over a small matter, the judge suggested to the counsel representing the parties that perhaps a compromise would settle the matter. As one of the parties was a rather deaf old lady, the counsel had to shout.

"His Lordship wants to know what you will take?" enquired the lawyer in a loud voice.

The old lady replied immediately, "I thank his Lordship very kindly," she said, "if it's no inconvenience to him, I'll take a brandy and some ginger ale."

I now tell you the story of a Magistrate who, set on giving the defendant before him a light sentence, asked the man about to be bound over if he had any friends who could act as sureties.

"The Almighty is my friend," the man replied.

"Yes, yes, but the point is whether you can give us a name of a friend living near."

"The Almighty is a friend and he is here, there and everywhere," replied the man.

"I know," said the Magistrate, "but I am afraid we have to think of someone of more settled habits."

Speaking of the Almighty, here is a story where he was called as a witness. At the end of a trial, the defendant was asked by the judge if he wanted to call any witness. He replied, "None, but my Maker who is well aware of my complete innocence." "Gentlemen," said the judge to the jury. "the prisoner is charged with stealing a watch. He calls a witness who does not appear. On the other hand, two witnesses saw him take the watch. Consider your verdict."

To conclude in a much lighter vein, let me tell you two true stories. The first is that of a young nun. Expelled from her Order for certain breaches of the rules of the convent, she appeared before a London court. The lawyer, who acted for the young girl, cross-examined the mother superior of the convent. He asked,

"And you said, among her offences, was the eating of a few grapes."

"Yes," said the mother superior, "and grapes are forbidden in a community consisting of nuns who have taken a vow of poverty."

"But eating a few grapes is not a crime," persisted the lawyer.

"That depends on your point of view," came the reply. "After all we all know what happened because a certain person ate an apple."

Next is the story of another Lord Chief Justice, again the present company excepted. The Lord Chief Justice had a reputation of being swayed by evidence of pretty witnesses. And so while presenting a particularly hopeless case, the lawyer (Khoo) put a pretty and blushing young girl into the witness box. For a few moments, the Chief Justice was quite distracted by the beauty before him, but catching sight of the look on the lawyer's face said, "Mr. Khoo (the lawyer), I do not mind admitting there may be occasions where testimony by this kind might have affected me, but that was a long time ago. I am now an extinct volcano." Irresistibly, the Lord Chief Justice's eyes were drawn back to the girl and Mr. Khoo, noticing this again, added, after a short pause, "I do not know, my Lord, but there might be a rumble in the old crater yet."

So be it.

HARI PALANG MERAH DAN BULAN SABIT MERAH SEDUNIA 1986*

Saya amat berbangga pada pagi ini kerana diberi penghormatan untuk mengambil tabik hormat dan memeriksa perbarisan tahunan PBSMM Cawangan Pulau Pinang sempena menyambut Hari Palang Merah dan Bulan Sabit Merah Sedunia bagi tahun 1986 ini. Perbarisan ini terdiri daripada 1,000 orang ahli-ahli Pasukan Bantuan Sukarela dan Belia.

Sukacita saya mengucapkan tahniah kepada Pengerusi, Pegawai-Pegawai dan ahli-ahli PBSMM Cawangan Pulau Pinang kerana telah bekerja keras bagi menjayakan Perbarisan ini yang mana saya percaya telah mengambil masa yang lama untuk merancang, mengatur dan berlatih bagi mencapai prestasi yang tinggi sepertimana yang kita telah dapat saksikan pagi tadi.

PBSMM Cawangan Pulau Pinang adalah satu dari beberapa Cawangan yang sangat aktif dan teguh dari segi pentadbiran, kewangan dan keahliannya. Cawangan ini telah giat menjalankan pelbagai aktiviti yang berterusan sepanjang tahun seperti Perkhidmatan Ambulan (secara Ad-Hoc), Bantuan Bencana Alam, tugas-tugas pertolongan cemas, rancangan derma darah, lawatan hospital dan bantuan-bantuan kepada orang-orang tua dan orang-orang cacat.

Saya difahamkan Cawangan ini telah menubuhkan beberapa pasukan sukarela di institusi-institusi pengajian tinggi seperti di Universiti Sains Malaysia dan Maktab-Maktab Latihan Perguruan termasuk kilang-kilang dan hotel-hotel bagi melatih penuntut-penuntut dan pekerja-pekerja dalam bidang memberi pertolongan cemas, bantuan bencana alam dan perkhidmatan-perkhidmatan masyarakat untuk meningkatkan pengetahuan dan kefahaman mereka dalam aspek-aspek perkhidmatan sukarela.

Dalam konteks ini, saya suka mengesyorkan agar Cawangan mengambil kesempatan ini menerapkan dalam program-program latihan dan kursus mereka unsur-unsur Undang-Undang Kemanusiaan Antarabangsa dan Prinsip-Prinsip Palang Merah dan Bulan Sabit Merah supaya perkara ini dapat disebarkan dengan seluas-luasnya.

Seterusnya saya mengambil kesempatan ini merayu kepada firma-firma, kilang-kilang dan orang-orang perseorangan agar dapat memberi sokongan terhadap projek-projek kutipan derma Cawangan ini terutama sekali projek

---

**Di Perbarisan Tahunan Persatuan Bulan Sabit Merah Malaysia (Malaysian Red Crescent Society) Cawangan Pulau Pinang, Pada 29hb Jun, 1986 Di Pulau Pinang.*

cabutan Loteri PBSMM Kebangsaan tahun 1986 yang akan dilancarkan dalam sedikit masa lagi untuk membolehkan Cawangan ini menjalankan khidmat-khidmat sukarelanya dan memberi bantuan kepada mereka yang memerlukan.

Akhirnya, saya mengambil kesempatan ini sekali lagi mengucapkan setinggi-tinggi penghargaan dan tahniah kepada Pengerusi PBSMM Cawangan Pulau Pinang, Encik Khoo Leong Hun, Pegawai-Pegawai dan ahli-ahli sekalian atas segala pengorbanan samada masa dan tenaga yang mereka telah berikan demi untuk kepentingan masyarakat keseluruhannya. Saya yakin dengan kepimpinan Pengerusinya yang bijaksana Cawangan Pulau Pinang akan terus berkembang dan berjaya.

I take this opportunity to read out to you the World Red Cross Day Message from our National Chairman, Y.M. Tunku Tan Sri Mohamed bin Tunku Besar Burhanuddin to all our Branches:

> "Every year on May 8, the Persatuan Bulan Sabit Merah Malaysia (Malaysian Red Crescent Society) joins 136 other National Red Cross and Red Crescent Societies throughout the World in commemorating World Red Cross and Red Crescent Day. The day marks the birthdate of Jean Henry Dunant, the man who was most instrumental in founding this International chain of Humanitarian Red Cross and Red Crescent Societies."

Each year a pragmatic theme is chosen to illustrate and convey the ideals of the Red Cross/Red Crescent as contained in the Red Cross and Red Crescent principles of Humanity, Impartiality, Neutrality, Independence, Voluntary Service, Unity and Universality. This year the theme chosen is blood donation and the slogan reads "Give Blood–Save Life". We in Malaysia view blood donation as an essential community service and thus have embarked on several projects to recruit blood donors and instill an awareness of the importance of donating blood.

This year is also the United Nations International Year of Peace. The Red Cross and Red Crescent Movement does not view peace simply as the absence of war, but rather as a dynamic process of co-operation among all States and peoples, co-operation founded on freedom, independence, a fair and equitable distribution of resources to meet the needs of people all over the world. Though peace, as a dynamic process of co-operation among all States and peoples, must necessarily be a collective responsibility, it nevertheless requires individual conviction and commitment.

It is noteworthy therefore that the Second World Red Cross and Red Crescent Conference on Peace held in Finland and Sweden in the autumn of 1984, re-dedicated its conviction to the promotion of its Programme of Action for Peace and adopted a Peace Message to the World Community. In the fostering of peace, our own Society's initiative consisted of a peace message conveyed through a specially composed song entitled "TAKE THE FIRST STEP" to peace.

In its day to day activities, the main thrust of the Malaysian Red Crescent Society (MRCS) is directed towards the four major areas — all contributing towards peace. These areas are:-

* Protection and Assistance

* Community Service

* Youth Activities

* Development

I am, therefore, on this auspicious day, appealing to all Red Cross and Red Crescent members to re-dedicate themselves to the high ideals of the Red Cross and Red Crescent movement. Let us "TAKE THE FIRST STEP" to peace.

Sekian, Selamat maju jaya.

THE PRESS, THE LAW AND THE COURTS

Saya telah diundang untuk berucap di kursus/bengkel bertajuk "Akhbar, Undang-Undang dan Mahkamah" dan seterusnya merasmikan kursus ini. Ini adalah suatu penghormatan bagi diri saya dan saya ucapkan setinggi-tinggi penghargaan.

Saya difahamkan bahawa Institut Akhbar Malaysia (A.I.M.) adalah sebuah badan yang menerima bantuan kerajaan dan bertujuan, antara lain, meningkatkan prestasi perkhidmatan para wartawan tanahair. Saya juga difahamkan bahawa kursus seperti ini sudah pasti akan memberi kesempatan kepada wartawan kita, khasnya para pemberita kanan mahkamah dan penyunting kanan memahami dengan lebih mendalam lagi masaalah yang mereka hadapi dalam menjalankan tugas harian masing-masing. Bahawasanya juga diharapkan dengan adanya kursus serupa ini prestasi penulisan dan pengliputan berita-berita mahkamah dapat dipertingkatkan serta laporan-laporan dapat dihasilkan dengan lebih tepat, jelas dan saksama.

At this point, may I turn to the topic for the Seminar, namely "The Press, the Law and the Courts". The topic is, to my mind, very wide and there is a great deal that we can speak of it. Conceivably it covers a very wide scope and would certainly stimulate and provoke an interesting and fruitful discussion. When I accepted the invitation to speak (probably a mistake), I had not fully appreciated the gravity of the task I had undertaken. It's too late to regret. I have accepted. The only choice open to me is to speak to you of what little I know. Hopefully I can live up to your expectations.

In the course of my speech I propose to deal briefly with laws which are pertinent to the subject at hand and also of relevance to you.

When speaking of the press, one invariably thinks of the freedom of the press.

Freedom of Speech as Fundamental Liberty under the Constitution

Freedom of speech and expression is one of the fundamental liberties enshrined in the Federal Constitution.

Article 10, Clause (1)(a) of the Constitution states:

At The Opening Of The Malaysian Press Institute's Course/Workshop At Wisma Bernama On 30th March, 1987.

"Every citizen has the right to freedom of speech and expression."

The Article does not of course expressly refer to freedom of the press, but as freedom of the press means the freedom to write or publish without censorship, the freedom of speech and expression referred to in the said Article must logically include freedom of the press.

Freedom of the Press: Incidence of Freedom of Speech

Freedom of the press as an incidence of freedom of speech is a provocative and challenging issue of our times. The importance of freedom of speech and expression cannot be overestimated because it lies at the foundation of all democratic governments for without free political discussion no public education is possible. Some say it is a cause for which men are willing to fight and die. The press obviously is one of the most powerful forces in the world.

Freedom of speech goes to the heart of the natural right of an organized freedom loving society to impart and acquire information. The essence of the right does not consist in merely making use of the human voice but lies in the ability to convey one's views to others. It follows that the right to freedom of speech and expression carries with it the right to propagate and circulate one's views and opinions. The freedom of the press includes the freedom of circulation—complete freedom to write and publish without censorship or restriction save such as is absolutely necessary for the preservation of society—its safety and security.

However, a freedom of such amplitude might involve risks of abuse. It is an abuse to incite violence and crime and political and social unrest and public disorder. The Government, by that I mean the legislative, executive and judicial limbs of the Government, however, shall have to be protected against unlawful conduct of the press. Accordingly, freedom of speech and of the press do not comprehend the right to speak or write on any subject whatsoever at anytime.

Limitations, Restrictions and Restraints

Freedom of speech and of the press are therefore subject to limitations, restrictions, restraints and prohibitions imposed by statutes and the common law. Restraints are imposed by the Federal Constitution, the law of contempt of court, the Penal Code, the Courts of Judicature Act 1964 (Revised 1972), the Printing Presses and Publications Act 1984, the Sedition Act 1948 (Revised 1969), the Cinematographic Films (Censorship) Act 1952 (Revised 1971), the Public Order (Preservation) Act 1959 (Revised 1983), the Internal Security Act 1960, the Official Secrets Act 1972, the Defamation Act 1957 (Revised

1983), the Copyright Act 1969, though the enumeration is not exhaustive. I shall highlight briefly some of these provisions.

Constitutional Restrictions

Like practically all the other fundamental liberties enshrined in the Constitution, freedom of speech and expression is not absolute. Article 10(2) qualifies that freedom in the following terms:

> "(2) Parliament may by law impose -
>
> Such restriction as it deems necessary or expedient in the interest of the security of the Federation or any part thereof, friendly relations with other countries, public order or morality and restrictions designed to protect the privileges of Parliament or of any Legislative Assembly or to provide against contempt of court, defamation, or incitement to any offence."

A great jurist William Blackstone said:

> "The liberty of the press is indeed essential to the nature of a free state; but this consists in laying no previous restraints upon publications, and not in freedom from censure for criminal matter when published. Every freeman has an undoubted right to lay what sentiments he pleases before the public; to forbid this, is to destroy the freedom of the press; but if he publishes what is improper, mischievous or illegal, he must take the consequences of his temerity."

The rationale for providing such restrictions on the freedom of speech and expression is readily comprehensible and I feel it does not require much amplification or elaboration.

Thus, there is a plethora of legislation in the country which trammel upon the freedom of the press to write and publish whatever it likes. The breach of the provisions of these laws carries with it penal consequences. I shall refer to some of these legislations in due course.

When we speak of the press, one, for obvious reasons, refers to newspapers. Our law defines "newspaper" to mean "any publication containing news, intelligence, reports of occurrences or any remarks, observations or comments, in relation to such news, intelligence or occurrences, or to any other matter of public interest, or any magazine, comic or other forms of periodical printed in any language for sale or free distribution at regular or irregular intervals." (Section 2 of the Printing Presses and Publications Act 1984). The object of the Act itself is to regulate the use of printing presses and the printing, importation, production, reproduction, publishing and distribution of publications and for matters connected therewith.

The Act covers a very wide spectrum of matters. In like manner the definition of "newspaper" too is very wide. The definition covers almost every kind of publication. The Act, as can be seen, imposes prior restraints. It prohibits the keeping for use or using a printing press unless a licence has been granted under the relevant provisions (Section 3). It also prohibits the printing, importation, publishing, selling, circulation or distribution, or offering to publish, selling, circulation or distribution, of any newspaper printed in Malaysia or Singapore unless there has been granted by the Minister in respect of such newspaper a permit under the relevant provisions (Section 5). Violation or contravention of or any disobedience to these provisions will result in penal consequences.

Other provisions found in the Act related to the topic at hand, *inter alia*, include those designed to control undesirable publications, prohibition of such publications with penal consequences, in particular for possession of such prohibited publications by any person (Sections 7 & 8).

The more serious provision, in fact the life and death of a newspaper, hang on Section 13, which empowers the Minister to revoke a licence or a permit granted under the provisions of the Act. Additionally "if the Minister is satisfied that any printing press in respect of which the licence has been issued is used for printing of any publication which is prejudicial to public order or national security or that any newspaper in respect of which a permit has been issued contains anything which is prejudicial to public order or national security, he may revoke such licence or permit without giving the person who is issued with such licence an opportunity to show cause why such licence or permit should not be revoked."

Writers have deliberated much on the topic, and, in particular have embarked upon considerable analysis on the question of restraints on the freedom of the press and have observed that the law regards and is right to regard this type of restraints as prior restraints that should be viewed with hostility.

In England, for example, licensing of the press under the Licensing Act was repealed in 1695 when the annual legislation under which the Stationer's Company used to control the publication of newspapers and pamphlets were not renewed. (See W.S. Holdsworth's *Press Control and Copyright in the 16th and 17th Centuries* (1929) 29 LJ 841). There has been no general censorship of the press since that time, nevertheless, there was no general or blanket sanction to freedom of expression.

In the United States prior restraints are rarely countenanced and there is a heavy presumption against their constitutional validity. It is difficult to rebut even in cases involving government secrets.

However, British law and, by and large, our law, adopts a more pragmatic approach.

In this country, the press enjoys a very substantial degree of freedom though subject to certain restrictions and restraints by way of legislative impositions. Such restrictions and restraints, however, shall have to be within the ambit or confines of the enshrined restrictive provisions of the Constitution.

While the Constitution is explicit about its guarantee of the right of free expression which includes freedom of the press the freedom, however, has its price in that the press shall have to police its own action. This is vital to secure integrity of journalism. Evidently the press itself must assume the responsibilities to ensure accuracy and fairness in reporting. Another factor of crucial importance is that while it is essential to act responsibly to secure accuracy and fairness in reporting, it must also make itself accountable for its own actions. Accountability is, in my view, fundamental to the integrity of journalism. If the press should lay down rules it should also decide how they are to be enforced. Lapses in the enforcement may give rise to disputes between the media and their critics. Some criticisms may well be justified. Some may not. Lapses in editorial judgments and failures to meet reasonable standards of accuracy and fairness may cause members of the public it serves to suspect the press' own ethical commitments.

By and large, it is accepted that the press has a vital role to play, namely, as public watchdogs and advocates.

But we must not forget that the press too has its weaknesses which the press itself should readily acknowledge. An American, Tom Johnson, the publisher of the *Los Angeles Times*, who previously held the position as Assistant Press Secretary to President Lyndon B. Johnson, Executive Vice-President and Director of the Texas Broadcasting Corporation and publisher of the *Dallas Times Herald*, had this to say in an article entitled *A Publisher Reflects on Freedom of the Press*:

> "The press has its weaknesses, and these must be acknowledged. We seek excellence, but no institution can rid itself of all imperfections. There indeed have been violations of journalistic ethics. Because the transgressions of one reflect poorly on all, each violation sounds an alarm throughout the profession. Instead of offering excuses or retreating behind the well-worn rhetoric of the people's right to know, we must always have the courage to recognize our errors and the wisdom to seek ways to correct them."

In my opinion the crucial questions that emerge and which should be subject to rigorous scrutiny at this Seminar are —

(a) whether we need more new laws, executive orders, restrictive court decisions to regulate the press and

(b) whether excessive legislative impositions and restrictions are conducive to or are in the best interest of our democratic way of life.

I had occasion to observe recently, during proceedings on an admission of a lawyer to the Bar, while speaking on the freedom of the individual with reference to fundamental liberty that -

> "A fundamental principle which is universally recognised is that of the freedom of the individual; where there is a conflict between freedom and any other rights or interests, then, no matter how great or powerful those others may be, the freedom of the individual must necessarily prevail. However, such freedom is not absolute and we do subscribe to what was stated by Lord Denning, namely that 'the freedom must be matched of course with social security.....and peace and good order of the community.'
>
> The freedom of speech or expression, as we all know, is one of the fundamental liberties which is enshrined in our Federal Constitution. ...
>
> Excessive encroachments or interventions would significantly undermine this fundamental principle and render it meaningless. ... We all live in a society under a system of parliamentary democracy and are subject to the laws of the land. We acknowledge that there will have to be legal restraints on the freedom of an individual by means of legislative impositions which are constitutionally permissible, and which are imposed primarily in the interest of security and public order. Nonetheless, these restraints being *ipso facto* exceptions should be subordinate to and not prevail over the fundamental principle."

I feel that serious thought should be given by the authorities before enacting new laws to avoid unnecessary or excessive restrictions or restraints—laws which may not be conducive to or in the interests of our democratic way of life. I hasten to add that the press itself must act responsibly. It is incumbent upon the press, as its primary responsibility, to avoid creating a situation which compels the authorities to introduce more new laws or executive directions. It is fundamental that the press adheres strictly to the concept of accountability. Moreover, it should also be its duty to behave properly and ethically. Where it has behaved improperly and unethically, an acknowledgement of it is essential to maintain its credibility. A free press should not abuse its privilege by violating the trust vested in it by the public and by our Constitution.

If it should fail to do so, it may mean that while it is willing to enjoy the privilege, it is not so willing to apply to itself the same standard it demands of others.

By and large, newspapers are the strongest influences in the communities or societies they serve. They expose folly, untruthfulness and crooked dealings. The press can demonstrate how in some cases decisions made by corporate bodies could create problems and cause dangerous and damaging consequences. Newspapers will serve public interest so long as the press' ethical principles place primary emphasis on that end. Further only by strictly adhering to these ethical principles can credibility be assuredly maintained.

If I may, I should also like to quote what the American writer I referred to earlier said:

> "I believe that most of the people—the ultimate beneficiaries of a free press—continue to look to us as a guarantor of their liberty. This support demonstrates a fundamental public confidence in our ability and determination to do our job, and do it well, within our constitutional framework. This is a source of satisfaction. It should not be an invitation to complacency."

At this juncture, may I propose to speak briefly on specific legislations which impose restrictions and shall then proceed to deal with two other matters related to the topic, namely, (a) press reporters in court and (b) contempt of court.

LEGISLATIVE RESTRICTIONS

A. Penal Code

Restrictions on freedom of expression may be found in the Penal Code, *inter alia*, under Sections 292, 293, 298A and Sections 499 to 502.

Section 292 prohibits the distribution, exhibition, circulation and so forth of obscene books, pamphlets, etc., with penal consequences, and also the importing of such publications, etc. These restrictions are designed to restrict indecent or immoral publications.

Section 293, on the other hand, is designed to prohibit selling, distributing or circulating to persons under the age of 20 years any such obscene object or publication.

A new Section 298A, recently introduced, prohibits by words either spoken or written, etc., in any manner causing or attempting to cause disharmony, disunity and so forth on grounds of religion. This section also provides penal consequences.

Sections 499 to 502 are offences relating to defamation. Section 499 makes it an offence for a person who either by words spoken or signs, representations and so forth, publishes any imputation concerning any person intending to harm, or knowing or having reason to believe that such imputation will harm the reputation of such person, etc.

Section 500 provides for the punishment while Section 501 deals with printing or engraving the defamatory matters and Section 502 deals with selling or offering to sell any such printed or engraved defamatory matters.

B. The Sedition Act 1948

Problems of national security are serious more so in our multi-racial society. The interest of cherished individual freedom and security of the State must be properly balanced. In the 18th century the British Government made great use of prosecutions for sedition in an attempt to restrict criticism of its conduct in the press. We in Malaysia have made use of the Act in a variety of situations. I do not propose to refer to all of them here.

The object of such law is to provide for the punishment of sedition. Although sedition is not defined, "seditious tendency" is defined as a tendency —

(a) to bring into hatred or contempt or to excite disaffection against any Ruler or against any Government;

(b) to excite the subjects of any Ruler or the inhabitants of any territory governed by any Government to attempt to procure in the territory of the Ruler governed by the Government the alteration, otherwise than by lawful means, of any matter as by law established.

(c) to bring into hatred or contempt, or to excite disaffection against the administration of justice in Malaysia or in any State;

(d) to raise discontent or disaffection amongst the subjects of the Yang di-Pertuan Agong or of any Ruler of any State or amongst the inhabitants of Malaysia or of any State; or

(e) to promote feelings of ill-will and hostility between different races or classes of the population of Malaysia; or

(f) to question any matter, right, status, position, privilege, sovereignty or prerogative, established or protected by the provision of Part III (Citizenship) of the Federal Constitution or Article 152, (National Language), 153 (Reservation of quotas for public service, permits, etc., for Malays, etc.), or 181 (Rulers' sovereignty) of the Federal Constitution.

Press journalists and publishers should be especially concerned with Section 4(c) of the Sedition Act, 1948. It prohibits the printing, publishing, selling, offering for sale, distributing or reproduction of any seditious publication — and there are penal consequences.

C. Internal Security Act 1960

You are, I am sure, familiar with the Internal Security Act 1960. It is enacted to provide for the security of Malaysia, preventive detention and so forth. In the context of the topic of the Seminar, the powers relating to subversive publications are of special relevance.

Under Section 22(1) the Minister, charged with the responsibility of printing presses and publications, may by order prohibit absolutely or subject to conditions the printing, publication, issue, circulation or possession of any document or publication which contains any incitement to violence or which counsels disobedience to the law or is calculated or likely to lead to a breach of the peace or to promote feelings of hostility between the different races or classes of the population or is prejudicial to the national interest, public order or security of Malaysia. In this regard it is to be observed that Section 24 provides the penalty for printing and publication in contravention of Section 22 and Section 25 provides for possession of documents in contravention of Section 22 and Section 27 provides for importation also in contravention of Section 22.

Again as you can see, the Minister's power is very extensive and so are the areas of restrictions covered by the section. Severe penalty is provided by law in the event of any contravention of these provisions.

D. The Official Secrets Act 1972

The law relating to the Official Secrets Act should indeed be very familiar to all of you by now. The Act has been enacted for the purpose of maintaining the safety of the security of the country. The necessity for such a law is universally accepted. Recently, the Act was amended to enable the Government to rule more effectively. It may well be true but the fact remains that the manner in which the law is to be enforced is very vital to society's well being under a democratic way of life.

The question that lurks in the minds of many is whether the amendments are strictly necessary, and if they are, whether they have been framed too widely so as to go beyond the protection of national safety and to cover all kinds of official acts unrelated to security. I do not propose to provide you with the answer — indeed I do not know what the answer is.

There is one aspect of the law, however, which merits special attention. I speak of it to emphasise the strictness of the restraints. Section 8(1) provides that any person who has in his possession or control any official secret or any secret official code word, etc., or any article, document or information which relates to the matters set out in paras (a) to (e), communicates directly or indirectly any such information to any foreign country to whom he is not authorised to communicate is guilty of an offence.

The offence is absolute in that the question of *mens rea* or guilty mind is not relevant. The position is the same in England, where it has been held in a judgment of the Court of Appeal that the offence is absolute. It is committed whatever the motive for disclosure is, and whether or not the disclosure is prejudicial to the State. The essence of the offence is the disclosure of confidential information.

Having regard to the strictness of the law, may I seriously commend that all pressmen be thoroughly conversant with the provisions of the Act for if they were to unwittingly flout these provisions, they will have to face very serious consequences.

E. Cinematographic Films (Censorship) Act 1952

The Cinematographic Films (Censorship) Act 1952 (Revised 1971) deals with censorship on cinematographic films to control exhibition and presentation. This includes production of any music, speech, etc. The penalty for contravention of the law, that is, for exhibiting, selling, distributing, etc., in respect of which a censorship certificate has not been granted is a sentence of imprisonment.

F. Public Order (Preservation) Act 1958

This is an Act not popularly known, nevertheless, it contains provisions which impose restrictions.

The Act relates to the maintenance and restoration of public order. The provisions of the Act are invocable during any period in which a state of danger to public order has been proclaimed by the Minister under Section 3. During such period it is an offence for any person in any place in Malaysia to do any act or utter any word, print, publish, sell, offer for sale, distribute, etc., or have in his possession any document containing any matter which is likely to prejudice the maintenance or restoration of public order.

G. Injunction (inhibits the exercise of free speech)

Another form of prior restraint is the discretionary process of preventive and remedial justice whereby a person is required to refrain from making or stop a future publication. It is what we call an injunction which is a form of judicial censorship. If an article is already published, an injunction may be issued to restrain further publication.

Court injunctions are frequently sought in certain cases to stop publication of a book or report in a newspaper.

In this connection may I invite your attention to the Supreme Court decision (SCCA No 342/85) in the *New Straits Times Press (M) Bhd* v *Airasia Bhd* (1987) 2 MLJ 36. I do so to illustrate the principles governing the issue of injunction in such cases.

In that case *Airasia* claimed damages against the *New Straits Times* for libel — allegedly contained in an article headed 'Danger on Model Job' and another headed 'Cops Check Model Jobs' published in two issues of the *Sunday Mail* dated 14.4.85 and 30.6.85 respectively. *Airasia* also sought an injunction to restrain the *New Straits Times* from publishing such articles. The learned judge in the High Court granted the injunction pending hearing of the action. The *New Straits Times* appealed to the judge to set aside the order. It was dismissed. The *New Straits Times* then appealed to the Supreme Court. The appeal was allowed. I presided at the Supreme Court hearing and delivered the judgment holding that the judge had acted erroneously in the exercise of his discretion when granting the injunction.

This case, like any other, turns not only on the facts but also the law. There were two articles involved. With regard to the first article headlined "Danger in Model Job", *Airasia* alleged that the *Sunday Mail* falsely and maliciously wrote and published the article and it meant that *Airasia* was a disreputable and non-existent company and that its directors were immoral, lewd and promiscuous people when offering employment to a girl, the intention being to procure her for immoral purposes. The second article headed "Cops Check Model Jobs", alleged that the *Sunday Mail* falsely and maliciously published the article and meant that *Airasia* were elusive, shady and dangerous characters whom members of the public must be protected from.

The *Sunday Mail* admitted the publications but denied that they were falsely and maliciously published. They also denied that these articles conveyed the meaning alluded to. They asserted that the matters set out in these articles were

(a) in substance true in fact, and

(b) matters of comment upon a matter of public interest.

The *Sunday Mail* supported their assertion with particulars setting out the case of a schoolgirl who responded to the advertisement but the offer by *Airasia* was for an unknown work and terms and also it was without interview.

One of the questions that called for determination was whether the assertations were on the facts pleaded sufficient to show that there was specific assertation of justification and whether there were sufficient particulars to support the defence of fair comment on matters of public interest.

The question we had to consider was whether an injunction ought to have been granted by the learned judge in a case where the defendant has sufficiently pleaded that he shall rely on a well-recognised defence.

It is settled law that the High Court may grant an interlocutory injunction restraining a defendant from publishing matter which is defamatory or of malicious falsehood. An applicant need not show that there has already been an actionable publication or that damage has been sustained. And in appropriate cases an injunction may be granted *ex parte* before the issue of a writ. (*Halsbury's Laws of England*, 4th Edition, Vol. 28, para 166). This power of the court, however, is a discretionary power and must accordingly be exercised judicially. In exercising such discretion, it is of cardinal importance to bear in mind that

> "Because of the Court's reluctance to fetter free speech and because the questions that arise during the proceedings, such as whether the meaning is defamatory, whether justification or fair comment are applicable and as to malice, are generally for the jury, interlocutory injunctions are granted less readily in defamation proceedings than in other matters and according to different principles." *Halsbury's Laws of England*, 4th Edition, Vol.28, para 167. (See *Quartz Hill Consolidated Gold Mining* v *Beall* 1882 20 ChD 501)."

In *Bonnard* v *Perryman* (1891) 2 ChD 269 at 284, Lord Coleridge, CJ delivering the judgment of the court in which Lord Esher, MR, and Lindley, Brown and Lopes, LJJ concurred emphasised that —

> "The right of free speech is one which it is for the public interest that individuals should possess, and, indeed, that they should exercise without impediment, so long as no wrongful act is done; and, unless an alleged libel is untrue, there is no wrong committed; but, on the contrary, often a very wholesome act is performed in the publication and repetition of an alleged libel. Until it is clear that an alleged libel is untrue, it is not clear that any right at all has been infringed; and the importance of leaving free speech unfettered is a strong reason in cases of libel for dealing most cautiously and warily with the granting of interim injunctions. We entirely approve of, and desire to adopt as our own, the language of Lord Esher, MR in *Coulson* v *Coulson* — 'To justify the Court in granting an interim injunction it must come to a decision upon the question of libel or no libel, before the jury have decided whether it was a libel or not. Therefore the jurisdiction was of a delicate nature. It ought only to be exercised in the clearest cases, where any jury would say that the matter complained of was libellous, and where, if the jury did not so find, the Court would set aside the verdict as unreasonable."

Bonnard's case and *Monson* v *Tussauds Ltd* (1984) 1 QB 671, were followed in *Crest Homes Ltd* v *Ascott* (1980) FSR 396, where the trial judge granted an interlocutory injunction against the defendant who said that he would justify his assertions. Allowing the appeal and discharging the injunction, the Court (CA) held: "(1) There was no reason to depart from the general rule that an interlocutory injunction will not be granted against a defendant in a libel action if he intends to plead justification unless the plaintiff can prove that the statement is untrue; (2) The plaintiff had not shown that the defendant's statement was untrue." Lord Justice Geoffrey Lane, sitting with Lord Denning, MR and Lord Justice Stephenson, stated that "the line of authority is long and weighty that interlocutory injunctions in these cases will not be granted unless the plaintiff shows that the defence of justification will not succeed."

Authorities do also show that the principle that there shall be no interim injunction if a defence is raised "applies not only to the defence of justification" (*Bonnard* v *Perryman*), "but also to the defence of privilege" (*Quartz Hill Consolidated Gold Mining* v *Beall* (1882) 20 ChD 501 CA), and "fair comment" (*Fraser* v *Evans & Ors.* (1969) 1 QB 349). "In accordance with the long established practice in defamation actions, the principles enunciated by the House of Lords in *American Cyanamid* v *Ethican Ltd* (1975) AC 396, relating to interim injunctions are not applicable in actions for defamation (*Herbage* v *Pressdram Ltd*, CA (1984) 1 WLR 1160, 1162)."

In our judgment, therefore, the learned judge had erred in law in exercising his discretion. He acted contrary to the established principles governing the issue of interim injunction in a libel action.

The principle that clearly emerges is that the question of libel or no libel is eminently a matter to be decided on the facts at the trial. So also is the question of the proper meaning to be assigned to the words used in a particular statement. To restrain a defendant before the questions are determined would amount to fettering with free speech. Indeed it is the importance of leaving free speech unfettered that the Court must be slow in issuing an injunction in a libel action.

The law quite relevant to the issue is the Defamation Act of 1957.

PRESS REPORTERS IN COURT

I now move on to the subject of press reporters in Court.

Lord Denning, in an article entitled *The Road to Justice*, had this to say on the subject:

> "Reporters are a familiar sight in all our courts. They cover not only important cases in the Supreme Court but the dullest cases in the High Court and the most trivial cases in the Magistrates' Courts. They take notes and make a fair and accurate report of the case in the press. The judge will be careful to see that the trial is fairly and properly conducted if he realises that any unfairness on his part or impropriety will be reported in the press. It is said that every judge who tries a case is himself on trial for he is being tried by those present to see that he gives the accused a fair trial. The reporter in Court is the watch-dog of justice. Bentham said that the security of securities is publicity. 'In the darkness of secrecy' he said 'sinister interest and evil in every shape have full swing. Only in proportion as publicity has place can any of the checks applicable to judicial injustice operate. When there is no publicity, there is no justice."

And to quote what has been said before —

> "Justice is not a cloistered virtue. She must be allowed to suffer the scrutiny and respectful even though outspoken comments of ordinary men."

Courts of Judicature Act 1964

It is an Act relating to the superior courts of judicature. Section 15(2) of the Act gives the Court control over some aspects of press coverage of proceedings. It provides that a Court may at any time order that no person shall publish the name, address or photograph of any witness in any cause or matter or any part thereof tried or held or to be tried or held before it, or any evidence or any other thing likely to lead to the identification of any such witness. Section 15(1) of the Act provides that the place in which any Court is held for the purpose of trying any cause or matter, civil or criminal, shall be deemed an open and public court to which the public generally may have access. I pause to mention here that in a recent case in England, *Regina* v *Felixstowe Justices, Ex parte Leigh and Another* (1987) 2 WLR 380 an issue which concerns the question of policy to withhold names of justices from journalists, was considered. Also considered was whether a refusal was lawful.

In that case the applicant, a journalist for a leading Sunday newspaper, sought to write an article about, *inter alia*, the variation in newspaper reports. He applied for judicial review by way of an order of *mandamus* directed to the clerk to the justices to reveal the names of justices and for a declaration that the policy of the justices, was contrary to law. In granting the application Watkins LJ said that

> "in exercising the inherent power of a court to control the conduct of its proceedings justices should neither discourage fair and accurate reporting of the proceedings nor depart from the general rule of open justice to any extent greater than the court reasonably believed necessary in order to serve the ends of justice; that open justice required that no member of a court could seek anonymity and the names of justices must not be withheld from the parties, their legal representatives, the press in court reporting the proceedings and a bona fide inquirer (post, pp.391 C-D, s93B). (Dictum of Lord Diplock in *Attorney-General* v *Leveller Magazine Ltd* (1979) AC 440, 449, HL(E) applied)."

I hasten to add that my summary of the English case would not be complete if I do not also mention that the court nevertheless held that the applicant journalist was not a journalist present in court to report proceedings before the justices but a journalist wishing to comment on the issue arising from the reports of the case appearing in other newspapers; for that purpose his standing in the proceedings was not sufficient to give him *locus standi* to apply for an order for *mandamus* to reveal the justices' names. But he, or possibly the press through him, as guardian of the public interest in open justice had a sufficient interest to give him *locus standi* to apply that the justices were not entitled to withhold their names. (*Reg* v *Inland Revenue Commissioners, Ex parte National Self-Employed and Small Businesses Ltd* (1982) AC 617, HL applied.)

Be that as it may, a court under the Courts of Judicature Act is given the power to hear any cause or matter or any part thereof in camera if the court is satisfied in the interest of justice, public safety, public security or property, or for other sound reason so to do. Under subsection 2 of Section 15 a court may at any time order that no person shall publish the name of any witness in any cause or matter tried or to be tried before it or any evidence likely to lead to the identification of any such witness. A person who acts in contravention shall be subject to penal consequences.

There is also one other particular legislation I should like to draw your attention to and that is the Women and Girls' Protection Act 1973 which allows the court discretion to hear proceedings in camera. The Act imposes stringent restrictions on newspaper reporting of proceedings under the Act. (See Sections 29 and 30 of that Act). Under Section 29, any court may in its discretion order an exclusion of any member of the public from the whole or part of an enquiry held under the Act and Section 30 clearly prohibits publications calculated to lead to the identification of any female person respecting the enquiry under the Act. Contravention of the prohibition results in penal consequences.

CONTEMPT OF COURT

Let me say a few words on restrictions imposed on those who wish to comment on Judges and Trials.

Any act done or writing published that tends to bring the authority and administration of law into disrespect or to interfere with litigation is a contempt of court. The press sometimes falls foul of the law of contempt.

The different classes of contempt are illustrated in *Regina* v *Gray* (1900) QB 36 where Lord Russel of Killowen CJ observed as follows:

> "Any act done or writing published calculated to bring a Court or a judge of the Court into Contempt, or to lower his authority, is a contempt of court. That is one class of contempt. Further, any act done or writing published calculated to obstruct or interfere with the due course of justice or the lawful process of the Court is a contempt of court. The former class belongs to the category which Lord Hardwicke LC characterised as scandalising a Court or a judge. That description of that class of contempt is to be taken subject to one and an important qualification.
>
> Judges and Courts alike are open to criticism and if reasonable argument or expostulation is offered against any judicial act as contrary to law or the public good, no Court would treat that as contempt of Court. The law ought not to be astute in such cases to criticise adversely what under such circumstances and with such an object is published; but it is to be remembered that in this matter the liberty of the press is no greater and no less than the liberty of every subject of the Queen."

The Courts, however, are not too sensitive or touchy in this respect. The dignity of the Court is not so frail as to be easily affected by casual remarks or comments. (see *Surrendranath* v *Nabakrishna AIR 1958 (Orissa):*

In *The King* v *Dunabin & Anor* (1935) 53 CLR 434 it was said:

> "The jurisdiction (of the power of the Court to punish for contempt of itself) is not given for the purpose of restricting honest criticism based on rational grounds of the manner in which the Court performs its functions. The law permits in respect of Courts, as of other institutions, the fullest discussions of their doings so long as that discussion is fairly conducted and is honestly directed to some definite public purpose. The jurisdiction exists in order that the authority of the law as administered in the Courts may be established and maintained."

Contempt of court is committed in two different ways. One way is to attack the judge or the Court generally, and level against them criticism which far exceeds the bounds of legitimate criticism. When the judiciary as such, or the judge in particular is so attacked, and the attack may contain various kinds of imputation, such a contempt is styled as scandalising the court itself. The other type of contempt is committed when there is an attempt to interfere with the course of justice, an instance in point would be publishing material affecting the party defending itself, while a case is pending. This amounts to obstruction or interference in the course of justice.

Where unjustified and excessive criticism of the judiciary is treated as a contempt of court, the ground on which it is so treated is that such unwarranted, unjustified and an unoccasioned malicious criticism tends to undermine the prestige and dignity of the judiciary. This is only one effect. Such criticism, if passed unnoticed has also the tendency to shake the confidence of the common man in the impartiality of the judiciary. It is the duty of every right-thinking citizen not to do anything consciously or unconsciously which will undermine that special position of the judiciary. (*Law of Contempt of Court* by K.J. Aiyar).

The power of the Court to punish for contempt of itself is contained in:

1. Article 126 of the Federal Constitution which reads:

   > "The Supreme Court or High Court shall have power to punish any contempt of itself."

2. Section 13(2) of the Courts of Judicature Act 1964 which reads:

   > "The High Court shall have power to punish any contempt of itself."

3. Under paragraph 26 of the Third Schedule of the Subordinate Courts Act 1948, Revised 1972, the Subordinate Courts can take cognizance of any contempt of court.

Comments in Pending Cases Sub-judice Matters

Comments in regard to the merits of a pending case, whether they be made in newspaper articles or through leaflets or pamphlets, or criticisms offered on public platforms, or by way of resolutions, should be scrupulously avoided.

The underlying rationale behind it is that the court having possession of the case will arrive at a conclusion, on the basis of the evidence and materials that will be placed on record by the parties to a litigation. Extraneous comments, based mostly on surmises or unauthorised versions furnished by interested parties, are of no avail, when the matter is to be adjudicated upon in a court of law.

Such extraneous comments may have the mischief of harming a party to a case if the comments have a tendency to prejudice a person and in favour of one party.

PRESS: THE GUARDIAN OF JUSTICE IN THE COURTS

The press, that is to say, newspapers play an integral role in the administration of criminal justice. One of the principal objects of a criminal prosecution is to punish the offender not only with a view to deterring him, but also to act as a general deterrent on others who might be tempted to commit a crime. The wide publicity given to judicial proceedings in the press not only helps to propagate the concept of deterrence, but also enlightens and educates the public of their civil rights and in the criminal law. A vigilant press, therefore, is an important adjunct to the administration of criminal and civil justice. There must indeed be a dynamic interaction between the Press and the Courts in the interests of the nation.

Among the mass media the Press retains a central position because of its unique capacity for serving as a focus of public opinion and in shaping attitudes in highlighting instances of injustices.

The Courts are institutions where justice is done through trials in an endeavour to seek the truth. Misrepresentation of facts by the press can do irreparable harm. This is especially so in our plural society where the play on racial feelings may create an undesirable situation. The Press is a powerful ally of the Court in its efforts to discover and disseminate truth; for the strength of a Court or of a nation lies in its ability to discover the truth, to speak the truth and to face up to it. The press must guard against half-truths, inflammatory and irresponsible coverage, which I must say, is rare nowadays.

To sum up – one cannot deny that the Press enjoys here in Malaysia a degree of freedom not found in some other countries. The Government stands by its democratic principles and cannot be said to have interfered with the freedom of the Press beyond the limits permissible under the Constitution, nor for the matter have the Courts influenced, intimidated or interfered with the Press. On this vital issue it is in the best interests of newspapers and journalists themselves to exercise discretion and self-discipline. Newspapers and journalists must avoid actions that might enrage public opinion and compel the authorities to take measures which might be detrimental to our democratic way of life.

Truth and fairmindedness, responsible and sensible reporting should be a keynote in the relationship between the Press and Courts.

THE ROLE OF ROTARIANS*

When I was invited to attend this dinner I had some reservations as to whether I should accept it as I had a distinct feeling that I would be made to pay for it in the form of a speech. I dread making a speech. It sounds strange coming from a judge. My fear has been that a speaker, especially a long-winded-after-dinner speaker, often makes a nuisance of himself. In this respect judges and lawyers may well be the worst offenders.

The story has it that a judge made a lengthy and tedious summing-up to the jury in a case of arson involving nuisance. The judge made a long drawn summing-up. When at last it was over, the jury was asked to retire to consider the verdict. The jury returned and the foreman, when asked, told the judge that they had found the accused guilty but would also like to thank the judge very much. "What for?" asked the judge. The foreman said, "Members of the jury would like your Lordship to know that not until we heard your Lordship's summing-up did we know what nuisance was". Be that as it may, I hope that present company is excepted.

May I say that my wife and I are indeed honoured and privileged to be invited to this very auspicious occasion, which is the official installation of the 21st Pudu Rotary Club President and, more importantly, to be among this distinguished gathering.

I have been to a few Rotary dinners and lunches and indeed I have spoken at one or two of them before. I am, therefore, quite well informed of the splendid services rendered by the Rotarians. Speaking of Rotarians, I am reminded of a story where not so long ago one of the Rotarian District Governors paid a visit to a timber concession in a remote part of East Malaysia. He hoped to set up a Rotary Club there. He was accommodated in the special section of the Long House. That night there was a loud noise on his door. He opened it to find a head-hunting tribal chief in full regalia. The Governor was quite alarmed. He asked the chief what he had to do to save his life. The chief replied, "I have not come here to eat you up even though our tribe has the best known cannibals in the country. I have a problem and I know you can help."

**At The Pudu Rotary Club Dinner Held On 13th June, 1987 At The Shangri-la Hotel, Kuala Lumpur.*

The District Governor was relieved. He discovered that the problem of the tribe was that they had all got rather sick of eating their victims cooked in the same way, i.e. they are boiled.

Upon enquiring further as to how he could help, the District Governor was told by the tribal chief:

> "All you have to do is to present our tribe tomorrow with the new Rotary Recipe Book."

The District Governor was puzzled and asked what that new book was. The tribal chief replied, "It is called 'One Thousand and One Ways to Serve Your Countrymen'."

On a serious note I wish to say this. I am aware of the excellent work the Rotarians do and I do know that they have carried out various activities and programmes beneficial to the community and all these were done in the spirit of community service. It is the manifestation of their thoughtfulness and helpfulness to others in the community.

Basically Rotarians are well known for their international service advancing, international understanding, goodwill and peace. And their vocational and youth service have helped to promote leadership development and growth. In so doing, they have played a very significant role in their dedication to the cause of humanity, a manifestation of their concern in the sphere of humanitarian works and a determination to serve to alleviate hardship. The very nature of their service constitutes, therefore, a vital factor in achieving peace.

The theme "United In Service And Dedicated To Peace" is in my view appropriate. It constitutes an affirmation of the role of the Rotarians in community service and of their desire to preserve peace. Upon such premises they work with full commitment to the spirit of peace and tranquillity free from any consideration alien to the principles governing Rotary movement.

I am confident that in an effort to advance unity in service Rotarians would continue to disseminate ideals and principles which inspire them nationally and recognisably and through their continuing action, throughout the world.

However, unity in service alone may not be a decisive factor and a complete answer to the attainment of satisfactory maintenance of peace. It is fundamental that Rotarians should also serve with dedication. The symbol of Rotary movement should not be merely symbolic. It should be a genuine symbol of hope, of a future that will be better and therefore more humane. The ideals and principles should be real and not mere lip service.

We all know that the world continually evolves, indeed rotates round and round and in that state transforms noble ideals which, like that of peace, are universally accepted and in turn are translated into tangible facts of the everyday life of individuals and nations. But what is vitally important is the application of that universal value, namely peace, to specific areas of actual circumstances where it could flourish. In the context of our society Rotarians can undoubtedly play their role very effectively if they feel constrained to explore the limit of family life and the life of the multi-racial community to discover opportunities for appropriate actions to dedicate their services in a way which are conducive to peace. And peace of course should sustain the ultimate objective.

In the spirit of service to the community, I would urge the organizations and institutions concerned to strive to do more in that direction to achieve such objectives. In particular the Rotarians should continue to be faithful to their principles and to give unselfishly to the service of Rotary and their ideals.

To conclude may I on behalf of all the guests thank our hosts for the generous hospitality they have extended to us.

FREEDOM OF THE PRESS*

I have a very easy and pleasant task to perform this afternoon. My job is to officiate at the closing ceremony of this Conference. Nevertheless, it is an honour which I truly appreciate.

Before I declare the Conference closed, may I sincerely congratulate Mr. T.S. Sidhu on his election as President of Lawasia. In the light of his track record, particularly in his involvement with Lawasia, he undoubtedly deserves the honour. I also regard his election as an honour for Malaysia, in particular, to the Bar Council of the States of Malaya. May I also congratulate the organizers for having successfully staged the Conference. They have put in a lot of work to make it a success. More importantly they have spared no efforts to make the participants' stay in this country, especially those from overseas, a pleasant and memorable one. I am confident that our overseas friends would bear testimony to this fact. I am also confident that our overseas participants would take advantage of their visit here not only to attend the Conference but also to see a little of Malaysia either before, during or after this Conference. It is my hope that when they return to their respective countries they will take with them pleasant memories of their stay here and always remember the theme of the song "Lawasia forever", "Through law, let us seek"; "Whether mighty or small; our fulfilment of justice for all, our fulfilment of justice for all".

The Conference is over and the discussions have ended, so are the exchanges of views and the deliberations but the search for justice will continue. The Conference, hopefully, has helped to identify problems which beset not only the courts and the legal profession but also the communities which the courts and legal profession serve. It has also helped to identify the problems besetting the lawyers' lack of integrity and discipline and on the other hand has helped to create greater awareness of the need to serve the profession with greater dedication and to achieve the highest degree of integrity. I am glad that the Bar Council of the States of Malaya has, in this regard, recognised the necessity for a review of the disciplinary provisions contained in the Legal Profession Act. Hence the appointment of the Bar (Disciplinary proceedings) Review

---

**At The Closing Ceremony Of The 10th Lawasia Conference On 3rd July, 1987 At The Putra World Trade Centre, Kuala Lumpur.*

Committee chaired by the former Prime Minister, the Honourable Tun Hussein Onn is most welcome. This action was necessitated by the fact that in recent times the conduct of members of the Bar has been the subject of public scrutiny and adverse publicity. The number of complaints have multiplied much and at an alarming rate. My view is that while it is true that the legal profession has a vital role to play in the enforcement of the fundamental liberties and human rights and while it is also true that they can do much to shape the processes of law, members of the legal profession must, however, strictly conform to and abide by an acceptable canon of ethics and etiquette to ensure a high standard of conduct for the legal profession.

It is satisfying to note that Mr Param Cumaraswamy in his paper on the legal profession has recognised the need for respectability and integrity of the Bar. I consider them to be prerequisites for lawyers if they are to play a meaningful role in the promotion of human rights. I fully subscribe to the view that respect, public or private, is not something which can be demanded but must be earned. It is therefore for lawyers to demonstrate not only by words but by deeds that they can provide quality service and that they can discharge their professional duties honestly and with integrity.

Now, one of the topics for discussion at the Conference was Press Freedom. Much had been said about it at this Conference. As we all know, freedom of the press is an incidence of freedom of speech. One's freedom of speech and expression, being fundamental rights enshrined in the Constitution, are matters of great importance.

Equally important are, in my view, the limitations, restrictions and restraints on such freedom. A freedom of such amplitude might involve risks of abuse. It is an abuse to incite violence, crime, political and social unrest and public disorder. The Government, by that I mean the legislative, executive and judicial limbs of the Government, however, shall have to be protected against unlawful conduct of the press. Accordingly, freedom of speech and of the press do not comprehend the right to speak or write on any subject whatever at any time. Hence the necessity to make provisions in the Constitution to impose restrictions upon such freedom arises.

The rationale for providing such restrictions on the freedom of speech and expression is readily comprehensible and I feel it does not require much amplification or elaboration.

At the opening of the Malaysian Press Institute's Workshop on 30th March this year while speaking on the subject of the *Press, Law and the Courts* I had this to say:

> "In this country, the press enjoys a very substantial degree of freedom though subject to certain restrictions and restraints by way of legislative im-

positions. Such restrictions and restraints, however, shall have to be within the ambit or confines of the enshrined restrictive provisions of the Constitution.

While the Constitution is explicit about its guarantee of the right of free expression which includes freedom of the press the freedom, however, has its price in that the press shall have to police its own action. This is vital to secure integrity of journalism. Evidently the press itself must assume the responsibilities to ensure accuracy and fairness in reporting. Another factor of crucial importance is that while it is essential to act responsibly to ensure accuracy and fairness in reporting, it must also make itself accountable for its own actions. Accountability is, in my view, fundamental to the integrity of journalism. If the press should lay down rules it should also decide how they are to be enforced. Lapses in the enforcement may give rise to disputes between the media and their critics. Some criticism may well be justified. Some may not. Lapses in editorial judgements and failures to meet reasonable standards of accuracy and fairness may cause members of the public it serves to suspect the press' own ethical commitments.

By and large, it is accepted that the press has a vital role to play, namely, as public watchdogs and advocates."

At this point I shall conclude. Before I do so, may I wish those who will be leaving, wherever they are going, Godspeed. And to all participants may I sincerely wish you good luck, good health and God bless you.

On that note, I declare the Conference closed.

MOOT COURTS AND ADVOCACY*

I am very pleased to be here today on the auspicious occasion of the opening of the Moot and I thank you for inviting me.

We all know that Moots are mock hearings and we also know that they should form an integral part of legal training. Undoubtedly they help to improve advocacy in students and what is more important is that they help to develop the mind for quick thinking in a given situation in court.

What is a Moot Court?

According to dictionary meaning a Moot Court is a Court where students discuss a hypothetical case for practice. To a law student therefore, participation in a Moot Court is a must particularly if it is his intention to practise as an advocate. Excellence in advocacy or, for that matter, in the sphere of any particular undertaking depends much upon a person's interest and motivation.

To achieve the greatest benefit, those participating in a Moot Court must regard it seriously as one would treat a proper court of law. By so doing, not only is a particular legal problem well expounded but it also improves the technique and method of presentation of a case.

In what respect would a Moot Court help?

No law school can teach the students all the answers to the difficult and complex questions and points of law which a lawyer will be faced with in actual practice. Knowing the law, of course, is a fundamental rule. Technique is acquired through experience. A lawyer has to be quick on the uptake and be ready to counter his opponent's arguments and not be caught without a sensible and logical reply. Presence of mind may only be acquired with practice and moots do help the future lawyer to be able to gauge his opponent's case from the line of his examination-in-chief, cross-examination, re-examination and any points of law raised or preliminary objection taken in the course of the proceedings.

Decorum is the cornerstone of a lawyer's behaviour. Regardless of who presides in a court of law you must give a good impression to the Court. Your appearance means a lot. You must dress neatly and not appear sloven. Be

---

**At The Opening Of The Moot Court*
-- Institut Teknologi Mara On 27th September, 1987.

well-groomed. You are a friend and an officer of the court and must assist the Court to arrive at the truth by your behaviour before the Court.

From experience I would say that one of the fundamental requirements of a good advocate is to secure the confidence and respect of the Court. In order to do so it is essential that you be (and in fact be) courteous, truthful, frank, fair and be even willing to confess ignorance or uncertainty should such an occasion arise. There is nothing disgraceful about being ignorant, indeed in not being infallible. I would say that sometimes a frank admission of ignorance is not out of place. Indeed, it is often greatly appreciated by the Court.

In my view our system of administration of justice is fundamentally an efficient and effective one. But I hasten to add that even the best of systems in any country cannot be said to be without any room for improvement. In order to achieve maximum efficiency any system needs the services of men and women of high calibre with a great sense of loyalty and dedication, to a point where they are ardent but realistic believers in the rule of law — conscious of the need to maintain a proper balance between individual liberty and legal control and to be further conscious of the fact that there can be no synthesis of liberty and law without justice. In the context of what I have just said my reference to the men and women of high calibre is not only confined to the judicial and legal officers but also to the advocates and solicitors.

Whilst in the past many of those engaged in the administration of justice had their training overseas (many still have), today many of our judicial and legal officers and young advocates and solicitors are the products of our own local institutions of higher education. And, needless to say, in the course of events and as time marches on they would assume greater and more responsible roles, eventually wholly responsible for the administration of justice. To maintain an efficient and admirable system, I firmly believe that the new generation lawyers should prepare and equip themselves with the necessary tools of trade. I refer in this regard to the command of the language.

Lord Denning said in his book *The Discipline of Law* that "to succeed in the profession of the law, you must seek to cultivate the command of the language—Words are the lawyer's tools of trade". Words are very important because they "are the vehicles of thought" and obscurity in thought inexorably leads to obscurity in language. It is therefore fair to say that the knowledge or wisdom that one has in his head is of no use to anyone unless he can communicate his ideas. It has been said that language, the greatest of men's inventions, is almost the only means we have to convey our ideas. Hence it is actually very important for those engaged in the administration of justice to be proficient in the language of the Court.

I have said all these to stress that those who have been trained overseas and are proficient in the English language but may not be quite proficient in the National language and equally those who graduate from our local universities who are more proficient in the National language but may not be so proficient in the English language should strive to cultivate a good command of the language in which they are not proficient.

May I also stress the need to have a very good command of the language of the Court be it English now or ultimately the National language or both. It is important not only to those already engaged in the administration of justice, lawyers included, but also to law students in our institutions of higher education who would in due course be engaged in the legal profession. They should, in my view, be fully conscious of the necessity to have a good command of both the National language and the English language. The latter's importance should not be under-estimated as it is now a universal language internationally used in business and the commercial sector and it is inevitable that practising lawyers will invariably be called upon to handle their clients' interest or business internationally in that language.

Now the plain truth is that when an advocate is pleading in any cause he is not stating his own views and indeed has no right whatsoever to do so. He is bound by very strict rules of conduct and an equally strict code of behaviour on how he conducts his case. These are designed to allow him to discharge his duty in the administration of justice without being false to himself or to his conscience and without failing in his duty to the community in which he lives.

The function of the advocate is to present one side of the case with all the skill he possesses so that the Bench or the judge and jury can compare his presentation with that of counsel for the other side and then decide, after full investigation, where the truth lies.

In a criminal case, an advocate who is prosecuting is to act as an impartial officer of justice in the fullest sense. Relevant and admissible evidence must be presented without bias. He must also make sure that the evidence in favour of the accused is before the court and is given the same prominence and emphasis as evidence tendered to show his guilt.

What is the duty of the advocate who shoulders the heavy responsibility of defending the accused on the gravest of all charges? It is his duty to devote himself completely to his task whatever he himself may think of the charges and to lay aside every other duty so that he may act constantly in the interest of the accused and say for him all that he would wish to say for himself. It is the duty of the advocate to press his arguments upon the Bench but not his opinion.

A reasonable and workable harmony and goodwill ought to prevail between the Bench and the Bar. Both are part of the same machinery of justice and the Bench must never be misled. Both are essentially men of law and, presumably, honour performing different functions aimed at one and the same end which is the administration of justice with dignity, courtesy and honour. These qualities should be seen and reflected in their respective conduct and behaviour. It is only then that they will earn the respect of the public.

May I wish you all success in your studies. I now declare this Moot open.

SILVER SCEPTRE PRESENTATION TO THE MUAR HIGH COURT*

May I respectfully thank Y.A. Hakim Dato' Mohd. Eusoff Chin for inviting me to this function this morning on the occasion of the presentation of the silver sceptre by the State Government to the High Court, Muar.

Traditionally, to a High Court, the sceptre is regarded as a pillar of strength in reflecting its independence and integrity to uphold justice.

The High Court is vested with the judicial power of the Federation under Article 121 of the Federal Constitution and is one of the limbs of the Government, the other two being the executive and the legislature. The presentation of the sceptre by the State Government is very significant in that it reflects the close rapport between the executive and the judiciary and the understanding and respect for each other.

I am very happy to note that Y.A.B. Menteri Besar Johore himself has found time to attend this function and to present the beautiful sceptre to the Court. I am also happy to say that the State Government has not only given close co-operation to the Courts but has also shown serious concern for our needs especially in regard to alienation of land for court houses. On behalf of the courts, therefore, I would like to extend a thousand thanks and our sincere appreciation to the Johor State Government. It is my hope that the close rapport that exists between the two would continue to be so.

Cases which are heard in the High Court Muar come from the Segamat, Muar and Batu Pahat districts. Since independence, the Johore State Government has achieved great success in its development by reason of which the volume of cases in Johore has increased. It was for that reason that a decision was made to place a judge in Muar commencing 1st August 1985. In view of the number of cases now being filed in court, I hope that lawyers would prepare their cases well and assist the courts in their speedy disposal.

There have been complaints by the public on the delay in the disposal of cases. May I say that we spare no efforts to find ways and means of speeding up

---

**At The Sceptre Handing Ceremony By The Johore State Government To The High Court Muar On 26th October, 1987.*

the disposal of cases but unfortunately the delay in the disposal of some cases is unavoidable in view of the shortage of support staff.

At the Judges' Conference held on the 19th-22nd August, 1985 I had put forward a proposal to increase the jurisdiction of the Sessions and Magistrates' Court and to establish a Small Claims Court. This was met with approval by the Government and Parliament has made the necessary amendments to the Subordinate Courts Act to give effect to the proposal. The increase in the jurisdiction of the Sessions Court would relieve the burden of the High Court. Now with the establishment of the Second Class Magistrate's Court, called the Small Claims Court, cases below RM3,000, with the simplification in the procedure, could be dealt with expeditiously.

Currently, a committee has been set up to look into ways and means of expediting further the disposal of cases. In particular, this committee is to look into the question of having additional High Court Judges, Sessions Court Judges and Magistrates and of course support staff such as Senior Assistant Registrars, interpreters, court clerks, bailiffs, process servers and so forth.

I take this opportunity to make some observations on the role of the courts. Primarily it is the duty of the courts to administer justice impartially between citizen and citizen and citizen and state according to law. In this respect there is no real distinction between the functions to be performed by Magistrates, Session Court Judges and Judges of the High Court. They are there to do justice. Closely related to the duty to administer justice impartially is the duty of each and every member of the judiciary to conduct himself in a manner that befits the dignity and standing of his office. This is necessary for the judicial officers to perform their judicial functions without fear or favour. It is important that judicial officers do not act in a manner that is likely to tarnish the image of the judiciary. There have been complaints of judicial officers making remarks that are uncalled for. To my mind they ought to refrain from making such remarks for by doing so they would not only lose the respect of the people who appear before them but such conduct would also tarnish the image of the judiciary. Such remarks, apart from hurting the people to whom they are directed, could also create a controversy. From the nature of our office we cannot reply to criticisms made in response to such remarks. Indeed we cannot afford to enter into a public controversy. Such being the case, we must rely on our conduct to be its own vindication. Be that as it may, nothing should, however, deter us from doing what the occasion requires provided that it is pertinent to the matter in issue.

In conclusion, may I once again express my grateful thanks to the State Government for the generous gift of the sceptre and may I also express my personal appreciation to Y.A.B. the Menteri Besar for having taken the time to be with us at this function.

UNITED IN SERVICE AND DEDICATED TO PEACE*

I have been asked to say a few words on behalf of the guests. It is on their account that I have been given this honour to speak. For myself, I deem it a very great privilege and pleasure and gladly perform this very pleasant task.

Be that as it may, there is still some doubt lingering in my mind as to whether the Rotary Club has made the right choice in asking me to speak. Contrary to some public expectations a judge is rarely a good speaker. Many of our judges are truly men of few words, unlike lawyers in the legal profession who have much to say. The short story I am about to tell you confirms this. A judge heard a case before him for seven days and during that time there had been great wranglings between the lawyers for the prosecution and the defense. When the case finally ended, the judge addressed the accused and said: "Your lawyer has much to say but I am not a man of many words. In actual fact I am a man of few words with long sentences. The sentence on you is fifteen years."

Many Rotarians have assembled here tonight. They are united in service and dedicated to peace. Founded upon those premises the guests have been invited to share the Rotary fellowship. Peace is, amongst others, defined to mean freedom from civil commotion. It also means public order and security. The opposite of peace is chaos. I believe no one in his right frame of mind would want to see chaos. Speaking of chaos, how many of us know the origin of that word? In this connection let me tell you a story.

A surgeon, a Field Marshal and a politician had a very liquid lunch together and entered into a very deep argument.

> "A surgeon's job is the oldest profession in the world," said the surgeon.
>
> "What makes you say that?" asked the Field Marshal.
>
> "Well," replied the surgeon, "when woman was created she was made from one of Adam's ribs and surely only a surgeon could do something like that."

**At The Rotary Club Kuala Lumpur Diamond Jubilee Banquet At Hotel Regent Ballroom, Kuala Lumpur On 21st November, 1987.*

"Nonsense!" snorted the Field Marshal. "Even before Adam and Eve there was a world and it is said that order was created out of chaos. Who else could do that but a soldier of the highest rank?"

"Ah!" said the politician, "but who do you think created chaos?"

Turning now to a serious note, may I sincerely say that tonight's occasion is indeed a very auspicious one. It is so because the banquet is held with the object of celebrating the Diamond Jubilee of the Rotary Club of Kuala Lumpur. But what makes it more auspicious is that the occasion is honoured by the presence of HRH The Sultan of Selangor who has kindly and generously consented to grace the occasion. It is the kind of occasion that Rotarians of the Rotary Club of Kuala Lumpur would wish to cherish long in their memories.

The theme of the Rotarians is: "Rotarians united in service, dedicated to peace." These few words bear much significance. Emphasis seems to rest on the words "unity, service, dedication and peace". It is rightly so for there can hardly be peace without unity, service and dedication. Great significance accordingly attaches to and revolves round that word "peace". Rotarians do make it their responsibility to promote peace, but the question is, should it be the business of Rotarians only? My view is and I believe it is yours too, that it is clearly the responsibility of every peace loving and law abiding person to promote peace and tranquillity, and to achieve positive results that responsibility should be dispensed faithfully and with full commitment. And in the context of our society, it should indeed be so if we are to achieve that goal.

Not very long ago, I was invited as a guest to the Pudu Rotary Club dinner and at that dinner I had made some observations which I would like to repeat here. At that dinner I remarked that Rotarians have played a significant role in our society. What has impressed me, indeed also a vast majority of other people, is their dedication to the cause of humanity, a manifestation of their concern in the sphere of humanitarian work and a determination to serve to alleviate hardship. All these, a reflection of the nature of their services, constitute vital factors to attain peace.

The theme "United In Service and Dedicated To Peace" is in my view appropriate. It constitutes an affirmation of the role of the Rotarians in community service and of their desire to preserve peace. Upon such premises they work with full commitment in a spirit of peace and tranquillity free from any consideration alien to the principles governing Rotary movement. I am confident that in an effort to advance unity in service, Rotarians would continue to disseminate ideals and principles which inspire them nationally and regionally and through such continuing action, throughout the world. However, unity in service alone may neither be a decisive factor nor a complete answer to the attainment of satisfactory maintenance of peace. It is fundamental that Rotarians should also serve with dedication. It is with a view to attaining excellence that it is important that the symbol of Rotary movement should not be left to be merely symbolic. It should be a genuine symbol of hope, of a future that will be brighter and therefore more humane. The exhortations of the final ideals and principles should be real and not mere lip service.

We all know that the world continually evolves, indeed rotates round and round and in that state transforms noble ideals which, like that of peace, are universally accepted and in turn are translated into tangible facts of the everyday life of individuals and nations. But what is vitally important is the application of that universal value, namely peace, to specific areas of actual environment where it could flourish. In the context of our society Rotarians can undoubtedly play their role more effectively if they are disposed to explore the limits of family life and the life of the multi-racial community to identify problems and consider avenues for more appropriate action to render services which would promote peace. And peace of course should be sustained as the ultimate objective.

To conclude, may I on behalf of all the guests thank our hosts for the generous hospitality they have extended to us.

PENTADBIRAN MAHKAMAH*

Saya berasa gembira kerana kita semua dapat berkumpul untuk Persidangan Majistret dan Pendaftar Mahkamah Rendah. Saya anggap semua yang hadir telah meneliti dan memahami aturcara-aturcara persidangan yang telah disediakan. Persidangan ini adalah bertujuan untuk meninggikan lagi mutu dan taraf perkhidmatan tuan-tuan dan puan-puan sekalian. Kertas-kertas kerja yang akan dibentangkan mulai hari ini akan disampaikan oleh penceramah-penceramah yang berpengalaman dalam bidang masing-masing dan akan merangkumi sedikit sebanyak pengetahuan dan pengalaman yang boleh dijadikan panduan oleh seorang Majistret dan pentadbir ketika menjalankan tugas-tugas mereka.

Tanggungjawab Majistret dan Pendaftar Mahkamah Rendah

Majistret dan Pendaftar yang di tempatkan di merata-rata daerah Semenanjung Malaysia merupakan sebahagian daripada anggota Jabatan Kehakiman, khasnya dan Kementerian Kehakiman secara am. Oleh itu, segala gerak geri dan tingkah laku sama ada dalam menjalankan tugas harian ataupun di dalam lapangan-lapangan lain adalah sentiasa diperhatikan oleh semua lapisan masyarakat. Jika Majistret atau Pendaftar tidak menjalankan tugas mereka dengan jujur, tekun dan ikhlas, maka bukan sahaja imej mereka akan terjejas tetapi imej badan kehakiman keseluruhannya akan turut terjejas.

Peranan seorang Majistret bukan sahaja untuk menjalankan tugas-tugas kehakiman di pejabat tetapi juga bertanggungjawab untuk memastikan pentadbiran kewangan di mahkamah masing-masing berjalan dengan licin dan teratur. Jika Mahkamah Sesyen dan Mahkamah Majistret terletak di bangunan yang sama, maka urusan Pentadbiran dan Kewangan akan dibantu oleh Pendaftar Mahkamah Rendah. Dalam hal ini, satu kertas kerja akan dibentangkan dan dibincang di Persidangan ini. Saya berharap, segala perkara dan masalah yang akan dibangkitkan oleh tuan-tuan dan puan-puan akan dapat diatasi dengan sebaik-baiknya.

**Di Pembukaan Persidangan Majistret Dan Pendaftar Mahkamah Rendah Di Awana Golf & Country Club Genting Highlands, Dari 25 Hingga 27 November 1988.*

Jabatan Kehakiman telah juga memohon kepada kerajaan supaya Pendaftar Mahkamah Rendah di tempatkan di mahkamah-mahkamah di mana terdapat nya dua orang Majistret atau lebih. Walaupun perkara ini tidak dapat dilaksanakan sekarang oleh kerana keadaan ekonomi negara baru sahaja pulih, tetapi sebaik sahaja permintaan ini diluluskan maka Majistret akan dapat menumpukan sepenuh masa dalam membicarakan kes-kes dan perkara-perkara berkaitan dengan pentadbiran serta urusan kewangan di mahkamah akan dikendalikan oleh Pendaftar Mahkamah Rendah.

Penggunaan Bahasa Malaysia di Mahkamah

Selaras dengan dasar Kerajaan untuk megembangkan penggunaan Bahasa Malaysia di negara ini, saya sendiri telah mengeluarkan arahan kepada semua mahkamah untuk menjalankan perbicaraan dalam Bahasa Malaysia secepat mungkin. Ibu pejabat telah menubuhkan Jawatankuasa Induk Penggunaan Bahasa Malaysia dan peranan jawatankuasa ini ialah untuk memastikan pelaksanaan penggunaan Bahasa Malaysia dapat berjalan dengan lancar. Semua mahkamah dikehendaki melaporkan ke ibu pejabat statistik mengenai perkara tersebut dari masa ke semasa. Semua pegawai yang bertanggungjawab di tiap-tiap mahkamah hendaklah mematuhi segala arahan yang dikeluarkan oleh Jawatankuasa Induk dari masa ke semasa.

Sistem Litaran

Kerajaan telah pun meluluskan sebanyak 14 jawatan Hakim Mahkamah Sesyen dan 26 jawatan Majistret. Baru-baru ini 398 jawatan sementara untuk kakitangan lain di mahkamah-mahkamah juga telah diluluskan. Mulai 1.1.1989, Hakim-Hakim Mahkamah Sesyen akan diarah bertugas selama beberapa hari dalam sebulan di Mahkamah Majistret termasuk Mahkamah Tertutup mengikut jadual yang akan ditentukan oleh ibu pejabat bagi mendengar kes-kes sivil dan jenayah. Kesemua kes sivil dan jenayah untuk Mahkamah Sesyen tidak lagi di daftar di ibu negeri atau di mana adanya Mahkamah Sesyen sahaja tetapi akan dikehendaki didaftarkan di daerah-daerah di mana adanya Mahkamah Majistret yang terdekat sekali. Di samping itu, semua kes sivil dan jenayah Mahkamah Sesyen yang sekarang telah pun didaftarkan serta menanti perbicaraan di Mahkamah Sesyen akan dipindahkan ke Mahkamah di daerah-daerah tertentu. Permohonan oleh mana-mana pihak untuk memindahkan kes sivil atau jenayah yang telah didaftarkan di Mahkamah Sesyen boleh juga dibuat secara lisan ataupun bertulis. Cara ini bukan sahaja dapat mengurangkan perbelanjaan orang awam kerana mereka boleh mendaftarkan kes di mahkamah yang terdekat dengan mereka, tetapi juga kes-kes dapat didengar dengan lebih cepat dan dengan itu dapatlah mengurangkan kes-kes tertangguh.

Hakim Mahkamah Sesyen yang dikehendaki membuat litaran ke Mahkamah Majistret yang akan ditentukan kemudian akan juga dikehendaki mendengar kes-kes sivil di bawah bidang kuasa Majistret. Tujuan ini ialah untuk membolehkan Majistret di mahkamah berkenaan mempunyai masa yang lebih untuk menumpukan perhatian kepada kes-kes jenayah dan dengan itu boleh mengurangkan kes-kes yang tertangguh. Bagaimanapun Majistret di mahkamah berkenaan akan bertanggungjawab mengeluarkan apa-apa saman ataupun urusan-urusan lain yang bersangkutan dengan kes-kes yang akan didengar oleh Hakim Mahkamah Sesyen. Dalam perkara ini, arah amalan akan dikeluarkan.

Jawatankuasa Tugas Khas Sistem Litaran

Berhubung dengan sistem litaran yang akan dilaksanakan mulai 1.1.1989 itu, ibu pejabat akan menubuhkan satu jawatankuasa khas untuk mengikuti perkembangan perjalanan sistem ini supaya ia dapat dikendalikan dengan lebih berkesan dan berfaedah. Dengan cara ini jawatankuasa tersebut bolehlah dianggap bukan sebagai satu pasukan naziran tetapi juga akan membuat kajian mendalam dari masa ke semasa jika terdapat apa-apa kelemahan dalam sistem ini.

Mahkamah Tertutup

Pada masa ini terdapat sebanyak 40 buah Mahkamah Tertutup di Semenanjung Malaysia. Sebilangannya mempunyai kakitangan yang mencukupi dan setengah lagi langsung tiada kakitangan. Dalam hal ini, tindakan akan diambil untuk menempatkan bilangan kakitangan yang dianggap perlu di Mahkamah Tertutup sekarang supaya ianya dapat berfungsi sepenuhnya seperti Mahkamah Terbuka. Mahkamah ini akan berfungsi sebagai Mahkamah Terbuka tiap-tiap hari kecuali hari kelepasan am, seperti yang ditetapkan di bawah Perintah 52 Kaedah 7 Mahkamah Rendah 1980.

Penangguhan Kes

Baru-baru ini saya telah mengeluarkan arahan berhubungan dengan penangguhan kes-kes sama ada oleh Majistret Kelas I atau II, Hakim Mahkamah Sesyen ataupun Mahkamah Tinggi. Saya menegaskan di sini bahawa tuan-tuan dan puan-puan hendaklah meneliti dan memahami sepenuhnya tujuan saya memberi arahan berhubungan dengan penangguhan kes-kes. Adalah diingatkan bahawa penangguhan ke-kes janganlah dijadikan amalan biasa tetapi sebagai kecualian sahaja dalam keadaan yang tidak dapat dielakkan dan mahkamah tidak boleh menjadi pihak utama menangguhkan kes-kes. Apabila mahkamah hendak menentukan tarikh perbicaraan satu-satu kes ia hendaklah berpandukan kepada tarikh-tarikh lapang di mahkamah dan bukan mengikut kehendak peguam atau pihak-pihak lain.

Kes-Kes Tertangguh

Adalah menjadi kenyataan bahawa kes-kes tertangguh amatlah perlu diselesaikan secepat mungkin. Kita mesti bersikap tegas terhadap semua pihak yang mengendalikan kes supaya permohonan penangguhan tidak akan dibenarkan dengan sewenang-wenangnya. Dengan cara ini maka sudah tentu banyak kes dapat diselesaikan dan kes-kes tertangguh akan berkurangan dari masa ke semasa. Penangguhan kes-kes dengan sewenang-wenangnya memberi kesan buruk kepada semua pihak terutamanya yang tertuduh di dalam penjara, dan saksi-saksi yang akan memberi keterangan. Tindakan seperti ini juga akan membazirkan wang. Walau bagaimanapun saya tidak menafikan bahawa ada masanya kes-kes untuk perbicaraan terpaksa ditangguhkan. Walaupun masalah kes-kes tertangguh bukan sahaja berlaku di negara kita bahkan di negara-negara lain juga, kita tidaklah boleh berdiam diri tetapi mesti bertekad dan mencari jalan mengatur serta mentadbir dengan berkesan supaya masalah kes-kes tertangguh dapat diatasi.

Alasan Penghakiman

Saya dapati ramai pegawai-pegawai tidak menulis dan menyediakan Alasan Penghakiman dengan segera. Ini amatlah mengecewakan dan saya telah memberi arahan kepada Pendaftar Mahkamah Tinggi supaya perkara ini tidak boleh diabaikan oleh mana-mana pegawai. Perkara ini akan diambil kira untuk pengesahan jawatan atau kenaikan pangkat jika sekiranya ada pegawai-pegawai yang sengaja melambatkan penyediaan Alasan Penghakiman atau menangguh kes-kes separuh bicara dengan sewenang-wenangnya.

Institusi Kehakiman

Jabatan Kehakiman dengan kerjasama Kementerian Kehakiman serta pakar-pakar daripada luar negeri telah pun membuat kajian yang mendalam untuk menubuhkan satu Institusi Kehakiman. (Institusi tersebut akan membolehkan persidangan-persidangan seperti ini diadakan lebih kerap), dan juga membuat kajian untuk meninggikan lagi mutu kerja Pegawai-Pegawai Kehakiman mengikut keadaan dari masa ke semasa.

Masa Waktu Pejabat dan Disiplin (Tatatertib)

Saya akan mengeluarkan arahan supaya semua Majistret dan Hakim-Hakim dikehendaki bersidang di Mahkamah Terbuka ataupun dalam kamar pada tepat 9.00 pagi tiap-tiap hari.

Semua pegawai hendaklah sedar dan memastikan bahawa mereka harus menjalankan tugas dengan penuh dedikasi, taat setia dan berakhlak mulia kerana ini akan memberi gambaran yang baik di kalangan orang ramai. Dalam membicarakan kes-kes, tuan-tuan dan puan-puan yang masih dianggap berusia muda sudah tentulah pernah menghadapi masalah di mana pihak yang berhadapan dengan tuan-tuan dan puan-puan di mahkamah mungkin berumur lebih tua. Oleh itu gerak geri, tutur kata yang dilafazkan oleh tuan-tuan dan puan-puan hendaklah tidak keterlaluan. Kita hanya perlu melafazkan perkara-perkara atau isu-isu yang bersangkutan dengan kes yang kita kendalikan sahaja dan elakkanlah daripada menyindir dan menyinggung perasaan sesiapa sahaja yang berhadapan dengan kita di dalam mahkamah. Saya sering kali terbaca di akhbar-akhbar dan juga kadangkala menerima aduan daripada orang ramai di mana terdapatnya sebilangan pegawai yang suka mengeluarkan kata-kata yang menyentuh peribadi mana-mana pihak yang tidak ada kena mengena dengan kes yang didengar. Ini hendaklah dielakkan sama sekali kerana kelakuan sedemikian akan menjatuhkan imej Jabatan Kehakiman.

Majistret sebagai ketua mahkamah masing-masing hendaklah selalu menasihati semua kakitangan untuk bekerjasama di pejabat tidak kira peringkat atau lapisan jawatan supaya jentera pentadbiran mahkamah tidak terjejas. Peranan kita ialah untuk melaksanakan pentadbiran keadilan dengan penuh kejujuran.

Tanpa kerjasama dan keikhlasan dari semua lapisan pekerja sudah tentu pentadbiran keadilan akan terjejas, dan oleh itu saya berseru kepada tuan-tuan dan puan-puan supaya menyedari hakikat ini.

Penutup

Saya berharap semua peserta akan mengambil bahagian dalam semua perbincangan mengikut aturcara yang telah disediakan. Tuan-tuan dan puan-puan bukan sahaja dapat bertukar fikiran tetapi dapat berkongsi pengalaman dengan rakan-rakan yang lain.

Saya sendiri merasa gembira kerana dapat bertemu dengan semua peserta. Saya sentiasa meluangkan masa untuk mengikuti segala perkembangan dan kemajuan di mahkamah dari masa ke semasa sama ada melalui pegawai-pegawai di ibu pejabat atau dari kakitangan di daerah-daerah.

Sebagai pengakhir kata saya ingin memberi sedikit pesanan kepada tuan-tuan dan puan-puan bahawa kita sebagai pemberi khidmat awam yang diamanahkan dengan tugas dan tanggungjawab hendaklah melaksanakan kewajipan dengan jujur dan dedikasi serta mematuhi prinsip Rukun Negara, khususnya Kesetiaan Kepada Raja dan Negara.

Saya sudahi dengan mengucapkan selamat bersidang dan terima kasih kepada kerajaan yang telah memberi peruntukan serta kepada semua pihak yang telah menjayakan persidangan ini. Dengan ini saya dengan sukacitanya merasmikan pembukaan persidangan kita mulai hari ini.

GUINNESS STOUT EFFORT AWARD*

Terlebih dahulu saya ingin merakamkan ucapan terima kasih kepada Guinness Malaysia Berhad kerana telah sudi menjemput saya ke Upacara Penganugerahan Dayausaha Guinness pada hari ini bagi menghargai seorang warganegara, Encik Tuah Johari Atan di atas sikap kegigihan beliau untuk mencapai cita-citanya.

Today, you have gathered here to honour a Malaysian for his outstanding achievement. He had ambition and he realised his ambition through dedication and hard work. Despite his physical handicap he achieved great success and was admitted to the Malaysian Bar as an Advocate and Solicitor.

Furthermore, despite his physical handicap, he has led a normal life. The lack of proper limbs has neither daunted nor prevented him from leading an active life.

It is clear therefore that as a man he had not allowed his physical limitations to hold him down. He not only believed that he could, but did do what any other person could. With the opportunity open to him and the determination to make it a success he did succeed.

I congratulate him on his remarkable and outstanding success. What is expected of him now is to continue to work harder towards greater heights and as a good citizen, to serve the country. As a Malaysian he should always be loyal to the King and the country. You have set the pace and it is indeed an example for others to follow.

I take this opportunity to express my heartfelt appreciation to Guinness Malaysia Berhad for their kind gesture and public spiritedness in presenting these Guinness Stout Effort Awards to those who have accomplished outstanding achievements in sports, business, education, nation-building as well as acts of bravery and integrity.

I am glad Guinness Malaysia Berhad has chosen to focus the minds and hearts of Malaysians towards the virtues of human nature. I say this because our attention is drawn daily to incidents and events which tell of human tragedy and suffering, of bigotry and discrimination, of hatred and violence, of in-

---

**At The Presentation Of The Guinness Stout Effort Award On 19th December, 1988 At The Kuala Lumpur Hilton.*

difference and apathy and other base characteristics of the human nature. We are bombarded on every side by news which pander to the negative aspects of mankind.

However, Guinness Malaysia Berhad affords us the opportunity to ponder upon the good that men and women can do or achieve for the benefit of society. This is a step towards positive thinking and a right perspective of the higher values of life which we should all cherish. It also helps us to re-align our thoughts, words and deeds so that we could seek the highest virtues for all mankind and in turn create the right conditions for a quality life.

The nation can be proud of achievers such as we have before us today. May we see more Malaysians of all ages and from all walks of life who are prepared to be part of this group of self-sacrificing, public-spirited, diligent and exemplary people.

MATRIMONIAL PROCEEDINGS AT MING COURT*

My learned friend Datuk Kam Woon Wah and Datin Kam and Mr. and Mrs. Chan Weng Kee have summoned our attendance tonight to this respectable Ming Court sitting in Kuala Lumpur to participate in the matrimonial proceedings between Chan Sze Loon (the applicant) and Linda Kam Thai Eng (the respondent).

They move to declare firstly, their profound appreciation to all distinguished guests present and secondly, to further declare that those who have failed to make their appearances, without just cause or lawful excuse, be in contempt of Ming Court.

They have craved your indulgence to move Ming Court for an undertaking that those who have graciously made their appearances and are comfortably seated be served with nothing less than a sumptuous dinner.

My learned friend Datuk Kam is on record to represent his faithful and better half and Mr. & Mrs. Chan (the outlaws) to stand before this Court to make a final submission. However, on the strength of a medical certificate certifying his inability to do so, leave has been granted that he be discharged. Hence, my being on my two old feet as substitute charged with a duty to expedite the proceedings and oppose any application for a postponement.

The truth behind Datuk Kam's inability to stand up before this Court is his nerve. He suffers from acute sadness and profound happiness — too sad to speak and too happy for words. He is sad to lose the respondent to the applicant and happy to secure a new son pursuant to and in accordance with law (hereafter and forever, no doubt, to be branded as son-in-law as far as Datuk Kam is concerned).

In the circumstances of this particular case, he now seeks the indulgence of the distinguished guests that I be allowed to urge you to give your blessings and henceforth make an order in terms as the applicant and the respondent think just and expedient. If you are too lazy to say much, just say the letters OIT.

**At Datuk Kam Woon Wah's Daughter's Wedding Dinner At Ming Court Hotel, Kuala Lumpur On 10 January 1989.*

Affidavits have been affirmed making a full disclosure of all material facts pertaining to the applicant and the respondent. Disclosures of these particulars do not, in my view, contravene the Official Secrets Act.

The applicant, the first party as hereinbefore described, is a male, very ready, very willing and very able. He is fair, tall and handsome. He is the son of Mr. & Mrs. Chan Weng Kee. The applicant was taught to read and write at the Victoria Institution. It had to be a good school for Sze Loon secured thereat the qualification to fly to London to improve his reading and writing, this time in law. The university examiners were very kind to him and quickly awarded him the LLB degree, and that saved him from LLD. That was in 1978. In 1979 the English Bar (it's not a pub) by the name of Lincoln's Inn thought fit, after Sze Loon spent enough time dining and wining, that he be called to that Inn. By coincidence it is the same Inn where I did my dining. Perhaps Sze Loon would agree with me that the food there was lousy. Back home Sze Loon was again made to read in Chambers to make sure that he knows that our laws are not so common. On his petition the Court admitted him as an advocate and solicitor of the High Court of Malaya in 1981. It is also disclosed in the affidavit that my learned friend Datuk Kam had also dined and wined in London but not at the Inn but in a temple. He chose the Middle Temple. Speaking of inns and temples, I am reminded of a Magistrate serving in Malaya some three decades ago who was seen on a number of occasions at functions dressed up in barrister's gown and wig. Another fellow Magistrate who had earlier been called to Lincoln's Inn was curious for he knew not that that Magistrate was a barrister. So he cabled his friend in London to check whether he was in any of the Inns or Temples. The cable came back with a negative reply but with a suggestion that he should try Holiday Inn or Air Hitam Temple.

That somewhat concludes my outline of the material particulars of the applicant insofar as his achievements in the field of law are concerned. I should, however, add that Sze Loon excelled not only in common law but also law that was not common such as equity. He also did some real law like real property and some unreal law like Roman law.

Now, as for the respondent Linda, she also learnt to read and write in Kuala Lumpur. But there was no evidence that she knew Sze Loon then. After she was found able to read and write, Datuk Kam, for some unknown reason and contrary to expectation, decided to pack Linda off to big island Australia in Adelaide. There she was to learn something useful to prepare herself to be a good wife, in particular, how to efficiently run a good house — strictly according to budget. She therefore secured herself a degree in economics. Thereafter Datuk Kam had a change of mind and felt that Linda should follow his footsteps, not as a politician and/or Senator but as a lawyer. That was why she landed at

Buckingham University. There the examiners were satisfied beyond any reasonable doubt that she deserved the honours in law. That was in 1980. The following year, after attending the traditional dinners, as expensive as ever but with no improvement in quality she was called to the Bar by the Middle Temple. Back home, following the footsteps of her father, she was admitted as an advocate and solicitor of the High Court of Malaya.

So much for material particulars. What is more significant to this auspicious occasion is the secret that led to the union culminating in holy matrimony. The facts unfolded give a clear picture that the romantic link started in chambers. Linda was reading in the chambers of Khoo Eng Chin. As a good daughter she used to call on her father regularly. Datuk Kam had a legal assistant by the name of Kiru — who is a close friend of Sze Loon. Sze Loon had heard of Linda and on the pretext of seeing Kiru he went to Datuk Kam's Chambers. Quite naturally he bumped into Linda there. For Sze Loon first sight was not enough and neither was it enough for Linda. So they had further sights. Rumour has it that Linda wanted her daddy to know of their plans. So one day she said to him:

> "Daddy, I simply love Sze Loon."
>
> She paused for a moment and then went on, "We might be getting engaged soon."
>
> "Has he got money?" asked Datuk Kam.
>
> "It is funny, Dad." said Linda.
>
> "Why did you say that?" asked Datuk Kam.
>
> "Well, he had asked that of you."

To conclude may I let some cats out of the bag.

Sze Loon was born in the year 1955 under the lunar sign of the sheep (25.10.1955). It is believed to be a very good sign. Support for this view is to be found in the *Handbook of Chinese Horoscopes* by Theodora Lau. It reads:

> "A person of the sheep year is called the good Samaritan of the cycle. He is righteous, sincere."

And it is good for Linda to know that "he is easily taken in by sob stories".

Theodora Lau also says that under this sign, he is mild-mannered, even shy. At his best, he is artistic, fashionable and a creative worker. At his worst, he tends to be easily overcome by his emotions.

Again, perhaps, Linda would be happy to know that the "sheep is known for his gentle and compassionate ways. He can forgive easily and be understanding about others' faults". I have splendid news for Datuk, Datin and Linda because a person born under this sign is "very fond of children". Next year Datuk Kam would certainly be a real Datuk.

Linda, on the other hand, was born on January 18, 1958 under the star Capricorn and the Chinese sign rooster. Theodora Lau has this to say:

> "All roosters are perfectionists in one form or another. They will have a sharp eye for details mixed with theoretical flights of fancy.... The female of this sign is usually more down to earth and less colourful in her aspirations. She is super efficient and will get things done with a minimum of fuss."

Sze Loon should be happy to know that a person born under this sign is reliable and has enormous amounts of energy to dedicate to any job she sets her sights on.

Jointly they have decided to proceed with their wedding in the year of the Dragon. There is, therefore, a splendid combination of the rooster, the sheep and the dragon. Theodora Lau has this to say about the year of the Dragon:

> "Orientals consider this to be an auspicious year to get married, have children and start a new business, as the benevolent Dragon brings good fortune and happiness."

On that note, may I ask everyone here to be upstanding to drink to the happiness and good fortune of the couple.

PENGGUNAAN BAHASA MALAYSIA DAN PROSEDUR MAHKAMAH*

Saya bersyukur ke hadrat Allah kerana dengan keizinanNya dapat kita bersama-sama pada hari ini dalam majlis pembukaan Bengkel Penggunaan Bahasa Malaysia dan Prosedur Mahkamah. Saya ingin mengucapkan terima kasih kepada pihak penganjur bersama iaitu Biro Terjemahan Mahkamah Agung, Kulliyah Undang-Undang, Universiti Islam Antarabangsa dan Persatuan Undang-Undang Universiti Islam Antarabangsa.

Ini adalah julung-julung kali Biro Terjemahan Mahkamah Agung, berganding bahu dengan sebuah institusi pengajian tinggi, untuk menganjur bengkel seumpama ini yang bertujuan memastikan pelaksanaan Bahasa Malaysia di mahkamah terlaksana dengan sempurna. Saya ucapkan syabas kepada mereka yang terlibat.

Usaha seperti ini seharusnya diteruskan bukan sahaja oleh Universiti Islam Antarabangsa sahaja tetapi juga oleh institusi-institusi pengajian tinggi yang lain bagi melengkapkan bakal-bakal peguam agar mereka benar-benar arif dan fasih dalam pertuturan Bahasa Malaysia yang berkualiti serta memastikan Bahasa Malaysia adalah setaraf dengan bahasa-bahasa lain yang telah berzaman-zaman digunakan dalam bidang kehakiman dan perundangan.

Dari apa yang saya diberitahu, tujuan bengkel ini ialah untuk mendedahkan para pelajar UIA kepada penggunaan Bahasa Malaysia di mahkamah serta melengkapkan diri mereka dengan istilah-istilah undang-undang yang mungkin buat masa ini masih samar-samar lagi bagi mereka.

Saya juga difahamkan bahawa bahasa perantaraan dalam jurusan undang-undang di UIA ialah Bahasa Inggeris. Ini disebabkan oleh pelajar-pelajar UIA terdiri daripada berbilang bangsa. Oleh itu adalah wajar Bahasa Inggeris menjadi bahasa perantaraan dalam pengajian mereka kerana ianya adalah bahasa antarabangsa. Keadaan ini mungkin menyulitkan pelajar-pelajar kita, yang apabila tamat pengajian mereka, terpaksa menggunakan Bahasa Malaysia.

Walua bagaimanapun saya yakin, bahawa kesemua pelajar undang-undang warganegara di UIA fasih dalam Bahasa Malaysia kerana ini adalah bahasa

---

**Di Majlis Pembukaan Bengkel Penggunaan Bahasa Malaysia Dan Prosedur Mahkamah Di Universiti Islam Antarabangsa Pada 1hb Mac 1989.*

ibunda. Sungguhpun begitu, kefasihan dalam bahasa sahaja tidaklah memadai bagi bakal-bakal peguam yang akan 'practice' di Malaysia. Adalah perlu bagi mereka melengkapkan diri sepenuhnya. Kini, Badan Kehakiman sedang mempergiatkan proses perlaksanaan penggunaan Bahasa Malaysia secara luas di Mahkamah Rendah hingga Mahkamah Tinggi.

Bidang undang-undang adalah suatu bidang yang khusus. Seseorang tidak dapat menjalankan tugasnya dengan hanya pandai bertutur sedangkan istilah-istilah undang-undang dalam Bahasa Malaysia tidak dapat dikuasainya. Jadi saya pasti dengan adanya kursus singkat seperti ini maka ianya dapat mendedahkan para peserta tentang undang-undang, istilah-istilahnya dan prosedur mahkamah dalam Bahasa Malaysia. Mungkin bengkel yang singkat ini tidak dapat mencapai kejayaan yang sepenannya dari segi menjadikan seseorang itu arif dengan istilah-istilah dan prosedur, tetapi sekurang-kurangnya membiasakan diri mereka kepada perkara-perkara yang disebutkan tadi. Ini adalah ibarat pepatah Melayu yang berbunyi "sediakan payung sebelum hujan".

Di Kolej atau di Universiti kita lebih terdedah kepada teori. Dalam bidang undang-undang, praktikal atau amali adalah sama penting. Terutama sekali dalam kes sivil di mana seseorang itu boleh kalah dalam guaman jika beliau tidak menguasai prosedur. Misalnya masa untuk mematuhi sesuatu dalam peruntukan-peruntukan tertentu adalah unsur yang amat penting dalam kes sivil. Kegagalan seseorang itu untuk mematuhi peraturan masa, boleh mengakibatkan kesnya dibatalkan.

Ahkir sekali saya ingin menyatakan bahawa dalam bidang undang-undang, mahupun bidang-bidang lain, kejayaan tidak datang menggolek. Kejayaan hanya dapat dicapai hasil dari kerja yang bersungguh-sungguh. Jadi, bagi memastikan kejayaan, saudara dan saudari hendaklah melengkapkan diri dengan menggunakan Bahasa Malaysia baik dari advokasinya mahupun dalam segi istilah.

Juga saya berharap bengkel ini akan membantu menggalakkan bakal-bakal peguam yang berkebolehan dan arif dalam penggunaan Bahasa Malaysia di Mahkamah. Memandangkan minat yang ditunjukkan oleh saudara dan saudari sekalian, saya percaya harapan dan azam saya untuk melaksanakan Bahasa Malaysia di Mahkamah dengan sepenuhnya menjelang tahun sembilan belas sembilan puluhan sejajar dengan aspirasi kerajaan dan rakyat tidak akan menjadi impian sahaja.

Dengan ini saya dengan rasminya membuka bengkel Penggunaan Bahasa Malaysia dan Prosedur Mahkamah.

PENGGUNAAN BAHASA MALAYSIA DI MAHKAMAH*

Alhamdulillah saya bersyukur ke hadrat Allah Subhana Wataala kerana dengan limpah keizinanNya kita dapat bersama-sama pada malam ini di Majlis Makan Malam Tahunan Pelajar-Pelajar Undang-Undang Institut Teknologi Mara 1989. Saya juga ingin mengucapkan terimakasih kepada Jawatankuasa Penganjur kerana sekali lagi telah mengundang saya dan isteri saya menikmati juadah-juadah yang enak dan tambahan pula diberi penghormatan kepada saya bagi memberi sepatah dua kata kepada peguam-peguam dan juga bakal-bakal peguam keluaran ITM.

Saya percaya ucapan saya tidak sempurna tanpa saya mengucapkan tahniah kepada pihak ITM yang telah berjaya mengeluarkan graduan-graduan lulusan undang-undang di peringkat diploma seramai 336 orang dan di peringkat diploma lanjutan seramai 129 orang. Tidaklah dapat dinafikan bahawa dengan terbentuknya sekolah undang-undang di ITM, bilangan lulusan undang-undang di kalangan Bumiputera telah meningkat. Bahkan banyak di antara mereka telah berjaya menjawat jawatan tinggi di badan-badan swasta dan awam termasuk juga badan kehakiman. Dengan ini jelas sekali bahawa ITM mampu mengeluarkan graduan-graduan yang berkaliber. Saya pasti ramai di antara saudara dan saudari yang hadir di majlis ini terdiri dari peguam-peguam yang sedang mengamalkan profesion undang-undang.

Izinkan saya menyentuh sedikit tentang pelaksanaan penggunaan Bahasa Malaysia di mahkamah walaupun isu ini kerapkali ditimbulkan. Sebagaimana yang diketahui, Badan Kehakiman sedang giat dalam proses melaksanakan penggunaan Bahasa Malaysia sepenuhnya di mahkamah. Di dalam bidang pentadbiran jabatan kehakiman, Bahasa Malaysia telah digunakan seratus peratus. Cuma bidang kehakiman (iaitu dalam perbicaraan di Mahkamah), akibat sebab-sebab tertentu, kita tidak dapat melaksana-kan penggunaan Bahasa Malaysia sepenuhnya buat masa sekarang. Walau bagaimanapun di Mahkamah Rendah, Bahasa Malaysia telah digunakan hampir seratus peratus. Di peringkat Mahkamah Tinggi dan Agung kita giat berusaha agar Bahasa Malaysia dapat digunakan seluas-luasnya.

**Di Majlis Makan Malam Tahunan Pelajar-pelajar Undang-undang Institut Teknologi Mara 1989, Pada 24 Mac 1989 Di Holiday Villa, Subang Jaya.*

Saya percaya bahawa saudara saudari sedar tentang hakikat ini dan tentu sekali telah berusaha melengkapkan diri dengan mempelajari istilah-istilah undang-undang yang tertentu. Kursus singkat yang bertujuan melatih diri dalam penggunaan Bahasa Malaysia di bidang perundangan dan kehakiman, sangatlah berguna kepada pelajar-pelajar yang akan tamat pengajian mereka. Jabatan Kehakiman sedia membantu sesiapa juga dalam usaha ke arah memperlengkapkan diri dengan penggunaan Bahasa Malaysia dalam profesion undang-undang.

Berkait dengan penggunaan Bahasa Malaysia di Mahkamah, wujud nada-nada sumbang yang mempersoalkan kemampuan Bahasa Malaysia untuk mengambil alih peranan Bahasa Inggeris sebagai bahasa mahkamah dan bahasa perundangan. Mereka bimbang kononnya undang-undang kita berasaskan Common Law Inggeris dan hanya Bahasa Inggeris sahajalah yang bersesuaian.

Kebimbangan ini tidak wajar kerana Bahasa Melayu (kini lebih dikenali dengan Bahasa Malaysia) telahpun menjadi bahasa undang-undang sebelum kedatangan penjajah. Di zaman kegemilangan Kerajaan Melayu Melaka, Bahasa Melayu telahpun mampu menjadi bahasa undang-undang. Kanun Laut Melaka digunakan pada masa itu oleh pedagang Eropah, Cina, Arab, India dan tempatan yang datang untuk berniaga. Dalam abad ke Lima Belas Bahasa Melayu sudahpun menjadi lingua franca.

Pengaruh kanun-kanun Melaka ini dapat di lihat dalam sejarah undang-undang di beberapa buah negeri Melayu iaitu Undang-Undang Pahang 1596, Undang-Undang Kedah dari tahun 1650 hingga 1784, Undang-Undang Johor 1789 dan Undang-Undang Sembilan Puluh Sembilan Perak 1878. Bahkan kebanyakan undang-undang ini ditulis dalam huruf jawi.

Di Indonesia sendiri Bahasa Indonesia diguna dengan jayanya dalam semua bidang. Jika suatu bahasa itu berkemampuan ia tetap berkemampuan samada dalam Common Law atau Sivil Law.

Saya ingin menarik perhatian saudara-saudari yang kita telah merdeka kira-kira 32 tahun lalu. Bahasa rasmi negara ialah Bahasa Melayu. Dalam bidang kehakiman Bahasa Melayu diberi nafas oleh Akta Bahasa Kebangsaan 1963/67. Ini bermakna pelaksanaan Bahasa Melayu di mahkamah bukanlah dengan tergesa-gesa.

Saudara-saudari adalah wajar bagi kita merdeka dalam erti kata sebenarnya. Tidaklah tepat jika kita menganggap apa saja yang kebaratan adalah bermutu. Pada pendapat saya, semua pihak hendaklah berusaha supaya Bahasa Malaysia mengambil tempat haknya dalam bidang perundangan dan kehakiman. Semua pihak hendaklah menerima hakikat bahawa Bahasa Malaysia adalah bahasa ilmu dan mampu menghadapi perkembangan zaman seperti mana Bahasa Inggeris.

Sebelum negara kita merdeka banyak orang termasuk orang-orang Melayu sendiri tidak yakin Bahasa Malaysia boleh mengambil alih peranan Bahasa Inggeris dalam pentadbiran, pelajaran, perundangan dan kehakiman. Terbukti bahawa sangkaan mereka itu tidak benar. Kini Bahasa Melayu digunakan seratus peratus dalam pentadbiran negara juga di Pusat Pengajian Tinggi. Di Parlimen sendiri Bahasa Melayu bukan sahaja dituturkan oleh kaum Melayu bahkan oleh kaum-kaum lain.

Pada hemat saya, Majlis yang indah ini adalah platfom yang baik untuk menyentuh sedikit berkenaan isu Common Law kerana saudara saudari yang terdiri dari peguam dan bakal peguam tidak patut keliru dengan salah anggapan dan salah pengertian mengenai kenyataan saya yang bersabit dengan isu ini.

Sistem perundangan kita ini adalah warisan penjajahan. Bila negara kita merdeka, sistem perundangan ini diwarisi terus. Sumber undang-undang kita berasal dari Common Law Inggeris dan undang-undang statut. Oleh kerana keadaan di negara kita telah berubah, maka undang-undang kita juga patut diubah selaras dengan aspirasi rakyat. Sebenarnya ada dua sistem undang-undang sekular yang terpakai di seluruh dunia, iaitu Common Law Inggeris yang dipakai oleh kebanyakan negara-negara Komanwel dan Amerika dan Civil Law yang dipakai oleh kebanyakan negara Eropah Barat serta Asia, termasuk Jepun dan Thailand adalah antara negara yang menggunakannya. Jadi Common Law bukanlah merupakan hak orang-orang Inggeris sahaja. Ianya sudah menjadi satu daripada dua sistem undang-undang universal.

Penggunaan Common Law di Semenanjung Malaysia adalah dengan penguatkuasaan S.3 Akta Undang-Undang Sivil 1956 (Disemak 1972). Seksyen 3(1)(a), (b) dan (c) memperuntukkan dengan jelas bahawa sekiranya tidak ada peruntukan yang telah dibuat atau akan dibuat oleh undang-undang bertulis, mahkamah-mahkamah di Malaysia hendaklah memakai Common Law dan kaedah-kaedah ekuiti yang ditadbirkan di England pada 7hb April 1956 bagi Semenanjung Malaysia (di Sarawak pada 12hb Disember 1949 dan Sabah pada 1hb Disember 1951). Seksyen 5 berkait dengan penggunaan undang-undang Inggeris dalam hal-hal komersial.

Baru-baru ini kenyataan saya mengenai Common Law telah disalah-ertikan. Saya hanya memperakui saranan yang dibuat oleh Tan Sri Prof. Ahmad Ibrahim yang menghendaki mahkamah membentuk Common Law kita sendiri dan Seksyen 3 Akta Undang-Undang Sivil 1956 dimansuhkan atau dipinda. Adalah tidak dapat dinafikan bahawa dalam kebanyakan kes-kes yang diputuskan oleh mahkamah-mahkamah kita, penggunaan undang-undang

Inggeris di bawah seksyen 3 tersebut adalah dengan syarat diizinkan oleh keadaan tempatan dan penduduknya dan tertakluk kepada penyesuaian yang dianggap perlu oleh keadaan tempatan.

Jadi bila kita mansuhkan seksyen 3 Akta Undang-Undang Sivil, maka mahkamah kita tidak lagi terikat dengan penggunaan Common Law Inggeris. Dengan pemansuhan seksyen 3 tersebut, mahkamah kita bebas menerapkan nilai-nilai hidup kita sendiri dan bukan dicampur-adukkan dengan nilai-nilai hidup asing bila membuat penghakiman. Dengan itu Common Law kita sendiri akan ujud dan berkembang dengan tidak terikat langsung dengan peruntukan yang mengambil kira undang-undang Inggeris.

Kini, tibalah masanya untuk Hakim-Hakim menyesuaikan diri dengan kehendak dan kepentingan negara. Undang-undang kita hendaklah berasaskan kepada nilai-nilai Rukun Negara, yang menjadi teras perlembagaan negara kita dan bukan undang-undang yang meliputi oleh unsur-unsur asing. Saya sedar bahawa kita tidak harus tergesa-gesa untuk mengubahkan suatu undang-undang. Kita perlu mangkaji dengan terperinci implikasinya kerana adalah menjadi tanggungjawab mutlak para hakim untuk bersikap adil tanpa mengira apa bangsa dan keturunan. Sebagai orang Islam kita hendaklah jangan lupa bahawa Allah menyuruh kita berlaku adil terhadap semua manusia bukan hanya kepada orang Islam sahaja. Nilai-nilai seperti inilah patut kita serapkan dalam Common Law kita nanti.

Saya harap setiap warganegara Malaysia akan menyokong setiap langkah yang dibuat bagi memastikan yang undang-undang kita benar-benar diputuskan berlandaskan unsur-unsur kita sendiri dan bukan mencirikan unsur asing. Namun, tidaklah dapat dinafikan bahawa ada unsur-unsur asing yang baik. Nilai-nilai sedemikian sepatutnya diterima jika bersesuaian, ibarat pepatah Melayu: "yang baik menjadi teladan dan yang tidak elok menjadi sempadan".

Saudara-saudari, saya harap dengan penjelasan ringkas tentang keadaan yang sebenar akan mengelakkan salah faham dan salah erti berkaitan dengan Common Law. Kita hendaklah jangan mempunyai sikap negatif bila usaha-usaha dibuat untuk membentuk Common Law kita sendiri.

Sekali lagi saya ingin tegaskan di sini bahawa kami di badan kehakiman tidak sekali-kali tergesa-gesa membuat suatu perubahan tanpa mengambil kira pandangan-pandangan yang membina dari sesiapa juga demi untuk menegakkan keadilan.

Baru-baru ini juga suatu kekeliruan telah timbul bersabit dengan perkara angkat sumpah jawatan DYMM Yang Di Pertuan Agong. Gambaran yang salah telah diberikan bahawa bakal DYMM Yang Di Pertuan Agong akan mengangkat sumpah di hadapan Ketua Hakim Negara dalam bulan April nanti.

Dalam sejarah kita DYMM Yang Di Pertuan Agong tidak pernah mengangkat sumpah di hadapan Ketua Hakim Negara kerana menurut Perlembagaan kita DYMM Yang Di Pertuan Agong dikehendaki mengangkat sumpah di hadapan Majlis Raja-Raja dengan kehadiran Ketua Hakim Negara.

Di bawah peruntukan Bahagian 4, Bab 1, Perkara 37, Perlembagaan Persekutuan, Malaysia Yang Di Pertuan Agong hendaklah sebelum menjalankan tugas-tugasnya, mengangkat dan menandatangani suatu sumpah jawatan yang dinyatakan dalam Bahagian 1, Jadual Keempat, di hadapan Majlis Raja-Raja dan dengan kehadiran Ketua Hakim Negara, Mahkamah Agung (atau jika ia tidak ada, dengan kehadiran seorang Hakim Mahkamah Agung terkanan selepasnya) dan sumpah itu hendaklah disaksikan serta ditandatangani oleh dua orang yang dilantik bagi maksud itu oleh Majlis Raja-Raja.

Saudara-saudari sekalian, saya berterima kasih kerana saudara-saudari sabar mendengar ucapan saya. Saya akhiri dengan pesanan kepada saudara-saudari supaya menghayati sikap-sikap murni seperti takwa, jujur dan amanah dalam kehidupan harian sebagai pelajar mahupun sebagai peguam. Kita hendaklah saling hormat menghormati kerana dalam bidang undang-undang, perbezaan pendapat itu adalah lumrah hidup. Dengan sikap sedemikian, profesion undang-undang akan terus unggul dan tidak diselubungi oleh emosi dan salah sangka.

Sekali lagi saya meminta maaf kepada saudara-saudari kalau-kalau ucapan saya tadi menyinggung perasaan atau terkasar bahasa.

SYARAT KEMAHIRAN DAN KEPINTARAN KEPEGUAMAN*

Saya bersyukur dan amat berbangga kerana diberi penghormatan untuk membuka Pertandingan Moot Kelima di antara Fakulti Undang-Undang Pusat-Pusat Pengajian Tinggi.

Pertandingan ini telah lama bertapak dan saya berharap ianya akan terus kekal sebagai sebahagian daripada ciri Pengajian Undang-Undang tempatan.

Di sini, saya bersama para hakim yang lain berasa gembira dan bersedia memberikan kerjasama yang mampu. Inilah julung-julung kalinya pertandingan moot seperti ini diadakan ditempat yang agak sesuai iaitu di Bangunan Mahkamah Agung sendiri. Saya percaya penghormatan yang diberi kepada Pertandingan Moot ini tidak akan disia-siakan.

I take this opportunity to say that the law courts exist to serve the interests of justice, and every law student is—or ought to be—aware of the gravity and sense of responsibility with which we approach that subject.

For me, the Constitution of Malaysia represents the necessary structure within which justice is secured in our society. Indeed, every judge takes an oath to "preserve, protect and defend" the Constitution. This can impose an invidious burden; but it is a responsibility that must in fact be shared by both the Bench and the Bar alike, if the Constitution is to function as it should. Conscious of what we owe to society we must do the best we can.

Dalam pertandingan seperti ini, kemahiran kepeguaman yang khusus amat diperlukan. Adalah diharapkan setiap pengamal undang-undang itu adalah seorang peguambela dalam ertikata yang sebenarnya, dan oleh yang demikian kepintaran dan kecekapan seseorang itu tertakluk kepada keupayaan berhujah yang boleh meyakinkan. Pada suatu masa yang lampau, mahkamah dapat dipengaruhi oleh hujah-hujah yang kononnya bernas dan munasabah tetapi tidak benar. Saya teringat kepintaran David Marshall, seorang peguam yang sering dicontoh. Hujah-hujahnya yang dikemukakan bagi pihak tertuduh menyebabkan Hakim atau Pendakwa begitu terpesona dengan kepintaran berhujah oleh peguam walau pun hujah itu tidak mempunyai merit dalam prosiding perbicaraan tersebut. Ini adalah keistimewaan dalam kemahiran

---

**Di Pembukaan Pertandingan Moot pada 30hb September 1989 Di Mahkamah Agung 2.*

kepeguaman. Tetapi ciri tersebut sahaja tidak menentukan seseorang itu sebagai peguam yang baik.

Memandangkan prosiding ini bersifat antarabangsa, maka ianya dijalankan di dalam bahasa Inggeris. Walau bagaimanapun, saya yakin bahawa penghujah yang berbahasa Malaysia yang mengambil bahagian dalam pertandingan ini tidak syak lagi dapat melakukannya dengan baik. Selagi laporan undang-undang digunakan, adalah perlu bahasa Inggeris digunakan. Kebanyakan prinsip undang-undang yang termuat di dalam Laporan Undang-Undang bukan sahaja dari United Kingdom malahan dari Australia, Canada, New Zealand dan Amerika Syarikat, dengan tidak mengenepikan India, Pakistan, Brunei dan Singapura. Masih perlu bagi kita menatapi jurnal-jurnal yang sedemikian. Walaupun saya dan para Hakim sedang giat berusaha meningkatkan penggunaan Bahasa Malaysia di dalam semua prosiding undang-undang, tidak dapat dinafikan bahawa dalam Bahagian Rayuan seperti yang menjadi pokok dalam pentandingan ini, kemahiran yang baik dalam bahasa Inggeris adalah perlu untuk memahami undang-undang. Ini adalah kenyataan yang mesti dihadapi. Usaha yang gigih perlu untuk menyediakan asas rujukan begi perbendaharaan kata undang-undang yang sentiasa berkembang, seperti kamus Undang-Undang dan Teks Undang-Undang dalam Bahasa Malaysia tetapi segala usaha-usaha sudah tentu akan mengambil masa yang lama. Seperti kata pujangga sesebuah negara tidak dibina dalam masa sehari.

I am very happy to see that the National University of Singapore is represented in this Competition. The legal systems of Malaysia and Singapore share a common origin, and even today reflect similar values. They are likely to develop in different ways, for the pressures within, and perhaps, the objectives of our two societies may differ; nevertheless, I believe that our aspirations for justice are the same. I welcome most heartily the presence of a distinguished Singapore judge, to assess the performance of our finalists tomorrow, and would like to say how much we appreciate his presence here.

Malaysia and Singapore are, after all, bound by more than the causeway. We belong to this great peninsula. Our commercial laws are similar, and are based on the common law we have adopted, adapted and developed over a century and more. Of course, because Islam is the religion of Malaysia, our law may develop slightly in a different way. This is a matter for the most careful and discreet consideration, in which there must be one of studied evolution, not impetuous revolution. Of one thing we can be sure, and that is our natural objectives of justice, harmony and peace within our societies must remain constant.

To that end the Bench and Bar, and, let me hope, all you youthful law students, are dedicated. May all of you enjoy your Moots here! But remember, these Moots are only games, a limited extension, if you like, of the recent Southeast Asian Games. As such, they offer useful training for the rigours, and often much abused profession.

Di sini saya dengan bangganya mengisytiharkan Pertandingan Moot antara Fakulti Undang-Undang ini dibuka dengan rasminya.

TOWARDS HEALTHIER UNDERSTANDING*

It gives me and my wife great pleasure to enjoy your wonderful hospitality and we are thankful for your kind thoughts behind this function. Perhaps it is appropriate for me to observe that generally speaking, the relationship between the Bar and the Bench is not as good as it could have been. However, this is not the forum to hold an inquest and pass a verdict over who is to blame. Without abusing your hospitality and without using the occasion to get involved in any never ending controversy, I take the liberty only to acquaint you with some of my personal views.

I am as much part of the legal system as each and every one of you present here. The Constitution, as promulgated by the legislature, reflects the will of the people and is supreme and sovereign above all of us. While our role and functions are different the ultimate objective, namely, to do justice, is the same. In this respect the Chief Justice and I and other Judicial and Legal Officers need your co-operation and understanding. The Supreme Court is like the quarterback in a football team (or like the halves i.e. the scrum half and the stand off half in a rugby team). It puts the play in motion, it guides others, it throws the ball but unless there is someone at the end to catch that pass and run with it, no actual headway is going to be made. We are all members of the same team but the rules of the game are to be observed. The office of the Lord President which I occupy, not by design, but due to a chain of unexpected circumstances, is not an Ivory Tower but only a Watch Tower. We, the members of the judiciary, are only the guardians of the Constitution which is the will of the people and not the masters. Any one of you with a genuine grievance relating to the operation of the legal system is always welcome to approach me or the Chief Justice or other judges and we will be attentive and do our best to remedy your grievance within the existing context. I appreciate that the recent events involving the judiciary and the Bar have not at all been a pleasant experience to any one of us, but a great majority of us feel that the time is overdue to promote a fruitful dialogue and healthier understanding. While time is the greatest healer of all

---

**At The Dinner Organized By The Legal Fraternity Of Wilayah Persekutuan And Selangor At Kuala Lumpur Hilton On 14th December, 1989 In Respect Of The Seri Setia Mahkota (SSM) Award Bestowed On Y.A.A. Tun By D.Y.M.M. SPB Yang Di-pertuan Agong Sultan Azlan Shah.*

wounds, it does not take many years, as in the case of the Communist Party, for any group to realise the mistake made and declare "amnesty" for common good.

In the whole exercise, I have no axe to grind against any one as my conscience and Allah are my witnesses. By convention and protocol I cannot condescend myself to step into the dusty arena of conflict but if and when an appropriate occasion arises, I will explain the truth behind certain wild, unkind and unfounded allegations circulated against me and others by sources from whom it was least expected in the ordinary course of human relationship and decency.

However, I hasten to add that I will not take this social event as waiving your organization's right to proceed in any manner as you think fit. As far as I am concerned, I have a job to do and I am trying my best to do it—to speed up the disposal of cases, clear the backlog, establish more courts, promote the use of Bahasa Malaysia with certain limitations and establish the best possible relationship with the other organs of Government. While I respect law, I am afraid that sometimes by virtue of our tradition and training we tend to see law in its abstract, symbolic nature. What we therefore need is acceptance of our uniqueness and independence by other social institutions. I stress that the legal system cannot exist by itself but must be viewed and analysed as an integrative mechanism which contributes a measure of co-ordination to society. The legal system receives inputs, such as goals, from the political system; in return it creates outputs of interpretation and legitimation. Its effectiveness in contributing to the integration of society, especially when such society is only developing to maturity, reflects, in part, the effective nature of its interchanges with the political system. Our legal approach should not be static but should be bound up, inextricably, with concepts of individual and social morality. It is rooted in a rapidly evolving society. It bows to the winds of fundamental social and institutional changes and in so doing reflects the essence of the ethics, culture, development and aspirations of society. When I was young I was told of a story of a young boy crying because he had only one shoe, not a pair for both legs. When the boy in turn saw one other without a leg, he could not help but feel how lucky he was. Likewise, I feel how lucky we all are in this society, in this country where we can enjoy a dinner in peace, notwithstanding our differences, unlike our unfortunate neighbours in the Philippines where I was ten days ago marooned in a hotel for four days living in anxiety with fighting going on in the city. What is the use of freedom in the abstract when unlimited freedom destroys the social fabrics.

Therefore from the common man's pragmatic point of view, our system of political institution is not bad at all in the context of our region. The centre of gravity of legal development lies not in legislation, judges and lawyers but in society itself. Many rules transplanted from other countries are contrary to the sentiments of our society and do not correspond to the interests or wishes of the people and the ruling elite. Our shape of rules clearly has more to do with history than with the present structure of society. The inescapable function of law is to help in avoiding and settling disputes for the moral, social or economic well being of society.

Enough is enough and I shall cease here thanking you for your hospitality, which I assume is directed to the institution I head.

KEDAULATAN UNDANG-UNDANG*

Terlebih dahulu saya bersyukur ke hadrat Allah Subhanahu Wata'ala kerana dengan limpah rahmatNya saya berada dalam keadaan sejahtera dan saya dapat hadir bersama-sama tuan-tuan dan puan-puan pada pagi ini.

Saya juga merasa sungguh bangga kerana diberi penghormatan oleh Persatuan Mahasiswa Fakulti Undang-Undang Universiti Kebangsaan Malaysia atau lebih dikenali dengan Perundang bagi menyampaikan ucapan dasar atau "keynote address" kepada perhimpunan para bijak pandai yang akan mengambil bahagian dalam Seminar Tahunan Undang-Undang dan Masyarakat Ke-3.

Saya juga mengucapkan syabas dan tahniah kepada Penganjur Seminar ini.

Pada hemat saya tajuk Undang-Undang dan Masyarakat ini sangatlah luas. Jadi apa yang saya akan memperkatakan adalah sub topik yang saya fikir relevan dengan hubungan masyarakat dan undang-undang. Adalah perlu disebut bahawa masyarakatlah yang membuat undang-undang melalui mandat yang diberi kepada wakil mereka di Parlimen. Dan jika mereka tidak memahami undang-undang maka soalannya adalah: Adakah menjadi tanggungjawab kita sebagai golongan yang arif dalam bidang khusus ini untuk memberitahu mereka sekurang-kurangnya tentang hak mereka di sisi undang-undang?

Saya tidak mungkin menyentuh kesemua aspek undang-undang dan masyarakat tetapi cukuplah sekadar apa yang akan disampaikan dalam skop masa yang terhad ini.

Apabila disebut undang-undang, apa yang sering terpampang di dalam ingatan kita ialah sistem kehakiman di mahkamah. Undang-undang itu sendiri sebenarnya menpunyai konsep yang luas. Ia telah lama wujud dan terus digunakan untuk mengekalkan keamanan dan ketenteraman dalam setiap masyarakat yang maju dan lebih-lebih lagi yang sedang berkembang. Namun demikian, jarang sekali kita mendengar undang-undang dikaitkan dengan pembangunan sesuatu masyarakat sedangkan kedua-duanya pada pendapat saya adalah suatu fakta fundamental yang tidak boleh dipisahkan. Di dalam sesuatu masyarakat, undang-undang adalah perlu sebagai suatu kesusilaan yang

---

*Di Seminar Tahunan Undang-Undang Dan Masyarakat Ke-3 Pada 6hb Dan 7hb Januari, 1990 Di Universiti Kebangsaan Malaysia.

mengawal perhubungan di antara ibu bapa dan anak-anak, dan di antara rakyat dengan kerajaan. Tanpa undang-undang, keamanan dalam masyarakat tidak mungkin wujud, sebaliknya kekacauan yang akan berlaku. Adakah tepat jika dikatakan bahawa keamanan hanya dapat diwujudkan di dalam sesuatu masyarakat melalui undang-undang yang berkuatkuasa?

Kita juga dapati bahawa undang-undang bukan sahaja menetapkan struktur dan jenis kerajaan yang memerintah, tetapi juga sebagai satu instrumen untuk Kerajaan mencapai matlamatnya. Kerajaan menjalankan kuasa-kuasa yang diperuntukkan oleh undang-undang, dan pelaksanaannya dijalankan oleh pihak-pihak berkuasa tertentu. Struktur jentera kerajaan dan pengawalseliaan kuasa dan kewajipannya adalah ditetapkan oleh undang-undang yang menerangkan bagaimana kuasa-kuasa ini dijalankan atau tugas-tugas ini dilaksanakan. Oleh yang demikian, adakah wajar dikatakan bahawa undang-undang adalah suatu himpunan kaedah-kaedah yang mengawal kesusilaan sesuatu masyarakat dan mengatur bentuk kerajaan di dalam sesuatu masyarakat? Dalam konteks ini, maka struktur dan jenis kerajaan sedemikian adalah apa yang dirujuk sebagai sistem demokrasi berparlimen.

Berhubungan dengan sistem demokrasi berparlimen, Kerajaan yang wujud dalam sesuatu masyarakat atau negara, mestilah mempunyai doktrin perasingan kuasa di antara Badan Perundangan, Badan Eksekutif dan Kehakiman. Parlimen yang diketuai oleh Yang di-Pertua membuat undang-undang, manakala Eksekutif yang diketuai oleh Perdana Menteri dan Kabinet akan memastikan pelaksanaan undang-undang sebagaimana yang dibuat oleh Badan Perundangan. Badan Kehakiman pula yang diketuai oleh Ketua Hakim Negara akan menjalankan pentadbiran kehakiman serta mentafsir undang-undang sebagaimana yang dibuat oleh Badan Perundangan, khususnya di antara rakyat dengan rakyat dan di antara rakyat dengan kerajaan. Kebebasan seseorang rakyat adalah bergantung kepada dua prinsip, iaitu seseorang rakyat boleh berbuat apa sahaja yang dikehendakinya dengan syarat dia tidak melanggar undang-undang substantif atau melanggar hak orang lain di sisi undang-undang; manakala pihak berkuasa, termasuk Kerajaan tidak boleh berbuat apa-apa selain daripada apa yang diperuntukkan dan dibenarkan oleh undang-undang. Soal yang timbul perlu adalah wajar atau tidak jika kita mengatakan bahawa sesuatu masyarakat yang berkembang adalah masyarakat sesuatu kerajaan yang strukturnya terikat kepada doktrin perasingan kuasa?

Soalan

Kewajipan dan taat setia rakyat adakah tertakluk kepada kedaulatan undang-undang. Kedaulatan undang-undang adalah suatu konsep yang menjadikan undang-undang suatu negara mengatasi kehendak mana-mana individu atau kumpulan individu, tidak kira bagaimana kuat pengaruhnya atau berapa banyak bilangannya.

Kedaulatan undang-undang menjelaskan bahawa semua orang adalah sama rata di sisi undang-undang dan berhak mendapat perlindungan yang sama rata di sisi undang-undang. Soalnya adakah tepat jika dikatakan masaalah tidak akan timbul jika undang-undang yang dikenakan adalah mengikut kehendak rakyat sesuatu masyarakat?

Berhubungan dengan kebebasan asasi, Bahagian II Perlembagaan Malaysia adalah berkaitan. Sebagai negara yang mengamalkan konsep demokrasi berparlimen, Parlimen adalah tertakluk kepada Perlembagaan kerana Perlembagaan merupakan undang-undang utama di negara ini. Konsep demokrasi yang dilaung-laungkan tidak akan memberi apa-apa makna jika tidak terdapat keseimbangan di antara kebebasan individu dan kawalan sosial. Kerapkali kita dapati di dalam sesuatu negara yang sedang membangun, sungguhpun kebebasan asasi individu adalah diiktiraf, pada masa yang sama, sekatan tertentu perlu dikenakan pada kebebasan tersebut demi keselamatan dan ketenteraman awam.

Perlembagaan bolehlah dikatakan sebagai undang-undang organik tetapi bukan statik di dalam sesuatu masyarakat yang berkembang. Ia mengandungi nilai-nilai unggul seperti kebebasan, keadilan yang sama rata yang tidak boleh ditafsir secara statik kerana apa yang betul pada hari ini mungkin tidak betul pada keesokan hari. Konsep hak dan kebebasan adalah berkait rapat dengan keadaan sosial masyarakat pada sesuatu masa dan tempat. Sekatan tertentu dan yang munasabah bolehlah dikenakan oleh undang-undang di atas kebebasan asasi seseorang individu. Adakah ini bermakna bahawa konsep kebebasan mutlak sebenarnya tidak wujud? Bagi diri saya anggapan sedemikian adalah berasas. Walaupun Perlembagaan menjamin hak rakyat, tetapi ia juga mempunyai kekecualian yang tidak terkandung dalam Perlembagaan, tetapi terkandung dalam undang-undang biasa. Oleh yang demikian, sungguhpun Perlembagaan memberi jaminan tentang kebebasan, keadilan yang sama rata, tetapi ia juga memberi kuasa kepada Parlimen untuk mengenakan sekatan dan batasan sebagaimana yang difikirkan perlu demi untuk menjaga keselamatan dan ketenteraman awam. Di sini saya ingin menekankan bahawa perlulah diadakan keseimbangan di antara kepentingan sosial dalam pencapaian kebebasan, keadilan yang sama rata dan kepentingan perlindungan kepada mereka yang akan terancam sekiranya ketiga-tiga sifat unggul tadi dibenarkan tanpa sekatan.

Kebebasan adalah suatu istilah yang komprehensif dan ia tidak terhad kepada kebebasan bergerak tanpa sekatan. Ia meliputi maksud kebebasan bergerak tanpa sekatan. Ia meliputi maksud yang luas sebagaimana yang diperuntukkan oleh undang-undang. Perlembagaan Malaysia telah menggunakan ungkapan "kecuali menurut undang-undang" di dalam peruntukannya untuk memberi maksud lain iaitu "kecuali mengikut prosedur yang ditetapkan oleh undang-undang". Dalam kes *Ong Chuan* lwn. *PP* [1981] 1 MLJ 64, Majlis Privy memutuskan bahawa "undang-undang" yang terdapat dalam rangkaikata "kecuali menurut undang-undang" mengandungi kaedah keadilan asasi iaitu hak untuk didengar. Dengan peruntukan ini, Parlimen telah diberi kuasa untuk membuat peruntukan mengenai undang-undang prosedur substantif sebelum kebebasan diri seseorang boleh dilucutkan. Ini disebabkan dalam mengekalkan demokrasi, suatu imbangan adalah perlu di antara kebebasan individu dan kepentingan masyarakat pada umumnya.

Berkaitan kebebasan berakhbar, ianya tidak diperuntukkan dengan nyata dalam Perlembagaan kita. Kebebasan akhbar adalah diiktiraf dengan meluasnya di negara-negara yang mengamalkan sistem demokrasi. Malangnya, kebebasan akhbar yang diberi itu sering disalahgunakan oleh pihak-pihak yang tertentu untuk kepentingan peribadi mereka. Sebagaimana yang kita maklum, melalui akhbar kita mengetahui apa yang berlaku di sekeliling, misalnya apakah undang-undang yang dibahaskan di Parlimen dan pelaksanaan sesuatu undang-undang itu apabila ia telah diluluskan. Melalui akhbar juga kita mengetahui keputusan sesuatu kes di Mahkamah.

Sungguhpun kita sedar akan pentingnya peranan yang dimainkan oleh akhbar khususnya dalam penyebaran maklumat kepada orang ramai, kebebasan akhbar tidaklah boleh diberi secara mutlak. Dalam negara yang sedang membangun, sekatan perlu dikenakan terhadap kebebasan akhbar demi untuk menjaga kepentingan sebahagian yang lain. Misalnya berkenaan dengan keselamatan negara, ianya perlu dikawal supaya tidak mendatangkan perasaan takut atau kebimbangan rakyat. Selain daripada itu, sebagai negara yang berbilang kaum, keharmonian hidup adalah perlu dikekalkan tanpa akhbar menimbulkan berita atau laporan yang boleh mewujudkan huru-hara dan ketegangan kaum. Oleh itu, demi keselamatan dan keharmonian negara, kawalan patut dikenakan ke atas kebebasan akhbar tetapi biarlah ianya munasabah. Tanpa sekatan, ia mungkin mendatangkan keburukan kepada negara kerana disalahgunakan oleh pihak tertentu. Walaupun kita mempunyai undang-undang khas untuk fitnah, slander dan hasutan bagi mengawal sebarang laporan yang tidak berasas, perlu ditekankan bahawa adalah wajar kebebasan akhbar digunakan dengan penuh tanggungjawab bagi pengeluaran laporan yang benar dan seimbang.

Bagi memelihara keseimbangan di antara kebebasan akhbar dan kawalannya, apa yang perlu diawasi adalah pemeliharaan hak-hak rakyat mengikut undang-undang. Rakyat perlu diberitahu maklumat mengenai negara, tetapi maklumat yang diberi itu biarlah munasabah bagi membolehkan rakyat turut serta memainkan peranan penting dalam pembangunan masyarakat.

Sekarang saya ingin menarik perhatian tuan-tuan dan puan-puan kepada soal Bahasa Melayu atau Bahasa Kebangsaan atau yang lebih dikenali kini sebagai Bahasa Malaysia dengan Bahasa Undang-Undang. Kita seharusnya tidak mempunyai sikap yang negatif terhadapnya. Maksud saya ialah kita tidak seharusnya lebih memikirkan tentang ketidakupayaan Bahasa Malaysia untuk menggantikan Bahasa Inggeris sebagai Bahasa Undang-Undang dan Bahasa Mahkamah. Sebaliknya, kita hendaklah memikirkan tentang kemajuan yang telah dicapai oleh Bahasa Malaysia sendiri dalam semua bidang. Bahasa Melayu telahpun menjadi Bahasa Pentadbiran, bahasa ilmu, tetapi perkembangan Bahasa Melayu di bidang undang-undang khususnya penggunaannya di mahkamah tidak terlaksana dengan pesatnya.

Keupayaan sesuatu bahasa itu untuk menjadi bahasa ilmu atau apa bahasa sekali pun bergantung kepada beberapa faktor. Yang terpenting ialah faktor sikap. Bagaimana sempurnanya sesuatu bahasa itu tidak akan bermakna jika sikap tidak mempercayai keupayaan bahasa itu sendiri masih bersemadi di lubuk sanubari masyarakat. Sikap tidak mahu berusaha untuk melaksanakannya juga adalah merupakan halangan besar kepada perkembangan bahasa itu.

Kalau kita kaji keupayaan Bahasa Melayu sendiri dari zaman silam hingga kini, sudah tentu bukan keupayaan Bahasa Melayu yang harus dipertikaikan tetapi keupayaan sendiri hendaklah ditilek kaji. Track rekod Bahasa Melayu adalah ternyata antaranya ialah Bahasa Melayu telah menjadi bahasa perantaraan antarabangsa di zaman Kesultanan Melayu Melaka dan juga Bahasa Undang-Undang seperti termaktub dalam Hukum Kanun Melaka dan Undang-Undang Laut. Kini Bahasa Malaysia ialah bahasa perantaraan kaum di Malaysia. Pusat pengajian tinggi telah membuktikan keupayaan Bahasa Melayu sebagai bahasa ilmu yang menerangkan hal-hal yang abstrak dan kompleks.

Bahasa Malaysia mempunyai khazanah perkataan yang luas dan mempunyai tidak kurang dari 30,000 perkataan. Bahasa hanya merupakan alat perantaraan dan tidak ada alasan mengapa Bahasa Malaysia tidak dapat digunakan di mahkamah.

Mutu undang-undang bukan bergantung kepada bahasa tetapi bergantung kepada penggunaan bahasa itu oleh golongan yang mengamal undang-undang. Oleh itu kualiti undang-undang adalah bergantung kepada kewibawaan seseorang peguam atau hakim dan kepada kefasihan mereka dalam bahasa itu. Kefasihan tidak mungkin datang menggolek, ia haruslah diusahakan. Buat permulaan sikap negatif pada diri sendiri haruslah dikikis.

Dalam pelaksanaan penggunaan Bahasa Malaysia di mahkamah tentu sekali soalan seperti ini melayang di fikiran segolongan besar pengamal undang-undang. Adakah penggunaan Bahasa Malaysia itu nanti akan menjejaskan mutu undang-undang? Pada hemat saya, soalan begini boleh dijawab oleh mereka sendiri jika sikap positif terhadap Bahasa Malaysia wujud. Saya berpendapat dan saya harap tuan-tuan dan puan-puan bersetuju dengan pandangan saya bahawa mutu sesuatu undang-undang itu bukan bergantung kepada bahasa tetapi ia bergantung kepada mereka yang berkecimpung dalam arena perundangan tidak kira para hakim, peguam atau para akademik. Pengalaman dan pengetahuan merekalah yang memainkan peranan penting dalam menilai mutu undang-undang. Lagipun fakta dalam undang-undang itu adalah dalam bahasa biasa yang dipertuturkan seharian oleh masyarakat.

Adalah tidak wajar bagi seseorang membuat perbandingan antara Bahasa Inggeris dan Bahasa Malaysia. Perkembangan Bahasa Inggeris tidak mempunyai rintangan tetapi sebaliknya Bahasa Malaysia telah menjadi mangsa penjajahan sehingga hampir hilang nilai ekonominya. Hanya selepas merdeka sahaja Bahasa Melayu dipupuk kembali sehingga didaulatkan di semua bidang melainkan di bidang perundangan dan kehakiman. Insya Allah suatu hari nanti Bahasa Melayu akan setanding dengan Bahasa Inggeris atau bahasa lain dalam semua bidang. Dalam peringkat peralihan ini usaha-usaha gigih telah dilakukan oleh semua pencinta bahasa. Baru-baru ini sebagai langkah awal untuk membuktikan bahawa Bahasa Malaysia mampu dan patut digunakan dalam bidang undang-undang, Kanun Jurnal Undang-Undang dalam Bahasa Malaysia telah diterbitkan bagi menampung kekosongan di dalam bidang ini. Ia merangkumi laporan kes dan glosari istilah yang diharapkan dapat memberi manfaat kepada pengamal undang-undang khususnya dan masyarakat am.

Akhir sekali saya harap dalam seminar ini, tuan-tuan dan puan-puan akan dapat mengenal pasti masalah-masalah di bidang perundangan dan kehakiman serta mencari jalan penyelesaian untuk membantu masyarakat memahami undang-undang supaya tidak lagi timbul salah tafsiran dan salah anggapan terhadap sesuatu undang-undang.

Dengan ucapan Bismillahirrahman nirrahim saya dengan sukacitanya merasmikan Seminar Undang-Undang dan Masyarakat Ke-3 ini dan berdoa agar diberkati Allah.

ETIKA DAN TINGKAH-LAKU PEGUAM*

Bersyukur saya ke hadrat Allah Subhanahu Wata'ala kerana dengan izinNya dapat saya hadir di majlis makan malam ini. Saya juga mengucapkan terima kasih kepada Persatuan Mahasiswa Fakulti Undang-Undang Universiti Kebangsaan Malaysia kerana sudi menjemput saya.

Saya difahamkan bahawa majlis ini diadakan untuk meraikan para graduan sulung dari fakulti Undang-Undang U.K.M. yang akan keluar meninggalkan Universiti tidak berapa lama lagi dengan ijazah undang-undang, Insya Allah.

Bilangan yang terlibat buat kali pertama ini ialah seramai 35 orang. Walaupun bilangan ini adalah kecil, ingin saya mengingatkan saudara-saudari yang berkenaan bahawa tanggungjawab yang dipikul oleh saudara-saudari adalah sangat berat. Saya katakan demikian kerana sebagai graduan-graduan sulung dari Fakulti Undang-Undang Universiti Kebangsaan Malaysia, saudara-saudari menjadi tumpuan perhatian semua pihak. Kemampuan saudara-saudari sebagai peguam akan diteliti dan mungkin mencorakkan pandangan masyarakat keseluruhannya terhadap lulusan undang-undang dari U.K.M.

Saya percaya Fakulti Undang-Undang U.K.M. sudah menjalankan tugas dengan bersungguh-sungguh untuk menentukan kejayaan. Kejayaan yang diperolehi bukan sahaja akan menentukan masa depan saudara-saudari dalam arena undang-undang negara, tetapi juga dalam menentukan kewibawaan Fakulti Undang-Undang U.K.M.

Saya difahamkan pendekatan pelajaran ilmu undang-undang khasnya di U.K.M., selain daripada yang diajar di pusat-pusat pengajian yang lain. Fakulti Undang-Undang U.K.M. selain daripada menyebar pengajian Undang-Undang Sivil yang biasa diajar di Fakulti Undang-Undang lain, juga menitikberatkan Pengajian Syariah, dan ini adalah satu kelebihan yang patut disedari oleh saudara-saudari sekalian semasa berkhidmat dengan masyarakat nanti. Dengan pengetahuan ini, saudara-saudari akan dapat membantu negara dalam usaha mempertingkatkan taraf perundangan syariah di seluruh negara.

Saya percaya saudara-saudari sudah membaca di akhbar-akhbar tentang usaha kerajaan mempertingkatkan taraf Mahkamah Syariah di negara ini.

**Di Majlis Jamuan Tahunan Ke-2 Fakulti Undang-Undang, Pada 13hb Januari, 1990, Di Hotel Holiday Inn (On The Park).*

Mereka yang terlibat dalam mahkamah ini telah diberi latihan dan saya percaya latihan itu akan diteruskan di masa-masa akan datang agar kemampuan pegawai undang-undang syariah ditingkatkan ke tahap yang lebih baik sejajar dengan undang-undang sivil yang sedia ada. Berhubungan ini, jelaslah behawa saudara-saudari dilatih di dalam kedua-dua bentuk perundangan yang mempunyai keistimewaan yang sewajarnya digunakan untuk kebaikan agama, bangsa dan negara.

Dalam mempelajari ilmu undang-undang, latihan akademik sahaja adalah tidak memadai. Saya berasa sukacita mendengar pihak Fakulti Undang-Undang U.K.M. telah memberi saudara-saudari latihan praktik yang luas untuk menentukan saudara-saudari akan dapat menyumbang dengan sebaik mungkin kepada dunia perundangan negara.

Saya percaya ada di antara saudara-saudari yang hadir pada malam ini yang akan menjadi pengamal undang-undang. Saya mengambil kesempatan ini untuk mengingatkan mereka yang benar-benar berminat dalam bidang undang-undang tentang beberapa perkara asas yang mesti mereka hayati. Pertama, memahami fakta-fakta kes berkenaan, iaitu dengan mengkaji fakta-fakta kes itu dengan teliti dalam semua aspek dan dari segala sudut. Kuasai dan serapkan setiap unsur bernas yang dapat diperolehi daripada pengkajian itu. Jika fakta-fakta kes difahami dan dinilai sepenuhnya, maka undang-undang yang terpakai bagi kes itu akan menjadi bertambah jelas.

Apabila saudara-saudari menyebut atau menulis mengenai sesuatu kes, pastikan bahawa isu tersebut tidak diselubungi dengan sesuatu yang separuh benar, palsu atau spekulasi, andaian atau syak wasangka untuk memberi gambaran bahawa anak guam tuan-tuan adalah tidak bersalah tetapi merupakan mangsa keadilan yang tidak berasas. Untuk menerima pendekatan seumpama ini samalah seperti menutup pintu-pintu kebebasan.

Sebagai peguam, tentu saudara-saudari bersetuju bahawa ada kalanya mereka boleh berubah pendirian di mana jika mereka menang dalam sesuatu kes, Hakim berkenaan dipuji tetapi jika berdasarkan kepada keterangan mereka kalah dalam kes itu, keadaan sebaliknya berlaku sedangkan keputusan itu mestilah diterima dengan tenang. Jika seseorang peguam kurang berpuas hati dengan keputusan yang diberi, maka beliau boleh beralih kepada remedi rayuan. Oleh itu, adalah wajar bagi seseorang peguam itu menahan diri daripada membuat tuduhan-tuduhan berat sebelah atau prasangka. Kedua, jika dipandang bidang kepeguaman dari aspek lain, apa yang perlu diingat oleh seseorang pengamal undang-undang itu ialah beliau mestilah berfikiran bijak, tajam dan pantas. Sekiranya beliau gagal hadir ke mahkamah atau gagal menimbulkan isu tertentu, beliau tidak sepatutnya kemudian melancarkan tindakan untuk mempengaruhi fikiran umum bagi menimbulkan keraguan terhadap seseorang hakim kerana telah tidak mempertimbangkan isu yang difikirkannya kini patut diberi pertimbangan. Apatah lagi seseorang hakim hanya dikehendaki memberi perintah mengenai perkara-perkara yang ditimbulkan di hadapannya sahaja.

Dalam mengemukakan hujah bagi menyokong sesuatu isu, peguam hendaklah menahan diri daripada memperbesar-besarkan perkara yang kecil. Beliau harus berhati-hati supaya hujahnya tidak lari daripada isu sebenar dan jangan sekali-kali menyuarakan isu-isu yang remeh-temeh atau yang tidak relevan dengan keputusan. Ketiga, saya patut tegaskan di sini bahawa kewajipan peguam ialah untuk mempertahankan imej dan kemuliaan badan Kehakiman. Jika para peguam tidak menghormati dan menerima keputusan mahkamah, apa lagi orang ramai. Haruslah diingati bahawa apabila para hakim mambuat keputusan, keputusan itu adalah dibatasi dan dikawal oleh undang-undang. Hakim-hakim yang tidak patuh pada undang-undang akan mengakibatkan gangguan pada sistem perundangan kita. Melainkan jika Parlimen meminda undang-undang berkenaan, hakim wajib memakainya walaupun litigan tidak dapat menerimanya. Sekiranya kritikan mengenai penghakiman tuan-tuan boleh diterima, penghakiman berkenaan hendaklah tetap dihormati supaya kedaulatan undang-undang dapat dipertahankan. Apa-apa kritikan yang melampaui batas kesopanan adalah suatu penghinaan khususnya kepada pihak berkuasa dan akan menyebabkan lemahnya kuasa Kehakiman.

Seterusnya, saya ingin mengambil kesempatan ini untuk menarik perhatian saudara-saudari kepada beberapa kejadian yang kurang menyenangkan. Saya fikir saudara-saudari tentulah dapat meneka apa saja yang saya maksudkan. Mereka yang memilih profesion di bidang undang-undang hendaklah bertindak sebagai peguam-peguam yang bertanggungjawab ke atas klien-klien mereka.

Akhbar-akhbar tempatan kebelakangan ini telah memaparkan beberapa peristiwa yang menunjukkan ada di antara peguam-peguam yang telah melanggar tatasusila sebagai peguam. Saya berharap saudara-saudari apabila diiktiraf menjadi peguam nanti, tidak akan terjerumus dalam kancah tamak haloba yang boleh menyeret saudara-saudari ke arah penyalahgunaan kuasa atau memperdayakan klien-klien saudara-saudari.

Saya percaya bimbingan yang diberi oleh mahaguru-mahaguru di Fakulti undang-undang U.K.M. telah menekankan betapa pentingnya sumpah profesion guaman itu dipegang dengan sekukuh-kukuhnya. Janganlah saudara-saudari sekalian mencemari nama baik profesion undang-undang sebagaimana yang telah dilakukan oleh segelintir mereka yang tidak bertanggungjawab dan tidak berperikemanusiaan.

Akhir kata, saya ingin mengucapkan tahniah kepada mereka yang akan keluar dengan kelulusan yang baik, sungguhpun saya tahu keputusan muktamad akan hanya menjadi kenyataan semasa akhir semester kedua ini. Tetapi oleh kerana tidak mungkin saya berpeluang bertemu saudara-saudari dalam keadaan seperti ini, saya ucapkan tahniah terlebih dahulu. Saya sangat berharap keseluruhan 35 orang yang dijadualkan lulus akan lulus dengan cemerlang.

Saya juga sekali lagi mengucapkan berbanyak terima kasih kepada pihak penganjur jamuan tahunan Fakulti Undang-Undang ini kerana sudi menjemput saya.

COMMON LAW: A MYTH OR REALITY*

I deem it a great honour, pleasure and privilege to be invited to address you at the opening session of this seminar. It gives me great satisfaction to see so many young, promising and welcoming faces at this function. At my time, some decades ago, I had to go to England to study law and today you are fortunate to have such education facilities at your doorstep. You would have realised that the university is the summit of our educational system. Be that as it may, university education is not the end of education itself. Philosophically speaking life is a continuous process of learning from others until we die. Malaysia is a country where youth predominates and therefore education plays a vital role in the future of our nation. As we are living in a crucial age, where the formation of a unique Malaysian culture and homogeneous spirit is being developed, the education imparted to the young at this point of our history may determine the future of the nation itself. It is thus important to remember that although the primary aim of education is to obtain knowledge, the greater underlying objective is to train you to develop a sense of balance. Conceivably only education can transform ordinary human beings into dedicated individuals capable of lifting themselves and their fellow beings to a sublime level of existence. It is in the nature of things that you, the young people, must one day take over from those who are now in positions of responsibility, authority and power. If, therefore, the youth are properly educated with good values and morals, the future of Malaysia would be even brighter, justifying a position of eminence amidst democracies of world countries.

Now, before I proceed any further, I must add a word of caution. Although I am before you today as Lord President and head of the judiciary, nothing that I say is to be interpreted as *ratio decidendi* (to use the lawyers' language) but only as *obiter dictum*. The views expressed are personal to me and are only meant for this occasion to inspire you to learn, research, achieve and serve. It must not be taken that I am laying down legal dogmas or undisputed truths which will be binding at any future occasion.

**At The Opening Of The Seminar On The Legal Profession On 24th February, 1990 At The International Islamic University, Jalan Universiti, Petaling Jaya, Selangor.*

The topic chosen by you for discussion, to put it very mildly, is very thought provoking and wide. Undoubtedly we can go on talking on the subject until the cows come home but on my part I only intend to make a small contribution to stimulate further thinking and discussion with the assistance of your distinguished academic staff. In my brief discussion I shall not bore you much with authorities we very often cite and rely upon but will leave it to you to develop whatever skeleton I place before you.

Now, let us turn our attention to the topic for today's discussion. As you all know section 3 of the Civil Law Act 1956 which has placed the reception of English Common Law on a statutory basis provides as follow:

> "(1) Save so far as other provision has been made or may hereafter be made by any written law in force in Malaysia, the Court shall —
>
> (a) in West Malaysia or any part thereof, apply the common law in England and the rules of equity as administered in England on the 7th day of April, 1956;
>
> (b) in Sabah, apply the common law of England and the rules of equity, together with statutes of general application, as administered or in force in England on the 1st day of December, 1951;
>
> (c) in Sarawak, apply the common law of England and the rules of equity, together with statutes of general application, as administered or in force in England on the 12th day of December, 1949, subject however to subsection (3)(iii):
>
> Provided always that the said common law, rules of equity and statutes of general application shall be applied so far only as the circumstances of the States of Malaysia and their respective inhabitants permit and subject to such qualifications as local circumstances render necessary."

Historically, the predecessor of section 3 can be traced back to 1878, when the Civil Law Ordinance of Penang, Malacca and Singapore formally incorporated, by reference, various portions of the English Supreme Court of Judicature Act, 1873, as well as the entire *corpus* of English commercial law.

In 1937, by the Civil Law Enactment No.3 of 1937, the Federated Malay States incorporated by reference, and in general terms "the Common Law of England, and the rules of equity..."

In 1951, the Civil Law Enactment of 1937 was extended and made applicable to the Unfederated Malay States.

In 1956, the Civil Law Act, 1956, restated the application of the English Common Law and rules of equity and, in addition, so far as East Malaysia was concerned certain "statutes of general application" were made applicable.

Given this legislative history, English Common Law has become so entrenched in our system of jurisprudence that in *Che Ani bin Hitam* v *P.P.* (1984) 1 CLJ 72, Raja Azlan Shah, LP (as he then was) when considering Articles 5, 8 and 13 of the Federal Constitution said that "it is firmly established that the word 'law' refers to a system of law which incorporates those fundamental rules of natural justice that had formed part and parcel of the Common Law of England that was in operation at the commencement of the Constitution".

In a recent speech delivered at a public lecture, Sultan Azlan Shah, (now the Yang di-Pertuan Agong) speaking about the legal effect of section 3 of the Civil Law Act said that:

> "English law was relevant only to the extent that it was made subject to modifications to suit local conditions."

His Royal Highness then added — and I respectfully agree with him — that:

> "Once a particular aspect of the law has been applied in Malaysia it becomes Malaysian law. And the Malaysian Courts when called upon to decide new issues relating to this aspect of the law, merely apply and develop the already existing laws of Malaysia."

Thus the Common Law has been, like the works of William Shakespeare, one of England's most successful exports.

It has, despite the disappearance of the English Empire, continued to dominate legal thinking not only in Caucasian countries like North America (except Louisiana), Canada (except Quebec), Australia, New Zealand, but also in Asian countries like India, Pakistan, Bangladesh, Brunei, Singapore and, of course, Malaysia.

Indeed, even decisions in Common Law countries like Australia, New Zealand and America have been cited with approval in our Courts. (See for example, *Murugesu* v *Michael Chong* (1978) 1 MLJ 23 and *B.A. Rao & Ors.* v *Sapuran Kaur & Anor* (1978) 2 MLJ 149.)

It has been said that the success of the Common Law overseas is largely due to the fact that wherever it went it found a legal vacuum. It is the lawyers' law of universal application. The Common Law has, in theory, no gaps or omissions, only a few silences which at any time, upon the suit of a litigant, the voice of the judge can break; an example is the evolvement of the common law duty of care and the tort of negligence which provided a legal right to compensation for personal injuries based on the concept of fault without the intervention of Parliament. Similarly, an earlier illustration of the same process is the history of equity developed by the judges as a gloss or graft upon the property law, thus adapting the law to serve the needs of society of the time without the necessity of destroying it.

But having said that, I must now address the question posed in the title to this discussion.

It appears to me that ours being an independent sovereign country, section 3 with its reference to "the Common Law of England and rules of equity as administered in England on the 7th day of April, 1956" cannot be defended politically. In other words, I advocate an assertion of Malaysian judicial independence and an important step towards establishing a sense of national identity is a repeal or an amendment of section 3.

In 1963, there was an article, *Filling lacunae in the Law* by L.C. Green where he said, "In view of the increased political stature of the two territories (i.e. Singapore and the Federation), and in anticipation of further changes likely to be effected with the establishment of Malaysia, it is now perhaps evidence of an out of date attitude as well as contrary to national prestige to make provisions for the supplementation of the local laws in the event of *lacunae* by means of reference to any 'alien' system, whether it be that of the former imperial power or not" (see (1963) MLJ xxviii). From various cases decided in Malaysia, we can see that the Civil Law Enactment did not help much to fill the l*acunae* in our laws.

In a thought provoking and erudite article entitled *The Civil Law Ordinance in Malaysia* Professor Ahmad Ibrahim said: "The lack of a civil law enactment did not prevent the filling in of *lacunae* in the law before 1937 and there is no reason why the *lacunae* cannot be filled even if the provisions of the Civil Law Ordinance were repealed. We then appealed to Malaysian judges to take into account the provisions of systems of law other than the common law and, in particular, the position of Muslim law of the land can be re-emphasised and adequately recognised." With respect, although Article 3 of the Federal Constitution provides explicitly that Islam is the religion of the Federation, ours is a secular state. Besides, the composition of the population in this country with its various ethnic groups who have acquired considerable political power and each with its customs and traditions dictates that it would be best to keep religion separate from the law.

But is a repeal of section 3 feasible? For more than one hundred years, through the judicial process, the Common Law has been applied by our Courts extensively so as to provide the foundation upon which our legal system has developed. It is a trite observation that if Malaysia is to continue its role as a viable member of the international community, its laws must also be internationally acceptable and this is especially so in the context of Commercial Law. Besides, the question that arises is whether a repeal of section 3 may place formidable difficulties in the way of lawyers when advising clients as to their rights and obligations and whether the law would generally become less certain and unpredictable with consequent difficulties for the Bench when faced with the task of declaring the law.

The further question that arises is whether it would be more feasible to amend section 3. Accordingly, the next question is this: what form should that amendment take bearing in mind the fact that the whole purpose and object of the Common Law is to do justice and its principles are of universal application?

In my opinion, apart from the considerations I have mentioned, section 3 in the form it now takes, with its reference to "of England" and "as administered in England on 7th April, 1956" (with its corresponding variations so far as it applies to Sabah and Sarawak) is unduly restrictive. These quoted words should therefore be deleted and the effect of this would be to further broaden the base of Malaysian Law thus encouraging the development of our common law; its particular application to be worked out as the occasion arises. In other words, if this approach is adopted no great harm will be done since our judges, whose task it is to apply the received law to local circumstances, would regard themselves as free to mould it to those circumstances just as much as Parliament would be free to modify existing laws to suit the changing needs of our Society.

It is appropriate for me at this point to urge you to note that there is a distinction that may be drawn between the "law in action" and the "law in books". The law in books sometimes does not bear much resemblance to reality. And further discussion of the topic you have chosen for today will, I believe, show the path for reform of the law. In the first place, you must not think of law in a narrow sense as something clearly defined and stated in print. It has been said in a broad sense that positive law lives in the common consciousness of people and that law is the reflection of the spirit of the people. You may wish to reflect whether they are fit and appropriate definitions of law. Whatever be the definition, the centre of gravity of legal development lies not in legislation, nor in juristic science, nor in judicial decision but in society itself. Irrespective of the truth of such wide thought provoking ideas, Common Law can be defined for the students' purpose, as that part of the legal system embodying judicial decisions of English judges from time to time based on precedents as distinguished from statutory law and law of equity. Then the controversy starts. Firstly, the term Common Law is very vague. Secondly, the expression Common Law can be used in a bewildering variety of senses. Thirdly, the so called Common Law of one nation which was or still is a British dominated territory will swerve from that of another and from that of England. Clearly, therefore, it can mean one thing to an Englishman, another to an Australian, American or Malaysian. Fourthly, the term can also be said to mean all those fundamental principles of English Law which were introduced into Singapore by the Second Charter of Justice of 1826 and into Malaysia more or less at the same time and ratified by the Civil Law Ordinance. Fifthly, the other factor that influences the choice of foreign law to be adopted and which is independent of the quality of law is language and accessibility of the law. There are other factors such as past history to be considered. In a book entitled *The Common Law in Singapore and Malaysia* (Edited by A.J. Harding) the author said in the opening paragraph as follows:-

> "One of the consequences of the establishment of the British maritime empire was the spread of English law into all those areas.... the legacy of English law which it left behind has in most cases not been rejected as some sort of *hereditas damarse*, but has been with varying degrees of enthusiasm accepted as providing the foundation upon which legal systems can be developed."

Perhaps it is safe to view the concept of Common Law as residing in the mental attitudes and habits of legal thought that historically developed in England and which are still refined by the admirers and followers of the Common Law Systems. Such attitudes are variable and imponderable and it is well nigh impossible to define common law with mathematical accuracy. Whatever be its definition, Common Law is something which has been borrowed unless we redefine the term as Malaysian Common Law incorporating all changes which we have adopted, followed, applied, interpreted, redefined, altered and tolerated and perhaps distorted for our purposes for which it was never originally intended. In this respect it is generally accepted in most places, that borrowing from a different jurisdiction has been the principal way in which law has developed.

Speaking on development of the Common Law, the Chief Justice of Malaya, Y.A.A. Tan Sri Datuk Hashim Yeop Sani at the opening of your Law Week on February 10, 1989 while touching on proviso (2) of section 3(1) of the Act had this to say:

> "It seems to me quite clear that the British drafters of the original Civil Law Act, 1956 anticipated the development of our own common law. The proviso to section 3(1) of the Act clearly enables our courts from the dates specified in that section to modify and develop the English common law as our own law. To my mind it was intended to encourage the development of our common law grounded on local values and not on British values. In such modification and development the courts may instill local values including Islamic values and the values of the various ethnic and religious communities in this country and the universal principles of justice and good conscience."

He referred to *Government of Malaysia* v *Lim Kit Siang* (1988) 2 MLJ 41 where he drew our attention to the role of our courts when applying the law of

England in that we should not apply the law of England blindly without comparing the basis of our own jurisdiction. He also pointed out that in his written judgment in that appeal he relied on section 3 of the Civil Law Act, 1956 to apply the common law principle in *Boyce* v *Paddington Boroughs Council* (1903) 1 Ch 119 on the *locus standi* of the respondent and had declined to follow the so called liberalised post-1978 doctrine of *locus standi* in English law until our law itself is amended.

The process of assimilation of English Law was accomplished by the Common Law concept of "reception". To cover this process, academics may use other expressions such as imposition, transplantation, infiltration and inoculation, etc. What we should concern ourselves with are the reasons for such reception. It may well be that the foreign law was chosen because of the general respect in which it is held. Could it also be said that underlying the question of receptability of a foreign legal system is a question of power, at the very least a spiritual and cultural power? Thus the position of the English Law was a position of power; the accepted law of a strong political power. It is for you to discuss whether that power is still real or not. Is there still remaining a living memory of it and its culture? It is also for you to deliberate whether that borrowing should be made or should be restricted.

Reverting to the topic of our discussion, I personally feel that the existence of the Common Law or Malaysian Common Law with all its adaptions cannot just be described as a fancy or myth and be summarily dismissed. It is a reality for the purpose of our discussion. Yet it does not mean that we, now being an independent nation, should be perpetually enchained to English Common Law doctrines. Beyond this, I cannot pretend to find any startling conclusion or decisive answer. The question we should apply our mind to is how English Common Law, the product of an alien culture and history, imposed or necessitated by the agency of imperial British rule can be improved to suit conditions vastly different from those in which it was created so as to assist in the overall development of our law. It is a question for consideration whether legislation by foreigners under the trialdom of precedents and analogies belonging to a foreign law, developed many thousand miles away under a different climate catering for a different civilisation is suitable under local circumstances, present and future. However, after several decades of increased consciousness in legal thinking of the distinctive character of the English Common Law and of the importance of maintaining its integrity, I subscribe to the view that a modification thereto cannot be done overnight in a piecemeal haphazard manner. We must also be conscious of the fact that changes should not be made purely to please a group or any vested interest. Permit me to say at this point that one underlying point to bear in mind is that the Common Law system in its development should instill more local values. Although our state religion is Islam, we follow a secular system of law except in the case of personal laws of Muslims where Islamic law and Adat are followed. The secular law is based on trial and error process and there are conflicts in certain areas between the Islamic and Secular System. While I personally cannot foresee any integration of the two systems, students should be aware of the situation to appreciate underlying factors behind such conflicts and to find ways to promote the co-existence of both the systems side by side. It is very important. I will quote a case of which I am sure many of you are aware. Islamic Law defines capacity to marry on the basis of adherence to the religion of Islam. English Law, on the other hand, proposes that the concept of domicile will fix or establish an individual as the subject of a particular legal system. An outstanding example is the famous *Nadra* case — Singapore Court of Appeal decision in 1951 in *Re Maria Huberdina Hertogh: Inche Mansor Adabi* v *A.P. Hertogh & Anor* (1951) MLJ 12; 164 CA. Maria had been left in Indonesia by her Dutch parents as a child during the Japanese Occupation in 1941. She was cared for and brought up as a Muslim girl by a servant of A.P. Hertogh the respondent. The respondent who lost contact with the child and her custodian guardian finally traced their whereabouts after the War and attempted to regain her custody which attempt was resisted by the girl's foster parents. At the time of the Court action the girl entered into a contract of marriage with the appellant in the present case. Her age at the time of marriage was 15 years. The Court was asked to decide on the validity of the marriage (which was valid under Muslim law). The Court found as a fact that the girl was an adherent of the Muslim religion. According to Dutch Law, the law of her father's domicile, she had no capacity to contract a valid marriage except with certain permissions which had not been obtained. The Court held that as the girl was a minor she had a domicile in Holland and the marriage was therefore declared a nullity. This was held to be so notwithstanding the fact that as far as Islamic Law was concerned the marriage was valid, under which system the consideration of domicile was irrelevant. Such conflicts are inevitable as neither system of law possesses any criteria for deciding which of the two definitions of personal capacity is to apply. The Court apparently gave the reason for its decision as being in the child's purported best interests. However, what such interests were do not appear from the face of the records.

Another factor we should bear in mind, when considering changes in the Common Law is the essential recognition that law and legal arrangements exist for the benefit of the community and not vice versa. Law is for the people. The people comprise, *inter alia*, of the business community who play a vital part in the national economic development. The Common Law System has already been integrated with the main spheres of commercial and fiscal laws. In this regard it seems intolerable that there should be any radical difference in the law of commerce and international trade on the two sides of the borders of Singapore and Malaysia or with any other commercial allies.

By so saying, I hasten to add that I am not unmindful of the need for changes. Even in England, the Common Law doctrines have been substantially changed, especially after that country joined the European Countries under the European Community Act 1972.

Let us bear in mind that Law is an institution of its society. It exists and is part of society. Hence it cannot be allowed to fall out of step with the needs or demands of societies. In fact the laws of each nation must be so particular to the people for whom they are made. Another point to bear in mind is the technology and use of the language. The continued use of English for legal purposes will only alienate people from the law and lawyers. As Lord President I have taken steps to implement the National Language in the Courts as fast as practicable although the response has not been as wholehearted as I desired. After independence, our legislature, Courts and the Attorney-General's Chambers have not been idle to tackle the problem of modifying English Law to suit the local needs.

You will observe that sections 3 and 5 of the Civil Law Act do not help us much in achieving our national aspiration. Under section 3, different laws are applicable to West Malaysia, Sabah and Sarawak. Section 5 also has different laws applying to the Federated Malay States, Unfederated Malay States, Straits Settlements, Sabah and Sarawak. Both sections had also hindered the usage of our National Language in court. Prof R.H. Hickling in his book, *Malaysian Law* at page 35 says that "In fact the language of Malaysian Law has been English for less than a hundred years. If a Malaysian jurisprudence is to develop, then the National Language — the medium from which the nation itself draws life — must effectively be adopted". He further said that yet the obstacle of the English Common Law remains formidable as the long and ever increasing rows of English law reports confirm. While the speedy retrieval of case law is now possible with computerization and new technology, the problem for Malaysia remains and can only be resolved by a confrontation between English and Malaysian Common Law, and a change in the structure of the legal profession itself.

To illustrate, may I point out that we have codified and put on a uniform basis the previous anomalous laws relating to marriage and divorce by promulgating the Law Reform Act 1976. We have incorporated many laws for consumer protection and stabilising industrial relations. We have followed the traditional concept of *locus standi* to suit the demands of our society. In the criminal legal system, we have amended the law relating to the heinous crime of rape. We had to incorporate a new concept of sedition and devise effective laws to deal with the menacing problems of drugs, abuse of freedom, growth of violence and exploitation of ethnical, racial, religious and language issues. Yet, there is a lot more to be done. In this context, what I wish to emphasise is that there is an undoubted need for change in the legal system — not rapid but slowly with caution. It has been said that the life of law has not been logic but experience. The creation of such changes is the responsibility of the society itself through their elected representative and others like the judiciary and also law teachers who are able to see things dispassionately. All legal rules are created by a cause. The cause is very often rooted in social, economic or political factors vital to the life of the society or its leaders. The reason for the continued existence of the present laws are often due to factors which have no direct connection to the life of the society. Sometimes the rules of law are in conflict with the best interests of the ordinary citizen and the ruling elite. Legal rules, once created, usually live on. They are often remote from the experience and understanding of non-lawyers. Some believe that the lawyers own financial interest and outdated professional outlook distort the legal system from what is desirable for the rest of society.

In view of the limited time available, I can only point out certain laws purely for illustrative purposes and they are not at all exhaustive. Our Penal Code is based on the Indian Penal Code and the Law of Contract similarly follows that of India. The Indian law framers drafted such laws based on the Common Law and took into consideration the social and religious moves of 19th century India which are radically different from that existing in Malaysia today. An example is section 84 of our Penal Code relating to insanity and section 86(2) relating to intoxication. Section 84 is broadly based on the MacNaughten Rules which themselves were the result of narrow outdated psychological views. Leaving aside such laws, we have modified the concept of natural justice and judicial review. Although puritans, unaware of the social needs of our developing nation may criticise some of these measures as repugnant the fact remains that such changes have been found necessary by the legislature because of the emergence of circumstances. The critics often fail to realise that as England has no written constitution, the judges are inevitably free to decide law under the disguise of declaring and interpreting the law. Here the situation is different. We have a written constitution, and if it clearly dictates intention by legislation, there is nothing much the judges can do except to carry out the wish and direction of the legislature which is accountable to the people whether the innovative legislation is in respect of judicial review or ousting the jurisdiction of the Court in favour of the policy oriented tribunals.

To conclude may I say that I do not wish to overstay your hospitality any further. The time is up to end my talk. My only request to you is that my thoughts be not misconstrued by being quoted out of context as there is a tendency with certain groups of people to attribute sinister motives and to find fault with me on all occasions as if I am a wolf in sheep's clothes responsible for all social ills, real or imagined.

The only purpose of my speech is to inspire you to achieve the ability for creative thinking and for development as future leaders of our nation.

I wish all of you a very exciting deliberation.

INTRODUCTION TO THE MALAYSIAN JUDICIAL SYSTEM*

1. Introduction

I thank you for the opportunity given to me to address you on the topic entitled "Introduction to the Malaysian Judicial System". Within the short time available, it is only possible to touch on the basic and elementary aspects of this complex subject. Law is not a string of rules to be studied in isolation. It is for you to question and help to develop them when the time comes after you study law by posing to yourselves, as future guardians of our society, issues like, "Is a particular law appropriate?" and "What are the alternatives?" No judicial system can ever be perfect but so long as there is a conscious effort to attempt to adapt to ensure continued harmony between law and nation building, we are moving in the right direction. Our judicial system did not evolve overnight from nothing. It has developed over centuries and has been moulded by cultural and political forces. Law serves the community and is a natural consequence of living together enabling people to know what is acceptable conduct and what is not. In any community there is a collection of shared values of right and wrong. Our judicial system is more complex than the English legal system as Malaysia is a melting pot of many cultures, religions and ethnic groups. For historical reasons, much of our local legislations are based on English models. While we acknowledge the wisdom of legal values of older jurisdictions like England, Australia and India we should be aware of the fact that these values do not necessarily reflect values cherished by our plural Malaysian society.

2. Stages of development of the Malaysian Judicial System

For historical purposes, the development of the Malaysian Judicial System can be roughly divided into four distinct stages viz:

1. British Colonial Rule (Pre-war period) 1786-1941.
2. Japanese Occupation (World War II) 1942-1945.

**At The 2nd Asean Law Students Conference On 20th June, 1990 At The International Youth Centre, Cheras, Kuala Lumpur.*

3. British Colonial Rule (Post War period) 1946-1956.

4. Independence and thereafter 1957-to date.

Such classification does not mean that before 1786 there was no law and order in our country but the system has been described as "rude justice" in Sir Hugh Clifford's report. The earlier laws were based on a variety of concepts like Hukum Syariah, Adat Perpatah, Adat Temenggong and various other systems. Be that as it may, the limited time at my disposal does not permit me to delve more into the historical aspects today. To those who are interested in further research, I can only invite their attention to two articles written on the subject. One of them is an article entitled *Administration of Justice in Malaysia* in *The Denning Law Journal* published by the University of Buckingham, which I wrote, when I was Chief Justice in 1987. Many changes have occurred since then in the legal system. The other is a very interesting article entitled *The Origins of the Malaysian Bench* by renowned Professor R.H. Hickling in the *Malaya Law Review Legal Essays* published in 1975.

3. **Present Judicial System**

For today's immediate purpose, let us look at the Judicial System as it is today. At the outset, let us remember that Parliament does not enjoy legislative supremacy like Britain which has no written constitution although in that country there is a movement to introduce a Bill of Rights. In Malaysia, the constitution is supreme to the extent stated in Article 4 of the Federal Constitution.

4. **Islamic Law**

4.1 Before I begin to talk on secular law, I must mention Islamic Law. Islam is not merely a religion. It embraces the whole life, comprising a legal, social and moral order. Article 3(1) of our Constitution reads "Islam is the religion of the Federation but other religions may be practised in peace and harmony." It may not be wrong to say that Islam in the old colonial days was institutionalised and bureaucratised.

4.2 **Islam as official religion**

A question may be asked as to the legal significance of Islam being the official religion of the country. In *Che Omar Bin Che Soh* v *Public Prosecutor (1988) 2 MLJ 55*, the Supreme Court considered the meaning of "Islam" or "Islamic Religion" in Article 3 of the Federal Constitution. In a single opinion of five judges, their Lordships noted that although Islam is a complete way of life covering all fields of human activities, this is not the meaning intended in the Constitution. British rule has introduced dichotomy into the Malay States, confining Islamic Law to operate as a personal law of marriage, divorce and inheritance for Muslims and secularizing public law. In their Lordships' view, the term in Article 3 of the Constitution means only such acts as are related to rituals and ceremonies. Their Lordships further rejected the contention of counsel in that case that because Islam is the religion of the Federation, the law passed by Parliament must be imbued with Islamic and religious principles. The Islamic Law as applicable to Muslims is administered by the Syariah Court as a separate and independent system.

4.3 The Constitution (Amendment) Act, 1988

The Constitution (Amendment) Act, 1988, among others, provided a new Clause (1A) to Article 121 of the constitution which provides that the High Courts and inferior courts established by Federal Law "shall have no jurisdiction of the civil courts in respect of the matters specified in the State List as set out in paragraph 1 of List II of the Ninth Schedule of the Federal Constitution". However, it should be noted that the parties before the Syariah Courts must be Muslims. The Syariah Courts have no jurisdiction where one of the parties involved is a non-Muslim, in which case, the matter may be brought before the civil court. Further discussion of this separate topic may perhaps be appropriately held on another occasion.

4.4 Power of Parliament to amend

Although Parliament is empowered to amend the Constitution any change must be carried out in accordance with the provisions of the Constitution. The validity of any legislative act can be questioned by the Courts but the conditions in Clause (3) of Article (4) must first be observed. For such purpose leave of a Supreme Court Judge as provided by Clause (4) is required.

5. Judiciary's role in respect of a proclamation of emergency

What is the judiciary's role in respect of a proclamation of emergency? Clause (8) of Article 150 of the Constitution (Amendment) Act 1981 leaves the Court with no discretion to review the action of the Cabinet. The said clause (8) reads:

> "Notwithstanding anything in this Constitution —
>
> (a) the satisfaction of the Yang di Pertuan Agong mentioned in Clause (1) and Clause (2B) shall be final and conclusive and not be challenged or called in question in any court on any ground; and
>
> (b) no court shall have jurisdiction to entertain or determine any application, question or proceeding, in whatever form, on any ground, regarding the validity of —
>
> i) a Proclamation under Clause (1) or of a declaration made in such Proclamation to the effect stated in Clause (1);
>
> ii) the continued operation of such Proclamation;
>
> iii) any ordinance promulgated under Clause (2B); or
>
> iv) the continuation in force of any such ordinance."

6. **Present structure of courts**

6.1 What is the present structure of the courts? The Superior Courts comprise of the High Court of Malaya, the High Court of Borneo covering Sabah and Sarawak, and the Supreme Court (Mahkamah Agung). The Supreme Court established on 1 January 1985 under the Constitutional amendment to Article 121 (2) is a final Court of Appeal.

6.2 **The Supreme Court**

The Supreme Court consists of the Lord President, who is the President of the Court, the two Chief Justices of the High Court, and the current number of Supreme Court Judges is nine. When hearing cases, the Court shall consist of not less than three judges or such greater uneven number as the Lord President may decide depending upon the complexity and gravity of the subject matter to be heard. The Supreme Court has appellate, original, referral and advisory jurisdiction.

6.3 **High Courts**

Article 121(1) of the Federal Constitution establishes two High Courts of co-ordinate Jurisdiction, namely the High Court of Malaya for the States of Peninsular Malaysia with its principal registry in Kuala Lumpur and the High Court of Borneo for Sabah and Sarawak with its principal registry in the two States as determined by His Majesty. For administrative convenience the High Court of Malaya is organized into Divisions dealing with specific types of cases. The vast majority of cases are heard by a single High Court Judge. The exceptions are those of a person charged with murder who is to be tried by a judge and jury unless the case is certified a security case and a charge under section 3(3) of the Kidnapping Act 1961 which is tried by a single judge with the aid of assessors. It should be noted that in Sabah and Sarawak where the death penalty is involved, the trial is by judge and assessors except in the case of the Dangerous Drugs Act 1952 and firearm offences under the Firearms (Increased Penalties) Act 1971.

6.4 **Jurisdiction**

The jurisdiction of the High Court is original, appellate and supervisory with unlimited criminal and civil powers. It has been the practice in the past that in criminal matters no case may be brought to the High Court for trial unless the accused has been properly committed for trial after a preliminary hearing in the Magistrates' Court although under section 418A of the Criminal Procedure Code an exception can be made at the instance of the Public Prosecutor. There are also exceptions dispensing with preliminary hearings for offences under the Essential (Security Cases) Regulations 1979 and Section 41A(1) of the Dangerous Drugs Act 1952. In this connection, it should be remembered that the Attorney-General is empowered to determine the Court or the venue in which proceedings may be instituted or to which they may be transferred.

7. **Sessions Court**

7.1 A Sessions Court is under the charge of a Sessions Court Judge. It is a court of general jurisdiction with authority to try criminal and civil cases.

7.2 **Civil**

It has jurisdiction to try suits where the amount in dispute or the subject matter does not exceed RM100,000 and more, unless the parties mutually consent.

7.3 **Criminal jurisdiction**

The criminal jurisdiction of a Sessions Court extends to all offences not punishable with death and it may impose any sentence of law except death.

7.4 Supervisory role

Under section 54 of the Subordinate Courts Act 1948 the Sessions Court is also vested with limited supervisory role over the Magistrates' and Penghulus' Courts.

8. Magistrates' Courts

8.1 There are two classes of magistrates. They are the First Class and Second Class Magistrates. The Second Class Magistrate performs minor functions and may include public servants and junior court officers in administrative duties.

8.2 The First Class Magistrate

The First Class Magistrate, who is legally qualified has jurisdiction to try all offences punishable with up to ten years imprisonment or with a fine. While they may try serious offences, their power of sentencing upon a finding of guilt is limited to five years imprisonment, a fine of up to RM10,000 and whipping of up to twelve strokes.

8.3 Civil matters

In civil matters they have the jurisdiction to try all litigation where the dispute or value of the subject matter does not exceed RM25,000.

8.4 Juvenile Court

Another important court is the Juvenile Court dealing with offenders between the ages of 10 years and 18 years. This Court, sitting with two advisers preferably including a woman, can try all offences except those punishable with death. The principle followed by the court is that youngsters need care and attention and that they should be treated differently from adults and with compassion so that they are rehabilitated thus preventing their development into criminals.

9. Small Claims' Court

9.1 Another court, which has been recently introduced is the Small Claims' Court. Although its name says "small" it deals with a large number of disputes between citizens, without many legal formalities and in an inexpensive and expeditious way. Started in 1986 in Kuala Lumpur, it has proved to be a source of friendly arbitration whenever possible to the benefit of the consumer. The court is manned by non-legally qualified — but experienced in human affairs — judicial administrative officers.

10. **Penghulus' Courts**

10.1 At the lowest rung in the hierarchy of courts in West Malaysia is the Penghulus' Courts established under the Subordinate Courts Act 1948. The Penghulu, appointed by the respective rulers, can in theory try all civil cases where the subject matter does not exceed RM50.00 in value. In practice this court no longer functions.

10.2 **Criminal jurisdiction**

The criminal jurisdiction of this court is very minimal, power being limited to a fine not exceeding RM25.00. Appeals against the decision of a Penghulu may be heard by a First Class Magistrate.

There is another court, peculiar to Sabah and Sarawak in East Malaysia, called the Native Court. Although important, time forbids further discussion on this topic. Before we close this topic, we must remember that there are various other bodies which, though not necessarily termed as courts, perform judicial functions. These are the Industrial Court, the Special Commissioners for Income Tax, the Labour Court, the Court Martial and the Mining Court. Some of these bodies are very important and are intended to relieve the ordinary courts of their work and to provide an adjudicial panel with expertise in the respective fields.

11. **Industrial Court**

Industrial courts come under the portfolio of the Minister of Human Resources. The Court is not bound by technical procedural rules and the Court shall have regard to the public interest, the financial implications and the effect of the Court's award on the economy of the country and on the industry concerned and also to the probable effect in related or similar industries. The Court should act according to good conscience and substantial merits of the case. Their action can be judicially reviewed by the High Court and Supreme Court.

12. **Court Martial**

12.1 The Court Martial possess jurisdiction over persons subject to service law—the general members of the armed forces including reservists and volunteers on duty and civilians employed by or accompanying regulars on active service. The Court is composed of senior army officers guided by a legally qualified officer from the Judge Advocate General's office. The Court Martial administers service law, based on the same jurisprudential principles of evidence and fairness but adapted to deal with military offences like absence without leave, desertion, insubordination and others of a similar nature.

13. Appointment of judicial personnel

13.1 Judges

His Majesty, acting on the advice of the Prime Minister and after consulting the Conference of Rulers, appoints the Lord President and Chief Justices of Malaya and Borneo, Supreme Court Judges and High Court Judges.

13.2 Sessions Court Judges

A Sessions Court Judge is appointed by the Yang di-Pertuan Agong on the recommendation of the appropriate Chief Justice.

13.3 First Class Magistrates

First Class Magistrates except those in the Federal Territories are appointed by the appropriate Ruler or Governor (now known as Yang di-Pertua Negeri) of each State where the Magistrate will preside. Judicial personnel of the subordinate courts are drawn from the Judicial and Legal Service. Appointment is made by the Judicial and Legal Service Commission.

13.4 Judicial Independence

Judicial independence and impartiality is ensured by the following constitutional provisions: judges of the Supreme Court and High Court hold office till 65 years of age but are removable by His Majesty on the limited ground of misbehaviour, etc., and that too, strictly in accordance with an elaborate procedure set out in Article 125 (3), (4) and (5) of the Constitution, which provides for the appointment by His Majesty of a tribunal consisting of not less than five judges or ex judges. Further, judges' salaries are not subject to annual approval by Parliament as in the case of a money bill. Judges' salaries and other benefits of office including pension may not be altered to their disadvantage after appointment. The conduct of a judge may not be discussed in either House of Parliament except in the restricted manner as laid down in the Constitution. Judicial Commissioners may be appointed by the Yang di-Pertuan Agong on the advice of the Lord President. They possess the same powers of a High Court Judge. A person cannot be invited to be a judge unless he or she has been an advocate and solicitor or a member of the Judicial and Legal Service.

14. Appeal System

14.1 Appeal procedure

Any human institution is bound to make errors and generally speaking there is at least one tier of appeal to minimise such errors. Appeals on questions of fact must be distinguished from questions of law. An appellate court is not easily persuaded to interfere with a decision on a question of fact as the trial judge or magistrate has the advantage of observing witnesses. On the other hand, the appellate courts are more readily disposed to identify errors in law and rectify them. Anyone convicted of an offence may appeal against conviction on a question of law or sentence imposed. Under section 50(1) of the Courts of Judicature Act 1964, the Public Prosecutor may appeal against any decision made by the High Court in the exercise of its original criminal jurisdiction including an acquittal.

14.2 Decisions of the Magistrate

Appeals from decisions of the Magistrate in both civil and criminal matters lie to the High Court. In civil appeals the amount in dispute or the value of the subject-matter must be in excess of RM10,000 except on a question of law. The same restrictions apply to appeals from the Sessions Court to the High Court.

14.3 The Supreme Court

The Supreme Court hears both civil and criminal appeals from decisions of the High Court. By virtue of section 68 of the Courts of Judicature Act, 1964 there are restrictions including a requirement of leave of the Supreme Court or High Court when the amount or value of the subject-matter is less than RM100,000. In criminal matters, where an accused has pleaded guilty and has been convicted on the plea, there is no appeal except as to the extent or legality of the sentence. Where a question of law of public interest is involved in an appeal from the subordinate court, any dissatisfied party may apply to the Supreme Court for leave to determine each question of law of public interest which has arisen in the course of the appeal and a decision of it by the High Court has affected the appeal.

15. **Reforms**

The legal system needs constant adaptations. The situation is being carefully monitored by the Chief Justices and me. The particular areas deserving attention include unrealistic and inequitable distribution of jurisdiction, more court houses, judicial and supporting staff, implementation of the National Language and clearance of the backlog of cases. In this context, I am happy to say that the delay in disposal of cases has been decreased considerably. An appeal to a higher court need not wait for years and in fact appeals to the Supreme Court from the lower courts are now disposed of in a matter of six months.

16. **Court Language**

In most of the developing societies laws are enacted and court judgments are delivered in a language not understood by the people, creating an unfair inequality between the educated minority and the uneducated multitude. In our process of nation building and adaptation of laws to meet the changing values, needs and demands of our society, the use of a foreign language hinders original thinking at times. If justice is to be a virtue and if it is to do good to the people, it should be done in the language of the people. While there is no intention to jettison wise judicial principles, which have now become part of our heritage, we are making all attempts to gear the machinery for the use of the National Language. Sometimes, we confront radical and subtle hostility from certain interested quarters in the implementation of our plans but we will not be deterred by such unhealthy trends. Also in our movement for legal development we sometimes meet cynical critics who do not realise that judges in developing nations bear the burden of balancing "golden" ideas such as the right of self-determination, freedom of religion, right of equal opportunity on the one hand and newfangled techniques of subversion and corruption on the other hand. All these problems generate great interest and a lot of havoc. Many of the problems are to be solved politically and there is no point in blaming judges for not roaring like lions.

No amount of judicial creativeness and activism will solve political problems. The aim of the judiciary is to work within the framework of the Constitution, dispensing justice at the lowest possible court in the least possible time with no — or the least possible — strain and stress to the participants.

ROLE OF THE LEGAL AND JUDICIAL SYSTEM TOWARDS A DYNAMIC AND EFFECTIVE ADMINISTRATION*

Before I begin, allow me to make two observations:

(1) The topic is complex and within the short time available it is only possible to give a very short introduction to the subject.

(2) Anything I say may or may not be fully applicable to the adverse circumstances you may be in as public administrators. What I say is only a drop in the ocean of knowledge and understanding and is by no means exhaustive.

My aim, therefore, is only to stimulate you and provide a base in your pursuit to improve your horizon of vision. If you should learn something from what you have heard, I hope your enhanced perspective and wider outlook will be generally beneficial to our nation.

A further observation I wish to make is that whatever I say should not be construed as the view of the judiciary and the Government. As you know, any decision in a dispute that comes before the court for adjudication will be determined based on the specific facts of the particular case after listening to arguments for and against each proposition. Therefore, anything I say must not be taken to be an authoritative guide but as a guide to inspire your own doubts and creative thinking.

It has been said by Francis Bacon that "If a man will begin with certainties, he shall end in doubts, but if he will be content to begin with doubts, he shall end in certainties". Before I move to the main topic for discussion today, let me make another observation. As public administration and law is interlinked closely, it may be necessary for me to express my views on administration and the civil service, which are not really within the province of the judiciary. However, the views expressed are those that I consider necessary to be introduced to establish a close connection between them. Such views are to be supplemented by your own research, experience and guidance from the executives from the civil service who are experts in the field of public administration.

---

*At INTAN, Bukit Kiara, Kuala Lumpur On 29th June, 1990.

Before we consider the proper role the legal and judicial system plays towards a dynamic and effective administration, it seems appropriate to begin with the question of what is law. Its definition seems to run in confusing circles. Some see it as fundamental principles of what we ought to do and which does not represent what we do. The critics of a secular legal system see it as an argumentative technique that is applied by skilful lawyers in the forum of courts seeking to escape from reality through alternate reliance on ceremony, formalities and verbal confusion. Notwithstanding such alleged defects, law is an indispensable ingredient of any society.

It is to be remembered that man is by nature a social being and at the dawn of civilisation he formed clans or tribes for the protection and survival of himself and the group of which he was a member. Once a group, clan or tribe is formed, rules are necessary to regulate the relationship of man with man and ensure order and peace within the group. A society cannot exist without such rules. For the purpose of our discussion today, the simplest way of describing law is to say that it is a system of rules which communities have adopted to guide their dealings with each other. Anyone who is able to keep to these rules will profit from doing so and those who break the rules will suffer in some way. For the sake of brevity, let us avoid any further abstract talk attempting to define law but deal with the reality of the Legal and Judicial System.

All legal rules are created by and for a cause. The cause of their creation is very often rooted in social, economic and political factors important to the life of the society at large or its leaders. As the values of society change in the course of development, some changes in the law are inevitable and it is when these necessary changes are made that law frequently becomes remote from the experience and understanding of the common man. If necessary changes are not effected outmoded rules will be kept in existence. The reason for any failure to effect changes could well be due to an absence of effective machinery for important changes or indifference or on account of some inherent juristic fascination with technicalities or a lawyer's self-interest.

The next question is the manner in which law plays its part in nation building, in particular, the harmonization of the diverse racial groups and ethnic divisions. As you can see, steps taken by our Government to forge a common identity in a plural society need not necessarily be compatible with the ideas of western democracy. But what seems necessary is to observe and monitor significant changes in our society's attitudes and to ensure that they are properly reflected in the law. A legal system that is out of step with its society will become ineffective and will hamper and frustrate progressive development. On attaining independence from colonial rule, the national leaders had and still have a tremendous task to perform. Their objectives are oriented to the twin objectives of maintaining a delicate but sustaining and improving balance between the seemingly conflicting and heterogeneous interests in a plural society where such balance should be sustained and improved to ensure economic progress and correct the imbalance between various groups. With these aims, certain concepts of outmoded legal theories have to be modified and reconciled.

With this introduction let me analyse very briefly the two basic concepts of law. They are (a) the separation of powers and (b) the rule of law, the supposed pillars of developed western nations.

(A) Doctrine of separation of powers

The doctrine of separation of powers is associated with Montesquieu, the French Philosopher. Put simply, the theory is that the three functions of government, that is to say, the legislative, the executive and the judicial organs should be discharged by separate bodies. To prevent tyranny and misgovernment, no two of the three functions should be entrusted to the same hands. But as you would have observed, even in Britain the separation of powers does not apply completely. An example of overlapping of functions is in the office of the Lord Chancellor. He is a member of the Cabinet, President (Speaker) of the House of Lords and Head of the Judiciary. The three powers are joined in his office and are exercised by the same individual. Likewise, the Cabinet as the centre of executive power in the State, is composed of ministers who must, by convention, be members of one or other of the House of Parliament. A rigid application of the doctrine would exclude all ministers of the Crown from membership of the legislature. Thus, in fact and in truth the Cabinet and legislature are closely and continuously associated with each other and the relationship may be described as a partnership in government rather than a separation. Now let us see how far the judiciary is independent. Even in England appointments to the High Court Bench are made by the Queen on the advice and recommendation of the executive and judges are removable from office on an address from members of both Houses of Parliament, many of whom are members of the executive. Judges also exercise an indirect power of "legislating" in the sense that they make new rules under the guise of "discovery" of law although a more appropriate word for it is "creating". They do so while carrying out their judicial function of interpreting laws and adjudicating upon disputes. The question that necessarily arises is whether in the strict application of the doctrine there is, in reality, an actual separation of powers even in a western democracy.

(B) Rule of Law

Let us now discuss the scope of the expression "Rule of Law". What we mean by Rule of Law may best be grasped by contrasting it with the opposite of it, i.e., the arbitrary uncertainty and unpredictable use of authority against any person or property unchecked by any other power or body. That state of affairs will lead straight to despotism or anarchy. The concept of Rule of Law was first expounded by Professor A.V. Dicey in 1885 by giving it three meanings. When analysed you will find that the validity of Dicey's theory was suspect even in his own lifetime.

In the welfare state, where the State controls man's affairs from womb to tomb, the executive is given very wide powers. Ministers and other executive bodies enjoy such wide discretionary powers by legislation. The Parliament may authorise a minister by statute "to act as he thinks fit" or "if he is satisfied". Words like "if necessary", "requisite" or "expedient" are found in new statutes. This practice is against Dicey's *first concept* of rule of law, forbidding "wide discretionary authority on the part of the Government". Dicey's theory opposed arbitrary power but emphasised supremacy of law. In Britain, for example, the IRA terrorism had made it necessary to create the Northern Ireland (Emergency Provisions) Act 1973 giving special powers to the police and army, even to detain suspected terrorists without trial.

Dicey's *second meaning* of Rule of Law is *equality before the law* or the equal subjection of all classes to the ordinary law of the land administered by the ordinary law courts. This theory is also not true. An illustration is the position of the Queen who cannot be sued personally in her own courts. Children under 10 years cannot be convicted of a crime and those between 10 and 14, can be convicted only in special circumstances. Another point of obvious inequality, perhaps of special interest to you, is the greater powers a number of officials have beyond those possessed by the ordinary citizen. The police, public health inspectors, factory inspectors, medical officers of health, inspectors of weights and measures, customs officers and so on enjoy such extra powers. Such law places the officials mentioned in a special position to the extent that there is no "equality before the law" as Dicey conceived.

Dicey's *third meaning* is that "The Constitution is the result of the ordinary law of the land (Common Law —Judge made law)". In view of legislation through Parliament this meaning is outdated.

By pointing out the impracticability of Dicey's concept of Rule of Law, I am not saying that his theory is totally wrong. His concept has served as a beacon towards a humanistic approach to law but the modern view is that those ideas have to be modified to fit into new environments. The English concept of separation of powers and rule of law need not bother us unduly as we have a written Constitution which is supreme. The court merely carries out its functions in accordance with the mandate given by the Constitution to it from time to time.

Having given a broad concept of the underlying principle of law, as conceived in the west, let us see how the local legal system can contribute towards a more dynamic administration of public service or administration.

The Legislature and the Executive

We discussed how a government can be broadly divided into the legislature, the executive and the judicial, each organ working in co-operation with the other and acting as a check and balance of each other. As explained earlier the relationship between the legislative and the executive organs is like a partnership. The exercise of the important functions of the Cabinet, including the supreme control of the national executive is influenced by the fact that the Cabinet is a group consisting of party representatives from Parliament. It is an important convention that a Cabinet which loses its support must resign. The value of this practice is that the Cabinet, through its control of the House of Representatives, can frame policies and pass them into law or raise funds necessary for government purposes. Some describe this system as "Cabinet tyranny" or "elected dictatorship". The system is that of "collective responsibility" of the Cabinet and it implies that the policy of a Minister in a particular ministry must be consistent with the policy of the Government as a whole. Although the Minister and ultimately the Prime Minister is responsible and accountable to the public for all actions in the name of the Government, the question is the manner in which they carry out their functions. In the light of present day workload and the complexities of administration, it is not possible for any minister to carry out his functions personally. It is also impossible for Parliament to supervise the different stages of executive action. Therefore, Parliament delegates some of its functions to subordinate authorities.

Delegated Legislation

Students of constitutional law will be too familiar with the concept of delegated legislation and the system of quasi judicial bodies known as administrative tribunals. Whatever be the form of such transfer of responsibilities to lower levels, the main performers behind the screen are anonymous civil servants. A civil servant is a Crown servant (other than the holder of a political or judicial office or a member of the armed forces) appointed directly or indirectly by the Crown and paid wholly out of funds provided by Parliament and employed in a department of government. The terms and conditions of their employment are contained in the General Orders.

Many civil servants belong to the administrative class. The senior civil servants advise the ministers on matters of policy. They are the backbone of administration and are responsible for a great number of decisions. Although the responsibility for taking such decisions is committed by the law to the ministers, these are in fact taken by civil servants, the real administrators in the Minister's name. In many cases they are taken without reference to the Minister personally. Except for a particular decision which is so important that a Minister's personal attention is appropriate (for example, preventive detention which concerns the liberty of the subject) the courts will accept the propriety of such a decision even though the Minister has not explicitly authorised the civil servant to make it. In this context, you may have to read the recent decisions of the Supreme Court on *habeas corpus*, which in my view supports the concept of the independence and impartiality of the judiciary within the limits allowed by the Constitution.

The impact of Law and the Judicial System in Administration

At this stage, it seems appropriate for me to direct my attention to the main topic of discussion today by posing this question—What is the impact of the ordinary laws and the judicial system in the administrator's performance of his duties? The expansion of government activities has necessitated an increase in administrators and administrative agencies charged with the various tasks involved in implementation of state policies and programmes. Before embarking on this discussion, I should observe that legal controls by ordinary courts are by no means the only form of regulating the actions of an administrative agency. There are many other economic and political controls such as public opinion, pressure groups and the mass media. One mode of political control is through the ballot box periodically every five years. The legislative body is thus accountable to the masses. In some cases, there may be a mixture of political and legal control.

An administrative decision and the Court of Law

Can the wisdom of an administrator's decision be questioned in a court of law? We have noted that under the doctrine of separation of powers, the judiciary should adjudicate on questions of law alone and should not delve into matters which are within the rightful province of the legislative or executive arm of government. It has been argued by academic writers that the dividing line between law and policy is difficult to draw. Professor A.V. Dicey insisted that the administration should remain subject to the ordinary law enforced by the ordinary courts. He, in keeping with his time, was opposed to collectivism — that is state intervention on behalf of the community at the expense of individual interests and liberties.

On the other hand, many look towards the courts as constituting an obstacle to effective and efficient administration because of their excessive formalism and insistence on adherence to rigid rules. How can the courts be convinced of potential threats of revolution and sabotage, as they insist on proof beyond reasonable doubt of such activities? One of the English critics of the legal system, Professor Griffiths, maintains with some confidence that the judges are most ill-equipped with regard to expertise in most areas of administration but also that they make political decisions, disguised as matters of law, because of their social and professional detachment and background. Such never ending disputes continue in England and I offer no further comments except to say that the issues are debatable. Let us revert to realities of the local situation. For the public to accept the abstract ideas of law there must exist symbolic conduct of a very definite pattern by a definite institution which can be seen and heard.

As administrators you are one of the mediums of communication and enforcement of law at grassroot level. You would have realised that good listening means not only hearing but also understanding with sympathy the problems of the rakyat. Your effectiveness lies in communication, leadership, teamwork and continuous self-analysis and keeping your political masters informed of the needs, demands and responses of the public. Without adequate public administrative officers like you, law is a toothless tiger. The civil servants, at this crucial stage of national development have a difficult job. They have a responsibility to develop new thinking, creativity in planning and budgeting in carrying out government programmes and projects. In doing so they have to grasp and appreciate the country's basic cultural and economic problems. In many matters the decision making is left to you by Parliament and not to the courts. You may find yourself adjudicating disputes as district officers do as rent officers to decide the "fair rent" of premises under the Rent Control Act 1966 and sometimes you have to decide over subordinates with regard to their promotion or dismissal.

Judicial review

Can courts hear appeals by an aggrieved party over your decisions? With regard to decisions made by you they may come to court by way of judicial review. In certain instances, e.g., for obvious illegality or procedural error the court may review your action.

There are many other areas where the administrators' action can be questioned by way of judicial review. What are these instances? What are the remedies available? In the first place, the person coming to the court must have sufficient interest to give him the right to sue the Government (*locus standi*). It is well established that public authorities and officials must act *intra vires* (within their powers).

Ultra vires doctrine

A person can only do what the law permits him to do. Any act done beyond the power entrusted by law will be declared *ultra vires* if the matter comes for judicial review. The scope of this doctrine has created judicial problems and it has been extended to cover many incidental contingencies. A body vested with discretionary powers acts *ultra vires*, if it acts in bad faith or for a wrong purpose or (in some cases) with gross unreasonableness or is materially influenced by irrelevant considerations or if it fails to have regard to relevant considerations. However, if you act honestly in making your decisions in quasi judicial disputes you should not worry about legal intervention as the courts will not interfere with your discretion by substituting their own opinion with yours. However, an issue of considerable importance that restricts the administrators' discretion is the need to observe an unwritten common law known as "natural justice", a very elusive concept. This concept embraces two main rules:

(1) The rule against bias (no man may be a judge in his own cause)

(2) Audi altram partem (both sides must be heard)

Many hold the view that the applicability of these rules has been invoked to an absurd extent, frustrating the decision making capacity of the administrators. The rules of natural justice can be stretched by courts but the consensus of judicial opinion is that natural justice in simple terms is only "fair play in action". Since ideas of fairness will vary and the range of factual situations in administration is very great, the law remains somewhat uncertain. According to English jurists natural justice imposes no more than a duty to observe minimum standards of procedural fairness. It does not require that decisions be right or be just or that proceedings be conducted openly in the public. Anyway, even these minimum standards of fair "adjudication" can be dispensed with or abridged by a clearly expressed legislative intention.

I shall now consider the technical aspects of judicial review. As explained earlier, there is no question of judicial substitution of an administrator's discretion and decision as in the case of an appeal from the lower court to a higher court. Control of administrative action by judicial review is exercised by what are known as the prerogative orders of (a) *mandamus* (b) *prohibition* (c) *certiorari* and (d) *declaratory judgment*. These are all discretionary remedies and the person seeking the assistance of the court through them must act speedily and must come to court with clean hands. I shall now deal with the four orders.

(a) *Mandamus* is an order issuing out of the High Court commanding (*mandamus*: we command) a person or body to exercise a duty imposed by common law or statute. For example, the order is available against a school principal who refuses to accept an application for admission of a student. Whether to admit him or not may be a discretion but a student is entitled to apply for the discretion to be exercised. (b) *Prohibition* is an order from the High Court to prohibit an inferior court or tribunal from continuing to exceed or threatening to exceed its jurisdiction. If a collector threatens to acquire somebody's land without complying with the procedural requirement of the Land Acquisition Act, 1960, such an order may be issued. (c) *Certiorari* is an order by which the record of decision of a judicial body is removed to the High Court to have its legality inquired into. The word *certiorari* means to be "informed" to enable the High Court to review the decision. It can be invoked to review an excess of jurisdiction or to correct errors of law on the face of the record. (d) *Declaratory Judgments* declare what the law on a particular point is and such judgments are not accompanied by any sanction or means of enforcement. As administrators, you ought to know that the principles of natural justice and judicial review are not available in certain circumstances. In instances where a decision entails the allocation of some resources, such as land, university places, industrial grants, discretionary licences where there may be numerous competitors and where policy consideration on the part of the administrator is predominant, natural justice consideration is not applicable provided the rejected applicant has an opportunity to make representations and has notice of rejection.

It is hoped that the above explanation will give you some insight into the working of the legal system. Unlike the United Kingdom, you need not be unduly concerned about judicial activism which frustrates the aspirations of dynamic administration. As stated earlier, our Constitution is supreme and the courts cannot exercise powers beyond those clearly entrusted to them. Before I conclude, there are some other aspects of law concerning public service which has some relevance to our topic. Any public servant carrying out his duties in good faith is given a degree of immunity by the Government Proceedings Act 1956. Likewise public servants should observe utmost confidentiality by complying with the rigid provisions of the Official Secrets Act. It may also be added that all civil servants enjoy the electoral franchise in common with all other adult citizens. They may vote in parliamentary and local elections but as you know there are necessarily some restrictions on their political activities. The law and convention require political impartiality in the public service. Confidence in that impartiality is an essential part of the structure of our Government.

May I also take this occasion to express some of the grievances the public have against administrators. Whether true or not, the complaints include lack of vitality, imagination, drive, initiative and creativeness. Added to the list is red-tape and adherence to precedent the net result being inflexibility. There are also comments that civil servants are guilty of excessive caution and self-importance protected by the anonymity of public servants. Let us remember the Malay proverb "Rasmi lalang semakin tinggi menunjukkan diri, rasmi padi semakin berisi merendahkan diri".

REDUCTION OF BACKLOG OF CASES

The question of backlog and delay in the disposal of cases has been raised from time to time and it is also a popular topic for discussion by the media. Quite frequently, it is made an item in the agenda at many judicial conferences. Those who administer justice, however, spare no efforts to achieve efficiency and speedier disposal of cases in their courts. It is clearly a matter of great concern to all connected with the administration of justice. It also appears clear that litigation often alters the lives of parties involved in it as well as other members of society. Where a case is delayed in its final disposition, it inevitably has serious effect on litigants, lawyers and judges. It would also reflect on the efficiency of the administration of justice. Besides, it compromises the quality of justice.

It is therefore fundamental that there should be speedy resolution of a dispute. Basically the question is the manner of solving this serious problem. The seriousness of the problem, of course, depends on the extent of the delay. What causes the delay may depend on the particular problem of judicial administration in each country. Problem common to all is the increase in the volume of cases. An increase in litigation may result in the inability of the courts to keep up with the increase due to shortage of judges, the court staff and other resources. On the other hand, delay could also be due to the courts not using their time effectively or perhaps it is due to poor organization and inadequate administration. It is for reasons of the latter that the courts must continually find ways to improve their administration.

The question is, what can we do to reduce delays? We all know that there are many pending cases and undue delays in their disposal. It is basically for this reason that we must give our special attention to this problem.

What is therefore necessary is to consider specific plans to solve what seems to me to be a very serious problem. Positive measures must be taken, for otherwise the whole process could get out of control.

Delay in trial courts, if allowed to continue will tarnish the image of the courts and result in loss of respect for the law. Delay in the disposal of cases clearly will not benefit the public, litigants, lawyers as well as the judges for as we all know delay devalues judgments, causes anxiety to litigants and results in loss or deterioration of evidence upon which rights are determined. By the same token there would be an increase in the cost of litigation. It is therefore the duty of the judicial administrators to formulate measures that have practical effect and produce tangible results. Such an effort will provide an effectively fair and expeditious system of case disposal.

Among the matters that call for consideration are —

(1) **The Court**

The court has an important role or responsibility in controlling the pace of litigation. The responsibility for controlling the pace of litigation should cover the control over postponement of cases. The essential emphasis should be in the judicial commitment to reduce delay. The goal is to be achieved by both the court under our system and the individual judge.

Under this head, matters that emerge for discussion are:

(a) the adequacy of existing resources such as courtrooms, registrars and support staff, etc.

(b) our rules and court procedures.

One of the fundamental elements necessary for a speedy disposal of cases, stressed time and again, relates to the court's control of cases described as case management. It covers matters such as:

(a) the need for effective supervision;

(b) formulation of procedures for early identification of cases that may be protracted and giving special administrative attention where appropriate;

(c) the adoption of trial fixing and also scheduling sufficient number of cases to ensure effective use of judicial time or minimising the fixing of cases so as to avoid overloading;

(d) the trials to commence on dates scheduled;

(e) a firm and consistent policy to minimise postponements.

As for court supervision, the responsibility is upon the court to press counsel and litigants to prepare a case for hearing without delay. In this regard the court should not lose control over litigation on account of failure on the part of counsel or litigants to observe the procedure, in particular, the process of getting cases ready for trial. The judge himself or a senior assistant registrar attached to a particular judge must supervise every case throughout its life to ensure that no unreasonable interruption occurs in its procedural development.

Complex cases require special handling. They must, at a very early stage, be identified (determined from the pleadings) and once this is done, they ought to be closely and continually supervised up to the time they are ready for trial, fixed for hearing and also disposed of. It may also be necessary in such cases, before they are heard, for a judge to secure agreement of parties on documents and the facts and issues to be tried. This will expedite the hearing of the cases.

(2) **The Bar**

Members of the Bar have a vital role to play in the speedy disposal of cases. What is required of them is total commitment and absolute co-operation.

Trial Date

The trial of a case should commence on the date fixed. Postponement should be avoided unless it is absolutely unavoidable. Counsel should be fully aware that the court means business and would be very slow to entertain applications for postponement.

Postponements have to be kept to a minimum. This is achieved through a firm control of the case by the court and the close co-operation given by members of the Bar. Applications for postponement will be less if counsel realise the inevitability of the trial being proceeded with on the date fixed.

Cases that come up for decision should be promptly determined. It is to be observed that a judge who is consistently prompt in his decision can cause the counsel to be prompt in his preparation.

In the event of a judgment being reserved with a written decision to be given, such written decision should be made available for delivery within the shortest possible time. By the same token, if a decision is appealed against, a written decision should also be prepared quickly, ideally not later than 4 weeks after filing of the notice of appeal.

There are many factors which contribute to the delay, one of which is the laxity shown by the court in allowing too much time for hearing before a case is brought to a conclusion. Counsel should be made to co-operate to keep to the date or dates allotted for the hearing of a particular case. Cases once commenced should be completed as soon as possible. Long adjournments should be discouraged. The reason is obvious. Facts are forgotten and their value will be considerably lessened as credibility of a particular witness would invariably depend on observation of the demeanour of that witness.

It is common practice for many judges to require or allow written submissions to be made by counsel. There is a danger in such a practice in that counsel tend to supply a very lengthy submission. Inevitably counsel for the opposite party would ask for time to reply and in that event much time would have elapsed in the process.

Apart from the matters that I have raised in this short observation, I do believe that there are certain provisions in our civil procedure rules which inhibit speedy disposal of cases. They are probably already outdated and must necessarily be amended or altered if we are to achieve our objective to expedite or speed up the disposal of cases. On this aspect the questions that arise are:

(1) Whether speedy disposal could be achieved under the existing laws and court rules;

(2) Whether such laws or rules have to be amended;

(3) Whether such laws or rules should be modified in certain areas to achieve effective and speedy disposal.

Existing resources

My view is that with the existing resources there is still a lot which could be done to reduce the backlog of cases. For a systematic approach a judge in each State should from time to time be supplied by the registrars with up-to-date information (data) on the number of cases pending and the extent of the backlog in his court. This is essential before any firm step can be taken to eliminate delay. The information is also necessary to identify the areas and the causes of the delay. Needless to say, it is necessary for a determination of the type of action to be taken. The availability of such information facilities not only more accurate assessment of the size of the problem but also the goal that can be achieved and the priorities that have to be accorded.

Leadership and motivation

There must be leadership and motivation. When I say leadership, I am referring to the position at State level and the individual judges. Very much depends upon their initiative and motivation. I must say that there has been a concerted effort on our part to dispose of the cases speedily. There is no room for complacency. Things must change and through our collective efforts we hope to bring about a change and move to a level where we can proudly say that justice is not denied as it has not been delayed.

Allow me to conclude by saying that there must be a changed attitude and new outlook so that all organs of Government can co-operate to create a better society. I thank all of you for patiently listening to me.

PERTANDINGAN MOOT: TUJUAN DAN KEPENTINGANNYA*

Saya merasa bertuah di atas undangan bagi merasmikan Pertandingan Moot di antara universiti-universiti tempatan bagi kali ke-enam.

Saya mengucapkan ribuan terima kasih kerana ini ialah sesuatu penghormatan bagi diri saya.

Kebetulannya pada bulan September 1989, saya telah di beri peluang memberi ucapan pembukaan Pertandingan Moot Ke lima antara Fakulti Undang-Undang Pusat Pengajian Tinggi di Universiti Kebangsaan Malaysia, malangnya saya tidak dapat hadir. Ucapan saya itu di baca oleh Yang Arif Hakim Dato' Siti Norma Yaakob.

Saya telah menyentuh tentang soal kepentingan keadilan, soal yang perlu diberi perhatian dengan penuh tanggungjawab oleh semua pihak. Sehubungan ini saya juga berkata:

> "For me, the Constitution of Malaysia represents the necessary structure within which justice in our society is secured. Indeed, every judge takes an oath to preserve, protect and defend the Constitution. This can—as I am myself only too well aware—impose an invidious burden; but it is a responsibility that must in fact be shared by Bench and Bar alike, if the Constitution is to function as it should. Conscious of what we owe to society, we do, indeed we must do, the best we can."

Bercakap tentang pertandingan moot, saya menekan bahawa:

> "kemahiran kepeguaman yang khusus amat diperlukan. Adalah diharapkan setiap pengamal undang-undang itu adalah seorang peguambela dalam erti-kata yang sebenarnya dan oleh yang demikian kepintaran dan kecekapan seseorang itu tertakluk kepada keupayaan berhujah yang boleh meyakinkan."

Sungguhpun begitu, perlu diingatkan bahawa Mahkamah tidak semestinya dipengaruhi oleh hujah yang hanya kononnya bernas dan munasabah tetapi ternyata tidak benar. Mahkamah tidak mudah terpesona dengan kepintaran berhujah sahaja jika hujah itu tidak bermerit. Jelas bukan ciri tersebut sahaja yang menentukan seseorang itu sebagai peguam yang cekap dan berkualiti.

**Di Majlis Perasmian Pertandingan Moot dan Sukan Antara Universiti-Universiti Tempatan 1990 Pada 22hb Disember, 1990 di Dewan Kuliah I Institut Pengajian Tinggi (Lama), Universiti Malaya.*

Dalam ucapan tersebut saya juga menarik perhatian kepada soal penggunaan Bahasa Malaysia di mahkamah. Sungguhpun Bahasa Inggeris perlu digunakan apabila sesuatu rujukan dibuat kepada prinsip-prinsip undang-undang yang termuat di dalam laporan undang-undang, maka tidak bermakna seseorang yang berhujah dalam Bahasa Malaysia tidak dapat melakukan dengan baik.

Pada hemat saya, adalah jelas pertandingan serupa ini menjadi sesuatu aspek terpenting "that forms an integral part of legal training".

Sebelum saya beralih ke sesuatu topik yang lain adalah perlu diingatkan:

> "To achieve greatest benefit, those participating in a Moot Court must regard it seriously as one would a proper court of law. Only by so doing, that not only the discussion of a particular legal problem may be well expounded but also improve the technic and method of presentation.
>
> No law school can teach the students all the answers to the difficult and complex questions and points of law which a lawyer will be faced in an actual practice. Knowing the law of course is a fundamental rule. Technic is acquired through experience. He has to be quick on the uptake and be ready to counter his opponent's arguments and not be caught without a sensible and logical reply. Presence of mind may only be acquired with practice and moots do help the future lawyer to be able to gauge his opponent's case line of examination-in-chief, cross-examination, re-examination and any points of law raised or preliminary objection taken in the course of the proceedings.
>
> Decorum is the cornerstone of a lawyer's behaviour. Regardless of who presides in a court of law you must give a good impression. Your appearance means a lot. You must dress neatly and not appear sloven. Be well-groomed. You are a friend and an officer of the court and must assist the Court to arrive at the truth by your behaviour before the Court.
>
> From experience I would say that it is necessary to secure the confidence and respect of the Court. In order to do so it is essential that you be (and in fact be) courteous, truthful, frank, fair and even willing to confess ignorance or uncertainty should such an occasion arise. There is nothing disgraceful about being ignorant, indeed in not being infallible. I would say that sometimes a frank admission is not one out of place, indeed it is often greatly appreciated by the Court."

Adalah diperhatikan bahawa sesuatu yang diperkatakan di sini adalah semata-mata pandangan peribadi dan tidak semestinya boleh diterima sepenuhnya. Walau bagaimanapun kata-kata yang dilahirkan mungkin berfaedah dan boleh diterima untuk menjadi bahan buah fikiran kita semua.

Saya akhiri ucapan ringkas saya. Didahului dengan ucapan Bismilahirahmanirahim saya merasmikan Pertandingan Moot Dan Sukan Antara Universiti-Universiti Tempatan 1990.

THE ROLE OF LAW IN NATIONAL INTEGRATION*

Saya amat bersyukur kepada Allah kerana dengan keizinanNya diberi peluang oleh Jawatankuasa Penganjur Seminar Undang-Undang dan Masyarakat Ke Empat untuk menyampaikan ucapan dasar dan seterusnya merasmikan seminar ini.

Perkara yang saya akan sentuh pada pagi ini ialah "Peranan Undang-Undang dalam memupuk Perpaduan Negara di Malaysia".

Dalam menyampaikan ucapan saya disini, izinkan saya untuk menarik perhatian mengenai beberapa perkara pokok perbincangan atas topik yang saya nyatakan tadi. Di samping itu, izinkan juga saya jelaskan bahawa janganlah para hadirin yang saya hormati sekelian salah anggap bahawa apa yang diperkatakan dalam majlis ini merupakan suatu perisytiharan kehakiman atau "judicial pronouncement" yang dibuat oleh Ketua Hakim Negara. Malah saya berdiri di sini, adalah sebagai rakyat biasa yang diberi penghormatan untuk melahirkan pandangan atau buah fikiran yang mungkin dapat kita bersama-sama menghayatinya.

Barangkali pada suatu hari nanti isu-isu yang dibangkitkan pada pagi ini berkemungkinan akan sampai ke peringkat Mahkamah Agung. Saya pasti bahawa isu-isu seperti perkara undang-undang dan perkara-perkara fakta (point of law and point of fact) yang dikemukakan ke Mahkamah Agung ketika itu akan diputuskan oleh panel hakim Mahkamah Agung bersandarkan undang-undang semasa yang terpakai ketika itu.

Para hadirin sekelian, topik yang saya akan membicangkan hari ini agak begitu konflek dan khusus maka saya mengambil kesempatan di sini untuk memohon izin untuk berucap dalam Bahasa Inggeris. Sebagaimana saya difahamkan bahawa proses pembelajaran dan pengajaran di Universiti Kebangsaan adalah dalam dua bahasa. Saya kira tidak menjadi masalah kepada para peserta seminar ini untuk mengikuti apa-apa yang saya katakan nanti.

Law and Society

The topic for discussion today is very complex and within the short time available it is only possible to express some basic issues relating to the subject. Be-

---

**Di Seminar Tahunan Undang-Undang Dan Masyarakat Ke-IV Universiti Kebangsaan Malaysia Pada 5hb Januari, 1991 Di Dewan Kampo, Pusat Belia Antarabangsa, Bandar Tun Razak, Cheras, Kuala Lumpur.*

fore we come to the specific role of law in national integration, we have to understand what is law and its connection with society. One of the many ways in which human activities can be distinguished from animal groups is by reference to social rules. Our behaviour towards others is closely regulated and controlled directly through moral standards, religious doctrines, social traditions and legal rules. As a typical example, let us take marriage. We are born with a mating instinct but it is through social and legal rules that such an instinct is channelled into a socially acceptable form of relationship known as "Marriage". Even a basic function like eating is in some way affected by law, in that the food we eat is required by legal rules to meet rigorous standards of purity and hygiene. A typical example before our eyes is the case of sale of fake mineral water offending the law. The definition of law is manifold. While jurists still argue what is law, it is defined for commonsense purposes in Jowitt's Dictionary as a "A rule of action to which men are obliged to make their conduct conformable, a command enforced by some sanction to acts or forbearance of a class". Without the rule of law and courts and the executive to enforce it we will be free to push and bully our fellow citizens who would be equally free to push and bully us, creating disorder.

Relationship of law to society

What is the relationship of law to society? Law is the spirit of the people and in particular to the people of each nation for whose needs and demands it is made. Although there is a historical reason for every legal development, law must progress in a rational and responsive way to harmonise with the aspirations of people. All legal rules are created by a cause rooted in social, economic or political factors important to the life of a nation. For example, capital punishment was abolished 25 years ago in England but our legislature believes in the effectiveness of such punishment to combat violent crimes such as murder and silent offences such as drug addiction. Law is an institution of its society, exists in society, is part of society and cannot be allowed to be out of step with society. The word "society" in this context is to mean people inhabiting a particular country. Law must correspond to the moral, social and economic condition of a society and be its expression.

Legal system

Let us now look briefly into our legal system. Malaysia's legal system has been shaped by events spread over a period of some six hundred years with three major systems emerging during this period. The first was the founding of the Malacca Sultanate at the beginning of the fifteenth century while the second was the period when Islam was spread to South East Asia with its impact in the indigenous culture. The most important event in modern Malaysia is the British Colonial rule with its constitutional government and the common law system. Unfortunately time does not permit us to delve into details of this source of law. Let us discuss how law can be modified to develop a united Malaysian Concept. The seminar held today gives everyone a limited opportunity to understand the role of law in our lives and the ways and means to develop our law and social order to operate in harmony and to be complementary to each other. It is important that our public in general should be instilled with a greater awareness as to the proper role of law. It must be remembered that the centre of gravity of legal and social development lies not in legislation nor in political science nor pronouncements by judges but in society itself. Such being the case, I wish to emphasise on some points which may be worthy of discussion to achieve the maximum benefit for this seminar.

Role of law

At the outset, let us remember some basic facts. Law is not a matter of words expressed in a foreign language or in archaic and formalistic jargons. In a developed country the role of law and courts is settled by its traditions, customs and conventions but in a developing society like ours the role of law is not an easy task. We cannot claim that our law is indigenous. It may not be wrong to say that until independence (to some extent even now), our law has been substantially a product of western civilization transplanted into our culture, habits and traditions. Western values need not necessarily be happily applicable to developing countries. Take the case of India which is a secular full fledged parliamentary democracy with fundamental liberty as the cornerstone of its constitution. The recent events spreading meaningless violence in the name of religion and democratic freedom show how futile it is to transplant western ideals. If one needs further examples, one need only look at Sri Lanka, Philippines, Bangladesh and a lot of other countries. As Malaysia is multi racial, multi cultural, multi lingual and multi religious, our aim is to produce a homogeneous society where there is equality for all people. The role of law in this context is not easy. I shall now consider the changes in some aspects of law which took place after independence to examine whether such changes are beneficial and justified and whether they can be accelerated.

Specific problems of developing nations

Before we come to the specific problems, let us discuss the points generally applicable to all developing nations. Most of the third world countries which became independent after the Second World War require different kinds of inputs and skills in the decision making process unlike developed nations.

Where there is a scarcity of resources like land wealth the executive has to cope with the problem of access to development and the even distribution of resources and wealth to produce equality not in paper alone but in practice. Our responsibility is great as concepts of democracy and rule of law, in the ultimate analysis, depend on access to and participation in development and growth. The role of law is not to produce abstract justice but social justice. That is the reason why in most developing countries the focus of judicial interpretation and judicial review has been modified or abolished and the social justice approach is being adopted. Further, the subject of rule of law in a developing nation, aiming to become a welfare state entail the conferment of wide discretionary powers to administrative agencies to implement large socio-economic goals. In a pluralistic society comprising diverse people, coming from different stock, speaking different languages, professing different religions and following different personal laws yet all under one flag, concepts such as fundamental rights (golden ideas in the West) often cause great unrest for the majority. In a developing country, for speedy development and achievement of minimum social objectives numerous laws have to be made creating new rights and obligations and offences overreaching traditional abstract values.

Malaysian Law after Independence

Let us now look at some of our laws passed after Independence. One of the laws introduced after Independence in respect of which members of the public can co-operate is the implementation of the National Language Act. An independent country should have a language it can call its own, a language that can help to bind the different racial groups together. Nobody ought to quarrel with the fact that such a language should be rooted in the soil and history of this country. The new law has not penalised anyone for a lack of knowledge of the National Language. The Malay language is aimed at simplicity and as a basic means of communication throughout the Malay archipelago. It was ill tuned to the incorporation of certain legal concepts but this does not imply that the language lacked a capacity for general refinement. All languages lend or borrow from each other in the course of human intercourse. With the advent of English and British colonial rule, the Malay language passed into an eclipse and it is fully justified that with the emergence of independence, the position of the National Language should be revived. In harmony with Article 152 of the Federal Constitution, the Education Act 1961 aims at "the progressive development of an education system in which the National Language is the main medium of instruction". In many developing societies, laws are written and judgments are delivered in English which are not understood by the majority of the people. This in consequence produces inequality between the educated minority and the uneducated multitude. In the circumstances, the courts have done everything possible to make Malay the court language. The full success of this scheme depends upon the co-operation of members of the legal profession and the public. Article 152 also safeguards the position of other languages by further providing that no person may be prohibited from using, otherwise than for official purposes, or from teaching or learning any other language. The Constitution does not prejudice the right of the Federal Government or of any State Government to preserve and sustain the use and study of the language of any other community in Malaysia.

It must be borne in mind that the creation of a national identity in a system where there are diverse racial groups and deep ethnic divisions is the principal task of the government. National unity is our overriding objective. Steps taken by the government to forge a common identity may not always be compatible with the idea of a liberal democracy. A legal system is never perfect and ours is no exception. Law is not a string of rules to be studied in isolation.

Security Legislations

Some major areas of the law the need for which some members of the public question are the Internal Security Act 1960, Emergency (Public Order and Prevention of Crime) Act 1969, Dangerous Drugs (Special Preventive Measures) Act 1985, Official Secret Act 1972 and a host of others restricting the traditional common law freedom of the citizen. No doubt these Acts strengthen the hands of the executive and it is not appropriate for me to commit one way or the other regarding the merits or otherwise of these laws lest what I say today for educational purposes be construed as the head of the judiciary entering into the forbidden political arena. The judiciary is only the guardian and not the master of the constitution. The justification claimed by the government for introducing such changes was that allowing courts to substitute the decisions of the elected government with their own meant that the country's security was not in the hands of the executive but the courts. It is trite that the courts are not experts on security. Another justification claimed for preventive detention legislation without trial is that very often witnesses are afraid to testify in open court because of a lack of civic sense and of a fear of reprisals. Although further discussion on this is outside the judicial boundary, I shall make a few comments on the general principle of freedom so that you can evaluate the need for such legislation to ensure security and stability to maintain the racial and religious harmony of our beloved nation.

Political scientists believe that freedoms conflict. To quote an example, the law on defamation which restricts freedom of speech increases the freedom of the individual in that it protects his reputation from untruthful statements. I hasten to add that this may be true legally but may be illusory in fact. Many in lofty positions may choose to ignore the false stories against them as vindication through the courts is a time consuming affair and the person who speaks ill may be looking for an opportunity for public attention to become a hero. Anyway, absolute freedom in all areas would restrict another person's freedom. The corollary is that there is only relative freedom in truth. Since there is a potential conflict between competing rights and freedom, it is imperative that a balance should be struck.

Freedom of speech and expression

In our Constitution, there is reasonable freedom to discuss or question affairs of the State except on matters relating to "sensitive issues". The Constitution upholds such restricted freedom. The court will act as a vigilant watchdog within the ambit of that freedom. A few critics point to the increasing degree to which the government and legislature go to interfere in the lives of individuals. Simple examples are legislation such as prohibition on drinking and driving and the obligation to wear a crash helmet on a motorbike or seatbelts in a car. These can be classified as a loss of freedom. But is it really so? It should not be forgotten that restriction of a person's freedom increases the collective freedom of many others to lead their lives in peace. Absolute freedom to question sensitive subjects is likely to create mass chaos and unrest as shown in our history two decades ago. Therefore, because of the potential conflicting freedoms, whenever one is faced with the question of whether a particular piece of legislation reduces freedom and infringement of so-called fundamental rights (according to western tradition) one must always ask himself the question "Is there a possible increase in somebody else's or community's freedom, which offsets the loss of freedom caused by the laws' limitation?" In undeveloped nations, people are less concerned with abstract individual freedom and are more concerned with freedom from the worst forms of arbitrary government. Emphasis on individual freedom arises from the West. However, experience has taught the West to realise that absolute freedom ought to be restricted in certain situations. For example, an irresponsible press can create havoc as mankind is not gifted with foresight and very often reach conclusions by using false data and imperfect reasoning by irresponsible mischief makers bent to sabotage society aiming to spread alarm and despondency for their own selfish interests. Crude advocates of individual liberty may even advocate liberty to smoke drugs as there is no victim of the crime other than the consumer himself. Even in Britain, the situation in Ireland has necessitated emergency restrictions overriding all Common Law liberties.

Collective social interest of the nation

Law may also be classified as something holding the balance of interests of various factors. The basic areas in a developing country are the interests of the individual and the collective social interests of the nation. The latter encompasses areas such as protection of religion, unification of various cultural and ethnic groups, existence of an effective legal order, changes of constitution through due process of law, national security and stability, upholding of moral, humanitarian and intellectual values, public health, welfare and so on. To conclude, in a democratic society law cannot be regarded as merely an arbitrary order imposed upon an undiscerning and unresisting public. Although law is formally found in constitutions and in all the formal regalia of the courts and enforcement agencies, it is also found in the human behaviour and attitudes because it is through such means that the primacy of the rule of law is acknowledged as a viable alternative to force and chaos with determination of opposing claims. Law deals with and is the product of the conduct of people in a society as explained earlier in my speech. Law is a relational science. It is a device allowing for the achievement of peaceful and orderly change. It is a means of facilitating unification of social change.

Role of the public in relation to Law

What is the role of the public in relation to law? Legislation and judicial decisions cannot by themselves perform miraculous changes in attitude, prejudices and socially structural arrangements based on ethnic, religious or racial considerations. In time, the educative impact of the law, spread by community leaders like you, may induce desirable changes in this problem area.

While we discuss national unity, let the basic ideology (supplemental to the constitution) embodied in the Rukun Negara be borne in mind. Following the unhappy events of May 1969, our then leaders caused this enlightened document comprising some twenty thousand words emphasising racial unity within a just and democratic society to be formulated to guide our lives. Its essence is set out in five brief principles emphasising belief in God, loyalty to the nation, the rule of law and good behaviour. We should never allow the spirit of Rukun Negara to fall into eclipse as it embodies the ideal concepts of a law abiding patriotic citizen.

The citizen's participation in the legal system can be in diverse manners. There is a growing need for awareness of law among the public. Educating them in the laws should be the primary task of those who are qualified. In this connection, running a weekly column on "You and Law" by the *New Straits Times* is a step in the right direction. The public can also assist in the detection of crimes by informing the authorities concerned in time. There are many cases of undiscovered crimes like child abuse of which the police may not be aware. Public apathy like the attitude of the three monkeys who speak, see and hear no evil is to be avoided. The police cannot solve all crimes without public support and co-operation. People should not be shy and be afraid of the courts and the police. Seminars like this can contribute in various other manners the nature of which is for you to deliberate. As you know, ignorance of the law is no excuse although it can be a strong mitigating factor for punishment. Instead of being ignorant of the law, the public should participate in the enforcement of law by helping in the prevention of crimes. Law must not be seen as criminal law alone punishing criminals but as a discipline regulating our whole life, existing for the benefit of the public and made by the representatives of the public.

Newspapers also have a heavy responsibility to draw the attention of authorities and citizens to incidents like cruelty to children, unhygienic conditions and other social evils which may remain unnoticed but for the newspapers' vigilance and investigative reporting. Punishment is not the only deterrent to crimes. Reward, in the form of public acclaim, especially by the mass media is another contributory factor to promote a "good Samaritan" attitude.

ANOTHER MATRIMONIAL PROCEEDING*

First, I take this opportunity to express my sincere thanks to Dato Kam Woon Wah and Mr. & Mrs. Ong Kong Lim for the kind invitation extended on this very auspicious occasion to my wife and me to be at this dinner tonight.

I recall January 10, 1989 when Dato Kam Woon Wah took out a subpoena to secure my attendance to testify in a matrimonial acquisition proceeding held at the grand chambers of the Honourable Ming Court. It was on a matter of acquisition into the Kam family of a male specie called Chan Sze Loon specifically and exclusively to be the life partner of Linda Kam Thai Eng. The parties having agreed to a consent order what remained then for me to do was to testify that the Kam family was joyous of the occasion and pleasantly disposed to express their profound pleasure and gratitude to everyone present at the proceedings and also to those who with just cause and lawful excuse were given leave of absence.

It may well be that the acquisition was successfully completed as no further particulars were applied for since then to show whether any progress had been made by the parties concerned i.e. Linda and Sze Loon to produce any issue or issues to elevate the status of Dato Kam to that of a real Datuk. If parties have not already done so it is ordered that they go down to business forthwith.

Now exactly two years afterwards another acquisition proceeding is at hand. This time the venue is no longer the Court Room of Ming but a grand ballroom. The choice is, presumably, because Dato Kam is acquiring into the Kam family a beautiful female specie called Gazel Ong Mei Yin to be lawfully chained to Andrew Kam Tai Yeow definitely to the exclusion of all others. The tie is effected with the full blessings and consent of the Ongs. A consent order having been made, again what remains for me to testify relates only to the Kams' and Ongs' desire to affirm their profound pleasure and appreciation to all assembled here tonight and also to those who with just cause and lawful excuse have been given leave of absence to witness today's proceedings.

I would further testify to the effect that the Kams and the Ongs had been given an undertaking by the Shang that in keeping with the high traditions,

---

**Address At Dato Kam Woon Wah's Son's Wedding Reception At The Shangri-la Hotel, Kuala Lumpur On 15th January, 1991.*

custom and style of the Grand Shang nothing less than the most delicious and sumptuous food would be served.

I have spoken much of the Ming, the Kams, the Ongs and the Shang but have not stated the real grounds why the proceedings are to take place on the 15th of January, 1991.

We are all aware that the Kams and the Ongs are peace loving people. Accordingly, peace and not war is foremost in the minds of the Kams and the Ongs, indeed in the minds of Gazel and Andrew also. Determined to keep in line with the United Nations Security Council Resolution, the Kams and Ongs have decided to place a deadline for Gazel and Andrew to be absolutely left in peace one minute past midnight tonight. The sign *DO NOT DISTURB* will be prominently displayed outside the door of the honeymoon suite. Incidentally, the other reason why this date has been chosen is because Tan Sri Haniff, the Inspector General of Police, will also be crossing another deadline one minute past midnight. Don't ask him how old he will be — he will not disclose it. As the IGP, Tan Sri has vast police powers but I know that even he will not consider removing the DO NOT DISTURB sign without a proper court order.

Perhaps it is appropriate that at this point I invite your attention to some of the unofficial secrets, the very personal particulars of the relevant parties; those who matter most in these proceedings.

In doing so, however, I would refrain from disclosing their dates of birth except to say that both are very young and naturally very ready, very willing and very, very able. Gazel and Andrew were both born in the Lunar year of the Ox. I am informed, after I looked up the *Handbook of Chinese Horoscopes*, that: "The Ox sign symbolises prosperity through fortitude and hard work. A person born during this year will be dependable, calm and methodical, with a resolute and logical mind. Basically an introvert he can turn into a commanding and eloquent speaker when the occasion arises (useful for Court Room appearance). It is also said that the Ox can be terribly naive about affairs of the heart. He cannot fully comprehend the entrapments of love, much less employ enticing strategy and other allures to plead his romantic cause" (I disagree and it is contrary to evidence). And, to Gazel, listen to this: "Don't expect lyric poetry and moonlight serenades from him".

In view of the personalities of an Ox it came as no surprise that both parties successfully graduated in law — Gazel at the City of London Polytechnic and Andrew at Buckingham University. While Gazel attended secondary school at Bukit Bintang, Andrew went to Methodist and St. John's and later United World College, Singapore and subsequently to Millfield School, England. At about the same time Gazel was at Clarendon School, Bedfordshire, England.

Before admission to the High Court of Malaya as advocates and solicitors both attended the Certificate of Legal Practice Course and that was where they met. You would notice that it is indeed a very practical course. That reminds me of Tan Sri Haniff who also attended the same course — but having been caveated by Puan Sri Hamidah a long way back when Tan Sri was in Pahang, Tan Sri is no longer subject to a registrable transfer.

After admission Gazel practised law at Messrs. Kam Woon Wah & Co., and Andrew wasted no time to assist her to practice. In a chamber application before his father, he sought an order that Gazel be the father's legal daughter (in-law, in fact). An order in terms was granted. On thé evidence before us there is no doubt that they will live happily ever after. I have some advice for Andrew now that he is securely tied up. Keep away from a piano, if you do not want a black eye. The story goes that a young man, newly married, was trying at a party to get the attention of a luscious young girl at the piano—while his wife was closely watching him. Being a bit clumsy he tripped and fell with his hands on the piano. The piano cover slammed down inflicting blue black marks on the young man's hands. The wife lifted him up with love and while doing so said, "Don't worry dear I'll place a piece of steak on your black eye when you get home."

"But I don't have a black eye," protested the husband. "Never mind," she said, "you'll get one when we get home."

And for you, Gazel, never describe him as a model husband.

The story goes that this newly married young lady was so proud of her husband that she told a close friend that her husband is a model husband.

"Now I understand," said the friend, "come to think of it I did see your husband with a very pretty model."

To conclude may I on behalf of my wife and everyone present once again congratulate the couple and Dato Kam and Mr. & Mrs. Ong.

PROFESION PEGUAM: TUGAS DAN TANGGUNGJAWAB*

Alhamdulillah, sekali lagi Persatuan Undang-Undang Universiti Islam Antarabangsa dengan kerjasama Bahagian Penyelidikan dan Sekretariat Bahasa Malaysia Mahkamah Agung menganjurkan "Kursus Pengenalan Profesion Peguam" dengan objektif-objektif yang tertentu. Pada hemat saya adalah tepat kursus serupa ini dianjurkan memandangkan perlaksanaan penggunaan Bahasa Malaysia di mahkamah secara praktikal bermula dari 1hb Jun 1990. Saya merasa amat bangga dan mengucapkan ribuan terima kasih kerana telah diberi peluang berucap diupacara perasmian Kursus ini.

Sebagaimana yang tuan-tuan dan puan-puan sekalian sedia maklum, untuk melahirkan peguam-peguam yang berkaliber, maka sudah sewajarnyalah generasi mahasiswa-mahasiswi jurusan undang-undang kini didedahkan dengan matlamat masa depan yang hendak dicapai. Justeru itu, melalui program sebeginilah mereka akan dapat menganalisa serta memahami dengan lebih dekat lagi tentang masalah-masalah di bidang perundangan termasuklah masalah pelaksanan penggunaan Bahasa Malaysia di mahkamah dan perumusan kaedah-kaedah yang paling efektif ke arah jalan penyelesaiannya.

Sukacita saya memulakan ucapan perasmian ini dengan menyentuh serba sedikit mengenai profesion peguambela dan peguamcara. Perlu diingatkan bahawa semata-mata memiliki sekeping ijazah di bidang undang-undang tidaklah mencukupi untuk menjalankan amalan sebagai peguambela dan peguamcara.

Dari segi undang-undang sebelum diterima masuk sebagai peguambela dan peguamcara, pemegang-pemegang ijazah undang-undang adalah dikehendaki menjalani tempoh latihan selama sembilan bulan dengan seorang peguambela dan peguamcara yang menjalankan dan telah menjalankan amalan secara aktif dalam Malaysia bagi tempoh yang tertentu. Latihan ini adalah untuk memastikan bahawa setiap pemegang ijazah undang-undang itu mempunyai pengetahuan dan pengalaman yang diperlukan untuk melayakkan mereka menjadi peguambela dan peguamcara.

Setelah menyempurnakan tempoh latihan tersebut, pemegang-pemegang ijazah undang-undang dikehendaki pula menjalani suatu upacara penerimaan

---

**Di Hari Perasmian Kursus Pengenalan Profesion Peguam pada 2hb Mac, 1991 di Dewan Kuliah I, Universiti Islam Antarabangsa.*

masuk sebagai peguambela dan peguamcara di Mahkamah Tinggi. Penerimaan masuk sebagai peguambela dan peguamcara di Mahkamah Tinggi sahaja masih tidak melayakkan seseorang untuk menjalankan amalan sebagai peguambela dan peguamcara melainkan ia mempunyai suatu sijil amalan yang sah untuk menjalankan tugas sebagai peguambela dan peguamcara. Sijil amalan ini dikeluarkan oleh Pendaftar Mahkamah Tinggi.

Mereka yang telah diterima masuk sebagai peguambela dan peguamcara menikmati keistimewaan-keistimewaan tertentu, di antaranya ialah hak untuk mengendalikan kes-kes di mahkamah dan di firma masing-masing bagi pihak anak guaman. Dengan keistimewaan-keistimewaan yang dimiliki, sudah semestinya seorang peguambela dan peguamcara itu mempunyai tanggungjawab tertentu yang perlu dilaksanakan. Diantaranya ialah tanggungjawab sebagai peguam dalam mana-mana prosiding di mahkamah dan tanggungjawab sebagai peguam di bawah Akta Profesion Undang-Undang 1976.

Seorang peguambela dan peguamcara diharapkan mengguna kecekapannya dan kemahirannya dengan sempurna terutama sekali semasa menjalankan kewajipan terhadap seseorang anak guaman dan mahkamah. Adalah juga menjadi kewajipan seorang peguambela dan peguamcara semasa menjalankan tugas-tugasnya berhadapan mana-mana pihak pengadilan, bertingkah laku sopan dan beradab, namun demikian tidak perlu takut mempertahankan kepentingan seseorang yang diwakilinya, kepentingan keadilan serta kepentingan dan keutuhan profesionnya, walaupun akibat yang tidak diingini mungkin menimpa dirinya.

Profesion seorang peguam dalam bidang perundangan amatlah terserlah. Sikap dan gerak-gerinya sentiasa diperhatikan dan diambil kira dalam menentukan kejayaannya. Penampilannya di mahkamah haruslah meyakinkan semua pihak dan kebijaksanaannya amatlah penting demi untuk mematahkan hujjah lawan. Justera itu setiap peguam haruslah menerapkan nilai-nilai peribadi yang tinggi ke dalam diri masing-masing. Perkara-perkara ini haruslah dimiliki oleh setiap peguam yang ingin menjadi peguam yang berkaliber. Akta Profesion Undang-Undang 1976 sendiri mempunyai peruntukan-peruntukan mengenai kesopanan, kelakuan dan tatatertib profesional peguambela dan peguamcara yang mengikat setiap peguam.

Profesion undang-undang adalah suatu profesion yang sangat di pandang tinggi di mata masyarakat. Anggota masyarakat menaruh kepercayaan penuh kepada para peguam untuk mengendalikan kes-kes mereka. Tetapi apa yang mendukacitakan ialah sejak akhir-akhir ini banyak sekali berlaku kes-kes di mana peguam telah menyalahgunakan kuasa yang ada pada mereka dengan menyelewengkan kepercayaan yang telah diberikan kepada mereka. Perkara ini haruslah dipandang serius kerana perbuatan para peguam tersebut telah mencemarkan nama baik profesion perundangan dan sudah tentu kita tidak mahu mendengar masyarakat mengeluarkan kata-kata bahawa "a lawyer is a liar".

Beralih kepada pelaksanaan penggunaan Bahasa Malaysia di mahkamah-mahkamah pada 1hb Jun 1990, pada hemat saya, bahasa adalah memainkan peranan yang amat penting di dalam profesion peguam, khususnya dalam membuat penghujjahan di mahkamah. Kini hampir keseluruhan perbicaraan di mahkamah telah dijalankan di dalam Bahasa Malaysia. Ini bermakna keupayaan Bahasa Malaysia di bidang undang-undang memang tidak boleh disangsikan lagi. Bahasa Inggeris hanya digunakan dalam keadaan tertentu dan untuk kepentingan keadilan sahaja. Usaha-usaha yang pesat juga sedang dilaksanakan oleh Jabatan Kehakiman bagi membantu memudahkan pelaksanaan penggunaan Bahasa Malaysia di mahkamah.

Kita seharusnya mengambil iktibar dari negara-negara yang mengamalkan bahasa ibunda mereka di dalam dan di luar mahkamah dengan secara menyeluruh. Kalau mereka boleh melakukannya maka tidaklah mustahil untuk kita menjadikan Bahasa Malaysia sebagai bahasa undang-undang di Malaysia.

Mahasiswa-mahasiswi Universiti Islam Antarabangsa jurusan undang-undang adalah dianggap golongan bakal-bakal peguam yang bertuah kerana sebahagian besar daripada mereka berupaya menggunakan Bahasa Malaysia dan Bahasa Inggeris. Namun demikian, mahasiswa dan mahasiswi sekalian haruslah terus berusaha untuk memperbaiki Bahasa Malaysia untuk kepentingan kerjaya masing-masing.

Dengan kesedaran kepentingan penggunaan Bahasa Malaysia di mahkamah kini dan tatasusila profesion peguam, maka saya benar-benar berharap agar program seumpama ini akan sentiasa diadakan sebagai satu kesinambungan untuk memenuhi cita-cita pihak-pihak yang berkenaan. Melalui program seumpama ini juga adalah diharapkan agar kita dapat melahirkan peguam-peguam yang benar-benar berkualiti pada masa hadapan demi untuk kepentingan keadilan.

Maka di sini saya, didahului dengan ucapan segala pujian kepada Allah SWT. dengan sukacitanya merasmikan pelancaran "Kursus Pengenalan Profesion Peguam".

CLAW THE FACTS*

Terlebih dahulu saya ingin mengucapkan ribuan terima kasih kepada Jawatankuasa Majlis Makan Malam Pra-Graduan, Kajian Pentadbiran dan Undang-Undang 1991 yang telah sudi menjemput saya dan isteri saya ke Majlis yang permai ini dan memberi penghormatan kepada saya melahirkan sepatah dua kata.

Sukacita saya mengambil peluang ini untuk mengucapkan tahniah kepada pihak ITM yang telah berjaya mengeluarkan graduan-graduan lulusan undang-undang. Kejayaan yang telah dicapai oleh ITM yang perlu diberi kepujian adalah pada hemat saya hasil peningkatan pentadbiran dan usaha-usaha gigih bertujuan mencapai satu tahap pengeluaran lulusan undang-undang yang membanggakan terutama sekali di kalangan bumiputra. Kejayaan adalah ternyata memandangkan banyak di antara mereka yang berkelulusan undang-undang telah pun menjawat jawatan tinggi dalam badan-badan swasta dan juga dalam kehakiman. Syukur Alhamdulillah.

Pada malam 24hb Mac, 1989 di Majlis yang serupa saya telah menyatakan bahawa ITM mampu mengeluarkan graduan-graduan yang berkaliber. Saya ulangi kenyataan sedemikian oleh kerana pada hemat saya, apa yang telah saya lahirkan dua tahun dahulu jelas terbukti. Saya juga percaya suatu hari nanti mereka yang mendapat kelulusan di ITM pasti memainkan peranan yang lebih bertanggungjawab dalam badan kehakiman khususnya di peringkat mahkamah-mahkamah atasan.

Setiap graduan yang telah mendapat didikan ITM sewajarnya berbangga kerana ITM adalah sesuatu institusi pengajian tinggi yang terbaik di rantau ini dan adalah jelas telah banyak menyumbangkan jasa terhadap negara terutama sekali dari segi pengeluaran graduan-graduan yang kian meningkat untuk menampung keperluan negara. Justeru itu ITM pada hakikat telah berjaya membuka peluang keemasan kepada warganegara terutama sekali orang-orang Melayu yang sebelum merdeka dahulu kurang menikmati peluang yang sedemikian.

Dengan bertambah pengeluaran graduan-graduan terutama graduan-graduan undang-undang berkaliber, saya yakin pencapaian serupa ini bukan

---

**Di Majlis Makan Malam Pra-graduan Kajian Pentadbiran Dan Undang-Undang ITM 1991 Di Pacific Ballroom, Hotel Pan Pacific Kuala Lumpur, Pada 26hb April, 1991.*

sahaja memenuhi kehendak negara bahkan akan membantu menyumbangkan tenaga intellektual sejajar dengan dan menandingi pertumbuhan ekonomi yang pesat.

Pada malam 24hb Mac, 1989 juga saya telah menyentuh sedikit tentang perlaksanaan pengguna Bahasa Malaysia di Mahkamah dan sebagaimana yang tuan-tuan maklum perlaksanaan penuh telah pun dikuatkuasa pada 1hb Jun, 1990 dan berjalan lancar. Sehubungan ini adalah tepat bagi saya memerhatikan bahawa walaupun demikian tidaklah wajar seseorang peguam mengabaikan kecekapan pertuturan dan penulisan dalam Bahasa Inggeris kerana sebagaimana kita semua maklum Inggeris adalah bahasa yang dipertuturkan diserata dunia — it's a universal language. Oleh yang demikian adalah manafaat bagi seseorang itu cekap dalam kedua-dua bahasa ini.

Saya beralih kepada topik "Practice in the Legal Profession". Benarkan saya melahirkan suatu pesanan yang penting kepada mereka yang akan praktis sebagai seorang peguam.

"Claw the facts." The paramount objective of "clawing the facts" of a case is to study them diligently, that is to say, with the utmost care in every aspect and from every angle, of tearing them about and of turning them inside out and mastering every ingredient of substance that is to be extracted from them. If the facts of a case are thoroughly well appreciated and digested the law which is applicable to the case tends to become reasonably plain.

Let me illustrate what I have just said by one or two examples. Late in 1973, in the United Kingdom, the question of an address for the removal of a judge — Sir John Donaldson, then President of the Industrial Relations Court and now Master of the Rolls, arose. In October of that year, that Court had made an order to sequester certain assets held in the political funds of the Amalgamated Union of Engineering Workers, but it refused to comply with the order. There then followed a campaign of criticism by trade unions and labour back benchers against Sir John and a motion was tabled in Parliament calling for Sir John's removal from office for "political prejudice and partiality". Sir John then broke judicial tradition by defending the decision of the Court in public when he made a speech at the Institute of Chartered Accountants' Dinner. In the course of the speech Sir John made the following preliminary remarks "As some members of the Union and some members of the public seem to have misunderstood what occurred, may I take this opportunity of setting the record straight". Sir John then explained that "neither the sequestrator nor the Court had any knowledge that this £200,000 was earmarked for a political or any other purpose". The motion in Parliament fell into abeyance when Parliament rose for the Christmas recess.

I mention the experience of Sir John to show how important it is "to claw the facts", that is to say, know all the material facts before you arrive at any conclusion. In Sir John's case his critics were not aware that neither the sequestrator nor the court knew that the funds sequestrated had been earmarked for a political purpose, yet they launched on their campaign to have him removed. In doing so, they had also breached the rule of natural justice which requires that each party be heard.

This brings me to a personal matter. I have been recently criticised severely by some members of the Bar for having admitted to the Malaysian Bar the daughter of a certain Minister of the Government on a day when many other petitioners were also admitted to the Bar by a judge of the High Court in Kuala Lumpur. Like Sir John, I too would like to set the record straight by directing my critics' attention to one cogent fact. I had no knowledge, at the time I made the order of admission and enrolment, that there were other petitioners who were on that very day seeking admission to the Bar before a High Court Judge.

In the absence of that element i.e. knowledge, there was no basis whatsoever to found an allegation of discrimination. An admission to the Bar by a Lord President or Chief Justice or any Supreme Court Judge of any particular person or persons by itself is not *per se* discrimination. The courts do accommodate occasional requests for a particular judge to preside at an admission ceremony which, where there is no objection to such an admission, is strictly a formality. Many such admissions had been made in the past.

Still on the subject of practice in the legal profession may I add that you are in name and in fact engaged in a learned and honourable profession. The discipline of law sharpens your power of analysis. Your training is such as to make you fit not only to understand but to communicate your understanding. If you study law alone as an independent source of knowledge but lacking in communication skills of that knowledge and also if you study law without appreciating the national history, economics and sociology you will not be able to make your contribution to the nation although you may be able to make a dignified living. If you do not have a balanced vision and a well-rounded competence you will just become a cog in the wheel of corporate society. You must realise that the future of our nation is in the hands of young people like you. In a time of rapid change you must avoid adjusting to every passing wind. On the other hand you must continue to grow which involves changes in attitudes. If growth is to be organic, it must be determined in part by important elements in our past. Through the study of our own traditions we retain a core of continuity out of which order and stability emerge and without which human personality and group organizations are liable to be broken down. While there should be changes from time to time such changes must be linked to the past if we are to retain a secure and stable identity. Yet we must be critical and creative and must not allow ourselves to be dominated solely by traditions. Be that as it may, we must be careful not to fall into the opposite error and sweep out all traditional vestiges. It is essential that you think for yourselves about the aspects of traditional practice which have value and relevance and those which are obstacles to the progress of our developing and plural society. One danger you have to watch is false and subtle propaganda in the name of freedom. Meanings of phraseologies like democracy, rule of law, freedom and sovereignty are elusive and capable of being distorted.

Tujuan saya di sini ialah untuk menekankan bahawa pelajaran itu tidaklah berakhir dengan pencapaian sesuatu ijazah atau diploma dan juga mengadakan sesuatu majlis makan malam seperti mana yang diadakan pada malam ini. Setiap negara perlu mengadakan undang-undang yang sesuai dengan keadaan tersendiri. Sehubungan ini tuan-tuan sewajarnya membantu dengan menyumbangkan kritik dan penyelesaian yang membina 'but be on the guard so that you are not carried away blindly by foreign ideals and also be on guard against what is spoonfed into your fresh and receptive brain by people whose views can destabilise what has been achieved by our leaders during the past three decades following independence'.

Saya akhiri dengan ucapan ribuan terima kasih dan maaf zahir batin.

CONSTRUCTION LAW*

It is a great honour for Malaysia to host the First International Conference on Asia-Pacific Construction Law. This privilege is clearly shared by the University Technology Malaysia, the principal organizer of the Conference and also the Institute of Surveyors, the Public Works Department, the Master Builders Association Malaysia and the Chartered Institute of Building Malaysian Branch as co-organizers. The University Technology Malaysia deserves to be congratulated for its pioneer efforts in organizing this Conference. I deem it a great honour to be invited to address the Conference. Before I move on I take this occasion to welcome those from overseas to our country. I wish to add that we are grateful for your esteemed presence and participation, and I congratulate those who have written thought provoking papers for the Conference. We are inspired and stimulated by the fact that this is not just an ordinary conference but an inaugural one, the brain child of great luminaries and illustrious economists presumably wizards of the construction industry in the Asian Pacific region. This country is indeed privileged to host this Conference.

Purpose of the Conference

This Conference is in my view very timely as Malaysia is on the threshold of an ambitious and successful economic planning programme. The construction industry is looking extremely bright and promising and I am confident that the Conference will be a great success and help in the progress of the construction scene in this region. No man is an island and the Conference is hopefully oriented towards decision makers in the industry including bankers, architects, engineers, quantity surveyors and manufacturers, suppliers both local and from overseas. In our objective to achieve economic progress particular attention shall have to be given to the role of law.

It is an established fact that the construction industry is a major economic factor in countries in the Asia-Pacific Region where constructions are effected on the basis of agreement by parties using either local or international contract forms and documents. It is with a view to deliberating on common problems arising therefrom and in that regard searching for acceptable solutions in con-

**At The First International Conference Of Asian-pacific Construction Law Held On 25th June, 1991 At Dewan Tun Hussein Onn Putra World Trade Centre, Kuala Lumpur.*

formity with law that this Conference is organized. What appears crystal clear therefore is that law plays a very significant role.

Role of Law

Law may be regarded as a benign facilitating mechanism, making transactions possible between men and solving awkward problems as they arise. Alternatively, law may be seen as a mechanism of social control regulating activities and interests in the name of community as an impartial institution for the furtherance and protection of the welfare of everyone. Law cannot operate in vacuum and the understanding of the law is not complete unless the subject matter is examined in close relationship to the social, economic and political contexts in which they are created and operate. Law must ideally correspond to the general economic conditions and be its expression. Law cannot be the spirit of the people unless it is a rational response to their needs and desires. Legal philosophers maintain that legal development lies not so much in legislation, juristic science or in judicial declaration of law but in society itself. Private arrangements whereby parties make their own agreement from social and moral consciousness will not be ignored by the courts provided such arrangements are not against public policy or illegal. Failure to comply with standardized formalities and practices of law need not necessarily be fatal in all cases.

Legal development and society

Legal development is often woven into the general fabric of society and law should rejuvenate itself by clearing away its own past. Society's values fluctuate dependant, among other reasons, upon economic and political conditions, the activity of the legislature and the energy and opinion of economic, spiritual and political leaders of society at a given time. No group enterprise is to be looked at in an isolated manner but in relation to the overall social structure and its maintenance through its activities as a consumer unit.

In the present context of world events, no single group occupies a self-sufficient position as both consumer and producer and middlemen are required for satisfaction of every need of the community. This interdependence is the keynote of social solidarity.

Objects of Law

One of the objects of law is to solve grievances by trying to restore the complainant to the position he was in prior to the dispute provided he is not at fault. Apart from the legal machinery a resolution to a conflict can be achieved within a framework of negotiation, arbitration and electoral battle, and many other ways like strikes or lockouts in a constitutional manner, without resort to violence. Law in a secular society like ours is not considered as divine. Justice which the courts are able to grant is only a tolerable accommodation and a balancing of conflicting interests of society. Courts are not a royal road to successful solution of all problems. It has been said by an American jurist that law is not logic but the embodiment of experience. The wills and actions of society are not regulated by convenience but by social necessity. Unless law is periodically changed to harmonise with rapid social changes in this atomic age it will remain static. Law and legal arrangements exist for the benefit of people and not vice versa. Law is for people including the business community.

Regional Development of Construction Law

I understand from the agenda that one important topic for discussion today is the regional development of construction law. In the light of successful co-operation among ASEAN countries, that should not be an impossible task. The quest for law is a task to be accompanied by all jurists in common each acting in a given sphere and using his own technique always inspired by a common ideal aimed at conforming to the general sense of justice—a justice founded on a reconciliation of all kinds of interests of private individuals and the community at large. The concept of an ASEAN Pacific region legal system knit together by a common system of basic values is ideal. However, sharp differences resulting from local historical backgrounds, social attitudes, national ideological and political ambitions have until recently prevented us from proceeding with success. Yet we now stand in closer partnership and the phenomenal achievements of modern means of transportation, science, technology and co-operation have created a regional sense of independence. There is an improved feeling of regional identity and cohesion. But the task is not easy and caution is needed before we implement any fundamental change.

Changes of legal concepts based on Common Law

It must be remembered that in this connection many of the English legal concepts based on common law have been recently changed and the effect of such changes cannot be ignored. By way of illustration let me quote some examples, which may be of interest to you, if you are not already aware. In *Smith* v *Bush* (1987) 3 WLR 889 the House of Lords distinguished the time honoured dictum of *Hedley Byrne* v *Heller and Partners Ltd* (1964) AC 465 and decided that valuers who prepared valuations for mortgage purposes but failed to exercise reasonable care and skill are liable for damages to house buyers who relied on the negligent valuation to their detriment, notwithstanding disclaiming liability. The House of Lords in August 1989 in the case of *Murphy* v *Brentwod DC*

(1990) 3 WLR 414, a new landmark decision in construction law, reversed the 12-year-old decision of *Anns* v *Merton L.B.* (1977) 2 All ER 492. In *Murphy's* case it was held, allowing the appeal, that, "where a defect was discovered before any injury to person or health or damage to property other than the defective house itself had been done, the expense incurred by a subsequent purchaser of the house in putting the defect right was pure economic loss; and that to hold that a local authority, in supervising compliance with the building regulations or byelaws, was under a common law duty to take reasonable care to avoid putting a purchaser of a house in a position in which he would be obliged to incur such economic loss was an extension of principle that should not, as a matter of policy, be affirmed (post. pp. 419D-E, 424A-B, 425F-426A, 428A, 429D-E, 432A, 433D-E, F, 435E-436A, 440G-H, 441D, 442E-G, 443H, 448E-G, 450C, 451E-F 457A-C)."

"*Per Curiam*. Such extension of principle would necessarily extend also to the builder of the house and would logically also extend to the manufacturer of a defective chattel. There is much to be said for the view that in what is essentially a consumer protection field the precise extent and limits of the liabilities that in the public interest should be imposed on the builders and local authorities are best dealt with by the legislature, as in the Defective Premises Act 1972 (post, pp. 419A-B, 429H-430A, 433C-D, 442D, E-G, 451C-D, 457C-D)."

In *Caparo Industries Pte* v *Dickman*(1990) 1 All ER 568 the House of Lords decided that an auditor owed no duty of care to an individual shareholder in the Company to buy more shares. While the changes may apply to us, subject to local interpretation by our courts based upon the unique circumstances of each case, let us now focus our attention on construction law.

Building contracts

In the case of building contracts there are many thorny areas where the law cannot be said to be absolutely certain. The last two decades have seen the rapid development of construction law. Although construction law is based on the ordinary law of contract, a sound knowledge of building contracts can be very useful to lawyers. Time prevents me from going into minute details but to appreciate the complexity of building law, which is not easy, let me point out some areas which have created problems in the building industry. These are, for example:–

(a) whether an estimate can be accepted as a firm offer;

(b) whether a letter of intent would give rise to a binding contract;

(c) what terms can be applied in a building contract;

(d) the need for the main contract and subcontract to exist with each other;

(e) what are the duties and powers of an architect especially in relation to issue of completion certificate;

(f) liquidated damages and extension of time;

(g) whether wasted expenditure can be claimed in the event of breach of contract;

(h) the scope of arbitration;

(i) whether direct payment to a sub-contractor is in order in view of the many conflicting decisions;

(j) the battle of standard forms;

(k) disruption and protected processing of claims.

Building contract problems

In this regard you may wish to refer to the book by Vincent Powell-Smith entitled *Some Building Contract Problems*. I would also like to mention that many of the cases before the courts indicate that the construction industry's business is carried on in happy indifference or ignorance of the rapid changes in law with the result that the industry is a major benefactor of the legal and consulting professions. As I do not wish to turn this Conference into a classroom I would however observe that there are, I believe, sufficient local professional literature dealing with these points and reading them will not only be useful but will also be an intellectual pleasure. I hope that you will not consider me irrelevant or legalistic if I say from my experience that contracting organizations are often very lax when it comes to completing contractual formalities. In the case of many large projects the work is nearly completed before the actual documents are signed. One interesting point peculiar to building contracts is the use of standard forms. Very often local housing developers do not realistically estimate expenditure and cash flow. At this juncture it seems appropriate to direct our attention to the use of standard forms.

Standard forms

With regard to standard forms, you may feel that the provisions are outdated. Terms and conditions are lengthy and printed in small type on the back of forms. This practice may be against a businessman's desire to keep it simple and avoid red tape. Businessmen neither have the time nor the ability to analyse the small prints. Humorously, it has been said that "You can settle any dispute if you keep lawyers and accountants out of it". Lord Denning analyses the problems by stating that: "The difficulty is to decide which form or which part of which form is a term or condition of the contract. In some cases the battle is won by the man who fires the last shot. He is the man who puts forward the latest terms and conditions and if they are not objected to by the other party, he may be taken to have agreed with them". Lord Denning adds: "If the differences are irreconcilable so they are mutually contradictory, then the conflicting terms may have to be replaced by a reasonable implication". His Lordship's views may be a bit farfetched as his suggestion may amount to the court rewriting the contract for the parties. Another problem I have come across occasionally is that many people do not read and digest standard form contracts, some make assumptions which had no basis in reality. I can only remind all concerned of the proverb "For want of a nail, the kingdom was lost".

International standard contract forms

In this regard, I note that this Conference will also consider the possibility of internationally agreed series of standard contract forms for use throughout the region. The thought is timely as one hardly finds any construction scheme which is not a joint venture with a foreign nation to the mutual advantage of the parties. Such participation promotes the economic growth worldwide.

Committee of experts

All said and done, solutions to problems arising from divergent legal systems is not easy to tackle and can be achieved only over a period of time. However, consideration can be given to this Conference delegating the task to appropriate committees of experts to start work on the basis. As an example of regional modification of laws, let me quote the example of the United Kingdom. The Treaty of Rome (1957) involving the United Kingdom Government, which established the European Economic Community, made provision, *inter alia*, for the harmonisation of the legal codes of member states to the extent required for the proper functioning of the common market. It is therefore only proper to consider the viability of Asia-Pacific legal systems being adapted to our regional requirement. I will not say it is a dream but it is a vision in the future horizon. No legal system can avoid borrowing and transplanting from other systems but the practical fact remains that the bulk of construction law is based on Anglo-Saxon law.

In Malaysia and Singapore we follow English Common Law where there is no statutory provision otherwise and where circumstances permit for historical reasons although, as time marches on, in addition to legislative developments we develop our own independent legal system which may be called Malaysian Common Law. As a first step, we have made it virtually mandatory to use the National Language in the Courts.

Arbitration or courtroom litigation

Leaving the question of modification and unification of laws on an Asia-Pacific regional basis, let me touch on the question of the practical effects of resorting to litigation instead of arbitration or settlement by other means. Adjustments of business relationship and dispute settlement by litigation has many disadvantages which sometimes outweigh the benefits. If a trial takes place the company may lose many days work from several key people. A breach of contract suit may settle a particular dispute but it may end in a "divorce" ending the "marriage" between the rival business parties. The executives have to face the prospect of being cross-examined in public. Finally after all, litigation may be a form of gamble. The outcome of a case depends on so many contingencies not capable of being accurately predicted. The lawyers can only indicate the degree of probabilities of success or failure. Even judges cannot hypothetically give an opinion as all cases are decided on the basis of the evidence and arguments of both sides.

In this context without embarking on a wide discussion, it is only fair to add that legal control with its "winner-takes-all" litigation are by no means the only form of regulating the actions of society. There is a complex framework of economic, administrative and political control by government, as a matter of necessity. The judiciary, in the name of creativity, cannot trespass into the rightful constitutional province of the executive or legislature. Policy planning, social services, equitable distribution of scarce resources and its disposal and similar matters are within such province. It is important that matters such as housing, transport facilities, environment, land use and planning industrial relations are organized, planned and managed on a collective public basis by government and its administrative units and agencies as they are consumed collectively.

Please permit me now to add some remarks on corollary matters which I wish to bring to your attention.

Professional ethics

I am sad to say without casting any aspersion on any group in particular that many professionals do not maintain ideal ethical standards. It must be realised that duty to a particular client or customer is outweighed by the duty to community. For example, architects have a responsibility for public safety and environmental considerations overreaching their duty to clients.

Economic aspects of construction industry

Incidentally but not irrelevantly in this context, I would like to add a few words which concern the industry as a whole. Apart from legal topics I wish to refer to the economic aspects of the construction industry, especially in relation to foreign participation. Historically, there is a close relationship between our countries' economic growth and that of the construction/housing industry. Foreigners are neither prevented nor restricted from participating in the local housing industry so long as their involvement is in accordance with the local laws and regulations that need to be adhered to. Their participation can be through direct involvement in housing development projects either solely or through joint ventures with local developers/agencies. Participation can also be through the provision of goods, services and expertise such as construction, management and consulting services. It will be superfluous for me to emphasise our capacity to use refined and sophisticated material both from the east and west. A look around Kuala Lumpur will convince you of the gigantic progress we have made.

It seems appropriate at this point that I touch briefly on the new Malaysian Development Policy outlined by our Prime Minister in Parliament on the 17th of this month. Emphasis is placed on socio-economic development for a better quality of life and national integration.

According to the Prime Minister, the second Outline Perspective Plan (OPP2) 1991-2000 which embodies the New Development Policy (NDP) signals the beginning of a new era in Malaysia's effort to make her a fully developed nation by the year 2020.

The Prime Minister has stressed the need for the Government to continue to be flexible and pragmatic in the implementation of its policies and programmes so as to create a favourable climate for better investment and for the economy to move towards higher levels of industrialisation — in particular to upgrade the country's infrastructure facilities.

While optimism seems to be the order of the day, the Prime Minister has cautioned that the private sector needs to rise to the occasion and play a more active role towards the realisation of our goal — taking advantage of the opportunities made available by the Government.

By and large Malaysia's growth and structural transformation targets towards year 2000 will hinge on the performance of the international economy, and if I may add, would conceivably hinge on the economic co-operation among the Asian-Pacific nations and Malaysia's ability to position itself to take advantage of the opportunity in world trade expansion.

Conclusion

To conclude, let me assure you that your entire deliberations will be watched with interest and your representations will be considered by the relevant authorities. It may well be that in certain areas of your suggestions the blessings of the Government and legislature will be needed. However, where justified and circumstances permit, I have no doubt that your suggestion will be favourably viewed.

I am afraid that I have already overstayed your hospitality and I now take leave and hope that we shall meet again at the next Conference. Let me pray that the initial enthusiasm shall not wither amidst professional preoccupation. May I wish those from overseas a safe journey home.

SUMBANGAN KEWANGAN BAGI PUSAT SPASTIK*

Mengadap DYMM Sultan Selangor Darul Ehsan.
Ampun Tuanku beribu-ribu ampun, sembah patik harap diampun.
Dengan segala hormat dan takzimnya patik bagi pihak Ahli Jawatankuasa Pengurusan Persatuan Kanak-Kanak Spastik Selangor Darul Ehsan dan Wilayah Persekutuan merafak sembah menjunjung kasih yang tidak terhingga di atas kesudian Duli Tuanku berangkat mencemar Duli bersama YM Che Puan Aishah ke Majlis Malam Kenangan Jasa ini.

Keberangkatan Kebawah Duli ke Majlis Makan Malam ini sudah pasti akan memberi inspirasi kepada semua yang berkenaan untuk menjayakan 'Malam Kenangan Jasa' ini.

Ampuan Tuanku,
Minat Kebawah Duli Tuanku di atas kebajikan kanak-kanak di Pusat Spastik sangat-sangatlah dihargai dan disanjung tinggi. Lebih-lebih lagi di atas minat Duli Tuanku mengikuti segala perkembangan dan kegiatan Pusat Spastik dari masa ke semasa. Duli Yang Maha Mulia Tuanku juga berangkat melawat Pusat Spastik setiap tahun disamping itu mengurniakan sumbangan kewangan.

Tujuan mengadakan 'Malam Kenangan Jasa' ini ialah untuk mengucapkan penghargaan kepada para dermawan atas sumbangan kewangan mereka dari masa ke semasa, disamping itu merayu sokongan kewangan mereka yang terus menerus supaya projek untuk memperluaskan bangunan dan bengkel dapat di sempurnakan dengan jayanya.

Projek untuk memperluaskan bangunan dan bengkel tersebut adalah difikirkan perlu supaya lebih lagi kanak-kanak spastik dapat menerima pendidikan, pemulihan serta rawatan dengan percuma. Bengkel yang baru dengan kelengkapan yang moden akan memberi peluang latihan untuk dewasa spastik. Projek ini bermula dengan pemberian sekeping tanah seluas 1.2 ekar oleh Kerajaan Negeri Selangor Darul Ehsan. Selepas itu rancangan telah diadakan untuk mengutip derma bagi membiayai projek ini dan setakat ini, derma lebih daripada satu juta ringgit telah dikutip. Kerja-kerja pembinaan untuk Projek ini telah ditangguhkan beberapa kali atas sebab-sebab yang tidak

---

**Di Persatuan Kanak-kanak Spastik Selangor Dan Wilayah Persekutuan Sempena 'Malam Kenangan Jasa' Pada 29hb November, 1991 Di Hotel Regent Kuala Lumpur.*

dapat dielakkan. Kini kos pembinaan untuk projek ini telah melambung ke hampir tiga juta ringgit dan sekurang-kurangnya satu juta ringgit lagi diperlukan untuk menjayakan projek ini.

Kerja pembinaan untuk Projek ini akan bermula pada awal tahun 1992 dan akan siap dibina pada akhir tahun 1993. Projek ini tidak dapat ditangguhkan lagi kerana kos pembinaan akan melambung lagi. Dengan yang demikian, sokongan yang penuh kepada projek ini amatlah dihargai.

Sebelum patik mengakhiri sekali lagi patik memohon ampun Kebawah Duli Tuanku dan merafak sembah menjunjung kasih di atas ampun perkenan Duli Yang Maha Mulia Tuanku berangkat menghaḍiri Majlis Makan Malam ini.

Dan juga patik ingin mengucapkan terima kasih kepada Dato' Lam Peng Chong, Pengerusi dan semua Ahli Jawatankuasa Pengelola atas usaha-usaha mereka untuk menjayakan Majlis Makan Malam ini. Terima kasih diucapkan kepada semua mereka yang telah memberi sokongan kewangan.

DARI ORDERLY KE KETUA HAKIM NEGARA*

Terlebih dahulu saya bersyukur ke hadrat Allah SWT yang telah mengizinkan kita semua berhimpun di majlis yang permai dan meriah ini. Dalam suasana yang meriah ini sukacita saya melahirkan ucapan ribuan terima kasih di atas kesudian pihak Kolej Pendita Za'ba, Universiti Pertanian Malaysia mengundang saya sebagai tetamu utama pada malam ini. Sukacita juga saya mengucapkan ribuan terima kasih bagi pihak isteri saya yang turut dijemput pada malam ini. Bagi diri saya, pemilihan untuk mengundang saya sebagai tetamu utama adalah sesuatu kehormatan yang saya sanjung tinggi dan Tuhan sahaja dapat membalas budi baik tuan-tuan dan puan-puan.

Saya diminta berucap sepatah dua kata mengenai perkara-perkara yang ada kaitan dengan peribadi, bermula dari tarikh saya kecil lagi hingga dewasa dan seterusnya ke hari ini. Jika saya diberi peluang untuk bercerita semua peristiwa yang telah berlaku dalam hidup saya selama enam dekad, tiga tahun dan sembilan bulan maka saya khuatir kita semua terpaksa bermalam di sini dan berkemungkinan saya akan sambung pada pagi esok. Oleh itu saya bercadang hanya berucap dengan ringkas sahaja dalam masa dua puluh minit yang dihadkan.

Saya dilahirkan di Kampung Nelayan, Kuala Perlis. Anak lelaki sulung kepada seorang guru sekolah Melayu dan ibu saya adalah seorang surirumah. Berayahkan seorang guru yang kemudiannya menjadi guru besar maka tidaklah hairan banyak penukaran tempat tinggal, dan oleh yang demikian saya dibesarkan khususnya di kawasan sekolah dari kecil hingga saya ke sekolah Inggeris di Alor Setar. Semasa berumur empat atau lima tahun saya dibesarkan di Kuala Perlis di Kampung Nelayan yang saya sebutkan tadi dan masih ingat satu peristiwa di mana saya hampir lemas dalam sungai waktu bermandi dan bermain bersama-sama dengan beberapa saudara kecil yang lain. Dan pada satu hari yang lain, saya bersama-sama dengan dua orang saudara juga berumur lima dan enam tahun hampir-hampir hanyut ke laut dalam sebuah perahu kecil.

Masa beredar dan genap sepuluh tahun saya telah diletak di bawah jagaan bapa saudara saya, guru besar Sekolah Melayu Kangar. Tujuannya adalah untuk diri saya dilatih dan membuat persediaan menghadapi peperiksaan untuk biasiswa ke sekolah Inggeris Alor Setar. Ini diadakan penghujung tahun 1939,

---

**Di Majlis Jamuan Malam Pendita Pada 3hb Januari, 1992 Di Dewan Makan, Kolej Pendita Za'ba, Universiti Pertanian Malaysia, Serdang, Selangor Darul Ehsan.*

di mana lebih kurang lima puluh orang memasuki peperiksaan dan seorang sahaja dikehendaki untuk melanjutkan pelajaran di Maktab Sultan Abdul Hamid Alor Setar. Dengan berkat Allah SWT. saya dipilih pada bulan Januari 1940 untuk masuk ke sekolah Inggeris dan tinggal di Asrama di kawasan sekolah. Selepas bersekolah selama dua tahun maka peperangan telah tercetus iaitu pada bulan Disember 1941. Oleh sebab Tanah Melayu ditakhluki Jepun maka saya terpaksa balik ke Perlis. Sekolah ditutup. Pada masa itu saya berumur lebih kurang tiga belas tahun. Dalam masa penakhlukkan Jepun sebilangan besar penuntut-penuntut Inggeris dan yang lain ke sekolah Jepun. Bersekolah selama lebih kurang tujuh atau lapan bulan, saya boleh dikatakan cekap berbahasa Jepun, mungkin lebih dari Jepun. Maka dalam zaman itulah banyak penukaran cara hidup bagi kebanyakan orang-orang Tanah Melayu termasuk juga bekas-bekas penuntut sekolah aliran Inggeris. Dalam pemerintahan Jepun, barang-barang keperluan susah didapati seperti beras, gula dan sebagainya. Bagi diri saya, selepas lapan bulan di sekolah Jepun maka saya diambil bekerja sebagai seorang Interpreter kepada Mr. Sakai San, C.I. di Polis Headquarters, Alor Setar. Orangnya berhati baik tetapi garang pada penjenayah. Saya bekerja di sini beberapa bulan sahaja. Pada satu hari seorang India ditangkap di atas syaki 'black marketing' dan telah disoal berkenaan dengan barang-barang yang dimilikinya. Beliau menyangkal tuduhan 'black marketing'. Mr. Sakai San tidak sabar lagi dan mengambil kerusi kayu di hadapan meja dan memukul orang India itu dan saya lihat darah mengalir dari sebelah kepala. Tetapi beliau tidak jatuh. Saya terus jatuh kerana tidak tahan melihat darah dan akibatnya saya berada di hospital lebih kurang sebulan (Shock). Ekoran dari peristiwa itu, saya terus berhenti kerja dan balik ke Perlis. Pada masa itu Perlis, Kedah, Kelantan berada di bawah pentadbiran Negeri Thai. Saya terpaksa memohon pekerjaan untuk tidak membuang masa dan meminta kerja sebagai kerani sementara dengan Sekretariat Kerajaan Negeri, malangnya permohonan saya ditolak. Sekretariat Kerajaan Negeri bersedia menerima saya sebagai Orderly. Dengan tidak memilih kerja, saya terima dan mula berkhidmat sebagai Orderly selama lebih kurang dua tahun hingga tamat peperangan pada tahun 1945. Pada hemat saya pengalaman ini banyak memberi manfaat pada saya.

Saya sebutkan awal tadi berkenaan pengajian bahasa Jepun. Saya dapati mereka bukan sahaja mengajar menerusi berbualan dan penulisan, tetapi guru-guru Jepun menggunakan teknik yang lebih baik untuk membolehkan penuntut-penuntut lebih fasih dalam bahasa Jepun. Ini adalah dengan cara lagu-lagu Jepun dan memahami makna lagu-lagu yang dipelajari.

Dalam masa pemerintahan Jepun oleh sebab kekurangan beras, gula dan sebagainya maka saya seorang yang kuat lari dari kecil lagi sering masuk pertandingan 'athletic' bagi kategori yang tertentu bertujuan memenangi hadiah yang tepat pada masa itu seperti beras, gula yang perlu bagi setiap isi rumah.

Peperangan berakhir pada tahun 1945. Selepas pemerintahan Jepun pada bulan Oktober, 1945 dan untuk menyambung semula pelajaran ke sekolah Inggeris selepas ditinggalkan selama tiga tahun lapan bulan, maka kami semua tidak dapat bertutur dalam Bahasa Inggeris dengan betul. Di waktu Pentadbiran Ketenteraan Inggeris—barang-barang keperluan seperti beras, gula dan sebagainya adalah kurang. Oleh itu penuntut-penuntut di asrama terpaksa diberi makan pulut, ubi dan sebagainya untuk menampung kekurangan beras.

When I was young I was under the influence of P. Ramlee and wanted to be a singer. But my real ambition was to be a lawyer. When I left school in 1950 I applied to the Perlis State Government for a scholarship to read law. I was not successful and joined the University of Singapore to do a course in Arts. My contemporaries include Tan Sri Thong Yew Hong, Rama Iyer, the late Hisham, Tan Sri Abdul Salleh and Tan Sri Hashim Yeop Sani who has just retired as the Chief Justice. In my examination I was referred in one subject. I again approached the State Government for a scholarship to read law but was turned down.

It is my father who was responsible for what I am today. I asked him to consider sending me to England to read law. My mother supported me and my father sold a piece of land of about seven acres and after securing about $6,000 from the Chartered Bank, Alor Setar, sent me to London. However, I had to learn Latin first before proceeding to England. My teacher in Latin was one Mr. Thiagarajah of 75, Pitt Street, Penang. He also assisted me in my application to join the Inns of Court. While learning Latin I stayed in Butterworth for about nine months in 1952. Ater that I left for London to sit for my Latin examination. But, on my arrival there I was told that it was no longer necessary to sit for the Latin examination. I then started on my law course at the Inns of Court.

In London things were not as rosy as I thought them to be—many items were being rationed. I stayed with Tunku Ahmad Yahya, the Chief Executive Director of Sime Darby and Dato' Dr. Osman Din who has now retired from Government service. I must also mention Tan Sri Jamil Rais who had become the State Secretary after having been Commissioner for Lands. He felt that I had not been fairly treated in the award of a scholarship and therefore asked my father to re-apply for one. Although there was some opposition to my application in the Scholarship Board the majority felt that I should be given the scholarship. I was given the scholarship and the fees that I had paid was refunded. For that reason Tan Sri Jamil Rais is my godfather.

I came back in 1956 and started service as a Magistrate. I have been the State Legal Adviser in three states. I have also served as the Chief Registrar and Parliamentary Draftsman.

Sekian, terima kasih.

PENTERJEMAHAN BIDANG UNDANG-UNDANG: KEPENTINGANNYA*

Saya bersyukur ke hadrat Allah SWT kerana dengan taufik dan hidayahnya dapat saya bersama-sama dengan tuan-tuan dan puan-puan dalam majlis ini. Tidak lupa juga saya mengucapkan terima kasih kepada urusetia majlis ini yang telah sudi menjemput dan memberi peluang kepada saya untuk menyampaikan sepatah dua kata dan seterusnya menyempurnakan penyampaian sijil kepada peserta yang telah berjaya dalam kursus penterjemahan modul undang-undang yang pertama ini.

Hadirin yang dihormati sekalian.
Ilmu dan teknologi merupakan wahana penting untuk membina sebuah negara. Dalam konteks negara kita yang sedang pesat membangun, pemindahan ilmu dan teknologi, terutama yang berasal dari Barat dan Timur begitu mendesak. Desakan ini hanya dapat dilakukan melalui pemindahan ilmu yang tentunya didokong oleh usaha penterjemahan.

Sejarah membuktikan bahawa kemajuan yang dicapai oleh tamadun barat sekarang ini diperolehi melalui pemindahan ilmu dari zaman kegemilangan Islam melalui penterjemahan karya sarjana-sarjana Islam. Usaha ini mempunyai kesinambungan dengan kemajuan pembinaan ilmu dan teknologi tinggi kini.

Bidang terjemahan bukan sahaja menjadi industri yang mencabar malah memainkan peranan penting bagi kemajuan pesat sesebuah negara seperti yang dicapai oleh Jepun. Dengan perkataan lain, kemajuan Jepun juga didokong oleh usaha penterjemahan ilmu dari tamadun Barat ke tamadun Timur. Demikian juga di Malaysia, bidang terjemahan telah mendapat tempat dalam industri ilmu sejak akhir-akhir ini dan pihak kerajaan juga memberikan galakan ke arah memperbanyakkan hasil terjemahan dari bahasa asing ke Bahasa Malaysia dalam pelbagai bidang ilmu. Sokongan kuat kerajaan terhadap industri terjemahan ini terpancar dalam Belanjawan 1992, dalam mana kerajaan telah meluluskan peruntukan untuk penubuhan Biro Terjemahan Negara.

**Di Dalam Majlis Penyampaian Sijil Kursus Penterjemahan Modul Undang-Undang (Dewan Bahasa Dan Pustaka) Pada 25hb Januari, 1992 Di Kelab Darul Ehsan.*

Hadirin yang dihormati sekalian.
Sebagaimana yang tuan-tuan dan puan-puan sedia maklum bahawa bidang kehakiman dan perundangan juga tidak terpisah dengan proses pemindahan ilmu dari bahasa asing terutamanya Bahasa Inggeris ke Bahasa Malaysia. Kita yakin bahawa proses ini akan berterusan sehinggalah Bahasa Malaysia dapat digunakan sepenuhnya dalam bidang kehakiman dan perundangan.

Pindaan kepada Seksyen 8 Akta Bahasa Kebangsaan 1963/67 dan pindaan kepada kaedah-kaedah mahkamah telah memberi kesan yang amat besar dalam mempercepatkan lagi penggunaan Bahasa Malaysia di bidang ini. Apabila pengumuman dibuat, bahawa bermula dari 1 Jun 1990, semua dokumen yang hendak difailkan di Mahkamah hendaklah dibuat dalam Bahasa Malaysia, maka pihak yang terlibat dalam perundangan terutamanya telah mula menunjukkan minat dan kesungguhan untuk menggunakan Bahasa Malaysia.

Perubahan yang berlaku ini ekoran dari pindaan ke undang-undang menyebabkan terdapatnya keperluan yang sangat mendesak kepada bahan rujukan undang-undang dalam Bahasa Malaysia sedangkan bahan-bahan tersebut tidak mencukupi. Keperluan ini hanya dapat dipenuhi jika usaha-usaha penterjemahan dalam bidang undang-undang dipercepatkan. Oleh itu saya berpendapat kursus yang diadakan ini adalah amat tepat memandangkan keperluan yang mendesak ini.

Mengenai bidang terjemahan undang-undang, saya berpendapat bahawa terjemahan bidang undang-undang lebih sukar dibandingkan dengan terjemahan bidang lain kerana ia bukan sahaja memerlukan kepakaran dalam bidang linguistik bahkan memerlukan pengetahuan yang mendalam tentang sistem undang-undang itu sendiri. Penterjemahan bidang undang-undang ini perlu dilakukan dengan setepatnya kerana kesempurnaan penggunaan bahasa menjamin tercapainya keadilan sepenuhnya. Oleh sebab itu, untuk menjadi penterjamah undang-undang yang baik, mereka haruslah menguasai bahasa sumber dan bahasa sasaran dengan baik dan memahami laras bahasa undang-undang teks sumber itu sendiri.

Dalam bidang penerbitan bahan undang-undang, kita dapat melihat usaha bersungguh-sungguh pihak Dewan Bahasa dan Pustaka dalam memperbanyak bahan rujukan undang-undang dan kegiatan, menyelaraskan dan memperlengkapkan istilah undang-undang dalam Bahasa Malaysia. Saya berharap Dewan Bahasa dan Pustaka akan terus memperluaskan peranannya sebagai badan penerbitan yang berpengaruh dan membantu mana-mana pihak yang berminat dalam menghasilkan bahan rujukan undang-undang yang lebih sempurna.

Akhir kata, saya mengucapkan tahniah kepada Dewan Bahasa dan Pustaka kerana menganjurkan kursus ini dan berharap Dewan Bahasa dan Pustaka akan terus mengadakan kursus seumpama ini pada masa akan datang. Kepada peserta kursus yang akan menerima sijil masing-masing pada hari ini, saya berharap pengetahuan yang diperolehi dapat membantu meningkatkan penghasilan bahan rujukan undang-undang.

PERKEMBANGAN UNDANG-UNDANG DAN MASYARAKAT KE ARAH WAWASAN 2020*

Terlebih dahulu saya bersyukur kehadrat Allah SWT. kerana dengan keizinannya kita berada dalam keadaan sihat dan oleh itu dapat bersama berhimpun di majlis ini.

Sukacita saya mengucapkan ribuan terima kasih kepada pihak penganjur persidangan ini kerana sudi menjemput saya dan seterusnya memberi penghormatan kepada saya untuk merasmikan pembukaan persidangan ini.

Sebagai permulaan, izinkan saya menyatakan bahawa, sebagai jenerasi muda, tanggungjawab saudara-saudari bukanlah untuk mencurigai nilai-nilai dan tradisi-tradisi lama, tetapi seharusnya menghidupkan semula nilai-nilai tersebut walaupun saudara-saudari menghadapi dilema-dilema dan masalah-masalah semasa.

Sebagaimana yang kita semua maklum, tajuk perbincangan yang saya akan memperkatakan hari ini adalah sesuatunya yang hangat diperkatakan pada masa kini (very topical). Tajuk ini sangat kompleks oleh yang demikian ianya memerlukan pertimbangan yang sangat teliti. Adalah benar jika saya mengatakan bahawa, tidak ada sesiapapun yang boleh meramalkan apa yang akan terjadi di masa hadapan dengan tepat, sama ada ramalan tersebut merentang dekad atau abad, melainkan Allah yang maha mengetahui. Sebagai insan biasa kita tidak boleh membuat ramalan. Kita perlu bertanggungjawab untuk membuat sesuatu dengan sebaik-baiknya dan pencapaiannya terserahlah kepada Allah, yang maha kuasa.

Pandangan-pandangan yang saya lahirkan adalah bergantung kepada jangkaan bahawa negara-negara perindustrian diuruskan dengan agak baik dan berjalan dengan teratur dalam tempoh beberapa dekad yang akan datang. Juga bergantung kepada tidak adanya sesuatu malapetaka antarabangsa.

Di sini saya mengambil peluang menggariskan sedikit garis dasar yang mungkin bagi para peserta sekalian untuk membincang dengan lebih mendalam. Faktor-faktor ini bukanlah konklusif ataupun komprehensif, tetapi bermaksud hanya, sebagai dorongan buah fikiran sahaja. Dalam konteks ini sebarang pandangan yang dinyatakan dalam ucapan ringkas ini, tidak seharus-

---

**Di Majlis Perasmian Seminar Undang-Undang Dan Masyarakat (Universiti Kebangsaan Malaysia) Di Dewan Tun Dr. Ismail, Pusat Dagangan Dunia Putra, Kuala Lumpur, Pada 27hb Januari, 1992.*

nya ditafsirkan sebagai pandangan-pandangan kehakiman. Pandangan-pandangan ini adalah pendapat persendirian.

Merujuk kepada tajuk perbincangan, maka soalnya adalah apakah yang kita faham mengenai undang-undang dan apakah hubungannya dengan masyarakat?

Salah satu unsur masyarakat manusia yang dapat dibezakan dengan kumpulan-kumpulan haiwan ialah peraturan-peraturan sosial. Apakah maksud "peraturan" dalam konteks ini? Peraturan yang dimaksudkan adalah peraturan yang menetapkan apa yang boleh, harus atau tidak harus dilakukan. Perlu diingatkan bahawa apa juapun definasi undang-undang, peraturan tersebut bukanlah suatu sistem tertutup yang beroperasi dengan cara tersendiri dan terpisah daripada konteks sosial. Pemahaman undang-undang tidak mungkin dicapai jika perkara tersebut tidak dikaji dalam konteks sosial, ekonomi dan politik dalam mana ia diujudkan, dikekalkan dan dilaksanakan. Bagi maksud perbincangan ini, istilah "masyarakat" pasti membayangkan pengumpulan manusia, institusi-institusi dan fenomena sosial yang lain di mana undang-undang didapati menduduki tempat ditengah-tengah dan mengaitkan kesemua susunan-susunan sosial. Tiap-tiap masyarakat bukan sahaja ada tabiatnya yang tersendiri bahkan juga perhubungan dan kepercayaan yang tertentu. Walaupun undang-undang adalah sesuatu teras yang melengkapkan struktur sosial, namun demikian ianya tidak boleh ditafsirkan sebagai sesuatu yang memisahkan kuasa-kuasa lain yang membentuk sesuatu masyarakat tertentu. Apakah faktor-faktor sosial lain yang membentuk mana-mana masyarakat? Sebahagian daripadanya adalah institusi-institusi politik seperti Parlimen, parti-parti politik, institusi-institusi ekonomi dan komersial, kesatuan sekerja, persatuan-persatuan pengeluar dan pembekal dan sebagainya. Bagi sesuatu sistem perundangan, maka sistem itu sewajarnya membayangkan keperluan, permintaan dan aspirasi masyarakat tersebut. Undang-undang sivil dan politik sesebuah negara adalah, secara umumnya, khusus bagi orang-orang di negara itu sendiri. Dan hanya secara kebetulan sahaja jika undang-undang di satu negara itu bersesuaian dengan negara yang lain.

Para hadirin sekalian,

Kita tidak boleh menilaikan moral dunia dengan menggunakan konvensyen Eropah mengenai hak-hak asasi manusia ataupun mana-mana piawaian seragam yang lain. Suatu contoh yang nyata ialah peruntukan yang terdapat dalam Perlembagaan Ireland yang melarang penceraian. Pada hemat saya, adalah jelas peruntukan ini bertentangan dengan hak kehidupan berkeluarga yang diperuntukkan di bawah Konvensyen Eropah yang membenarkan seseorang individu itu mencari seorang suami atau isteri yang lain, sekiranya perhubungan mereka telah gagal.

Sehubungan ini, maka perlu kita memikir secara kritikal berdasarkan kepada pengalaman di negara-negara membangun seperti Vietnam, Sri Lanka, Pakistan, dan dikebanyakan negara di Afrika, samada konsep berorientasi Barat yang elusif seperti "kedaulatan undang-undang", "pemisahan kuasa" dan "demokrasi" boleh diterima-pakai keseluruhannya oleh negara-negara membangun tanpa sebarang sekatan.

Dalam konteks ini, perlu juga kita merenungi konsep-konsep seperti konsep kebebasan. Adakah ini bermakna kebebasan daripada penyekatan kuasa arbitrari daripada pihak berkuasa sahaja, atau kebebasan itu meliputi kebebasan daripada beberapa perkara lain seperti kebebasan daripada kemiskinan, kepapaan, kejahilan dan buta huruf.

Seperkara lain yang perlu dikaji yang berkaitan dengan kedaulatan undang-undang ialah penggunaan kuasa budi bicara. Adalah dipercayai umum bahawa sesebuah negara kebajikan moden memerlukan pengagihan kuasa-kuasa budi bicara yang luas mengenai pentadbiran untuk melaksanakan matlamat-matlamat sosio-ekonomi yang baru. Dicey, seorang pakar undang-undang perlembagaan Inggeris berpendapat bahawa pihak pentadbiran tidak semestinya mempunyai kuasa budi bicara dan apa yang perlu ialah menerima pakai polisi-polisi perundangan yang digubal oleh badan perundangan. Pada hemat saya, ini tidaklah benar lagi kerana 'in reality' mustahil bagi badan perundangan menjangka dan membuat peruntukan yang lengkap untuk semua kemungkinan yang boleh berlaku.

Tuan-Tuan dan Puan-Puan yang dihormati,

Suatu perkara yang sewajarnya dibincangkan dengan teliti ialah perkara-perkara mengenai kuasa budibicara dan perlaksanaan polisi. Soalnya "Haruskah badan kehakiman menjadi pengadil yang memberi keputusan muktamad? Adakah wajar bagi pemimpin negara-negara membangun di dunia ketiga memandang sempit mengenai fungsi-fungsi kehakiman daripada apa yang sebenarnya dibayangkan oleh demokrasi itu sendiri? Bolehkah mahkamah dikhaskan sebagai authoriti untuk menyemak (review) pengawasan golongan elit pentadbiran dan politik dalam sesuatu perkara yang mereka lakukan dengan niat bersih untuk kebaikan am?"

Dalam suatu sistem demokrasi *bona fide* dan praktik, pemerintahan oleh pihak majoriti haruslah mendapat sokongan. Kerajaan akan menjadi suatu rangka kosong sahaja sekiranya badan perwakilan rakyat yang sah dilantik dinafikan hak dan keupayaan menyahut hasrat rakyat. Sehubungan ini, soalan mungkin timbul mengapa badan Kehakiman sungguhpun bebas membuat sesuatu penghakiman diberikan suatu kuasa mutlak untuk menolak sesuatu keputusan tertentu badan eksekutif yang mewakili rakyat yang majoriti? Penglibatan mahkamah dalam isu-isu tersebut telah dikritik atas alasan bahawa mahkamah kekurangan sumber-sumber dan kemahiran yang biasanya ada dalam makluman badan perundangan dan eksekutif sahaja.

Apa yang saya nyatakan bukanlah sesuatu pandangan yang spesifik. Ia hanya bertujuan menegaskan bahawa di masa hadapan kita mungkin perlu mengulang kaji konsep-konsep yang mempunyai tali perhubungan antara satu sama lain seperti peranan badan eksekutif, perundangan kehakiman termasuk peranan para peguam.

Perlu diingatkan bahwa Undang-undang merupakan lambang rakyat dan rakyat ialah hasil sesuatu negara. Kesemua peraturan undang-undang diujudkan di atas sebab-sebab tertentu. Sebab pengujudan peraturan-peraturan lazimnya berpunca dari faktor-faktor sosial ekonomi atau politik yang penting kepada kehidupan masyarakat atau pemimpin-pemimpinnya. Sebenarnya, undang-undang merupakan suatu institusi masyarakat, wujud dalam masyarakat dan adalah sebahagian daripada masyarakat dan tidaklah seharusnya terpisah dengan masyarakat.

Sehubungan dengan tajuk perbincangan, persoalan mungkin timbul mengenai perhubungan di antara undang-undang dan sasaran ekonomi. Ekonomi perusahaan persendirian telah memaksa undang-undang dalam negara-negara kapitalis untuk menganggap bahawa 'individual economic pursuit' dalam rangka undang-undang akan menghasilkan 'economic advantage' yang maksima bagi setiap orang. Tujuan utama undang-undang pada suatu ketika, adalah untuk memelihara undang-undang harta benda dan kontrak, serta hak-hak individu dalam mana individu-individu boleh memilih kepentingan mereka sendiri. Ini melibatkan anggapan bahawa semua anggota masyarakat adalah bebas dan boleh menjalani "their affairs with others free and equal in terms of their bargaining position". Justeru itu, jika manusia dibiarkan bebas dan sama bebas maka perdagangan akan maju dan ekonomi negara akan berkembang. Sebaliknya ada yang mengatakan bahawa kecenderungan untuk campur tangan oleh pemerintah secara terhad akan mempercepatkan kemajuan ke arah pencapaian matlamat ekonomi berdasarkan keuntungan bersama kepada masyarakat, sungguhpun ada kalanya akan melibatkan sedikit pengorbanan hak-hak individu. Campur tangan begini oleh pihak berkuasa adalah perlu untuk mengimbangkan peluang-peluang yang tidak seimbang yang mungkin berlaku dalam sesuatu masyarakat. Contoh-contoh campur tangan oleh kerajaan ialah penswastaan, projek-projek pembangunan, pembetulan ketidak-seimbangan ekonomi, pemeliharaan undang-undang dan ketenteraman di-dalam masyarakat yang berbilang kaum, menghadkan kebebasan mutlak untuk kebaikan bersama, perkhidmatan kesihatan dan lain-lain lagi.

Beralih kepada tajuk seminar hari ini, soalan yang relevan ialah apakah faktor-faktor utama yang mempengaruhi perkembangan undang-undang dan masyarakat menjelang Wawasan 2020?

Apakah pembangunan dan perubahan-perubahan yang boleh kita harapkan menjelang tahun 2020?

Memandangkan perubahan-perubahan pesat yang kita saksikan di seluruh dunia, saya percaya dalam beberapa dekad yang akan datang, suatu era yang penuh dengan penyambungan dan perubahan akan berlaku. Sebagai tunggak generasi yang akan datang, saudara-saudari sekalian tidak semestinya dihalang oleh 'fixed habits or negative habits' tetapi mestilah berfikiran positif, mempunyai sifat ingin tahu, kemahuan yang kuat, dan reseptif. Walaupun di kebanyakan negara wujud ketidakstabilan. Kita harus berbangga bahawa kita mengharungi pertumbuhan ekonomi yang pesat, kehormatan dan kesejahteraan di kalangan masyarakat majmuk. Kita telah mencapai pengikhtirafan antarabangsa sebagai negara contoh bagi negara-negara yang membangun. Kita telah menjadi suatu masyarakat pengeluar barangan yang mengekspot barangan ke pasaran antarabangsa dan mempunyai suara di dalam hal-hal antarabangsa. Hasil daripada kepintaran dan keberanian pemimpin-pemimpin kita dan polisi kerajaan kita, ekonomi kita terserlah sebagai salah satu kuasa yang paling dinamik, stabil dan berharapan baik di rantau ini.

Malaysia akan terus menggalakkan pelabur-pelabur asing untuk mengambil bahagian sebagai rakan kongsi tulus di dalam pembangunan. Semestinyalah kita dapat menghasilkan peningkatan pertumbuhan ekonomi dan penglibatan kita di dalam ekonomi dunia.

Soalnya adalah adakah kesan-kesan praktikal yang akan dibawa oleh perubahan-perubahan ini memerlukan, di masa yang akan datang, sukatan pelajaran perundangan diberi penekanan yang lebih kepada pengurusan kewangan antarabangsa, bank, insuran, perkapalan, perdagangan luar, undang-undang awam antarabangsa dan undang-undang antarabangsa. Besar kemungkinan akan terdapat banyak perubahan-perubahan kepada undang-undang dan peraturan sosial, kesemuanya mungkin membawa kebaikan. Latihan bakal-bakal peguam di atas asas yang sama sewajarnya diberi pertimbangan yang serius. Ada kemungkinan menjelang tahun 2020, terdapat berlebihan para peguam. Oleh yang demikian para peguam baru perlu bersedia mempelbagaikan kemahiran mereka di dalam bidang perindustrian dan lain-lain bidang tanpa menghadkan diri mereka kepada kerja mahkamah sahaja. Kini, terdapat berbagai cara untuk mendapat kelayakan sebagai seorang peguam, dengan latihan daripada berjenis-jenis institusi tanpa sebarang keseragaman.

Tuan-tuan dan Puan-puan yang dihormati,

Sememangnya banyak perubahan perlu dilakukan dalam sistem undang-undang dan perundangan dalam dekad-dekad akan datang. Dalam undang-undang di England sendiri banyak perubahan mungkin dilakukan bagi mencerminkan perubahan struktur kepada Komuniti Ekonomi Eropah. Undang-undang jenayah kita pula, perlu diperketatkan bagi mencegah peningkatan jenayah kolar putih yang semakin berleluasa dengan perkembangan bidang korporat. Bagi mengimbangi pertumbuhan korporat yang pesat, lebih banyak tanggungjawab spesifik perlu digubal untuk golongan profesional, khususnya Juruodit, Akauntan, Penilai dan Jurukur dan lain-lain lagi, bagi tujuan mencegah penyelewengan daripada berlaku. Begitulah juga, mengenai penagihan dadah dan ancaman penyakit AIDS, sudah pasti beberapa cara untuk mencegah perkembangan suatu masyarakat yang permisif perlu dirancangkan.

Saya berpendapat bahawa pertumbuhan ekonomi akan mengujudkan lebih banyak pertikaian dan mungkin akan melahirkan masyarakat yang gemar mendakwa di mahkamah seperti di Amerika. Keadaan ini tidak syak lagi akan memerlukan lebih banyak Mahkamah atau tribunal lain untuk menimbang-tarakan pertikaian.

Dalam menuju ke abad yang kedua-puluh satu, sistem perundangan Malaysia perlu ditaksirkan mengikut ciri-ciri Malaysia. Keinginan untuk merujuk kepada teks-teks terkenal Inggeris, Amerika dan India akan berkurangan. Jurisprudens Malaysia semakin berkembang, para peguam Malaysia mestilah membuat penilaiannya sendiri terhadap konsep dan prinsip jurisprudens Malaysia yang semakin berkembang, untuk memberikan penyelesaian yang paling adil kepada klien mereka dan Mahkamah. Tradisi-tradisi yang lepas boleh dikekalkan di mana perlu, tetapi bukan dengan kemunculan amalan-amalan feudal dan lapuk. Di masa hadapan, kita sepatutnya boleh menunjukkan suatu model Undang-Undang Malaysia, dengan menggunakan prinsip-prinsip asas Perlembagaan dan Rukunegara sebagai panduan.

Kesimpulannya, saya ingin menegas bahawa pandangan-pandangan di atas tidak perlu disifatkan sebagai kebenaran abadi tetapi hanya sebagai pokok perbincangan bagi para peserta seminar ini. Sebagaimana yang telah saya sebutkan, topik ini adalah luas dan tidaklah mungkin bagi saya dapat bentangkan secara terperinci dalam ucapan dasar saya dengan masa yang terhad. Seterusnya saya difahamkan bahawa masih ada anggota-anggota profesional yang lain yang akan mengambil bahagian dalam seminar ini yang boleh memberi panduan kepada tuan-tuan dan puan-puan dalam perbincangan nanti.

Akhir sekali saya menyatakan bahawa semua kejayaan undang-undang bergantung kepada kemahiran berhidup di dalam masyarakat berbilang kaum dan ugama dengan mengamalkan sikap penyesuaian dan penyerapan untuk hidup dalam rukun dan damai. Generasi yang membangun perlu sedar akan nilai-nilai hakiki hak kebudayaan orang lain dengan tidak memaksakan cara hidup mereka sendiri ke atas orang lain.

Dengan ucapan bismillah, saya dengan sukacita dan besar hati merasmikan Persidangan ini.

EVOLUSI/PERUBAHAN SISTEM PERUNDANGAN MALAYSIA*

Mengadap Kebawah Duli Yang Maha Mulia Pemangku Raja Perak, Raja Nazrin Shah Ibni Sultan Azlan Muhibbuddin Shah. Patik dengan segala hormat dan takzimnya merafak sembah memohon perkenan Kebawah Duli Tuanku untuk patik memberi sepatah dua kata kepada para hadirin sekalian.

Saya bersyukur kehadrat Allah SWT. kerana dengan keizinanNya kita bersama-sama dapat hadir di Majlis Jamuan Tahunan Persatuan Mahasiswa Undang-Undang UKM (PERUNDANG). Terlebih dahulu saya ingin mengucapkan ribuan terima kasih kepada Jawatankuasa Penganjur kerana sudi menjemput saya ke majlis Jamuan Tahunan Undang-Undang ke IV ini dan seterusnya diberi penghormatan untuk berucap kepada para hadirin sekalian yang terdiri daripada para akademik, pengamal undang-undang dan bakal-bakal peguam.

Pada hemat saya majlis seperti ini seharusnyalah diadakan berterusan. Di samping dapat menjamu selera, saudara saudari juga dapat menyambung sillaturrahim antara satu sama lain dengan bertukar fikiran baik dari segi ilmu undang-undang mahupun hal ehwal semasa. Sudah tentu sekali pengamal undang-undang yang turut hadir di majlis ini tidak berkeberatan untuk memberi kata nasihat kepada para pelajar hasil daripada pengalaman-pengalaman mereka yang mana tidak dapat dipelajari di bilik-bilik kuliah. Usaha seumpama ini sangat berkesan bagi membantu dan mendedahkan para mahasiswa sebelum melangkah keluar menceburi bidang undang-undang sepenuhnya.

Sistem perundangan di negara kita telah menghadapi pelbagai ujian sejak lebih empat dekad. Banyak pindaan dan perubahan telah dilakukan kepada perlembangan dan undang-undang selaras dengan perkembangan ekonomi, sosial dan politik. Sehubungan ini, ahli undang-undang mungkin mula berfikir untuk mewujudkan suatu sistem perundangan yang lebih berorientasikan Malaysia setelah sekian lama bergantung kepada sistem perundangan negara lain, khususnya dari Britain dan India, hasil kesan peninggalan sejarah. Malahan peruntukan Seksyen 3 dan 5 Akta Undang-Undang Sivil 1956 dengan

---

Di Majlis Jamuan Tahunan Undang-Undang Ke IV (Universiti Kebangsaan Malaysia) Di Concorde Ballroom, Hotel Concorde, Kuala Lumpur Pada 15hb Februari, 1992.

jelas memberi ruang kepada undang-undang Inggeris menyelinap ke dalam undang-undang kita. Apa yang berlaku ialah kita akhirnya telah memakai 'common law' dan kaedah ekuiti bersama dengan tradisinya. Teori 'common law' yang terawal di England jelas menunjukkan bahawa hakim-hakim mengisytiharkan kewujudan undang-undang mengambil kira adat tempatan pada masa itu.

Bagaimanapun, sudah tiba masanya para ahli undang-undang di negara kita khususnya graduan-graduan yang lahir dari universiti-universiti tempatan memikirkan suatu sistem perundangan yang lebih berlatarbelakangkan Malaysia dan adat-adat tempatan.

Kita seharusnya sedar bahawa masyarakat Malaysia hari ini adalah jauh berbeza dengan kehidupan masyarakat di England mahupun India beberapa kurun yang lalu. Sudah tentunya terdapat beberapa kejanggalan jika kita terus mengamalkan hukuman-hukuman yang hanya dilaksanakan oleh masyarakat asing yang jauh berlainan kehidupannya.

Beralih kepada jenis-jenis hukuman yang wajar dikenakan kepada para penjenayah kecil, maka ahli undang-undang perlu memikirkan alternatif kepada hukuman penjara yang kita amalkan sekarang yang mengakibatkan berlakunya kesesakan di penjara-penjara seluruh negara.

Di dalam konteks ini, kerajaan sentiasa menggalakkan usaha-usaha murni dari berbagai pihak untuk memberi cadangan-cadangan positif dan membina bagi memantapkan sistem perundangan negara kita. Menjelangnya Wawasan 2020, saya harap kita akan mampu mewujudkan suatu sistem perundangan yang pragmatik dan cekap yang boleh dibanggakan bersesuaian dengan aspirasi kerajaan bagi melahirkan sebuah masyarakat yang dinamik dan berhemah tinggi.

Memandangkan undang-undang merupakan suatu elemen yang amat penting di dalam masyarakat sesebuah negara, maka adalah wajar sekiranya para pengamal undang-undang, ahli-ahli akademik dan juga para mahasiswa undang-undang bergerak seiringan di dalam menyelesaikan segala masalah yang timbul. Badan perundangan dan kehakiman adalah komponen-komponen yang amat penting di dalam negara kita yang mengamalkan sistem demokrasi berparlimen. Malahan masyarakat keseluruhannya menganggap bahawa kedua-dua badan ini adalah suatu badan yang mulia. Kemuliaan ini sudah pasti akan tercemar sekiranya terdapat perselisihan faham di antara ahli-ahlinya sendiri. Adakah perselisihan ini akan diperhatikan oleh masyarakat amnya. Ini sudah tentu akan memberi gambaran yang buruk terhadap keharmonian sistem perundangan negara kita.

Tiada siapa yang dapat memelihara kemuliaan sistem perundangan kita melainkan kita sendiri. Mahasiswa-mahasiswi undang-undang yang bakal keluar sebagai pengamal undang-undang diseru supaya dapat berfikiran matang dalam proses memutuskan sesuatu perselisihan yang timbul. Adalah amat memalukan sekiranya seorang warganegara memberi gambaran yang negatif kepada dunia luar, tanpa memikirkan kesannya terhadap perkembangan ekonomi, politik dan sosial negara. Sebaliknya adalah menjadi tugas setiap warganegara untuk bersama-sama memberi penerangan kepada dunia luar akan usaha-usaha kita di dalam membangunkan negara yang tercinta ini. Kita tidak seharusnya membiarkan emosi dan sentimen mempengaruhi cara kita bertindak dan berfikir.

Dengan perkembangan masyarakat dan negara yang begitu pesat di dalam bidang perindustrian, keperluan kepada sesuatu pentadbiran undang-undang yang baik adalah elemen utama di dalam memastikan kemajuan negara akan dicapai kelak.

Oleh yang demikian, sekali lagi ingin saya mengucapkan syabas dan tahniah kepada Persatuan Mahasiswa Undang-Undang Universiti Kebangsaan Malaysia yang bukan sahaja bergiat di dalam masyarakat kampus malahan telah berjaya menempatkan persatuan ini (PERUNDANG) di tengah-tengah masyarakat keseluruhannya.

Akhir kata adalah diharapkan majlis ini akan berjaya mencapai segala natijahnya.

Ampun Tuanku, patik sekali lagi merafak sembah dan memohon ampun dan maaf jika ada sesuatu yang tidak kena dan terkasar bahasa dalam ucapan patik sebentar tadi.

GUIDED BY THE CONSTITUTION*

Saya dimaklum bahawa Majlis Makan Malam ini diadakan untuk meraikan hari jadi saya. Bagi seorang yang umurnya kian meningkat saya mungkin lebih berminat mengelak sesuatu keraian di mana umurnya yang sudah lanjut itu diketahui umum.

Minggu lepas saya menghadiri satu majlis hari jadi seorang yang umurnya meningkat 60 dan apa yang merisaukannya adalah the problem of having to sleep with a grandmother.

Walaupun begitu saya merasa terharu dengan keikhlasan penganjur-penganjur yang telah bersusah payah menganjurkan Majlis ini. Saya hanya dapat mengucapkan ribuan terima kasih kepada semua yang bertanggungjawab.

It may well be that this dinner is held because the organizers feel that I need one since the Bar Council no longer invites me for their dinners. Whatever it is, it is clear that tonight's dinner is a social event organized by friends or friendly parties who feel that we ought to get together mainly to promote goodwill and friendship and to establish a close rapport between members of the Bar and the judiciary. Given the assurance that this gathering is not an Annual General Meeting, I feel confident that I will be allowed to go on without interruption.

I do not propose to speak on courts or discord. I do not propose to speak on law or rules of natural justice. I do not even propose to speak on meetings—general or extraordinary and its summary judgment.

As an after dinner speaker I should perhaps stand up, speak up and shut up. Many have made fun of after dinner speakers. A story I was told concerns a speaker who, confident that his assistant had prepared yet another good speech, stood up and proceeded to give his hour long speech most brilliantly. He went on and on reading and after two hours the guests began to leave. The speaker was affronted and complained to his assistant. "That's because I gave you the duplicate copy of the speech as well," was the response from the assistant.

**At The Dinner Organized By Members Of The Legal Fraternity To Celebrate His Lordship's Birthday On 15th May, 1992.*

The short point leans therefore in favour of short speeches. The lesson to be learnt is that we all have so much to do that wisdom demands that we talk less but act more to get things moving. The principle underlying it, I believe, could be applied to many real-life situations. I realise that this is not an occasion for theoretical speech-making but one for merrymaking. Yet, I cannot refrain from saying a word or two thanking you for your kind thoughts and sentiments. I assume all of you know the background which has made me a controversial personality. This situation arises from the difficult position I am holding and the responsibilities that are imposed on me by the Constitution.

Judges bear the burden of striking a balance between the individual right and social collective right, between the pressing needs of development and the human hardship. However, a developing society is often saddled with certain problems which can only be solved politically. No amount of judicial pontification will solve them. In this dilemma, a judge like myself cannot aspire to win popularity as there can hardly be any consensus of what is absolutely right. I am guided only by the Constitution and my conscience. Clearly I am only a bare trustee of the powers of the judiciary given by the Constitution. Judges are therefore only watchdogs of the Constitution. I have always tried to do my best as humanely as possible but I do not claim to be perfect. It is my belief that anybody is entitled to disagree with me and criticise me but they need not be disagreeable and there is room for courtesy, decorum and goodwill. In the process of disagreeing, I for one acknowledge human limitations and therefore always make myself available for cordial discussions for the common benefit.

I have wished many times over that in performing the functions entrusted upon me the Almighty grants me the serenity to accept things I cannot change; the courage to change the things that I can; and the wisdom to know the difference.

Whether I am right in my philosophy and beliefs and succeed in my endeavour to change things I can is a matter for history to judge.

Suffice if I say that we have had a sumptuous dinner and a very pleasant evening. I say this very sincerely and I have much to be grateful for to all friendly parties and may I also express my sincere appreciation on behalf of the grandmother, my wife.

BUILDING INDUSTRY DISPUTES AND ARBITRATION*

I am greatly honoured to have been invited to deliver the opening address at this seminar. As the time available to me is very limited and I am well known for my brevity — and in view of the complexity of the subject, I shall only cover some elementary aspects of building industry disputes and arbitration. I shall confine this short address to highlighting certain aspects of the arbitrator's role and their relationship to the courts in very general terms. Even in doing so I will not attempt to deprive you of the opportunity to listen and learn from the main speakers. In particular, I would join the organizers to welcome the distinguished speaker from overseas Justice Neil Kaplan, who is the Vice-President (Overseas) of the Chartered Institute of Arbitrators and also the local speakers and Discussion Panellists — Miss P.G. Lim and Professor Vincent Powell Smith.

The first matter that arises for consideration is the role played by arbitrators in an arbitration. As you all know, an arbitration is the reference of a dispute between not less than two persons for determination, after hearing both sides in a judicial manner, by another person or persons, other than a court of competent jurisdiction. Yet, arbitrators are not on par with judges as the powers of the former are only those that have been entrusted to them specifically by virtue of the respective clause or clauses in the arbitration agreement. Moreover, their role is also different from that of judges. The arbitrators need not follow ordinary rules of procedure rigidly. Nevertheless, they cannot act contrary to the fundamental principles of public policy, principles of natural justice and rules of evidence. For example, where one of the parties to an arbitration attempts to communicate with the arbitrator without the knowledge of the other party, the arbitrator should refuse to hear the case or be influenced in any manner by such communication. Another difference is that an arbitration is a private tribunal for settlement of disputes and the general public need not be admitted if there is objection to such a course by any party to the reference. Needless to say, any person who assists a party to the arbitration may be present.

**At The One-day Seminar On Building Industry Disputes And Arbitration On 31st July, 1992 At The Card Room, Royal Selangor Club, Kuala Lumpur.*

Although the jurisdiction and the inherent powers of the arbitrators are not as wide as that of judges, they perform an equally responsible function. In this context may I quote what Lord Denning said about arbitrators interpreting trade clauses: "On such a clause, the arbitrator is just as likely to be right as the judge, probably more likely." In another context a former Lord Chief Justice in the United Kingdom, Lord Goddard said: "... in one sense, he is the anti-thesis to a court. A person goes to arbitration because he does not want to go to court. Therefore, he sets up his own private judge to decide the case but the arbitrator is not deciding as a judge, he is deciding as an arbitrator and the procedure, rights and all the matters are to be found in the Arbitration Act." As is often thought, an arbitrator need not necessarily be a legally qualified person. He may well be a member of the engineering profession or someone similarly qualified. The usual requirements are that an arbitrator (a) is not connected to any of the parties (b) has the necessary expertise in the particular field and (c) has experience in the specific area of dispute. In fact, the appointment of a non-legal person may be advantageous. One of the conventional reasons for solving disputes by arbitration, for example in the constructjon industry is that a judge's or lawyer's general expertise may not be adequate enough to deal with the more complex and specific problems that may arise. The effect of such a hearing before a legally qualified person, without the necessary professional knowledge will result in extra time being taken by the judge to assimilate the facts in order to arrive at a decision.

The arbitration procedure maximises the use of experts and professionals by placing them in the judgment seat in a new procedural format instead of in the witness box.

In the context of experts being arbitrators, I must add a word of caution. It is welcome for an arbitrator to use his expertise in respect of general matters. That may be the very reason why he was chosen to act as an arbitrator. Nevertheless, the rules of natural justice demand that even though the arbitrator is a qualified expert he cannot use his own knowledge on matters which are likely to form the subject of the decision unless he has communicated them to the parties to the dispute for their comments. If an arbitrator is convinced by a point which has never been raised by either side, it is his duty to put it to all parties concerned so that they may have an opportunity to comment on it. If the arbitrator is relying on his own personal experiences in favour of one party then he should invite the other side to comment on it. The arbitrator cannot give evidence to himself.

Another point which may interest you is the extent of the court's jurisdiction over an arbitrator's award. I would say that as a matter of general approach, the courts strive to uphold an arbitrator's award. We do not approach them to find fault with meticulous legal eyes trying to pick holes. Our aim is to uphold awards and not strike them down. As a general rule, judicial interference is justified only of it is shown that the arbitrator had clearly misdirected himself in law or had reached a decision which no reasonable arbitrator would have reached, e.g., where the arbitrator had obviously ascribed the wrong meaning to the contract or any clause or where the award is unusual. The court will interfere if there has been a serious and irreparable misconduct on the arbitrator's part, that is, where there have been procedural lapses causing substantial miscarriage of justice. Another example is where there has been bias on the part of the arbitrator.

It is important for you to know that generally speaking, we follow Commonwealth precedents in arbitration matters as disputes often involve commercial interests of other nations. Basically the courts are not inclined to "open up, revise and even rectify" certificates of engineers or architects. Arbitrators have an extra advantage in this respect in that they can review and revise such matters in a way that the courts do not normally do.

The courts permit arbitrators to exercise their powers as widely as possible consistent with the actual wording of the arbitration clause. Very recently, the Court of Appeal in England held that an arbitrator is empowered to grant relief in respect of operative mistake, misrepresentation or negligent misstatement. The courts always bear in mind the sanctity of the parties' right to decide their own affairs. This does not mean that the court will tolerate any party to oust its power of ultimate judicial control. Justice is a vague concept in commercial relations and it does not mean that the courts should lightly deprive a party of his contractual right in relation to an agreed and clearly intended method of solving the dispute.

One vexing question that often arises is the grant of stay of court proceedings pending arbitration where parties have resorted to the court for adjudication without going for arbitration. Generally speaking, if there appears to be a clear submission to arbitration, an application for stay will be granted if made promptly and in good faith.

As I said earlier, the arbitrator's power is limited by the provisions of the arbitration clause whereas the courts have an inherent jurisdiction to do what is required to do justice to the parties. One of the main setbacks of the Arbitration Act is that no provision is made for arbitration disputes to be consolidated and heard together in the same way as civil actions are consolidated and heard in the courts, if found necessary. The practical remedy is to have a suitable arbitration clause in each of the relevant main and sub-contracts for such a procedure.

It is appropriate to mention at this stage that under our law there is a provision in the Courts of Judicature Act empowering the High Court to refer to a special referee for inquiry or report any question arising in any cause or matter, other than a criminal proceeding by the Public Prosecutor provided—

(a) that all the parties interested who are not under disability consent;

(b) if the cause or matter requires any prolonged examination of documents or any scientific or local investigation which cannot, in the opinion of the High Court, conveniently be conducted by the Court through its ordinary officers; or

(c) if the question in dispute consists wholly or in part of matters of account.

However, this provision is seldom invoked as judges feel that proceedings in a cause or matter before the Court may be further delayed by such a reference. Instead, the court would prefer experts to be called as witnesses before it to testify on the cause or matter.

I am inclined to favour a much greater role to be played by arbitrators to resolve disputes between parties as this would certainly help to reduce the volume of litigation which invariably congests the court system.

The courts currently play a significant role in supervising arbitration proceedings and giving effect to awards made by arbitrators. There is no doubt that the courts would continue, within the powers vested in them by law, to play their role as effectively and efficiently as possible particularly to meet the needs of this country's rapid commercial and industrial development.

A seminar such as this would certainly help to create a greater awareness of the benefits of determination of disputes by arbitration and would even encourage parties to contracts to ensure the inclusion of provisions for reference to arbitration of disputes arising under the contracts.

Before I conclude, let me emphasise another important aspect of arbitration. A unique advantage of arbitration is that informal arbitration proceedings need not create much bitterness and hostility between the parties as in court cases. An arbitration is ideally carried out in a friendly atmosphere without much ado so as not to jeopardise the relationship of parties. It that way they can carry on with their business dealings after settling their differences amicably. Unwanted publicity can be avoided in arbitration. The sitting can be arranged at a place and date convenient to parties. The arbitrator's calendar will not usually be as preoccupied as that of the courts thus resulting in a faster settlement of disputes.

I believe I must stop now without misdirecting myself as to the interpretation of an opening address. Before I conclude, I must emphasise that I am satisfied with the effectiveness of the arbitration system operated locally and I am impressed with the integrity, impartiality, practical wisdom and common sense of the arbitrators especially in relation to the construction industry. Be that as it may, I am sure that no human mechanism and institution can reach total perfection and that there will always be room for improvement. The identification of weaknesses in the existing system is therefore one of the primary functions of a seminar of this nature. It is my hope that seminars like this will periodically be held by other professional bodies also so as to widen the scope of the citizen's participation in the legal machinery. As law is not the monopoly of the legislature, judges or lawyers it demands the support and vigilance of each and every citizen for successful nation building.

SILVER JUBILEE OF MALRA, SARAWAK*

Saya dahului dengan ucapan salam sejahtera. Saya juga ucapkan ribuan terima kasih di atas kesudian Pengerusi, Cawangan Sarawak dan juga Pengerusi, Penganjur yang telah mengundang saya untuk hadir di Majlis Silver Jubilee Celebration MALRA Sarawak Branch ini. Saya anggapkan jemputan dan kehadiran saya sebagai kehormatan bagi diri saya sendiri yang saya sanjung tinggi. During the last twenty-five years very significant achievements have been made by MALRA Sarawak Branch. While I stand before you and give credit to the people who had the vision to start a Branch in Sarawak I am equally proud and appreciative of the people who are at the helm of the branch today and who have translated the vision by providing relief to the most neglected members of society in the state. I take this opportunity to thank the President, Y. Berbahagia Dato Ang Lai Soon and his committee for the sacrifices they have made in meeting the challenges of the times with absolute commitment and dedication.

The idea of starting a Branch in Sarawak was mooted in 1965 and through the relentless efforts of the late Tan Sri T.H. Tan and our Secretary-General an Inaugural General Meeting was held on 1st November, 1966 in Aurora Hotel and an Executive Committee was elected under the Chairmanship of Dr. Rosalla.

Yesterday we visited the beautiful and well laid out Rajah Charles Brooke Memorial Hospital. At the turn of this century there was no Rajah Charles Memorial Hospital, but there was a hospital called "LEPER CAMP". It was situated at the 5th mile, Penrissen Road which at first accommodated about seventy "INMATES". A fund was set up in 1917 in memory of the second Rajah, Sir Charles Brooke. As a result of generous public subscription, it was possible to start a new settlement on Satang Island, as a personal memorial to the Rajah.

The building complex on the island was completed in 1924 and the transfer of the patients' residence from 5th mile, Penrissen Road to Satang Island took place in the same year. The island was not self-supporting. Communication to and from the island was extremely hard and dangerous even during the day. It was for this reason that efforts were made to secure another site. On the 10th of

---

**At The Silver Jubilee Celebration Of The Malaysian Leprosy Association (Sarawak Branch) On22nd August, 1992 At The Sarawak Plaza, Kuching, Sarawak.*

October, 1925 the patients were transferred to the present site at the 13th mile, Penrissen Road.

The present site was clearly the best choice. Permanent dwellings began to take shape in 1926. Most of the buildings then were built by the patients themselves from the materials salvaged from Satang Island with, of course, the help of the Government, which had been responsible for the running of the "Camp".

It is universally accepted that human energy is a driving force for all human achievements. The energy of an organization is released and directed by the vision, mission, values and goals which the organization sets for itself. The objectives are commonly identifiable for an organization's existence. These objectives no doubt inspire dedication. My view is that the Sarawak branch has set an exemplary example in providing relief and rehabilitation to the unfortunate victims of leprosy. I am confident that by the year 2000, with your zeal and dedication, leprosy can be completely controlled if not wiped out.

As I stand before you I am reminded of a story regarding Mahatma Gandhi. The Minister of Health once invited Mahatma Gandhi to come and open a new leprosy hospital. Gandhi thought for a moment and said that the Prime Minister should do it and added, "I will come to close the hospital once the ignorance has been wiped out and the patients cured."

I hope that the time will come when I too can happily perform that function by which time MALRA would have fulfilled its objectives.

MALAYSIAN LEPROSY RELIEF ASSOCIATION*

Leprosy, whether as a disease or a divine curse or a combination of a number of prejudices and superstitions has been in Malaysia from the fifteenth century although there is no conclusive documentary proof on it until from about the middle of the last century, and the only means of treatment then was complete isolation.

Although the main Leprosarium was established in Sungei Buloh in 1929-1930, patients were still governed by a leprosy ordinance called 'An-Enactment to declare the law relating to lepers dated 20th October, 1926' and revised in 1935. This law is still in force even though it has not been applied in recent times.

Up to the second half of this century, due to a lack of concerted and co-ordinated global attention, leprosy did not get the scientifically research-orientated attention it is getting today, and was treated as a disease apart. Among those "who walked alone" were not only leprosy patients, conceivably their acute loneliness was not unrecognized, but others in leprosy work were also feeling the same sense of loneliness. Medical men in leprosy work were alone, leprosy workers were alone, leprosy institutions were treading an isolated path and workers were feeling the sense of neglect amongst other social workers.

This sense of isolation was clearly felt by all types of leprosy institutions and workers who were involved in leprosy work "for its own sake". These institutions and workers regarded leprosy work as a national problem and gave the best possible treatment and relief to leprosy patients. They were rendering the type of service which Mahatma Gandhi described as something which is not merely a form of medical relief but an act of selfless service that could transform the frustrations in life into a joy of dedication and personal service.

In late 1958 and early 1959, Dr. K.M. Reddy with the help of Apex Club of Kuala Lumpur formed the Malaysian Leprosy Relief Association (MALRA) under the Chairmanship of Tan Sri T.H. Tan.

In the course of launching MALRA, it was realised that there was almost a total and complete ignorance of leprosy and on top of it there was a tremendous prejudice against it. The very first thing that the Association realized was

---

**At The Silver Jubilee Celebration Of The Malaysian Leprosy Association (Sarawak Branch) On 23rd August, 1992 At The Sarawak Plaza, Kuching, Sarawak.*

that the whole problem of leprosy in Malaysia revolved around prejudice. It was also further realised that if this problem was to be tackled successfully the patients would have to come forward voluntarily for treatment. It was the Association's hope that with proper and systematic treatment the disease could be arrested and would eventually be wiped out.

Every available resource was utilised in the war for a mental revolution—including the participation of school children, teachers, labour officers, welfare officers, hospital assistants, nurses, medical officers and religious centres and institutions. A membership of 75,000 school children with the help of mosques, churches, temples and gurudwaras contributed much to our massive endeavour.

At the same time, MALRA took recognition of the manifold needs of the patients and ex-patients upon their discharge and the members of the family while breadwinners are undergoing treatment.

The peripheral needs of patients which did not fall within the scope of the hospitals was met by MALRA. These included newspapers in different languages, monthly pocket allowances for patients in decrepit wards and subsidy for artificial aids such as spectacles and hearing aids. MALRA then introduced different financial assistance schemes for ex-patients who were unemployed, for members of family of in-patients, for their school going children as well as for those who required vocational training.

As an incentive for patients to come for regular follow-up treatment, MALRA gave financial aid such as subsidy for their transport.

To provide income for MALRA and at the same time job opportunities for patients and ex-patients and dependants MALRA opened rubber estates, oil palm estates, flower gardens and poultry farms where the patients learn to become self-reliant and become useful members of society. It was also through MALRA's efforts that the Government launched the National Leprosy Control programme as the Association was able to show that it is important not to dehabilitate patients so that the need of rehabilitation does not arise.

I might say today that the wall of prejudice and ignorance has not quite disintegrated, like the Berlin Wall, but there are already many cracks and I believe it would not be long before it comes tumbling down and a new thinking emerges. The patients themselves were taught not only to seek treatment but also to be self reliant and useful and also to contribute to the well being of the society.

Turning now to the current role it is clear that in order to maintain pressure on the work of prevention and eradication of leprosy MALRA shall have to direct its attention particularly to five areas of work during this decade. They are:

1. Orientation of upper secondary school students in prevention work:

2. Increase the use of mass media, especially radio and TV for non-formal education on leprosy:

3. Minimise defaulter rate in collaboration with Medical/Health Staff:

4. Assist and encourage the screening of contact of new cases:

5. Advocate the screening of all immigrant workers for H.D. (all other communicable diseases).

MALRA plans to sponsor school health clubs in collaboration with the Ministry of Education involving upper secondary school students. It will initiate this programme in a few premier schools in Peninsular Malaysia and then allow it to expand. MALRA's inputs would be know-how and financial support for activities such as inter-school debates, poster and essay competitions, exhibitions and periodical talks. Integration of some preventive aspects of H.D. into civic courses will be examined with the relevant authorities. Primary prevention can be best introduced at this level.

Efforts to change public attitude and prejudice against leprosy has to be relentlessly pursued. T.V. and radio are effective methods of communication. The usefulness of this modern technology must be optimised. Generally, in order for messages to trickle down to grass-root level, the output of information must be sustained on a regular basis. For this purpose MALRA will consider buying radio and TV time, while maintaining other methods of dissemination of information on leprosy. Money will have to be spent but it is firmly believed that money spent on publicity will yield good results in the long term.

Encouraging and ensuring discharged patients to continue follow-up treatment is yet another area where MALRA will intensify its intervention. Defaulters often attribute their failure to continue treatment to lack of funds. But in this regard MALRA is already providing transport subsidy for such patients. Depending on the need, this programme will be expanded. The current defaulter rate is 11% in Peninsular Malaysia. If this problem is not drastically contained first then two negative results will follow. The defaulters may communicate the disease to other persons they are in contact with or develop a drug resistant condition. Even annual incentives may be considered for patients who continue regular treatment during a given year by way of nutritious drinks, vitamins, etc.

Screening of the contacts of new cases, especially the immediate members of the family is urgent. Only regular messages on the TV and radio regarding

H.D. can convince these persons that H.D. is just another disease and that they should go for immediate medical screening to the nearest skin clinic or hospital. Some incentives may also be worked out for those who come forward voluntarily for medical screening.

The main form of transmission of H.D. disease is from person to person. The basic prevention thrust is to cut off the chain of communication or link by treating the patient until his condition is rendered negative.

Besides, local untreated patients being potential carriers, a new group has emerged in the person of the 'immigrant worker'. A few have been identified as H.D. patients and are currently receiving treatment.' The numbers unidentified will remain unknown.

An effective method of control would be to screen all legal immigrant workers from endemic countries before they are allowed to work in the country. MALRA should strongly advocate this measure, otherwise, half a century of efforts by both MALRA and the Ministry of Health may be nullified.

Another area where MALRA is working together with international agencies is in the prevention of deformities. While the implementation of multidrug therapy (MDT) has been increasing steadily, particularly in developing countries, the disenchantment with regard to the rehabilitation situation has not diminished. The major need has been to develop practical methods and approaches and also to apply all the available knowledge to prevent disabilities and rehabilitate the patients.

The main cause for concern towards leprosy is the disability it produces with its serious physical and social consequences. While the emphasis on the recent treatment technology of multi-drug therapy (MDT) to reduce the occurrence of the disease is well justified, we should not forget that for a long time to come we will have to live with the problem of patients who are disabled in addition to dealing with those already disabled. This means that we not only have to apply all the existing technologies and approaches available but also seek and develop new and better technologies and approaches.

Conceivably early detection of the disease and its prompt treatment are essential to prevent disabilities occurring among leprosy patients. However, in the practical world of today, a significant number of patients will continue to present themselves for the first time with already damaged nerves, with or without deformities. Unless we are able to develop appropriate strategies and responses to the disability problem, the control programmes are likely to be discredited for neglecting a very important human problem. A major justification for increase action on the rehabilitation front is the social component resulting from stigma which occurs in many cultural contexts and which further compounds the patients' problem.

The problem of leprosy and its disabling consequences in Asia are indeed immense. Of the 4.2 million registered leprosy cases in the world 3.4 million or 81% live in Asia. In terms of disabled leprosy patients, this amounts to anywhere between 600,000 to over one million persons needing attention. This pool of disabled individuals is constantly being maintained through new additions despite eliminations due to natural death among the disabled. Therefore, the major concerns presently are:-

1. How to prevent and treat disability among leprosy patients;
2. How to orient leprosy patients to take care of their hands, feet and eyes;
3. How to develop intervention strategies by the State as well as by the society so that lepers affected do not get dehabilitated from their familial, economic and social situations;
4. How to develop low cost rehabilitation services for the disabled persons suffering from leprosy.

For this purpose a Working Group has been set up by Rehabilitation International. Members of this Working Group come from countries like China, Malaysia, India, Sri Lanka and Nepal and other countries in Africa and Latin America may be requested to accept membership of this Working Group. Financial support for this Working Group will come from WHO & ILU.

It is with earnest hope that I look forward to this Working Group studying and devising and recommending proper strategies that will translate the dream of completely controlling, if not eradicating, leprosy by the end of this century. For this purpose it is important that every individual plays his or her part.

As St. Paul tells us "A man can have the Gift of Prophecy, can understand all the mysteries of life and have enough faith to move mountains, but without charity, he is nothing. The greatest of great things in life is charity — charity of mind that understands, forgives and cares for others".

With these words I thank you all.

UNIFORMITY OF DRUG LAWS IN ASEAN COUNTRIES*

It is a great honour and proud privilege for me to have been invited to inaugurate the Conference of Parliamentarians and other representatives of ASEAN countries assembled with a view to considering the preparation of a draft legislation for the uniformity of drug laws on drug abuse. On this occasion, I regret that owing to my preoccupation by virtue of the office I am holding, I cannot effectively contribute to your deliberations except to wish you success. On my part I shall give you a glimpse of my personal views with regard to the general need for regional co-operation on drug abuse. In giving such views, I must confess in all humility that my experience in the social field relating to drugs is, unfortunately, limited and cannot match up with your expertise. Yet, I venture to give my suggestions not for adoption but hoping that they will stimulate your thoughts. At the outset, I must say that your task cannot be achieved overnight but what you discuss at this conference can make a very significant step in the right direction. I am well aware of the tremendous efforts you have made since 1967 and the progress achieved so far. In adopting changes, no member nation need be frightened of losing its legal sovereignty. In most of the nations law has developed through a process of legal transplant. This happens when a country borrows laws and legal principles from another country. Any person using his own law must understand that a study of comparative law can help in a better understanding of his own law and in its improvement. Regional liaison and study can open the doors to all countries in the region to harmonise legal concepts on matters of common interest. Drug menace is a problem and it is a problem which cannot be solved in an isolated manner. This is particularly so in view of the geographical affinity of the ASEAN nations, improved communication facilities and the varied types of transport used. To illustrate the suggestion for unification, let me quote an example. Under the Singapore Law of Criminal Procedure a suspect in a criminal investigation must give his explanation to the alleged crime as soon as he is arrested. Otherwise, any defence which he raises at the hearing of the case is legally presumed to lose its credit-worthiness. This recent change in procedure in Singapore should be seriously studied, perhaps with a view to adoption by other

**At The Conference On Common Legislation On Drug Abuse In Asean Countries Held On 24th August, 1992 At Parliament House, Kuala Lumpur.*

countries, at least as far as drug offences are concerned. My experience is that there is no shortage of fantastic defence stories which the court is bound to consider as the law now stands.

Apart from the the penal and administrative laws what requires consideration are the social factors which contribute to the solving of the menace. It could be quite relevant to know how society responds to an individual's abuse of drugs. In this regard the factors that need to be borne in mind are, *inter alia* childhood environments, psychological precipitants, peer group influences, psycho sexual problems and cultural heritages. This list can never be comprehensive as even "creativity" can be a cause for drug abuse. Some artists, musicians, composers and poets take drugs because they claim that their creativity is heightened. Psychedelic drugs, LSD and cannabis give them a different interpretation of what they are trying to translate into art, music and poetry.

In your deliberations, you must bear in mind that as representatives of the people, your power is unlimited and you must dispel all notions that judges and courts can perform apparent miracles. The conventional role attributed to the courts has been recently questioned by the Lord Chancellor of England, Lord McCluskey. He argues that it is up to Parliament to give a clear and more definite mandate to the courts especially in relation to criminal cases. He says in his thesis about *Law, Justice and Democracy* that "The public are told that sentencing is for judges. That would be acceptable if judges knew what mystic principles guided their actions. But they don't. And it is the public who pay for prisons, who are the victims of crime and who have to live in the community with criminals and to maintain families of offenders. Should the public have so muted a voice?" Lord McCluskey concludes by stating that Parliament, which knows better should issue more mandatory directives as they bear a responsibility to the community. By quoting him, I am not saying I am entirely in agreement with him but it may be a matter for you to think about.

One vexing problem is the question of the death penalty for trafficking cases. Most countries in the ASEAN region impose mandatory death sentences for drug trafficking. However, for various reasons, the punishment is not implemented rigidly as it is done in Malaysia, Indonesia and Singapore. It may be that Brunei does not have to face a serious drug problem for apparent reasons. This may give you some food for thought. I feel that whatever legislative measures are adopted, the full success in diminishing the problem depends on cooperation and public education. Personally speaking, I fear that drugs and Aids are two modern evils equivalent to harm caused by nuclear warfare. Let me at this point say that you should not be terribly frustrated if your objective is not achieved by one or two sittings. Probably, some more conferences of this nature will have to be called or the task has to be delegated to appropriate sub-committees. For the present, you will no doubt achieve your objectives if you have agreed at policy level leaving the technical working for others to formulate and you should be proud that the full effects of your deliberations may only be experienced later. Let us hope that by the year of Vision 2020, there will be a uniform set of laws and administrative policies agreed and implemented. A very recent landmark achievement is the reported agreement this month between senior police officers of ASEAN member nations to have joint operations including exchange of information on drug trafficking and smuggling. The police representatives who met in Brunei have recommended to their respective Governments the setting up of an ASEAN police force (Aseanpol). I am sure you will closely follow the developments on this proposal.

In conclusion, I personally feel that I will be trespassing into your jurisdiction and abusing your hospitality if I go on speaking, covering areas which you know better than me. Let me be permitted to emphasise that the material content of any legal system is to reflect the needs or demands of society, as well as customs and conventions embodying fundamental values of societies which are conditioned by historical and even religious factors. For example, the Philippines legal system seems to be a combination of customary usages, the Roman Civil Law and Anglo-American Common Law. On the other hand, the legal systems of Singapore, Malaysia and Brunei originated from the Common Law of England. Thailand and Indonesia follow legal doctrines based on "civil law" elements importing influences of European continental traditions. I believe that your aim is to achieve positive results and to proceed conservatively and it is not your intention to replace one national law with a supposed super regional law. Your immediate aim should be to promote closer relations, co-operation and mutual understanding and promotion of uniform laws as far as possible. The centre of gravity of legal development lies not in juristic science but in the needs of the public of which you are better judges than the courts. Although I seek your permission to leave at this stage, I shall be following your deliberations with interest. Let me assure you that as far as our judiciary is concerned, you can be sure of our co-operation at all times without attempting to find hair-splitting abstract and academical arguments.

PERUNDANGAN DAN KEHAKIMAN SYARIAH DAN SIVIL*

Terlebih dahulu saya mengucap kesyukuran ke hadrat Allah SWT. kerana dengan limpah rahmatnya dapat saya bersama-sama di majlis yang mulia dan bersejarah ini. Izinkan juga saya mengucapkan ribuan terima kasih kepada ahli-ahli Jawatankuasa kerana telah sudi mengundang saya untuk merasmikan forum ini. Sesungguhnya ini adalah kali yang pertama Seminar Perundangan dan Kehakiman yang terdiri daripada dua aliran yang pernah diadakan. Dua aliran yang dimaksudkan di sini ialah perundangan dan kehakiman syariah dan sivil. Kedua-dua aliran ini telah wujud di negara kita semenjak kedatangan penjajah British, manakala sebelum itu undang-undang Islam telah wujud dan diterima pakai di seluruh tanahair dan Kepulauan Melayu. Selepas kedatangan penjajah British, undang-undang sivil telah diperkenalkan dan mengambil kedudukan penting berbanding dengan undang-undang Islam yang telah dipakai sebelum daripada itu. Walau bagaimanapun, Mahkamah Syariah tidak dihapuskan sama sekali bahkan telah berjalan beriringan dengan undang-undang sivil, khususnya undang-undang keluarga Islam.

Untuk mengembalikan kedaulatan undang-undang Islam atau Syariah, langkah-langkah telahpun diambil untuk meningkatkan bidangkuasa Mahkamah Syariah dari masa ke semasa. Dengan terpindanya Perkara 121 Perlembagaan Persekutuan, Mahkamah Sivil tidak lagi mempunyai bidangkuasa ke atas Mahkamah Syariah. Dengan lain perkataan, Mahkamah Sivil tidak lagi boleh menukar atau membuat pindaan ke atas keputusan yang dibuat oleh Mahkamah Syariah mengenai perkara-perkara tertentu yang dibawah bidangkuasanya. Aliran perundangan dan kehakiman syariah berjalan dengan sendirinya tanpa diganggu oleh Mahkamah Sivil. Pengadilan syariah dan pengadilan sivil di negara kita telah menjadi dua aliran perundangan dan kehakiman yang berjalan berseiringan. Sesungguhnya adalah mustahak bagi kedua-dua aliran ini tidak bercanggah di antara satu sama lain. Y. Bhg. Tan Sri, Dato'-Dato', Tuan-tuan dan Puan-puan, pada pendapat saya dengan pindaan kepada Perkara 121 Perlembagaan, tidaklah bermakna bahawa semua undang-undang yang ada dan terpakai di negara ini dapat dilaksanakan mengikut kehendak-kehendak hukum syarak, tetapi sebaliknya undang-undang yang

---

**Di Dewan Muktamar Pusat Islam Malaysia, Kuala Lumpur, Pada 12hb. Oktober, 1992.*

tidak bersesuaian dengan hukum syarak dan juga adat istiadat yang menjadi amalan di negara ini hendaklah terlebih dahulu diberi pertimbangan untuk dipinda jika wajar. Ini merupakan satu tugas yang amat berat kepada ahli-ahli perundangan di negara ini.

Buat ketika ini, walaupun terdapat pembahagian yang jelas antara fungsi Undang-undang Sekular dan fungsi Undang-undang Syariah, namun begitu, dalam beberapa segi masih lagi terdapat konflik antara kedua-dua sistem ini. Satu contoh ialah seksyen 51 Akta Undang-undang Pembaharuan 1976 (Law Reform Act 1976) yang dicadangkan dipinda, di mana salah satu pihak itu telah memeluk agama Islam, mana-mana pihak baik'yang telah menjadi Islam mahupun bukan Islam, boleh memohon ke Mahkamah Tinggi untuk mendapatkan penceraian. Pindaan yang dicadangkan ini bertujuan menyelaraskan semangat dan objektif Perlembagaan. Konflik juga boleh timbul berhubungan dengan perkara-perkara probet dan pentadbiran pusaka. Selagi Undang-undang Sekular tidak dipinda, nampaknya Mahkamah Syariah mempunyai bidangkuasa untuk mengendalikan Undang-Undang Islam yang ada kaitan dengan pewarisan sahaja dan tidak termasuk kes-kes berkaitan dengan alang dan wakaf.

Saya difahamkan bahawa Bahagian Hal Ehwal Islam, Jabatan Perdana Menteri telahpun menubuh satu jawatankuasa yang terdiri dari pakar undang-undang sivil dan syarak di negara ini untuk meneliti undang-undang yang ada supaya dapat diserap dalam pelaksanaan amalannya untuk keadilan semua undang-undang baik undang-undang sivil maupun undang-undang syariah sendiri.

Saya juga suka menarik perhatian semua peserta yang menghadiri forum ini bahawa satu prinsip undang-undang, iaitu, keharmonian, keadilan, keadaan semasa, tempat dan masyarakat mestilah diambilkira semasa membincang dan membahas sesuatu isu yang berkaitan dengan undang-undang. Ini bermakna sebagai sebuah negara di mana rakyatnya berbilang bangsa dan agama, keturunan dan berlainan sosio-budaya maka adalah perlu setiap usaha untuk menonjol dan memperkenalkan satu-satu undang-undang yang baru mengambilkira keadaan-keadaan yang saya sebutkan demi mengekalkan keharmonian dan kesejahteraan hidup rakyat di negara ini.

Dari pandangan peribadi saya, dalam sesuatu masyarakat majmuk seperti masyarakat kita, adalah bermanfaat dan menguntungkan bagi seseorang itu mempelajari Undang-undang Perbandingan (Comparative Law). Ianya berfaedah apabila seseorang itu menjalankan kajian dalam sejarah atau falsafah perundangan. Adalah penting bagi kita untuk memahami nilai budaya dan keagamaan kaum lain. Lagi pun, pengetahuan tentang agama Islam khususnya boleh menyumbang ke arah pembinaan hubungan baik antara satu agama dengan agama lain di samping mengujudkan konsensus dalam segi nilai-nilai kemanusiaan.

Ahli-ahli hukum barat yang berfikiran bebas telah mengikhtirafkan Undang-undang Islam sebagai salah satu daripada sistem perundangan dunia moden yang sangat baik yang boleh mentadbirkan hal-ehwal manusia dengan adil. Walaupun konsep-konsep asas Undang-undang Islam tidak boleh diubah-ubah, namun begitu, dalam beberapa aspek tertentu ianya boleh disesuaikan mengikut keadaan, misalnya berhubung dengan adat resam, hak membuat kontrak (dalam konteks dunia moden) dan peraturan-peraturan pentadbiran. Saya tidak percaya kesukaran akan timbul untuk membuat pengubahsuaian dan peraturan untuk membolehkan sistem perundangan Islam berinteraksi dengan baik dengan sistem sekular yang terdapat di dunia moden ini. Dalam Islam terdapat ajaran yang ditujukan kepada seluruh manusia yang menghendaki manusia mencapai lebih daripada hanya mengujudkan masyarakat yang adil sahaja. Islam menghendaki manusia sentiasa bersyukur atas segala rezeki yang dilimpahkan ke atas mereka oleh Allah, dan membahagi-bahagikan rezeki itu sesama manusia dengan cara adil dan saksama. Dalam dunia sekarang ini di mana terdapatnya jurang yang besar antara puak yang miskin dengan puak yang kaya dan kemusnahan nuklear yang sentiasa mengancam manusia, ajaran ini memberi makna kepada mereka yang berfikiran waras dan terbuka. Tujuan saya menekankan aspek-aspek ini bukanlah untuk memperkecilkan mana-mana ajaran agama yang lain sama ada secara terus atau secara implikasi, tetapi dilihat sebagai seorang rakyat biasa memberi pandangannya bahawa Undang-undang Syariah merupakan undang-undang yang boleh disesuaikan untuk mengujudkan sistem perundangan yang lain.

Sebelum saya mengakhiri ucapan ini izinkan saya menyatakan bahawa adalah mustahil bagi saya untuk menyentuh semua aspek masalah peralihan yang dihadapi dalam tempoh perubahan berikutan dengan pindaan Perlembagaan baru-baru ini yang memberi Undang-undang Syariah status yang berasingan. Antara masalah-masalah ini ialah sesuatu yang berkaitan dengan Undang-undang Syariah di peringkat kebangsaan, latihan Hakim-hakim Syariah dan langkah-langkah untuk menggabungkan sistem-sistem yang berlainan melalui persetujuan dan rundingan. Pada hemat saya tidak dapat dinafikan bahawa mana-mana sistem perundangan mestilah berubah dari masa ke semasa supaya bersesuaian dengan perubahan zaman. Bagi negara kita, saya berpendapat kita bertuah kerana dapat mengekalkan sistem perundangan kini yang telah membekalkan asas di mana sistem perundangan kita dapat dibentuk, perbaiki dan diperkembangkan, meskipun konsep-konsep asal berkemungkinan diubah mengikut keadaan.

Oleh itu dengan melalui forum seperti ini yang bertemakan synergi syariah dan sivil, saya berpendapat usaha ke arah persefahaman antara dua aliran perundangan di negara ini iaitu di kalangan syariah dan sivil dapat digabung dan diperkukuhkan antara satu dengan lain. Dengan itu secara tidak langsung atau secara 'low profile' akan dapat memberi fahaman kepada masyarakat tentang kedudukan dan perjalanan undang-undang di negara ini. Usaha-usaha Kerajaan untuk meningkatkan pemakaian undang-undang syariah dan kedudukan Mahkamah-mahkamah Syariah di negara ini amatlah perlu disokong oleh semua pihak.

Akhirnya saya mengucapkan syabas dan tahniah kepada Bahagian Hal Ehwal Islam, Jabatan Perdana Menteri kerana telah mengambil inisiatif untuk mengadakan seminar ini dan saya berharap seminar seperti ini akan dapat diadakan dari masa ke semasa.

LEGAL EDUCATION IN MALAYSIA*

Introduction

Terlebih dahulu izinkan saya mengucap tahniah kepada Fakulti Undang-Undang yang telah genap dua puluh tahun. Over the past twenty years, the Faculty of Law as the pioneer law school in Malaysia has achieved great heights. A number of its students have done the Faculty proud by excelling in both the private and public sectors. Many of them are now holding high positions in the judicial and legal service, big corporations and also in the Faculty itself. I believe the current dean of the Faculty is also a graduate of the Faculty. The achievements secured by these students speak much for the reputation of the Faculty and evidently is a reflection of the standard of education of the institution.

Graduates proficient in English-National Language

The Faculty is also the pioneer in producing a new breed of graduates, i.e. graduates who are proficient in both the English Language and the National Language. As we are all aware, Bahasa Malaysia has become the official language of the courts although English may be used with the court's leave where the interests of justice demand. Thus, the availability of these graduates has contributed to the successful and smooth implementation of the usage of the National Language in the courts. The Faculty and the students should therefore be proud of their role in attaining this national aspiration. The Faculty has also contributed much to the publication of legal literature especially in the Malaysian laws. These are but a few of the achievements of the Faculty over the past twenty years. I am sure that law teachers and students, both past and present, are proud of these achievements and of the fact that the Faculty has become one of the best law schools in the country and in this region.

Foreign and local Universities

Today, however, the Faculty of Law in the University of Malaya is no longer the only law school training our future lawyers and legal officers. Several other law schools have been set up in the country producing law graduates. Further-

---

**At The Seminar On Legal Education In Malaysia Organized By The Faculty Of Law, University Of Malaya On 20 October 1992.*

more, every year, a great number of students leave for overseas to read law in foreign universities. Those who are unable to do so take up what is known as distance learning courses by way of correspondence. The availability of the various avenues leading to a law degree has resulted in the upsurge of the number of lawyers seeking admission to the Bar. In Kuala Lumpur alone, the number of petitions for admission to the Bar in the year 1991 was 705 and the number for the year 1992 up to the month of September is 618. These figures speak for themselves about the number of lawyers the country is producing at the moment. With the diversity in the curriculum and the different emphasis placed in the legal education programmes undertaken by each of the law schools and with the large number of students graduating each year, I believe it is time that we address ourselves to the future of legal education in this country. There is no denying that the time is ripe that we take stock and review the role of our law schools.

Important Issues

A number of important issues need to be addressed. Are the law schools geared towards the manpower needs of the country? Are they in line with the national aspirations? What are the changes that need to be made in the light of the Government's objective to achieve an industrialised nation status by the year 2020? While it is generally accepted that the standard of legal education of the law schools in Malaysia is high, the time has come for the objectives of each of the law schools in the country to be clearly defined. The question that arises is whether each of the law schools should play the same role or some specifically different role. Should we not consider the establishment of a common post-graduate centre to train these graduates? In this regard, the needs of the profession as well as the needs and expectations of the country have to be considered. Are we going to have too many lawyers? Has any projection been made in this regard? Do we have enough lawyers specialising in specific fields? Are the law schools placing sufficient emphasis on the specific areas of the law where expertise is required? These and many more questions need to be asked and answers to them have to be found. I am confident that this seminar will address a number of specific issues pertaining to this matter.

Legal Education and Social Aspects

I take the liberty to point out at this stage that the duty imposed on our own law schools in regard to legal education should not be confined to the teaching of the principles of law only. It should be widened to cover the social aspects. Topics like ethics and social responsibilities should be made part and parcel of the legal education. I believe that the legal profession has always been looked upon with respect by the society. However, as of late, adverse publicity on the unethical conduct of lawyers has frequently been highlighted in the press. We hear of various types of white collar crimes committed by lawyers. If left unchecked, I fear that public confidence in the legal profession would erode with the result that the respect that should be accorded to the legal profession will diminish. It is thus important that colleges inculcate the principles of professional ethics and standards in the students.

Legal Aid

On the topic of legal aid, I am of the view that it should be made part of the curriculum of legal education so as to instill the values of a caring society in our law graduates. In a caring society there would be more volunteers who would come forward to provide legal aid to those who cannot afford to pay for legal services. It is often said that the legal profession is a lucrative profession but, sad to say, over the years much emphasis has been rested on status and gain. Conceivably financial interest and pursuit of self interest has become the goal of many lawyers. It is therefore appropriate for the lawyers as a body to review the well being and role of a lawyer and the contribution that they can offer to society.

In other words, a balance should be struck between the interests of society and the personal interests of lawyers. The emphasis on personal interest may lead to a situation where in some cases lawyers discharge themselves in court just before the hearing because of the failure of the clients to pay the fees. In those circumstances the courts have no choice but to allow cases to be postponed to enable the "abandoned" client to get another lawyer or to secure the money to pay his lawyer. This will contribute to the increase in the backlog of cases.

Continuing Legal Education

I now turn to the topic of continuing legal education which would be discussed at this seminar. For obvious reasons a law graduate does not cease his legal education upon graduation. The learning process therefore has to continue. Law is, after all, not static. It grows. This is especially so in countries like ours where the law is continuously being developed so that it may have an identity of its own to suit the nation. Even in the established branches of the law, many changes are taking place — changes in the decisions of the courts and in the interpretation of the laws. No matter how we practise the law—I use the word "practise" here in a broad sense to cover law teachers, advocates and solicitors, legal officers, corporate advisers or bank officers—we need to be up to date with these changes. Continuing legal education can take the form of a formal course for a fixed duration or even by way of one day seminars and workshops. Whilst I agree that not much has been done by way of such courses in this country even for magistrates, sessions court judges and judges of the superior Courts, the judiciary has now embarked upon a plan to organize specific courses specially tailored for our newly recruited magistrates and the plan is to eventually provide refresher courses for magistrates and judges. This course, known as the induction course, is actually only a two-week course. Participants are given talks on the various aspects of legal practice such as advocacy skills, principles of sentencing, ethics of the courts, etc. Upon completion of the course, the officers are then sent to the various courts to resume their duties. Such courses are designed to assist these officers in the discharge of their duties in a more effective and efficient manner. Continuing legal education is clearly necessary to keep lawyers well abreast of the trends and changes in the growth of current development of the law. Much could be achieved through seminars and programmes designed to update and review their skills and knowledge and to explore new and developing areas of law and procedure.

Research Institutes

Updating of legal education, to my mind, is a necessary process if we are to produce efficient lawyers. Positive policy is needed. There must be law institutes which are devoted to research to secure solutions to complex international policy problems involving governments and other multinational corporations especially in the field of economic development, foreign investment and loans, transfer of technology, arbitration, intellectual property and so forth.

Speaking of development and continuing legal education in the ASEAN countries with different judicial and legal systems, it is my view that countries in this region with similar legal and judicial systems could work closely together to provide continuing legal training beneficial to all of them subject, of course, to the reservation that the legal institutions in each country may have to tailor their legal education to meet the needs and aspirations of the particular nation. The close co-operation between countries with similar judicial and legal institutions, however, would help secure a continuing exchange of opinion on matters concerning new developments and legal devices and adaptation of all means to new solutions and so forth. Generally speaking, I believe that the law schools are appropriate institutions to organize refresher courses on selected areas of the law. This can be done jointly with the Bench, the Bar and other professional bodies.

Conclusion

Before I conclude permit me to say that law as the foundation and index of civilisation is crucial to the wellbeing of a community. Speaking of law and legal education, it is appropriate to quote what Shah Khabruzzaman from Bangladesh said in his opening paragraph in a paper presented by him at the 10th Lawasia Conference in Kuala Lumpur in July 1987 with which I subscribe as follows:–

> "A concomitant to this situation is the education of man in law. There must be a continual process in educating man in law and to keep him in track with the latest trends and developments in the domain of law noticeable in the developed countries of the world. The importance of legal education has assumed a significant dimension in the fast flow of social and political events in the developing countries including countries in the Lawasia region. A sound solid legal education system is the only safeguard to the pursuit of a peaceful life of civilised existence. It is, therefore, essential that legal education should be imparted to the people of this region for establishing a Rule of Law for a better and prosperous future."

Ladies and gentlemen, in conclusion, I wish each of you present at this seminar a fruitful and stimulating discussion. May your deliberations and the decisions at this seminar contribute further to the development of legal education in this country.

Dengan ucapan Bismillah saya resmikan pembukaan seminar ini.

ETIKA PROFESION*

Etika profesion: Apakah ertinya?
Mengikut kamus etika bermakna sesuatu sistem dasar akhlak atau tingkah laku (kesusilaan). Maka dengan itu etika profesion adalah sesuatunya yang dikaitkan dengan tingkah laku.

Dalam apa-apa profesion sekalipun etika adalah sangat penting untuk menjamin kehormatan sesuatu profesion—lebih-lebih lagi, dalam profesion undang-undang.

Dalam bidang profesion undang-undang pula kejayaan seseorang itu semestinya dipandang juga dari segi kebolehannya menegakkan prinsip-prinsip keadilan kerana ini adalah suatu ciri istimewa profesion ini. Sebagai ahli golongan profesion undang-undang, ia merupakan suatu bukti ikrar janji yang serius dan mulia, oleh kerana, mereka yang mempunyai kemahiran dan pengetahuan khusus dalam menjalankan amalan undang-undang semestinya bersedia untuk berkhidmat kepada orang awam, dengan berpegang kepada etika yang paling tinggi, melebihi dari apa yang diperlukan daripada rakyat biasa, pendek kata ia sewajarnya bersedia menerima tanggungjawab sepenuhnya terhadap mereka yang memerlukan khidmat mereka.

Dalam hal ini maka seseorang yang berkenaan perlu menghayati unsur-unsur yang tertentu selain dari moral tinggi dan rasa penuh tanggungjawab kerana ini pada hemat saya, boleh menjadi benteng pertahanan daripada gejala-gejala buruk.

Etika profesion undang-undang bukan sesuatu subjek yang diajar di universiti-universiti tetapi ini tidak bermakna kurang pentingnya dan tidak juga bermakna seseorang itu tidak mungkin menjadi peguam yang berwibawa kerana etika profesion undang-undang khususnya adalah soal sikap.

Sikap takut kepada tuhan, amanah, jujur dan ikhlas adalah di antara nilai-nilai yang menjadi teras kepada Etika Guaman. Ketiadaan nilai-nilai yang saya sebutkan tadi boleh menghakiskan kepercayaan orang ramai terhadap profesion guaman. Jika keadaan ini wujud sudah tentu keluhuran undang-undang seperti digariskan dalam rukun negara akan tidak bermakna lagi.

**Program Kursus Induksi Khusus Pegawai Kehakiman Dan Perundangan Di INTAN, Bukit Kiara, Kuala Lumpur, Pada 23hb Oktober, 1992.*

Dalam usaha melahirkan peguam-peguam yang bermutu serta menepati nilai-nilai yang tersebut tadi, penekanan terhadap etika guaman harus diberikan di peringkat awal lagi iaitu di peringkat pengajian tinggi. Pelajar-pelajar tidak seharusnya berorientasikan peperiksaan sahaja tanpa kesedaran tentang tanggungjawab yang harus dipikul apabila keluar dari institusi pengajian tinggi tersebut.

Kita tidak dapat nafikan bahawa manusia berusaha untuk mengejar kekayaan material tetapi untuk diseimbangkan dengan kejayaan kerohanian adalah amat penting. Tidak seimbang jika kita mempunyai peguam-peguam yang pintar dan bergeliga tetapi nilai kerohanian dan moral yang rendah.

Etika yang saya sebutkan tadi merangkumi bukan sahaja seseorang peguam tetapi lebih-lebih lagi seseorang yang berkhidmat sebagai Timbalan Pendakwa Raya, Penolong Kanan Pendaftar dan Majistret. Buat malam ini saya akan tumpuhkan khas kepada mereka yang berkhidmat sebagai majistret.

Perlantikan seorang Majistret: Seseorang majistret adalah dilantik di bawah seksyen 78 Subordinate Courts Act 1948. Section 78 of the Act specifically provides that only a fit and proper person shall be appointed. However, the law does not define what a "fit and proper person" is. Presumably, it must mean that before a person is appointed he must be a person of good character, of good repute, possessed of honesty, integrity and of an unblemished conduct. The description necessarily warrants quality. A fit and proper person should accordingly be a fit and proper person for the post. He should be so for in that capacity he has to shoulder very heavy responsibilities. He has to dispense justice and in that capacity he is the symbol of justice.

To administer justice impartially: Primarily, it is the duty of the courts to administer justice impartially between citizen and citizen and between citizen and state according to law. In discharging his function, a magistrate must not only be impartial but must also conduct himself in a manner that will not give the appearance of partiality, i.e., he must show that he is absolutely free from any suspicion of being partial. Impartiality and an appearance of it are supreme judicial qualities. It is significant to note that impartiality or the appearance of impartiality should, of course, be accompanied by an ability to give a properly considered judgment.

Independence of the Judiciary: It is of cardinal importance that the independence of the judiciary be maintained for it is infinitely related to the whole system of our government which is based on the rule of law and entrenched in the doctrine of separation of powers, namely, that of the legislative, executive and judicial. The concept of the independence of the judiciary is inherent in our system of government and must necessarily be respected and should not be lost sight of if we are to appreciate the values of democracy and the rule of law. In other words, all the three organs must discharge their respective functions to sustain the rule of law and a democratic government. The value of an independent judiciary, however, would be seriously eroded if essential judicial functions are removed from the courts and entrusted in the hands of administrative authorities. As you can see it is vitally important that the judiciary maintains its independence as it is crucial to the administration of justice. The concept is applicable to all levels of judicial administration. To ensure judicial independence certain qualities are demanded of a magistrate before he is entrusted with judicial functions.

Threats to the Independence of the Judiciary: May I at this juncture observe that there are occasions when members of the public have expressed concern over increasing threats to the independence of the judiciary in the courts at all levels. This is understandable in view of what I have just stated. The importance of the independence of the judiciary needs no exaggeration as the community's interest would clearly depend on whether a judge or a magistrate is able to play and maintain the role of an impartial umpire and to act in a manner consistent only with established concepts.

In view of the importance of the office of a magistrate public impression must not be ignored, for otherwise we cannot maintain public respect. Public impression of the performance of a magistrate is most crucial because it is at that level in our system of administration of justice that the majority of the members of the public first get in contact with the actual working of the law. Their impression of justice is invariably formed from their experience in these courts. Magistrates must therefore bear this in mind at all times.

Sewajarnya seseorang majistret itu sedar bahawa segala gerak geri, tingkah laku sama ada dalam menjalankan tugas harian ataupun di dalam lapangan-lapangan lain adalah sentiasa dalam pemerhatian semua lapisan masyarakat. Jika majistret atau pendaftar tidak menjalankan tugas mereka dengan jujur, tekun dan ikhlas, maka bukan sahaja imej mereka akan terjejas tetapi imej badan kehakiman keseluruhannya akan turut terjejas.

Justice and Rule of Law: What is justice?

Lord Denning in his lecture entitled *The Road to Justice* published in 1955 posed this question and then said -

> "What is justice? That question has been asked by men far wiser than you or me and no one has yet found a satisfactory answer. All I would suggest is that justice is not something you can see. It is not temporal but eternal. How does man know what is justice? It is not the product of his intellect but of his spirit. The nearest we can get to defining justice is to say that it is *what the*

> *right-minded members of the community*—those who have the right spirit within them—*believe to be fair.*"

The basic problem is where to draw the line and how to maintain a proper balance between individual liberty and legal control.

Judicial ethics: Before I speak on some aspects of the ethics of the profession which is particularly relevant to magistrates, may I at this point say that "seseorang majistret itu bermula perkhidmatannya dalam perkhidmatan awam dan semua tatatertib yang mungkin diambil adalah menurut apa jua peruntukkan dalam General Orders. Dan tindakan tatatertib mungkin diambil terhadap sesuatu perbuatan majistret yang bertentangan dengan mana-mana peruntukan dalam General Orders. Selain dari peruntukan tertentu maka seseorang majistret perlu, memandangkan kedudukannya sebagai hakim mematuhi etika kehakiman."

Free from bias: A magistrate whose role is to impartially umpire a case should be free from bias. An allegation of bias may emanate from or be levelled at a magistrate by a party to a suit or an accused in a criminal case. An allegation of bias may well have arisen from the magistrate's own conduct or certain utterances made by him in or outside the court. It could also be on account of his relationship with a particular person. I am not saying that close association *per se* gives rise to a suspicion of bias but an allegation to that effect may in certain circumstances be justified, where, for example, a magistrate associates very freely or openly with a particular lawyer who frequently appears before him. An impression may be formed that the lawyer would receive special treatment from the magistrate. It is in a situation such as this that a party to a civil suit may feel that, if the lawyer representing the other party is a bosom friend of the magistrate, he may not get a fair hearing and would therefore feel justice would not be done. Where, therefore, there are grounds for a party to entertain a suspicion that justice cannot under those circumstances be done, the matter should not at all be viewed very lightly. You are fully aware that justice must not only be done but must manifestly be seen to be done. A magistrate should remember that he is entrusted with the duty to dispense justice and it is therefore necessary for him to conduct himself in a manner that would give no room for suspicion that justice can no longer be meted out by him. I would hasten to add that a magistrate is not of course expected to be hostile to lawyers. Generally speaking he should maintain a close rapport with members of the Bar for they too have a role to play in the administration of justice.

Patient and courteous: One of the qualities demanded of a magistrate is patience. He should afford a fair and patient hearing to a case before him. Be that as it may, he has to exercise a firm control over the proceedings and should not succumb to an attempt on the part of any lawyer to unnecessarily protract a proceeding. A magistrate should be courteous but firm.

Bertugas dengan dedikasi: Semua pegawai hendaklah menyedari dan memastikan bahawa mereka hendaklah menjalankan tugas dengan penuh dedikasi, taat setia dan berakhlak mulia kerana ini akan memberi gambaran yang baik di kalangan orang ramai. Dalam membicarakan kes-kes, tuan-tuan dan puan-puan yang masih dianggap berusia muda sudah tentulah pernah menghadapi masalah di mana pihak yang berhadapan dengan tuan-tuan dan puan-puan di mahkamah mungkin berumur lebih tua. Oleh itu gerak geri, tutur kata yang dilafazkan oleh tuan-tuan dan puan-puan hendaklah tidak keterlaluan. Kita hanya perlu melafazkan perkara-perkara atau isu-isu yang bersangkutan dengan kes yang kita kendalikan sahaja dan elakkanlah daripada menyindir dan menyinggung perasaan sesiapa sahaja yang berhadapan dengan kita di dalam mahkamah. Saya sering kali terbaca di akhbar-akhbar dan juga kadangkala menerima aduan daripada orang ramai di mana terdapatnya sebilangan pegawai-pegawai yang suka mengeluarkan kata-kata yang menyentuh peribadi mana-mana pihak yang tidak ada kena mengena dengan kes yang didengar. Ini hendaklah dielakkan sama sekali kerana ia akan menjatuhkan imej Jabatan Kehakiman.

Remarks and interruptions: I shall finally speak on a matter concerning remarks and interruptions made in the course of a trial. A magistrate's duty is to try a case and in so doing he ought to play the role of an impartial umpire. He is not expected to say too much and should of course refrain from making uncalled-for-remarks—the sort that could be hurtful to those who appear before him. In certain instances the remarks made by a magistrate could even touch on a matter which is very controversial and could attract criticisms. It is therefore desirable that a magistrate should stay out of public controversy. That being the case, the magistrate must rely on his conduct to be its own vindication. Be that as it may, it is true that a magistrate is not free from criticisms. Indeed he is very vulnerable and is exposed to criticisms. Nevertheless nothing should deter him from doing what the occasion requires provided it is pertinent to the matter in hand.

Judges and magistrates are entrusted, on behalf of the community, to weigh conflicting interests; to weigh on the one hand the respect due to the confidence in the profession and on the other hand the ultimate interest of the community in justice being done. It does not speak well of a magistrate to talk too much. In this regard I feel it incumbent upon me to cite the case referred to by Lord Denning in his book *The Due Process of Law* at page 58—the chapter dealing with the conduct of judges with special reference to the judge who talked too much, to illustrate my point.

In *Jones* v *National Coal Board* (1957) 2 QB 55, the widow of a coal miner who was killed after the roof of a coal mine had fallen on him claimed damages. The case was tried by Hallet, J. who dismissed the claim. She appealed. One of the grounds of appeal was that the judge's interruptions had made it impossible for her counsel to put her case properly. The Board under cross-appeal also raised as one of the grounds the issue that the judge's interruptions prevented the Board from having a fair trial. Speaking for the whole Court, Denning, LJ (as he was then) had this to say:

> "No one can doubt that the judge, in intervening as he did, was actuated by the best motives. He was anxious to understand the details of this complicated case, and asked questions to get them clear in his mind. He was anxious that the witnesses should not be harassed unduly in cross-examination, and intervened to protect them when he thought necessary. He was anxious to investigate all the various criticisms that had been made against the board, and to see whether they were well founded or not. Hence, he took them up himself with the witnesses from time to time. He was anxious that the case should not be dragged on too long, and intimated clearly when he thought that a point had been sufficiently explored. All those are worthy motives on which judges daily intervene in the conduct of cases, and have done for centuries.
>
> Nevertheless, we are quite clear that the interventions, taken together, were far more than they should have been. In the system of trial which we have evolved in this country, the judge sits to hear and determine the issues raised by the parties, not to conduct an investigation or examination on behalf of society at large.....however a judge is not a mere umpire to answer the question 'How's that?' His object, above all, is to find the truth, and to do justice according to law;.....And Lord Greene MR who explained that justice is best done by a judge who holds the balance between the contending parties without himself taking part in their disputations. If a judge, said Lord Greene, should himself conduct the examination of witnesses, 'he, so to speak, descends into the arena and is liable to have his vision clouded by the dust of conflict': see *Yuill* v *Yuill* (1945) p.15 at 20, (1945) 1 All ER 183, 61 TLR 176.
>
> Yes, he must keep his vision unclouded. It is all very well to paint justice blind, but she does better without a bandage round her eyes. She should be blind indeed to favour or prejudice, but clear to see which way lies the truth: and the less dust there is about the better. Let the advocates one after the other put weights into the scales—the 'nicely calculated less or more'—but the judge at the end decides which way the balance tilts, be it ever so slightly..... So also it is for the advocates, each in his turn, to examine the witnesses, and not for the judge to take it on himself lest by so doing he appear to favour one side or the other: see *R.* v *Cain* (1936) 25 CrAppRep 204; *R.* v *Bateman* (1946) 321 CrAppRep 106 and *Harris* v *Harris* (1952), Times, 9

> April; Judgment of the Court of Appeal No.148 by Birket LJ especially. And it is for the advocate to state his case as fairly and strongly as he can, without undue interruption, lest the sequence of his argument be lost: see *R* v *Clewer* (1953) 37 CrAppRep 37. The judge's part in all this is to hearken to the evidence, only himself asking questions of witnesses when it is necessary to clear up any point that has been overlooked or left obscure; to see that the advocates behave themselves seemly and keep to the rules laid down by law; to exclude irrelevancies and discourage repetition; to make sure by wise intervention that he follows the points that the advocates are making and can assess their worth; and at the end to make up his mind where the truth lies. If he goes beyond this, he drops the mantle of a judge and assumes the robe of an advocate.....".

Adalah harapan saya pesanan-pesanan ini akan dipertimbangkan dengan halus-halus dan diambil kira setiap masa tuan-tuan dan puan-puan menjalankan tugas. Insya-allah jika diamalkan dengan perasaan dedikasi dan bertanggungjawab maka perkhidmatan yang tuan-tuan dan puan-puan curahkan kepada negara akan diberkati Allah (S.W.).

USAHA MENINGKATKAN PENERBITAN BAHAN UNDANG-UNDANG DALAM BAHASA MALAYSIA*

Terlebih dahulu saya ingin mengucapkan ribuan terima kasih kepada pengerusi dan Jawatankuasa Pelancaran Buku Undang-Undang Yang Kedua Dewan Bahasa dan Pustaka kerana sudi mengundang saya untuk turut hadir pada Majlis ini serta memberi peluang kepada saya merakamkan sepatah dua kata dan seterusnya melancarkan buku pada pagi ini.

Tuan-tuan dan para hadirin sekalian,

Majlis yang diadakan pada pagi ini memang kena pada masanya. Setelah kira-kira tiga tahun badan kehakiman melaksanakan penggunaan Bahasa Malaysia sepenuhnya di Mahkamah di Semenanjung iaitu bermula pada 1 Jun 1990 maka segala usaha untuk mencapai matlamat ini amat saya alu-alukan.

Perkembangan Bahasa Malaysia di Mahkamah dapat dikaitkan dengan satu peristiwa penting dalam sistem perundangan negara, iaitu pindaan yang dilakukan pada Seksyen 8 Akta Bahasa Kebangsaan 1963/1967 yang berkuatkuasa pada bulan Mac 1990. Pindaan terhadap Akta inilah yang membawa kepada penguatkuasaan dasar penggunaan Bahasa Malaysia dalam bidang kehakiman dan undang-undang di semua peringkat mahkamah di Semenanjung. Dengan penguatkuasaan pindaan Akta ini juga kita dapat menyaksikan betapa pesatnya usaha-usaha untuk meningkatkan penggunaan Bahasa Melayu dalam sektor kehakiman ini. Atas pelbagai usaha ini kita sewajarnya berterima kasih kepada semua pihak yang prihatin terhadap aspirasi rakyat dan negara untuk mendaulatkan penggunaan Bahasa Malaysia dalam semua aspek kehidupan masyarakat majmuk di negara kita ini.

Saya berasa amat bangga dengan peranan Dewan Bahasa dan Pustaka yang berusaha untuk menjayakan pelaksanaan penggunaan Bahasa Malaysia di mahkamah yang begitu menonjol sekali. Sehingga kini saya difahamkan bahawa Dewan Bahasa dan Pustaka begitu giat menerbitkan pelbagai bahan dan rujukan dalam bidang undang-undang. Ini termasuklah penerbitan buku-buku teks dan rujukan undang-undang, buku istilah undang-undang, jurnal undang-undang iaitu Kanun untuk memenuhi matlamat tersebut. Saya juga di-

---

**Di Majlis Pelancaran Buku Undang-Undang Kedua Pada 31hb Oktober, 1992 Di Balai Seminar, Dewan Bahasa Dan Pustaka, Kuala Lumpur.*

maklumkan bahawa dalam rancangan lima tahun penerbitan buku undang-undang, Dewan merancang untuk menghasilkan sekurang-kurangnya 100 judul buku undang-undang sama ada karya asli mahupun terjemahan, dan juga glosari undang-undang. Saya juga difahamkan bahawa pihak Dewan Bahasa dan Pustaka baru-baru ini turut membuat kajian untuk mengenal pasti kemajuan dan tahap penggunaan Bahasa Malaysia di kalangan para profesional undang-undang dan di kalangan pelajar undang-undang di institusi pengajian tinggi di negara ini. Apa yang saya harapkan ialah hasil laporan kajian tersebut akan membolehkan tindakan susulan dan mengenal pasti langkah yang perlu diambil untuk meningkatkan tahap penggunaan Bahasa Malaysia dalam bidang perundangan.

Sehubungan dengan itu, saya mengambil kesempatan mengucapkan syabas dan tahniah kepada Dewan Bahasa dan Pustaka di atas kejayaan semua pihak yang menyelenggarakan penerbitan bahan undang-undang. Usaha ini dapat dibuktikan dengan bertambahnya dua puluh judul lagi buku undang-undang yang akan dilancarkan pada pagi ini. Saya juga ingin mengambil kesempatan di sini mengucapkan terima kasih dan tahniah kepada penulis, penterjemah, penyunting, ahli-ahli panel penasihat/penilai buku undang-undang dan para petugas yang menggembelengkan kepakaran, tenaga dan masa masing-masing dalam menerbitkan buku ini. Saya berharap usaha ini akan diteruskan dengan lebih gigih lagi supaya pencapaiannya lebih cemerlang dari segi kualiti mahupun kuantiti. Dan dalam Majlis ini juga kita sewajarnya memberi penghormatan khusus kepada Yang Berbahagia Prof. Tan Sri Dato' Ahmad Ibrahim yang telah memberikan sumbangan yang amat besar dalam bidang undang-undang di negara ini. Malah di Dewan Bahasa sendiri Prof. Tan Sri terlibat secara langsung sebagai pengerusi panel penilai/penasihat buku undang-undang, saya juga difahamkan Prof. juga akan dilantik sebagai Penyunting Lembaga Majalah Kanun. Semoga usaha Prof. Tan Sri ini akan menjadi teladan kepada kita semua.

Tuan-tuan dan para hadirin yang dihormati sekalian,

Menyentuh tentang keupayaan dan tahap penggunaan Bahasa Malaysia di kalangan hakim dan peguam, sukacita saya menyatakan di sini bahawa golongan ini kebanyakannya boleh bertutur tetapi tahap penguasaan dan penggunaan bahasa tersebut berbeza mengikut latar belakang diri masing-masing. Penggunaan Bahasa Malaysia di kalangan hakim dan peguam adalah berbeza. Para hakim lebih cenderung berbincang dan berurusan dengan kakitangan dan rakan-rakan dalam Bahasa Malaysia. Tetapi di kalangan peguam khususnya Bahasa Inggeris lebih banyak digunakan. Namun begitu penguasaan Bahasa Malaysia di kalangan peguam semakin bertambah baik. Saya harap mereka yang masih belum dapat menguasai Bahasa Malaysia mengambil langkah segera untuk mengatasinya.

Tuan-tuan dan para hadirin yang dihormati sekalian,

Bahan bacaan bidang undang-undang yang bertulis dalam Bahasa Malaysia memang boleh didapati sekarang terutamanya buku-buku terbitan Dewan Bahasa dan Pustaka. Tetapi, jumlahnya masih lagi belum mencukupi untuk menampung keperluan golongan hakim, peguam dan para pelajar undang-undang di institusi pengajian tinggi. Oleh itu, usaha yang lebih giat perlu diambil untuk menambah bahan-bahan bacaan tersebut. Beban ini tidak sepatutnya ditanggung oleh Dewan Bahasa semata-mata. Sebaliknya penerbit-penerbit lain seperti penerbit universiti dan penerbit-penerbit swasta boleh turut serta menambah penerbitan bahan-bahan undang-undang ini.

Dalam usaha memperbanyakkan buku-buku dalam bidang undang-undang ini saya menyeru pakar dalam undang-undang supaya tampil ke hadapan menulis buku dalam Bahasa Malaysia untuk memperbanyakkan bahan bacaan tersebut. Dengan penggunaan Bahasa Malaysia di mahkamah dan penulisan laporan serta buku-buku bacaan akan terhasillah nanti laras bahasa undang-undang yang mantap.

Dengan ini saya yakin jumlah judul dan kualiti bahan-bahan penerbitan dalam bidang undang-undang dalam Bahasa Malaysia akan dapat dipertingkat lagi dan sekaligus faktor ini akan mempercepatkan penggunaan Bahasa Malaysia di mahkamah seperti yang kita cita-citakan selama ini. Dengan ini saya mengakhiri ucapan ini dan dengan lafaz Bismillah hirrahmannirrahim melancarkan dua puluh judul buku undang-undang penerbitan Dewan Bahasa dan Pustaka dengan rasminya.

THE ROLE OF JUSTICES OF THE PEACE*

It is a great honour for me to be invited to address you on the occasion of the National Convention of Justices of the Peace (JPs), Malaysia. The last occasion I had the privilege to do so was on 5th March, 1989. Since then we cannot fail to notice that our nation has achieved tremendous economic and social progress among developing nations to the extent that we are now a force to be reckoned with in international matters. Yet, we cannot afford to be complacent and every Malaysian should continue in the task of nation building. In that process, what is the function of elite bodies like yours comprising of distinguished men in national development? In this context, a quotation from the late American President, John F. Kennedy becomes relevant. He asked Americans, "Ask not what your country can do for you, ask what you can do for your country." In my humble view the same poser applies to all of us.

At this juncture of our emergence as a developed nation in the global arena, there is a need for greater unity among the people of this region. After 35 years of independence, we ought to have achieved full national unity of our multiracial and multi-religious society notwithstanding the practice of democratic institutions geared to create a Malaysian consciousness. Our actions in the field of economic development and social services are the embodiment of our desire to preserve this institution for the happiness and betterment of our people. We must have the ability to reconcile and govern the speed and nature of changes taking place oriented towards Vision 2020. For such contribution, what power and opportunity do the JPs have? To answer the question let us look at the historical origin of Justices of the Peace and their powers.

Locally, Justices of the Peace are, in the main, the creation and legacy of the colonial administration. In England, the office of a Justice of the Peace has a very long history as an institution in the legal system. A Royal Proclamation in 1195 set up Knights of the Peace to assist the Sheriff in the maintenance of law and order. This was the origin of Justices of the Peace. Initially, they were selected from "good and lawful men" "assigned to keep peace" holding administrative rather than judicial authority. From 1496, Justices were permitted to try

---

**At The 2nd National Convention Of Justices Of The Peace, Malaysia On 1st November, 1992 At The Royal Lake Club, Kuala Lumpur.*

minor summary criminal cases locally. In England, a JP who is also known as magistrate should live within fifteen miles of the area where he is sitting. In their sittings, JPs are assisted by a qualified barrister or solicitor of at least five years standing. A JP, probably because of his lack of educational qualification, cannot sit on the Bench alone. The number of summary cases heard annually by JPs and paid magistrates, who are very few, is approximately two million, which is 95% of all criminal cases tried in England and Wales. It is estimated that there are over 26,000 lay magistrates known as JPs. The inclusion of laymen in the legal system is generally felt to be an excellent arrangement, since it ensures that the law, in particular, criminal law, is kept in close contact with representatives of the public, who are affected by it. It is argued that this helps to preserve a respect for law throughout the community.

In Malaysia, in the main, there are almost a dozen statutes empowering JPs with varying powers which are hardly exercised. Since 1953, JPs may issue search warrants against premises and persons, apart from themselves entering and searching the premises, when they have good reason to believe that suspected premises are kept or used as common gaming houses. The same powers are given to JPs when dealing with bookmakers, their authority being vested on them by the Betting Ordinance 1953. In view of the risks involved in such operations, it is not surprising that the exercise of such powers has fallen into disuse. Unlike magistrates and senior police officers, they have no protection against unruly elements. In the name of assisting members of the public, JPs are entrusted with witnessing certain documents. This is more of a status symbol function. Two commonly used powers are attestation of loan documents in the case of illiterate borrowers under the Moneylenders Ordinance 1951 and authentication of Power of Attorney under the Power of Attorney Ordinance 1949. Other powers which are not commonly exercised are attestation of alteration in agreement with the crew of a ship under the Merchant Shipping Ordinance 1952 and administering oath to an election agent in respect of election expenses under the Election Offences Act 1954. Their extra respectability and responsibility for community welfare over and above ordinary citizens are recognised in them being granted powers equivalent to a Public Prosecutor and similar dignitaries on an optional basis. The laws stipulate that a court shall not take cognizance of any offence under the Children and Young Persons Act without the written sanction of a Public Prosecutor or upon a complaint made by (among others) a JP. One very useful power for the community where JPs can contribute immensely is that they may visit prisons in their state to examine prisons and prisoners. They are empowered to question them and make observations in a Visitors Book for the attestation of visiting JPs.

There are other persons entrusted with the same powers as stated above. They are usually paid for it unlike the JPs. That may be the reason why JPs are handicapped in making their social impact. Another reason for their inactivity in the legal arena may be due to the fact that in England the system of lay public judging their own peers through the jury and JP system has existed for more than 700 years. The sociology of people are conditioned for the system to operate. The English have no language or racial problems to the extent that the nations in the East face. The most important power of the JPs according to the statute book is the provision of Part IX of the Subordinate Courts Act 1948 under which they may be authorised to act as second class magistrates.

Incidentally, there is nothing significant in the position of a second-class magistrate that any increase in their number will make any major contribution to the legal system. In practice, they are usually public servants and junior court officers who have no legal qualification but are engaged in administrative or quasi-judicial duties such as granting bail or mentioning cases in places where there is no resident magistrate. In law, they are empowered to try criminal offences where the maximum punishment imposed is no more than twelve months imprisonment. If he tries such offences, his power is limited to a maximum of six months imprisonment and a fine not exceeding RM1,000 or a combination of both. Where he is of the opinion that the accused who is found guilty should receive a heavier penalty then he can impose, he may transfer the case to a first-class magistrate.

There have been many suggestions that in suitable cases, some of the JPs could be gazetted as second-class magistrates to conduct inquests, hear traffic cases or sit in quasi-tribunals. I refrain from offering any positive promise in this request as the whole issue is for the Government to decide. All I can say is that the problem needs consideration and study at Parliamentary level. I wholeheartedly agree that law should never remain stable but must be modified to meet the changing circumstances..

The fact that the participation of JPs in the legal administration in England or Australia has produced excellent results does not mean that it can therefore automatically be adopted in this country. The jurisprudential theory is that political and civil laws of each nation must in fact be particular to the people for whom they are made. The fact that the title of JPs is mentioned in many pieces of legislation does not by itself create any practical privileges or rights. We have to consider the JPs educational qualifications, age structure, the availability of alternative manpower, supporting staff and facilities and a host of other social repercussions.

Meanwhile, are all doors closed to JPs for public service? Are their talents being wasted? Not so. It is for your organization to create a climate of public opinion to recognise and avail your services. Those who are suitable can sit as arbitrators, if the parties choose them for resolution of disputes. They can be unofficial ombudsmen and serve as the link between Government, local authorities and the members of the public. They can be personal examples of national unity, ignoring ethnic or cultural considerations. There are so many social evils like drug menaces and juvenile delinquency where by virtue of their elite status, JPs can contribute by voluntary leadership participation. By pointing out these avenues, I should not be taken to oppose their appointment as judicial officers or in similar capacities. Personally, I know many of you whose common sense and wisdom is greater than that of many new judicial officers I know. What I emphasise is that any change of policy will need approval at a collective higher level so as to ensure efficiency and administrative cohesion and co-ordination. In conclusion, I wish your convention all success. My grateful thanks are due to you for your kind invitation and patient listening.

VISIT OF THE RT. HON. LORD DONALDSON*

First of all, may I on behalf of everyone present here welcome the Rt. Hon. Lord Donaldson of Lymington (formerly the Master of the Rolls, Court of Appeal, England) and also his charming lady Dame Mary Donaldson to Kuala Lumpur.

May I also say that my wife and I are delighted to welcome our special guests, Lord Donaldson and Dame Mary Donaldson and the British High Commissioner, Mr. Duncan Slater to this lunch. My wife and I are honoured by their acceptance of the invitation to attend this lunch.

To most of us present here, Lord Donaldson needs little or no introduction at all. He succeeded Lord Denning as the Master of the Rolls of the Court of Appeal in 1982, a post he held until his retirement in late 1992. Lord Donaldson became a judge of the High Court in 1966 after a distinguished career as one of the most outstanding members of the Bar specialising in Commercial Law. He put to full use his wide experience at the Bar in the Commercial Division of the High Court. Through his numerous judgments, he soon established himself as one of the leading Commercial Law judges in England.

Lord Donaldson was also actively involved in various other associations and bodies relating to Commercial Law, namely the British Insurance Law Association and the British Maritime Law Association. One of his main contributions was the volume on insurance law in *Halsbury's Laws of England, Third Edition.*

Lord Donaldson has recently been appointed as the Chairman of the newly established Financial Law Panel. He continues to be a Privy Councillor and since his retirement as the Master of the Rolls, he has been hearing a number of appeals to the Judicial Committee of the Privy Council.

What, however, is little known to most of you here is the equally illustrious career of Dame Mary Donaldson. She has the sole distinction of being the first woman to become the Lord Mayor of the City of London. She is actively involved in numerous bodies related to Medicine and is currently the Chairperson of the Government appointed Interim Licensing Authority for Human Invitro Fertilisation and Human Embryology. Dame Mary Donaldson is also

---

**Welcome Speech On The Visit Of The Rt. Hon. Lord Donaldson On 15th December, 1992.*

the Chairperson of the Banking Ombudsman Council and more recently she was appointed as a Member of the Press Complaints Commission.

For her distinguished career and her services to the nation, she was awarded the high and prestigious award of GBE by the Queen.

On behalf of all of you, my wife and I wish both Lord Donaldson and Dame Mary Donaldson a pleasant stay in our country.

I am also happy to inform you that Lord Donaldson has graciously agreed to speak briefly. I am confident that by reason of his vast experience and, of course his wisdom, some of the ideas that he would be sharing with us would be most useful particularly in the areas of case management and the clearing of the backlog of cases. It now gives me great pleasure to call upon Lord Donaldson to address you.

PERANAN HADIAH KEWARTAWANAN DALAM MENINGKATKAN IMEJ DAN PRESTASI PERTUBUHAN MEDIA*

Terlebih dahulu saya bersyukur ke hadrat Allah SWT. kerana dapat kita berhimpun di Majlis Hadiah Kewartawanan Malaysia pada pagi ini. Sehubungan ini, sukacita saya mengucapkan ribuan terima kasih kepada Institusi Akhbar Malaysia penganjur Hadiah Kewartawanan Malaysia yang telah sudi menjemput saya menyampaikan hadiah kepada mereka yang berjaya memenangi hadiah-hadiah tertentu.

Majlis penyampaian Hadiah Kewartawanan Malaysia 1991 pada hari ini dianjurkan oleh Institusi Akhbar Malaysia atas tajaan Malaysian Tobacco Company. YB Menteri Penerangan adalah Penaung majlis ini.

Hadiah Kewartawanan Malaysia ini diadakan tiap tahun sejak 1980 dengan tujuan:

(a) Memberi hadiah kepada kewartawanan yang menghasilkan tugas yang cemerlang;

(b) Meningkatkan lagi mutu kewartawanan;

(c) Memaparkan usaha-usaha wartawan dalam beberapa bidang tertentu yang telah diterbitkan di media massa.

Terbukti beratus-ratus wartawan telah menerima anugerah Hadiah Kewartawanan Malaysia sejak skim ini dimulakan, termasuk enam wartawan yang memenangi Hadiah Kajai.

Mulai tahun 1988 anugerah Tokoh Wartawan Negara diperkenalkan. Hingga kini dua orang telah menerima anugerah kewartawanan yang tertinggi ini untuk mengenang jasa perkhidmatan dan kecemerlangan mereka dalam bidang kewartawanan tanahair. (Kedua-dua tokoh tersebut hadir di majlis ini—Tan Sri Haji A. Samad Ismail dan Tan Sri Lee Siew Yee).

Hadiah Kewartawanan Malaysia merupakan satu-satunya skim yang diakui sebahagian besar pertubuhan media massa di Malaysia, untuk mengiktiraf kecemerlangan para wartawan dalam menjalankan tugas masing-masing. Usaha-usaha penganjur sewajarnya dipuji.

**Di Majlis Penyampaian Hadiah Kewartawanan Malaysia Pada 21hb Disember, 1992, Di Crown Princess Hotel, Kuala Lumpur.*

Malangnya jumlah bahan penyertaan yang diterima oleh penganjur beberapa tahun kebelakangan ini tidak menunjukkan ada perubahan yang menggalakkan. Saya menyeru supaya pertubuhan akhbar bersikap lebih serius untuk menyertai skim Hadiah Kewartawanan Malaysia, memberi lebih "masa dan tenaga" untuk memilih bahan-bahan penyertaan dan menguruskan hal-hal berkaitan dengan skim ini.

Sungguhpun begitu sukacita saya menyatakan bahawa ada contoh-contoh baik ditunjukkan oleh sesetengah akhbar yang mengambil berat untuk meningkatkan imej pertubuhan media mereka melalui skim Hadiah Kewartawanan Malaysia ini. Jumlah bahan-bahan penyertaan yang mereka kemukakan dalam beberapa kategori yang dipertandingkan sangat menggalakkan.

Ini menunjukkan penyertaan mereka dalam skim Hadiah Kewartawanan Malaysia tidak bergantung semata-mata kepada "masa dan tenaga" tetapi juga pada kemahuan dan, yang lebih penting, sikap ingin berlumba-lumba untuk meningkatkan imej pertubuhan masing-masing dan sikap bersedia untuk memberi peluang dan penghargaan kepada wartawan masing-masing kerana kecemerlangan dalam menjalankan tugas mereka.

Dengan sukacita saya menyeru ketua-ketua pengarang supaya memberi perhatian lebih kepada skim Hadiah Kewartawanan Malaysia kerana skim ini adalah anjuran akhbar-akhbar Malaysia sendiri, melalui Institusi Akhbar Malaysia, untuk faedah kaum wartawan Malaysia.

Saya difahamkan dalam Majlis Institusi Akhbar Malaysia ada wakil-wakil akhbar. Oleh yang demikian jika ada sesuatu perkara yang tidak memuaskan mengenai skim Hadiah Kewartawanan Malaysia ini wajarlah perkara-perkara itu dikemukakan, dibincangkan dan diambil keputusan bersama. Inilah salah satu cara yang baik untuk mengekalkan dan meningkatkan lagi mutu skim Hadiah Kewartawanan Malaysia ini.

Setelah enam tahun (sejak 1987) mengetuai panel-panel hakim, saya ingin mengemukakan pandangan yang difikirkan memberi faedah kepada kaum wartawan amnya mengenai skim Hadiah Kewartawanan Malaysia ini:

a) Skim Hadiah Kewartawanan wajar diteruskan dalam apa juga bentuk atau format yang sesuai yang disetujui oleh kaum wartawan, oleh kerana ia boleh menggalakkan kaum wartawan berusaha lebih giat lagi untuk mencapai kecemerlangan dalam menjalankan tugas masing-masing.

b) Ketua-ketua pengarang diseru memberi perhatian sewajarnya kepada skim ini untuk tidak menafikan peluang wartawan yang bertugas di bawah mereka menerima penghargaan kerana kecemerlangan mereka dalam menjalankan tugas;

c) Perlu diadakan suatu sistem di pertubuhan akhbar masing-masing untuk membolehkan atau memudahkan urusan penyertaan skim Hadiah Kewartawanan Malaysia ini. Pada pendapat saya, sistem seperti ini tidak banyak memerlukan tenaga dan masa. Apa yang perlu adalah suatu sistem yang praktik di pertubuhan akhbar masing-masing dan bukan sistem yang canggih.

d) Jika ada perkara-perkara yang perlu diperbaiki atau diadakan (jika belum diadakan lagi) untuk kebaikan kaum wartawan amnya dan skim Hadiah Kewartawanan Malaysia ini khasnya maka saya menyeru supaya syor dikemukakan kepada penganjur skim Hadiah Kewartawanan Malaysia.

Malaysia adalah di antara beberapa negara sahaja di rantau ini yang mengadakan skim Hadiah Kewartawanan Malaysia pada tiap-tiap tahun, seperti skim "Pulitzer Prizes in Journalism" di Amerika Syarikat dan "British Press Awards" di United Kingdom. Tradisi yang baik ini sewajarnya dikekalkan supaya ia menjadi insentif kepada kaum wartawan Malaysia untuk meningkatkan lagi prestasi mereka dalam berbagai bidang profesyen masing-masing. Sekian.

KEPERLUAN PENGKHUSUSAN BAGI MENGHASILKAN KEPAKARAN GUAMAN*

Terlebih dahulu saya bersyukur ke hadrat Allah SWT kerana dengan keizinan-Nya dapat kita berkumpul bersama untuk mengeratkan lagi tali silaturahim di antara satu dengan lain.

Dengan sukacita saya mengucapkan ribuan terima kasih kepada Presiden dan Ahli Jawatankuasa Persatuan Peguam-Peguam Muslim Malaysia yang mana telah sudi menjemput saya dan isteri saya ke Majlis pada malam ini dan seterusnya memberi penghormatan untuk berucap sepatah dua kata.

Sesungguhnya saya ingin mengucapkan tahniah dan syabas kepada mereka yang terlibat didalam penubuhan Persatuan ini. Banyak faedah dan peranan yang boleh dimainkan melalui Persatuan dan banyak idea baru yang berguna boleh disalur dan di timba dari cendekiawan melalui Persatuan. Apa yang jelas adalah, semangat cendekiawan di kalangan ahli-ahlinya dapat dipupuk, bimbingan dan tunjuk ajar dari peguam-peguam kanan dapat diberikan pada peguam-peguam junior yang baru melangkah ke alam pekerjaan atau profesion ini.

Pada hemat saya, melalui Persatuan juga pertukaran fikiran, idea, pendekatan dan tindakan ke arah sesuatu yang positif khususnya dalam menegakkan keadilan dan keluhuran undang-undang dapat dibuat secara bersama. Apa yang membanggakan saya ialah Persatuan ini dengan nada berani telah bertindak seiring dengan Dasar Pelajaran Kebangsaan di bidang perundangan dan juga di Mahkamah.

Saya difahamkan berbagai aktiviti telah dijalankan pada tahun 1992/1993 dan Persatuan ini telah juga mengambil peranan yang penting bagi memajukan penggunaan Bahasa Malaysia di bidang undang-undang.

Sebenarnya sebahagian dari masyarakat kita masih takut dengan perubahan, masih tidak yakin dengan kemampuan atau keupayaan Bahasa Malaysia sebagai bahasa perhubungan yang boleh digunakan di Mahkamah atau di sektor yang lain. Saya yakin di mana ada kemahuan di situ ada jalan. Hendak seribu daya tidak seribu daleh. Pokoknya usaha harus dipertingkatkan. Kalau

---

**Di Majlis Makan Malam Tahunan Persatuan Peguam-Peguam Muslim Malaysia pada 8hb Januari, 1993, di Kelab Darul Ehsan, Ampang Jaya, Selangor.*

lidah ibunda kita adalah lidah Melayu dan kita mampu atau berkeupayaan menguasai bahasa asing, masakan bahasa yang menjadi bahasa ibunda kita sukar kita gunakan. Kalau bangsa Indonesia boleh asimilasikan dan menerima bahasa kebangsaan mereka di pelbagai bidang urusan kenapa kita tidak boleh?

Semua pihak sedar bahawa bahan-bahan rujukan dalam Bahasa Malaysia masih berkurangan. Maka di sinilah terletaknya peranan penting Persatuan. Buku-buku perundangan perlu diterjemahkan ke dalam Bahasa Malaysia dan peguam-peguam harus digalakkan menulis atau menterjemahkan buku-buku ke dalam bahasa untuk membantu masyarakat kita memperluaskan pengetahuan mereka di bidang perundangan. Kalau bangsa Jepun boleh melahirkan generasinya yang maju dan dinamik hanya dengan berpandukan buku-buku terjemahan, saya yakin masyarakat Malaysia juga boleh diubah dengan kaedah yang sama. Pokok pangkalnya adalah terletak pada sikap masyarakat kita. Sebenarnya peranan terjemahan tidak seharusnya dibebankan kepada Dewan Bahasa dan Pustaka sahaja tetapi sepatutnya kita berganding bahu untuk bekerjasama ke arah itu.

Dengan tujuan berkhidmat untuk Bangsa dan Negara maka adalah wajar peranan ini dilaksanakan di atas nama Persatuan dengan kerjasama dan bantuan semua ahli—Supaya perlaksanaan ini dijalankan dengan sempurna dan berkesan, maka saya mencadangkan penubuhan suatu tabung yang diberi nama 'Tabung Perlaksanaan Bahasa Malaysia' diurus oleh Persatuan di bawah suatu Badan Trustee.

Kita sedar negara Malaysia adalah sebuah negara yang berbilang kaum dan Bahasa Malaysia adalah bahasa rasminya. Kita juga sedar bahawa bahasa kedua iaitu Bahasa Inggeris mempunyai kepentingannya yang tersendiri. Walau bagaimanapun setiap warganegara Malaysia haruslah memberi sumbangan untuk mendaulatkan bahasa dan budaya Malaysia.

Sememangnya wajar sekali kita menggunakan Bahasa Malaysia sebagai bahasa perundangan kerana undang-undang adalah landasan yang menegakkan keadilan sesuatu bangsa dan negara. Adalah tidak adil sekiranya penghakiman dan perbicaraan dilaksanakan ke atas seseorang yang tidak faham apa yang dibicarakan, hanya atas alasan kita menggunakan bahasa asing, sedangkan kita ada alternatif yang ideal bagi menyelesaikan masalah tersebut.

Walaupun masyarakat antarabangsa tidak memahami Bahasa Malaysia, ini tidak bermakna undang-undang negara kita lebih mundur. Maju atau mundurnya sesuatu undang-undang adalah terletak pada tahap keadilannya dan bukan bergantung kepada bahasa yang terpakai.

Undang-undang sebenarnya adalah panduan yang boleh menjamin keadilan manusia sejagat. Undang-undang adalah peraturan yang telah digariskan untuk menjamin perjalanan hidup yang sempurna. Seharusnya undang-undang tidak menyusah atau membebankan masyarakat sehingga mereka takut dengan Mahkamah atau pihak berkuasa.

Bidang perundangan adalah satu bidang yang mana bahasa memainkan peranan yang penting. Oleh itu, kita berharap masyarakat perlu faham maksud yang kita ingin sampaikan dan bahasa tidak harus mengelirukan pendengar. Dalam hal ini saya bersetuju dengan Presiden Jimmy Carter dalam perutusannya pada tahun 1978 meminta supaya semua agensi kerajaan Amerika Syarikat menulis dalam 'plain English' supaya ianya dapat difahami oleh mereka yang dikehendaki melaksanakan peraturan tersebut dan bukannya bahasa yang panjang-panjang, berbunga-bunga, bahasa yang jarang didengar sehingga pendengar terpaksa merujuk di kamus ataupun encyclopaedia.

Walaupun negara mencapai kemerdekaan iaitu hampir genap 37 tahun sahaja, perkembangannya yang cepat tidaklah dapat dipertikaikan. Kita berbangga kerana anak muda Malaysia menempuh kejayaan dalam pelbagai profesion. Pertengahan abad 20 adalah merupakan era yang banyak memberi kesan kepada golongan profesional. Revolusi sains telah mewujudkan pengkhususan yang kian pesat bagi manusia memahami ilmu yang baru lagi kompleks.

Bagi bidang guaman saya ingin menyarankan supaya agihan guaman dibuat mengikut pengkhususan tertentu. Biar kecil bidang kita asalkan ada pengkhususan tertentu. Walau bagaimanapun, apa yang harus kita sedar ialah masyarakat umum lebih yakin pada sesuatu yang besar, yang 'established'. Dalam hal ini saya berpendapat setiap peguam haruslah berusaha menjadi seorang berpengetahuan dalam sesuatu bidang tertentu. Pelbagai bidang ini akan digabung di bawah satu unit yang besar yang berupaya memberi perkhidmatan yang baik dalam apa jua masalah serta memenuhi permintaan semasa.

Buat masa kini, Malaysia amat memerlukan pakar guaman di pelbagai bidang. Ramai peguam-peguam pakar, khususnya Bumiputra diperlukan bagi memberi perkhidmatan nasihat di bidang pengswastaan (privatisation) dan persyarikatan (corporatisation). Peranan peguam pakar adalah untuk mengenalpasti, menganalisa dan menyelesaikan isu-isu perundangan serta implikasinya terhadap badan-badan yang akan diswastakan. Undang-undang yang melibatkan persyarikatan dan pengswastaan adalah bidang yang kurang diceburi oleh peguam tempatan.

Pada hemat saya tibalah masanya bagi peguam-peguam tempatan mempertingkatkan kemampuan masing-masing dibidang yang khusus yang sekian lama dimonopoli oleh peguam-peguam asing. Malaysia sangat memerlukan lebih banyak pakar-pakar dalam bidang korporat, mergers, takeovers, patent marks, trademarks, copyright. 'International off-shore financial centre' seperti di Labuan, Sabah amat memerlukan khidmat profesional umpamanya khidmat bank, syarikat amanah (Trust company) akauntan dan juga khidmat guaman. Peluang bagi golongan profesion mengambil bahagian dalam aktiviti yang diwujudkan oleh kerajaan terbuka dengan amat luas sekali.

Kita juga memerlukan pakar dalam bidang perdagangan antarabangsa di mana misalnya, pengeksport barangan Malaysia boleh mendapat nasihat guaman mengenai undang-undang perdagangan antarabangsa negara-negara maju seperti Amerika Syarikat dan EEC, agar dengan ini dapat memberi peluang dan galakan kepada pengeksport negara kita menembusi pasaran mereka dengan mudah.

Kita juga memerlukan kepakaran guaman khusus bagi penyelesaian pertikaian perdagangan (commercial dispute) yang buat masa kini diselesaikan secara litigasi (litigation), yang mana kaedah ini terlalu membebankan mahkamah yang sememangnya dibebani dengan pelbagai kes. Implikasinya kes lambat diselesaikan dan akhirnya menjejaskan prestasi keputusan atau tindakan sesuatu syarikat atau pertubuhan.

Umumnya masyarakat perdagangan dan industri pembinaan sekarang ini lebih gemar menyelesaikan pertikaian perdagangan atau kontrak melalui proses timbangcara (arbitration) yang lebih cepat sebab arbitrator adalah pakar dalam bidang tertentu disamping adanya privasi, kerana penyelesaian seringkali dibuat dalam mesyuarat secara tertutup. Kepakaran yang ada pada kita sahaja dapat menyakinkan pihak tertentu untuk melantik kita bagi menyelesaikan masalah mereka.

Berhubungan dengan pentadbiran Mahkamah Syariah, saya difahamkan masih terdapat ketidakselarasan dalam perlaksanaan undang-undang berkaitan. Usaha untuk mengemaskinikan undang-undang syariah haruslah dipergiatkan khususnya yang bersangkutan dengan hartanah. Penyelesaian kes-kes mal yang memakan masa yang panjang haruslah diatasi. Jalinan yang jitu dan kerjasama yang padu antara pihak yang terlibat dengan mahkamah sivil dan mahkamah syariah harus dipertingkatkan. Kepakaran, ketelitian dan kecepatan disamping keadilan dalam membuat pertimbangan akan membuatkan masyarakat merasa terlindung bila berurusan dengan mahkamah syariah dan lebih yakin dengan pentadbiran undang-undang Islam.

Akhir kata adalah besar harapan saya semoga Persatuan Peguam-Peguam Muslim Malaysia dapat memainkan peranan yang sebaik-baiknya dalam menegakkan kedaulatan undang-undang negara dan aspirasi bangsa Malaysia yang tercinta.

UNDANG-UNDANG DAN SISTEM KEWANGAN SALING BERGANTUNG*

Saya berasa amat berbangga sekali pada hari ini kerana dijemput oleh Urusetia Seminar Undang-Undang Dan Masyarakat untuk merasmikan Seminar Tahunan ini, yang merupakan satu seminar tahunan pelajar Fakulti Undang-Undang, Universiti Kebangsaan Malaysia. Terima kasih saya ucapkan kepada pihak Urusetia kerana sudi menjemput saya sekali lagi bagi merasmikan seminar yang cukup bermanfaat kepada semua golongan pelajar terutamanya pelajar Undang-Undang.

Syabas dan Tahniah juga saya ucapkan kepada Perundang kerana mempunyai inisiatif serta daya usaha untuk terus menjayakan serta memperdalamkan pengetahuan mereka dalam usaha menghasilkan Graduan Undang-Undang yang bertanggungjawab, berkaliber serta berdedikasi. Melalui program-program seperti inilah, akan dapat melatih serta membuka pemikiran pelajar terhadap dunia luar yang sebenar dan serba mencabar ini.

Sesungguhnya tema tahun ini bertajuk "Undang-Undang Dan Sistem Kewangan Malaysia" amatlah tepat dengan perkembangan negara kita Malaysia yang sedang pesat membangun. Oleh itu perkembangan Undang-Undang dan Sistem Kewangan akan berkembang serentak, ke arah melahirkan satu sistem pentadbiran negara yang lebih teratur dan stabil.

Undang-Undang dan Sistem Kewangan adalah dua unsur yang saling bergantung selain daripada kestabilan politik, dalam menjamin perkembangan ekonomi negara yang teratur. Anasir-anasir seperti rasuah, penipuan serta berbagai-bagai lagi jenayah korporat, jika tidak dibendung secara total melalui Undang-Undang, sudah pasti akan melemahkan dan melumpuhkan Sistem Kewangan dan ekonomi sesebuah negara.

Jenayah kolar putih adalah satu dari gejala-gejala yang menjadi racun dalam perkembangan ekonomi Malaysia. Dari penyalahgunaan wang, penipuan kad kredit hinggalah kepada pemalsuan sijil-sijil saham serta berbagai-bagai lagi bentuk penipuan adalah faktor yang membebankan pihak penguatkuasa undang-undang dalam mencari jalan penyelesaian. Seminar seperti

---

**Ucapan Perasmian Seminar Undang-Undang Dan Masyarakat VI Universiti Kebangsaan Malaysia Pada 11hb Februari, 1993.*

ini diharap dapat menjelaskan serta mendedahkan masalah ini dengan cara yang lebih berkesan supaya dapat menimbulkan kesedaran kepada peserta-peserta, dalam membantu usaha menyekat kejadian ini dari terus berleluasa dimasa-masa akan datang.

Seminar seperti ini juga sudah pastinya akan mendedahkan para pelajar kepada tokoh-tokoh penting dalam bidang perundangan seperti peguam-peguam, hakim-hakim dan penggubal undang-undang itu sendiri. Seterusnya saya amatlah mengharapkan agar seminar ini dapat manfaat oleh kesemua peserta dan menjadi landasan pemikiran yang rasional lagi jitu.

Mengenai fikiran yang rasional dan jitu, maka teringatlah satu kisah di mana seorang doktor sedang berehat dan bercakap-cakap dengan seorang peguam di sebuah Kelab Golf. Doktor ini mengadu kepada peguam itu bahawa beliau selalu saja ditanya oleh ahli-ahli Kelab ketika beliau berehat setelah main golf mengenai penyakit itu dan ini yang mereka hadapi. Doktor berkata hal ini tidak menyeronokkannya kerana orang-orang ini tidak datang ke kliniknya dan in menjejaskan pendapatannya. Doktor meminta pendapat peguam berhubungan hal tersebut. Peguam itu menjawab. "Itu senang saja, hantar bil kepada mereka yang bertanya." Doktor sangat gembira dengan nasihat peguam itu kerana ianya merupakan satu syor yang baik. Dua hari yang kemudian doktor pula menerima satu bil dari peguam itu 'as consultation fee'.

Pemikiran kisah tadi bolehlah dikatakan jitu tapi tidak rasional.

Untuk mengakhiri maka dengan lafaz Bismillahirrahmanirrahim saya merasmikan Seminar Undang-Undang Dan Masyarakat VI dengan rasminya.

CABARAN BIDANG GUAMAN*

Saya mengucapkan berbanyak-banyak terima kasih di atas kesudian pihak penganjur program ini menjemput saya bagi merasmikan pembukaan program tahunan "Pertandingan Moot dan Sukan Antara Universiti," kali ke lapan, 1993.

Apa yang pihak penganjur program ini lakukan adalah satu langkah yang sungguh cemerlang kerana program ini merangkumi dua perkara penting yang menjadi pelengkap (compliment) antara satu dengan yang lain.

Moot merupakan satu latihan membahaskan secara 'hypothetical' sesuatu kes manakala sukan pula merupakan satu latihan gerak badan yang memerlukan ketangkasan serta tenaga. Untuk menyebatikan kedua-dua unsur ini maka seseorang itu seharusnya mempunyai otak yang cergas dan badan yang sihat. Sekiranya kedua-dua unsur ini wujud di dalam tubuh mahasiswa/mahasiswi maka saya percaya mereka boleh menjadi peguam yang berkaliber kerana badan yang sihat boleh mewujudkan ketahanan dan kecergasan mental. Seterusnya mereka dapat menerima kekalahan umpamanya jika kalah dalam sesuatu kes di mahkamah dengan semangat kesukanan, kerana di dalam sesuatu perbicaraan ada dua pihak yang bersengketa, dan sudah tentu ada satu pihak yang tidak berpuas hati dengan sesuatu keputusan.

Apabila tuan-tuan dan puan-puan meninggalkan kampus masing-masing setelah tamat pengajian, tuan-tuan dan puan-puan akan menjadi manusia yang sibuk menjalankan tugas masing-masing. Jadi melalui program ini tuan-tuan dan puan-puan dapat berkenalan di antara satu sama lain yang mana melalui program tahunan seperti ini diharap akan dapat menjalinkan silaturrahim yang berkekalan. Dengan cara ini juga sesuatu masalah klien dapat diselesaikan sekiranya pihak yang lain itu kliennya diwakili oleh peguam yang dikenali. Seperti kata pepatah "tak kenal maka tak cinta". Sekiranya sesuatu penyelesaian ini dapat dicapai di luar mahkamah, maka penyelesaian itu amat dialu-alukan bukan sahaja oleh klien masing-masing tetapi juga oleh pihak mahkamah yang sentiasa sahaja dihujani dengan kes-kes yang kian bertambah.

**Ucapan Perasmian Majlis Pembukaan Tahunan Pertandingan Moot Dan Sukan Antara Universiti Kali Yang Ke 8, 1993 Universiti Islam Antarabangsa Pada 20hb Februari 1993.*

Untuk mencapai cita-cita menjadi peguam yang berjaya dari segi material maka aspek spiritual atau rohaniah perlu juga diambil kira. Allah memerintahkan agar hambanya berusaha mencari kesenangan di dunia di samping membuat persediaan untuk akhirat. Sehubungan ini, semasa menjalankan tugas-tugas sebagai peguam sama ada di sektor awam atau swasta, maka etika guaman, tatasusila, budaya dan moral tidak harus dilanggar hingga tercemar nama profesyen.

Cabaran masakini dalam bidang guaman amatlah mencabar. Ini adalah hasil dari kemahuan manusia yang komplek, teknologi yang canggih serta pembaharuan dalam berbagai-bagai bidang. Mahu atau tidak, profesyen undang-undang, sama juga dengan profesyen-profesyen yang lain, hendaklah peka kepada perubahan zaman. Namun begitu, sebagai peguam, tugas utama kita ialah bagi mewakili dan menasihati klien kita dengan jujur, tepat serta mengendalikan kes sebaik mungkin mengikut undang-undang dan peraturan yang sedia ada dengan mengenepikan kepentingan sendiri. Kalau seseorang peguam itu dapat melakukan kesemua ini, profesion guaman akan dapat semula menduduki mercu kegemilangannya sebagai pembela bagi yang tertindas.

Dunia yang menunggu di luar kampus nanti adalah lebih mencabar dan tidaklah seindah seperti yang seseorang itu mengharapkan. Dunia kampus adalah penuh dengan idealisma dan utopia. Berkaitan dengan apa yang saya sebutkan ini teringat saya kepada satu kisah yang saya terbaca dalam Readers Digest yang dipetik dari Virginia Law School Report yang ceritanya begini: A law School Professor said to a graduating class, "Three years ago, when asked a legal question, you could answer in all honesty, 'I don't know'. Now you can say, with great authority, 'It depends'."

Untuk mengakhiri saya dengan lafaz Bismillah hirahman nirrahim, merasmikan Pertandingan Moot dan Sukan Antara Universiti kali yang ke-8 Tahun 1993.

Sekian, wabillahi taufiq walhidayah wassalamualaikum w.b.t.

RELATIONSHIP BETWEEN UNIVERSITY STAFF AND STUDENTS*

I thank you for giving me the liberty to say a few words. I shall not spoil the happiness of the occasion and your hospitality with a serious speech.

When I was a student I got the distinct impression that generally in the universities, the relationship between students and academic staff is one of love and hate. And yet we all know that a university is a key institution—a factor in the process of civilisation providing the continuity and expansion of knowledge by which each generation climbs up on the shoulders of the last. Therefore, one should not make much of the friction between staff and students. Friction of this kind should indeed be a method of sharpening the academic knife, carving its way into the hidden realms of knowledge. This is what it should be in the nature of things especially in the law faculty as students are earmarked to be the leaders of tomorrow's world. As a self-governing community within a society and with a responsibility to society, a university must abide by the rules that society lays down for its conduct. Each university in turn is bound by its foundation charter. A university organization shall have to face the problem of establishing a unity of interest between the academic staff and students in order to cater for effective channels of communication. In this context, let us pause and ponder over the respective roles of the academic staff and students. The academic profession probably enjoys less substantial financial rewards. Anyone who has an inclination towards teaching is probably influenced by a dedication to the pursuit of truth and the dissemination of knowledge. As for the students, generally they arrive as raw recruits knowing very little about what lies ahead of them and the sudden transition from school to university may well be an alarming experience. What therefore are the factors that underlie the relationship between academic staff and students? Numerically students form by far the largest part of the university. Upon entering the university they do not generally aspire to be social leaders but to give priority to acquiring some of the skills that its dons and administrators already enjoy. As students are temporary members and the academic staff long term members, the staff therefore assume that they have a stake in its stability. In

---

**At The Law Society Of The International Islamic University, Petaling Jaya On 31st March, 1993 At Dewan Cempaka, Kelab Darul Ehsan, Jalan Ampang, Kuala Lumpur.*

such a state, however, it is not open to argument that one party is superior or subordinate to the other. What seems important is that there must be a mutual desire to strengthen the relationship between the parties and the area of dedication of each party should be towards the pursuit of truth and acquisition of knowledge either by teaching or by studying. Fundamentally, creative and independent thinking, tolerance to dissent, mutual accommodation and understanding and trust is imperative for this process.

I am of the view that a university should be a place which can offer its best to all its members, not just for a select few who are equipped to demonstrate the doctrine of survival of the fittest.

As law undergraduates your role is very important in the task of nation-building to achieve Vision 2020. You have to be prepared and be equipped fully to meet the challenges ahead.

Another aspect I wish to touch upon tonight is that social events of the type I witness today is an essential part of university life as it strengthens the relationship between the dons and the students. In the absence of such organizations, it can only be supplied through an active and competent student union offering, among other things, facilities for sporting and cultural activities.

Sebagai pesanan, let me say this—that besides law in books, you should apply your mind to law in action when you complete your studies. Law is a social process, a complex of human activity with cause and effect with the past and present.

VISIT OF THE RT. HON. LORD MACKAY*

My wife and I and members of the judiciary and their spouses who are assembled here tonight are delighted to have had this opportunity to welcome your Lordship and Lady Mackay on the occasion of your short visit to Kuala Lumpur. A majority of us on the Superior Court Bench received our professional training in the United Kingdom and are therefore always conscious of the long tradition of friendship and co-operation between Britain and this country. Although such ties between us took their root in different historical circumstances, they are sound and enduring. The tie is strengthened by the fact that Britain and Malaysia are both democratic nations within the Commonwealth with strong commitments to industrial development, investment and trade. Both countries do recognise the fundamental importance of a free enterprise system and both are involved in promoting new technology. In addition, we share a fundamental commitment to the rule of law. Broad similarities exist between our legal systems although each has to contend itself with separate issues. While Britain has to take cognisance of European Community Laws, we have to harmonise our system with Islamic Syariah Law. Despite the means being different, the end of achieving justice is the same and I am confident our close affinity will continue. This is reflected in the close relationship in the field of commerce and investment and in the multitude of Malaysian students who are currently in Britain.

I now turn to something less serious. We are gathered here tonight to honour his Lordship Lord Mackay and Lady Mackay. I therefore take the liberty to say one or two words about our Guest of Honour. Most of us are aware of the immense contribution Lord Mackay has made and still continues to make in the legal field and the inspiration he evokes.

Those of us who heard the Lord Chancellor's speech yesterday at Shangrila Hotel when he spoke of the recent developments in commercial fraud trials and the need for trials to be considerably shortened would appreciate the Lord Chancellor's deep knowledge, legal acumen and wisdom expressed in his typi-

---

**At The Dinner In Honour Of The Rt. Hon. Lord Mackay Of Clashfern, The Lord High Chancellor Of Great Britain And Lady Mackay At Hotel Istana, Kuala Lumpur On 2nd April, 1993.*

cal lucid style. Many of the points raised provided eye openers for us for improving our own system even though our problems may not be similar.

His Lordship Lord Mackay started his legal career as a practising Scottish lawyer to become the Lord Chancellor of England. Although the modern Scottish Law is derived from Roman Law with different traditions from English Law, Lord Mackay was no stranger to English Law, having appeared before the House of Lords in many leading cases and having become a Lord Advocate.

When Lord Mackay was appointed Lord Chancellor, Britain then was witnessing changes in the political, social, economic and legal fields which few would have anticipated as possible at the start of the decade. Lord Mackay's appointment was rather unexpected. Be that as it may, Lord Mackay proved to be a dynamic leader with a great vision of the future. He has a profound respect for history and tradition and would not lightly seek to tamper with it. Yet, Lord Mackay feels free to question the ways things are done within such a framework. Although not bent on change for its own sake, Lord Mackay did not feel constrained to introduce reforms, when necessary. A great believer in free enterprise, Lord Mackay made the legal fraternity of all descriptions adapt to changing circumstances and rethink their role radically.

In the legal arena, the period when Lord Mackay assumed responsibility as Lord Chancellor was certainly turbulent. There were colourful events such as allegations of miscarriage of justice arising mainly from the *Birmingham trials* and the backlog of cases. There were feelings of unrest and clamour for drastic reforms. Among the many reforms Lord Mackay made, to mention a few, are diminishing the historically oriented difference between solicitors and barristers, opening the doors of High Court judgeship to solicitors, changing the system of legal aid schemes, reviewing of solicitors' conveyancing monopoly and probate, modifying barristers' exclusive right of audience, improving criminal trials and listing, appointing more judges, civil justice reviews and many other sweeping changes.

I would say that in so far as Lord Mackay's contribution and his help to the Government in building a just legal service is concerned, the role assumed is not that of an architect but of a humble bricklayer. The task was onerous yet it was performed steadily. "Behold the turtle. He makes progress only when he sticks his neck out."

In the judicial circle in Malaysia we admire Lord Mackay and indeed we admire the western liberal and democratic approach to jurisprudence, but being a developing nation, it will be too premature for us to adopt all changes blindly without considering the local social ethos. For example, we cannot insist on a specified number of days limit to start a trial as in Scotland. We cannot have the luxury of jury trial in all cases because of the heterogenous culture of our people. Preventive detention may be regarded as undemocratic but, viewed in the light of local conditions, it is unavoidable in rare cases when people try to subvert a democratically elected Government. On attaining independence, we had to introduce our National Language in the Courts. This was necessary to make the question of law intelligible to the masses. I mention these points to emphasise that it is equally necessary that our aspirations be appreciated in its true perspective.

May I, on behalf of all judges and their spouses, wish his Lordship Lord Mackay and Lady Mackay a very pleasant stay in Malaysia. My wife, I and my fellow judges are privileged by his Lordship's inspiring presence tonight together with the charming Lady Mackay. It is a great honour for us and I hope the short time we spend together will be valuable as symbolic of our common objective in the business of searching for justice and dispensing it.

KEPENTINGAN UNDANG-UNDANG PERDAGANGAN ANTARABANGSA*

Bersyukur kita kehadrat Illahi, kerana dapat kita bersama-sama sekali lagi pada tahun ini meraikan bakal-bakal graduan undang-undang, Institusi Teknologi MARA. Saya difahamkan bahawa Majlis Makan Malam ini adalah kali yang ke 25 yang dianjurkan oleh Kajian Pentadbiran Dan Undang-Undang, ITM. (KPU).

Saya pasti tahun ini juga adalah tahun bagi KPU, ITM menyambut ulangtahun ke 25 Jubli Perak. Saya ucapkan setinggi tahniah.

Sebagai sebuah sekolah undang-undang yang tertua di Malaysia saya berkeyakinan penuh bahawa KPU, ITM dapat mengekalkan mutu graduan-graduannya yang bakal menjadi peguam di negara ini. Peranan yang dimainkan oleh KPU, ITM adalah amat mencabar kerana selain daripada mengeluarkan graduan-graduan yang akan mengisi kekosongan di profesyen perguaman, ITM juga mengeluarkan bakal-bakal peguam bumiputra yang bermutu, berkaliber dan yang lebih penting sekali ialah mereka yang bertanggungjawab terhadap profesyen guaman. Selain daripada itu, bakal peguam bumiputra ini juga mestilah mampu bersaing dengan peguam-peguam bukan bumiputra yang lain apabila mereka memulakan kerjaya mereka sebagai peguam.

Malaysia bukan sahaja sebuah negara yang sedang pesat membangun, ia merupakan sebuah negara di mana sebilangan besar penduduknya terdiri dari generasi muda. Oleh kerana kita kini sedang berada di dalam era yang genting, pengajaran yang diberikan kepada generasi muda kita pada ketika ini khususnya akan menentukan masa hadapan negara ini.

Sebagai bakal peguam, saya ingin memberi sedikit nasihat dan pandangan kepada saudara dan saudari.

Sejak kebelakangan ini, kita menyaksikan trend ekonomi antarabangsa sudah berubah di mana di arena perdagangan antarabangsa, "global trade" tidak lagi menjadi prinsip asas tetapi adalah lebih mirip kepada regionalism. Penubuhan Kesatuan Eropah, menyaksikan satu gergasi perkumpulan ekonomi yang telah bergabung untuk membentuk satu kumpulan ekonomi yang kuat

---

**Di Majlis Makan Malam Tahunan (tahun Ke 25) Pelajar Undang-undang, Institusi Teknologi Mara Pada 16hb April, 1993, Di Crown Princess Hotel, Kuala Lumpur.*

di dunia kini. Selain daripada itu perkumpulan-perkumpulan lain seperti NAFTA (North American Free Trade Area) dan lain-lain kumpulan telah juga menunjukkan trend "regionalism".

Sementara di dunia sebelah sini pula, kita pasti dengan tertubuhnya AFTA (Asean Free Trade Agreement) akan menambahkan lagi pertumbuhan ekonomi di kalangan negara-negara Asean. Selain daripada itu kita juga harus mengambil kira cadangan Perdana Menteri kita untuk menubuhkan EAEC (East Asia Economic Caucus) yang bertujuan untuk mempertingkatkan lagi perdagangan antarabangsa di dunia sebelah sini.

Tuan-tuan dan puan-puan, perkembangan-perkembangan baru ini ada kaitannya dengan profesyen guaman. Apabila perdagangan antarabangsa menjadi fokus utama kepada negara-negara yang berdagang, maka undang-undang perdagangan antarabangsa juga pasti menjadi penting bagi tujuan melicinkan urusniaga-urusniaga perdagangan.

Oleh itu, saudara-saudari haruslah pada masa ini bersiap sedia dan memperlengkapkan diri untuk menghadapi cabaran-cabaran sebagai peguam di bidang undang-undang perdagangan antarabangsa pada masa hadapan.

Apa yang saya maksudkan ialah kita tidak harus menumpukan profesyen guaman secara domestik sahaja kerana pasaran pekerjaan di bidang profesyen guaman hendaklah diperluaskan meliputi peringkat antarabangsa. Pada ketika ini, Malaysia masih lagi kekurangan peguam di bidang undang-undang antarabangsa. Oleh itu saya ingin menyarankan supaya saudara-saudari mengambil peluang ini sebagai satu insentif dan motivasi untuk memperluaskan lagi skop profesyen guaman. Sehubungan ini dan untuk mencapai tujuan di atas, saudara-saudari hendaklah bertekad untuk memperlengkapkan diri saudara-saudari dengan segala ilmu yang ditimba dari sekolah undang-undang dan apabila keluar kelak mengamalkan ilmu tersebut.

Keperluan utama sebuah negara yang sedang membangun adalah pertumbuhan ekonomi yang stabil. Keadaan ini hanya dapat dicapai sekiranya penduduknya mempunyai kemahiran yang mencukupi untuk menggunakan sumber-sumber alam semulajadi negara dan untuk maju di dalam perdagangan antarabangsa. Menurut analisa terakhir, sumber-sumber alam semulajadi adalah tenaga manusia terlatih.

Pada pendapat saya, ITM telah memainkan peranannya tanpa membelakangkan bahawa pengajian undang-undang adalah berkait rapat dengan perkembangan ekonomi, domestik dan antarabangsa.

Seperkara lagi mesti saya memperkatakan di sini ialah tanggungjawab saudara-saudari. Pada hemat saya, saudara-saudari mestilah sentiasa memelihara nama baik profesyen ini yang kini sedang merosot akibat sikap tidak beramanah dan tidak bertanggungjawab di kalangan peguam-peguam tertentu.

Akhir kata saya ingin mengucapkan ribuan terima kasih kepada jawatankuasa penganjur Majlis Makan Malam 1993 kerana menjemput saya dan isteri saya ke Majlis ini. Saya juga ingin mengucapkan selamat maju jaya kepada bakal-bakal graduan undang-undang ITM.

MINAT SPB YANG DI-PERTUAN AGONG DALAM PERKEMBANGAN BADAN KEHAKIMAN*

Mengadap Seri Paduka Baginda Yang Di-Pertuan Agong.
Ampun Tuanku, sembah patek pohon diampun. Patek bagi pihak YAA Hakim Besar Malaya Tan Sri Datuk Gunn Chit Tuan, YAA Hakim Besar Borneo Tan Sri Datuk Amar Haji Mohd. Jemuri bin Serjan, para hakim, dif-dif jemputan dan pegawai kehakiman menjunjung kasih yang tidak terhingga di atas ampun perkenan Tuanku mencemar Duli berangkat ke Majlis Santapan/Makan Malam yang tidak sepertinya pada malam ini.

Juga bagi pihak YAA Hakim Besar Malaya dan YAA Hakim Besar Borneo, para hakim, pegawai-pegawai kehakiman serta kakitangan Mahkamah Agung/Tinggi, patek menjunjung kasih di atas ampun perkenan Tuanku Berangkat membuat lawatan rasmi ke Mahkamah Agung/Tinggi di Bangunan Sultan Abdul Samad pada hari esok.

Limpah perkenan Tuanku mencemar Duli ke Majlis Santapan pada malam ini sesungguhnya amat menyerikan Majlis ini. Keberangkatan Duli Tuanku khususnya memberi kesempatan kepada hakim-hakim untuk beramah mesra dengan Duli Tuanku.

Di atas limpah perkenan Duli Tuanku berangkat ke Mahkamah Agung di Bangunan Sultan Abdul Samad esok maka patek percaya ini adalah sesuatunya peristiwa yang akan menempah titik sejarah kerana inilah kali pertama dalam sejarah negara di mana seorang Raja yang pernah menyandang jawatan Ketua Hakim Negara melawat Mahkamah Agung dalam tempoh pemerintahannya sebagai Yang Di-Pertuan Agong. Patek, para hakim dan pegawai kehakiman sekalian berasa amat terharu, gembira, bangga dan terhutang budi di atas penghormatan yang dikurniakan oleh Tuanku kerana peristiwa keberangkatan Tuanku ke Mahkamah Agung esok akan merupakan satu peristiwa yang tidak dapat patek semua lupakan sepanjang hayat.

Patek sekalian juga berbangga, dan terhutang budi di atas usaha gigih Tuanku lah maka Bangunan ini diubahsuai dan Mahkamah Agung ditempatkan di Bangunan Sultan Abdul Samad yang indah dan menarik ini.

**Sembah Ucapan Menjunjung Kasih Di Majlis Makan Malam Pada 29.4.1993 Di Hotel Shangri-la, Sempena Lawatan Seri Paduka Baginda Yang Di-pertuan Agong, Sultan Azlan Shah Ke Bangunan Sultan Abdul Samad Pada 30th April, 1993.*

Patek dan para hakim serta pegawai kehakiman sedar bahawa walaupun Tuanku sudah tidak lagi bersama dalam badan kehakiman, Tuanku tetap dan terus mengambil berat terhadap pembangunan dan perkembangan Badan Kehakiman dan mahkamah-mahkamah di seluruh negara.

Juga sehubungan ini, patek berbangga kerana nama Tuanku dilafazkan dan disebutkan saban hari di mahkamah-mahkamah di seluruh Malaysia oleh kerana banyak penghakiman-penghakiman Tuanku telah disiarkan dalm jurnal undang-undang.

Fenomena ini berlaku khususnya kerana Tuanku telah banyak membuat keputusan dalam kes-kes penting yang menjadi tunggak perundangan negara kita. Kebijaksanaan dan keunggulan Tuanku dalam menulis penghakiman amat menarik sekali dan ini merupakan kelebihan yang ada pada Tuanku yang sukar dimiliki oleh orang lain.

Shakespeare berkata "some men are born great, some achieve greatness and some have greatness thrust upon them". Kemasyhuran Duli Tuanku bukan saja kerana kelahiran Tuanku tapi kemasyhuran Tuanku itu adalah pencapaian kejayaan dari semua perspektif.

Pada hemat patek, Tuanku telah berjaya menempah sejarah kerana terdapat 280 kes yang diputuskan oleh Tuanku dilaporkan dalam jurnal undang-undang yang merangkumi kesemua aspek perundangan yang sama ada secara langsung atau tidak langsung telah menyumbang kepada perkembangan pesat sistem perundangan negara kita sejak merdeka.

Tetapi ciri penting yang ada pada Tuanku ialah sifat dan sikap adil baginda. Sifat ini terserlah di dalam kes *P.P.* v *Tengku Mahmood Iskandar & Anor* (1973) 1 MLJ 128 Tuanku Raja Azlan Shah ketika itu Hakim Mahkamah Tinggi berkata "...there is only one kind of law in the country to which all citizens are amendable. With us, every citizen, irrespective of his official or social status, is under the same responsibility for every act done without legal justification. This equality of all in the eyes of the law minimises tyranny." Prinsip ini ditekankan lagi oleh Tuanku di dalam kes *P.P.* v *Datuk Hj. Harun bin Hj. Idris No. 2* (1977) 1 MLJ 15 bila mana Tuanku enggan mengambil kira kedudukan seseorang individu dalam meringan hukuman bagi kes-kes yang berat dan Tuanku berkata "...I repeat what I had said before. The law is no respector of persons."

Duli Tuanku dalam satu lagi kes termasyhur yang melibatkan isu perlembagaan iaitu kes *Loh Kooi Choon* v *Government of Malaysia* (1977) 2 MLJ 187 FC telah menyarankan bahawa "the constitution is not a mere collection of pious platitudes and that it is the Supreme law of the Land embodying three basic concepts; one of them is that the individual has certain fundamental rights upon which not even the power of state may encroach. The second is the distribution of sovereign power between the States and the Federation ... The third is that no single man or body shall exercise complete sovereign power, but that it shall be distributed among the executive, legislative and judicial branches of government, compendiously expressed in modern terms that we are a government of laws not of men".

Beberapa tahun yang lalu, ketika menulis mengenai peranan raja-raja berperlembagaan di Malaysia, Tuanku menyebutkan bahawa seorang Raja "has no absolute power. He is responsible to Allah and subject to the principles of Islam". A Muslim Ruler cannot expect loyalty from his subjects if in carrying out the royal command, he is required to violate the moral values of his religion. For, as Muhammad is reported to have said "there is no obedience in sin. It is only in virtue". In the same article, Duli Tuanku quoted the writings of other eminent jurists who said that the Yang di-Pertuan Agong is a "visible symbol of unity in a remarkably diverse nation. The office of Yang di-Pertuan Agong has provided for the first time a living national symbol to a society whose people differ racially, culturally and linguistically". These were not mere empty rhetoric words alone. Duli Tuanku has proved by example the value of these ideals.

Institusi kehakiman yang merupakan salah satu cabang dalam sistem pemerintahan demokrasi adalah satu institusi yang bebas—iaitu bebas dalam membuat keputusan berlandaskan perlembagaan, undang-undang, peraturan-peraturan dan kaedah-kaedah yang ada. Sehubungan ini patek dan semua para hakim berikrar menumpahkan taat setia kepada Raja, Negara dan akan memelihara, melindungi serta mempertahankan Perlembagaannya dan patuh kepada Rukun Negara.

Sebagai mengakhiri sembah ucapan ini patek, para hakim, pegawai-pegawai kehakiman dan hadirin sekalian mendoakan semoga Tuanku serta Tuanku Permaisuri berada di dalam keadaan sihat sejahtera agar pemerintahan Tuanku membawa kemakmuran, keadilan dan kesejahteraan kepada rakyat dan negara.

Ampun Tuanku. Sembah patek pohon diampun. Wabilahitaufiq walhidayah wassalamualaikum.

LEGAL EDUCATION, LEGAL RESEARCH AND SPECIALIZATION, LEGAL REFORM AND THE JUDICIARY*

May I take this opportunity to speak very briefly on Legal Education, Legal Research and Specialisation, Legal Reform and the Judiciary which are all very closely connected.

Legal Education

I gather that presently a large number of Malaysians are pursuing their legal studies in various private colleges with a view to obtaining the Bachelor of Laws (LLB) External Degree conferred by the London University. Upon successfully passing the LLB examinations, those who wish to enter the legal profession would, under the present law, be required to take the Certificate of Legal Practice (CLP) Examination. In order to prepare themselves for that Examination, these LLB holders would either enrol for the CLP course of studies at the University of Malaya or at some other private college.

In my opinion, the CLP course of study is extremely beneficial although it is not easy to pass. Holders of the London University LLB Degree may not, as a general rule, have a firm grasp of some aspects of Malaysian laws, or for that matter, an adequate understanding of the basic precepts of the Malaysian legal system itself—as their three years of study would have steeped virtually in the common law system prevailing in the United Kingdom. Thus, to quote an example, graduates who have recently returned from a three years' stay in the United Kingdom with their LLB scrolls would find, to their horror, that their knowledge of English land law, family law or probate is of little practical value back home in Malaysia.

For these graduates, therefore, the CLP course of study effectively fills the void and closes the "knowledge gap" in their studies. Upon passing the CLP Examination they are reasonably equipped to enter into private legal practice.

The problem, however, remains. Not all LLB graduates from the United Kingdom enter into private legal practice. A large number of these graduates join the government or enter the corporate world as legal advisers or legal

---

**At The Official Launching Of The "All Malaysia Reports" On 5th May, 1993 At The Malaysian Petroleum Club, Podium Block, Dayabumi Complex, Kuala Lumpur.*

managers. For them, the risk of a continuing or prolonged "knowledge gap" with regard to Malaysian law is very real.

With the benefit of wisdom based on hindsight, and with the hope that this unhappy state of affairs could be overcome it is my view that private colleges in Malaysia which offer these English law degrees be asked to incorporate, in their curriculum, legal subjects relevant to the Malaysian ethos and society. Thus, for example, subjects such as Malaysian Legal System, Malaysian Constitutional Law, Malaysian Commercial Law (to name a few) could be made either as mandatory or optional subjects for the students to take alongside their usual LLB core subjects offered by the United Kingdom based universities.

Legal Research and Specialisation

The traditional view is that legal research is the private domain of the academia. Whether this traditional view holds good as Malaysia leaves the 20th century and enters the third millennium is something which every member of the legal profession ought to ponder about.

I believe that the willingness to carry out legal research is the spark that will ignite the flame which will in turn show the way for our lawyers to attain a status known as "legal experts". Such expertise does not come easily or quickly. It takes will-power, it demands discipline and hard work and it requires guts. Inevitably it takes time, but time is available if one knows how to organize one's affairs and to manage one's time.

Many others before me have spoken on the need for Malaysian lawyers to enhance their skills and attain specialisation in various fields—such as international trade, off-shore banking, aviation law, marine insurance, admiralty, shipping and intellectual property, to name a few.

As Malaysia emerges to play a more important role in international affairs, in terms of political, strategic and commercial matters, I take the liberty to repeat the call that it is imperative for Malaysian lawyers to keep pace with these developments.

Legal Reform

Malaysia does not, like the United Kingdom, have a permanent Law Reform Commission. What we have is a Commissioner for Law Revision. Many people may have mistakenly believed the latter to be discharging the functions of the former.

Our daily papers now carry extensive reports of various legislative reforms in the offing—environmental law being the latest example. Earlier this year and last year we saw new laws being enacted by Parliament such as the Direct

Sales Act 1993 and the Securities Commission Act 1993. Several existing legislations have also been revamped on a major scale—such as the Co-operative Societies Act, the National Land Code and the Companies Act.

There has also been talk of amending some other statutes such as the Bankruptcy Act and the Evidence Act, but to-date we do not have any details. There were also suggestions made by several quarters to amend some provisions of the Civil Law Act—such as sections 3 and 5 (the application of English common law, equity and commercial law) and section 28 (no damages for loss of future earnings for people over 55 years).

Opinions are divided as to whether Malaysia ought to have a Law Reform Commission or not. Cogent reasons have been put forward in support of both points of view—for and against. It is not for me to say whether the Government ought to decide one way or the other. But should the Government decide one day to establish such a Law Reform Commission, it is hoped that Malaysia would then choose to chart its own strategies and develop its own legal priorities—and not, as sometimes had happened in the past, of adopting wholesale whatever "reforms" that had been made in England or in some other Commonwealth country.

Any law, before it is adopted and made part of our law requires careful consideration to ensure its suitability viewed in the context of our society and local conditions. It should be adopted if it meets the objects of the government to create a just society.

The Judiciary

On the judiciary, I would like to make some observations on the subject of written judgments. The need for written judgments to be issued as expeditiously as possible need not, for obvious reasons, be stressed. What I would also like to touch on is the need for written judgments in the subordinate courts. We know that according to the present practice, Sessions Judges may not feel disposed to write written judgments in full, setting out the facts of each case, the applicable law, their actual decision (the judgment) and the grounds of their judgment unless there is an appeal against their judgment to the High Court. The same thing could be said of the Magistrates' Court.

A great proportion of criminal cases however is dealt with by the Magistrates' Courts and the Sessions Courts. My view is that in appropriate cases, I repeat, in appropriate cases, Sessions Judges and Magistrates should endeavour to write out their judgments in full—whether there is an appeal pending or not from such decisions. It is only by so doing that we can develop professionalism in the judiciary. Furthermore, such a practice would provide the judicial officers with the necessary training and practical experience which would equip them well later in their career, particularly when they are elevated to the High Court Bench. I do realise that much time would be taken but time is what you make of it.

These are some of my random personal thoughts and views for this afternoon. I hope that those present here would find the time to reflect further on what I have said and contribute their own views and ideas on the matter.

Untuk mengakhiri saya dengan perkataan Misnillahi Rahmani Rahim dengan rasminya melancarkan the *All Malaysia Reports*.

THE ESTABLISHMENT, JURISDICTION AND POWERS OF THE SUPREME COURT OF MALAYSIA*

Before I speak on the subject of the Establishment, Jurisdiction and Powers of the Supreme Court of Malaysia, may I, with the greatest respect, convey the heartiest congratulations from the Prime Minister and Government of Malaysia and also my heartiest congratulations on behalf of the Malaysian Judiciary to the Supreme Court and the Government of Turkey on this auspicious occasion of the celebration of the 125th Anniversary of the Supreme Court. In view of its old establishment, there is very little doubt in anybody's mind of its maturity and wisdom.

For me personally and on behalf of my wife, I take this opportunity to express my most sincere thanks and appreciation for the invitation extended to me to attend this auspicious occasion. It is our privilege to be in this beautiful country. Indeed it is an honour to our judiciary and the Malaysian Government for the invitation extended to me.

The subject I shall speak on is entitled "The Supreme Court of Malaysia, its Establishment, Jurisdiction and Powers". Before I do so, it is perhaps useful for a better appreciation of the topic to relate briefly, by way of introduction, the background of my country, the system of government, the people and the country's judicial structure from the date of her independence in 1957 to the date of the establishment of the Supreme Court.

Malaya (a Malay peninsula) is geographically situated in Asia, to be more precise, in South-East Asia, bordering Thailand in the North, in the East by the China Sea and in the West by Sumatra separated by the Straits of Malacca. In the southern tip of the peninsula is the Island of Singapore.

Pre-31 August 1957 (date of our independence) Malaya was under the British and comprised of the four Federated Malay States and the five Unfederated Malay States. Each of these states was ruled by a Malay Ruler (the Sultan). There were also the two Straits Settlements of Malacca and Penang. Malaya achieved its independence on 31st August, 1957 with a written Constitution referred to as the Federal Constitution of Malaya. Basically Malaya was a Federation of eleven states with a Central Government at Kuala Lumpur.

**On The Occasion Of The 125th Anniversary Of The Turkish Supreme Court On 12th May, 1993.*

Malaysia practises parliamentary democracy with a constitutional monarch. A King is elected from amongst the nine Malay Sultans to hold office for five years. At Federal Level, there are two Houses of Parliament—the House of Representatives and the Senate. At State Level, there is a single legislative body. The judiciary is one of the three organs of Government, and as I said earlier, provisions relating to the judiciary are enshrined in the Constitution in Chapter IX.

Fundamental to our Constitution is Article 3(1) which makes Islam the religion of the Federation but other religions may be practised in peace and harmony in any part of the Federation. Article 4 provides that the Constitution is the supreme law of the Federation and any law passed after Independence Day which is inconsistent with the Constitution shall, to the extent of the inconsistency, be void.

Entrenched in the Constitution are, *inter alia*, provisions relating to fundamental liberties such as liberty of the person, the prohibition of slavery and forced labour, protection against retrospective laws and repeated trials, equality before the law, prohibition of banishment and freedom of movement, freedom of speech, assembly and association, freedom of religion, rights in respect of education and rights of property.

Under the Chapter that deals with the judiciary provisions are made on matters such as the judicial power, constitution of the Supreme Court, the establishment of the High Courts, the appointment of superior Court judges, oath of office, qualifications, tenure of office and the restriction on Parliamentary discussion of conduct of judges. There are two other important provisions in the Constitution relating to jurisdiction of the Supreme Court which I shall refer to shortly.

In 1963, pursuant to Article 2 of the Federal Constitution which allows Parliament to make laws to admit other States to the Federation, Singapore, Sarawak and Sabah were admitted to the Federation making up altogether a Federation of thirteen States, nine States each with a Sultan as the Head of State and the other four States each with a Governor. However in 1965, Singapore left the Federation of Malaysia and became an independent State.

Malaysia today consists of two territories, the Peninsular Malaysia and the Borneo States in Borneo bordering Indonesian Kalimantan. Malaysia has a population of approximately 18 million comprising of people of diverse races. They consist of the Malays, the Chinese, the Indians and others.

THE COURT STRUCTURE

(A) (1957-1963)

The court structure during this period consisted of the subordinate courts, that is, the magistrates' court with limited jurisdiction in both criminal and civil cases and the sessions courts with higher jurisdiction than that of the magistrates' courts. Both these courts are presided by legally qualified persons.

The High Court is a superior Court with unlimited jurisdiction in both criminal and civil cases. The High Court also hears appeals from decisions of the subordinate courts. The highest court then was the Court of Appeal which was presided by the Chief Justice sitting with two other judges of the High Court to hear appeals from a decision of a single judge. It also heard references on points of law of public interest.

(B) (1963-1984)

When Sabah, Sarawak and Singapore joined the Federation in 1963, the Constitution was amended to provide for the establishment of three High Courts in Malaya, Singapore and Borneo, each with a Chief Justice. The Constitution was also amended to provide for the establishment of a Federal Court headed by a President called the Lord President. Members of the Federal Court comprised of the Lord President, the Chief Justices of the three High Courts and seven Federal Judges. When Singapore left Malaysia in 1965, the two High Courts of Malaya and Borneo continued.

The Federal Court was then not a supreme court as such as its decision was subject, with leave, to appeal in certain cases to the Privy Council in London. The decision of the Privy Council was communicated to the Yang di-Pertuan Agong (King) in the form of an advice as to whether to allow or dismiss the appeal. However it was the highest court for Malaysia.

Over the years the number of appeals to the Privy Council decreased for reasons, *inter alia*, that it was costly for the parties and was also time consuming. As for criminal appeals it was quite apparent that these appeals mainly revolved around questions of fact and the Federal Court decisions were not invariably interfered with. As a result the Government decided that appeals to the Privy Council in criminal cases be abolished. The Government also decided to abolish appeals to the Privy Council in constitutional matters. The Privy Council was left to deal only with appeals in commercial and civil cases.

(C) 1st January, 1985

Sometime in 1984 the Government decided that the Privy Council would cease to hear appeals from Malaysia and the Constitution was accordingly amended to make provisions for the establishment of a Supreme Court of Malaysia. It was so established as from 1st January, 1985.

The Supreme Court now consists of the Lord President as President of the Court, the Chief Justices of Malaya and Borneo and seven other Supreme Court Judges. The Supreme Court sits mainly in Kuala Lumpur. Apart from its jurisdiction to hear appeals from decisions of the High Court in criminal and civil cases, the Supreme Court is also empowered to hear references on points of law of public interest which may have arisen in the course of appeals in criminal matters heard by the High Court. The other powers of the Supreme Court which, to my mind, are very important are those that are provided by Articles 128 and 130 of the Federal Constitution:

> "128.(1) The Supreme Court shall, to the exclusion of any other court, have jurisdiction to determine in accordance with any rules of court regulating the exercise of such jurisdiction—
>
> (a) any question whether a law made by Parliament or by the Legislature of a State is invalid on the ground that it makes provision with respect to a matter with respect to which Parliament or, as the case may be, the Legislature of the State has no power to make laws; and
>
> (b) disputes on any other question between States or between the Federation and any State.
>
> (2) Without prejudice to any appellate jurisdiction of the Supreme Court, where in any proceedings before another court a question arises as to the effect of any provision of this Constitution, the Supreme Court shall have jurisdiction (subject to any rules of court regulating the exercise of that jurisdiction) to determine the question and remit the case to the other court to be disposed of in accordance with the determination.
>
> (3) The jurisdiction of the Supreme Court to determine appeals from a High Court or a judge thereof shall be such as may be provided by federal law."

An Act of Parliament, called the Courts of Judicature Act 1964 is such federal law relating to superior courts of judicature.

> "130. The Yang di-Pertuan Agong may refer to the Supreme Court for its opinion any question as to the effect of any provision of this Constitution which has arisen or appears to him likely to arise, and the Supreme Court shall pronounce in open court its opinion on any question so referred to it."

There have been quite a number of cases decided by the Supreme Court on the validity of laws made by the Legislature, in particular, by the State Legislatures. A recent case where I presided, sitting with four others, was the case of

Dewan Undangan Negeri Kelantan & Anor. v *Nordin bin Salleh & Anor.* (1992) 1 MLJ 697.

Before concluding, I take the opportunity to once again express my appreciation for the invitation extended to me. Thank you.

PERANAN JURUBAHASA DAN PENTERJEMAH*

Saya amat berbesar hati kerana diberi peluang merasmikan Mesyuarat Agung Dwitahunan Kesatuan Jurubahasa dan Penterjemah. Saya difahamkan bahawa Kesatuan ini adalah salah satu daripada Kesatuan tertua yang didaftarkan tetapi disebabkan beberapa masalah penubuhannya telah dibatalkan. Namun demikian, atas daya usaha beberapa orang ahli, Kesatuan ini telah ditubuhkan semula di Johor Bahru dalam tahun 1988 dan semenjak itu dua (2) Mesyuarat Agung Dwitahun telah diadakan. Mesyuarat ini adalah kali yang ke tiga.

Perlu saya tekankan di sini bahawa bagi membolehkan sesebuah Kesatuan itu bertahan lama, anggotanya-anggotanya mestilah mempunyai dedikasi. Cogankata "satu untuk semua dan semua untuk satu" harus disematkan di hati setiap ahli.

Sekarang saya ingin menjelaskan sedikit sebanyak mengenai pentingnya peranan Jurubahasa dan Penterjemah dalam pentadbiran keadilan di Jabatan Kehakiman. Pegawai-Pegawai Kehakiman adalah mustahak dalam mengendalikan tugas-tugas menegakkan keadilan. Kelulusan akademik dan latihan yang diterima adalah bersesuaian dengan keperluan ini. Namun demikian tugas ini pasti gagal dengan tiadanya kakitangan sokongan yang amat diperlukan dalam pentadbiran keadilan. Disinilah pentingnya peranan Jurubahasa. Tidak boleh dinafikan bahawa di Mahkamah Rendah Daerah, hampir semua kerja-kerja perkeranian seperti pengeluaran resit denda, pengemaskinian rekod, pengendalian dan simpanan barang-barang kes, terjemahan dalam mahkamah dan proses perbicaraan mahkamah adalah dilaksanakan oleh Jurubahasa. Tanpa Jurubahasa fungsi Badan Kehakiman untuk menegakkan keadilan pasti akan lumpuh. Saya sendiri pernah menjadi jurubahasa pada zaman pemerintahan Jepun dulu. Oleh itu saya memahami akan kesukaran dan kesulitan yang dihadapi oleh Jurubahasa. Saya perlu sebutkan di sini bahawa walaupun kesulitan demi kesulitan dihadapi oleh Jurubahasa, kesetiaan mereka kepada Badan Kehakiman tetap teguh dan saya ingin melihat kesetiaan ini dikekalkan.

Saya masih ingat akan kesulitan dan ancaman yang dihadapi oleh badan kehakiman apabila Jurubahasa Mahkamah melancarkan mogok dalam tahun

---

**Mesyuarat Agung Dwitahunan Ke 3 Kesatuan Jurubahasa Dan Penterjemah Di Bangunan Dewan Perhimpunan Cina Selangor, Pada 20hb Jun, 1993.*

1974 dan akibatnya menjejaskan hampir keseluruhan Sistem Perkhidmatan Keadilan. Kes-kes tidak dapat dibicarakan dan terdapat rasa tidak puashati di kalangan orang awam.

MEMORANDUM

Saya difahamkan oleh Ketua Pendaftar bahawa Jabatan Kehakiman dan Kementerian Undang-Undang menyokong penuh tuntutan Kesatuan sebagaimana terkandung di dalam memorandum yang telahpun diserahkan kepada JPA. Buat masa ini JPA telah mempertimbangkan cadangan-cadangan yang terkandung di dalam memorandum berkenaan dan sebagai Ketua Badan Kehakiman, tentulah saya mengharapkan jawapan yang menggalakkan daripada pihak berkuasa tersebut. Jawapan yang ditunggu telahpun diterima. Melalui suratnya bertarikh 24hb. Mei, 1993 pihak Jabatan Perkhidmatan Awam telah bersetuju menambah STPM sebagai salah satu kelayakan masuk. Dengan memasukkan STPM (HSC) perkhidmatan ini masih lagi kekal di dalam tarafnya yang dahulu cuma perbezaannya ialah pemegang STPM berpeluang menyertai perkhidmatan Jurubahasa dan akan terus dibayar gaji yang setaraf dengan pemegang STPM.

Walaupun skim perkhidmatan bertarikh 24hb. Mei, 1993 itu tentu sahaja tidak dapat memenuhi aspirasi dan harapan tuan-tuan dan puan-puan sekalian tetapi terimalah dahulu sebagai tanda muhibbah di antara kedua-dua pihak Kesatuan dan Kerajaan. Pintu rundingan tentu sahaja masih terbuka dan dalam hubungan ini saya percaya Seksyen 13 Akta Tribunal Perkhidmatan Awam dapat digunakan untuk cuba mengatasi masalah tidak puashati Kesatuan.

PERKEMBANGAN KERJAYA.

Jurubahasa akan tetap memainkan peranan penting dalam Badan Kehakiman oleh kerana Malaysia adalah sebuah negara yang berbilang kaum. Memandangkan pembangunan pesat dan kemasukan ekspatriat dan bangsa asing ke negara ini, keperluan bagi Jurubahasa akan terus meningkat. Sebagaimana diketahui, pembangunan biasanya akan membawa kepada litigasi di mahkamah, dan dalam hal ini saya menggesa Kesatuan ini supaya melengkapkan diri dan bekerjasama dengan Unit Terjemahan Kementerian Pendidikan yang telahpun menubuhkan satu Bahagian khusus bagi menterjemah hasil karya kesusasteraan asing ke dalam Bahasa Malaysia dengan tujuan memajukan lagi Bahasa Kebangsaan kita. Saya menjangkakan masa depan yang cerah bagi Jurubahasa yang boleh bertutur dalam bahasa Jepun, Eropah dan bahasa-bahasa negara Asia lain. Perkara ini perlu diberi perhatian serius bagi perkembangan kerjaya yang lebih cerah.

Berkenaan dengan prospek dalam Jabatan ini, sukalah saya merakamkan ucapan terima kasih kepada pihak Kerajaan yang telah bersetuju menambahkan jawatan kenaikan pangkat untuk Jurubahasa sebanyak 30 jawatan di Semenanjung Malaysia. Keputusan Kerajaan itu adalah terkandung di dalam Waran Perjawatan Bil. 73/93 yang berkuatkuasa mulai 1.3.1993. Pecahan pembahagiannya adalah seperti berikut:–

> Mahkamah Tinggi Malaya–Ditambah tujuh jawatan Jurubahasa dalam Gred N7
>
> Mahkamah Sesyen Malaya–Ditambah tiga jawatan Jurubahasa dalam Gred N7
>
> Mahkamah Majistret Malaya–Ditambah dua puluh jawatan Jurubahasa dalam Gred N7.

Saya berharap dan penuh yakin bahawa pengisian jawatan kanan itu nanti akan menjadi perangsang kepada tuan-tuan dan puan-puan untuk bekerja dengan lebih cemerlang lagi.

Sukalah juga saya memberi jaminan bahawa saya dan Bahagian Pentadbiran Mahkamah Agung/Tinggi adalah sentiasa peka dan mengambil berat kebajikan saudara/saudari semua.

KAEDAH-KAEDAH PESURUHJAYA SUMPAH, 1993.
Kaedah-Kaedah ini mula berkuatkuasa pada 1.4.93 dan diwartakan untuk mengawal-selia Pesuruhjaya Sumpah. Secara tradisi dan amalan, Jurubahasa diberi keutamaan untuk dilantik sebagai Pesuruhjaya Sumpah di Jabatan Kehakiman memandangkan bidang tugas dan pengetahuan mereka di bidang undang-undang. Saya mengesyorkan kepada kerajaan supaya elaun Pesuruhjaya Sumpah sekarang ini sebanyak RM25 yang dibayar semenjak 1974 dikaji semula dan dinaikkan kepada RM100 sebulan.

Akhirnya, saya ingin menekankan bahawa Badan Kehakiman akan sentiasa dianggap sebagai sebuah institusi yang agung dan mulia selagi Jurubahasa yang merupakan sebahagian daripada anggotanya mengekalkan imej yang ada sekarang dengan melaksanakan tugas-tugas mereka secara jujur, penuh dedikasi dan tanpa rasa gentar. Dengan yang demikian mereka juga membantu pembangunan negara secara tidak langsung.

Saya ucapkan Selamat Maju Jaya.

Dengan ini saya dengan sukacitanya merasmikan Mesyuarat Agung Dwitahun ini.

Sekian.

KEPENTINGAN LAPORAN MAHKAMAH AGUNG*

Izinkan saya mengucapkan ribuan terima kasih kepada the management and staff of Asia Pacific Publications Sdn. Bhd., Kuala Lumpur, kerana mengundang saya ke Majlis Pelancaran Laporan Mahkamah Agung [1993] 1 LMA.

We are gathered here today to witness the birth of a new law journal—Laporan Mahkamah Agung which it is my privilege to launch.

Laporan Mahkamah Agung (LMA) is a new law journal on the Supreme Court judgments and all matters related to it. It is intended to cater to the needs of both the government and the private sector. The object of the journal is to provide them with easy access to the judgments of the Supreme Court. These judgments, being the judgments of the highest court in the country, are binding on all other lower courts and thus become precedents and act as a guide for the courts below. As such, it is very important that they be made accessible to as many parties as possible, in particular, to the members of the legal profession, both in the public and private sectors and the various government agencies dealing with the members of the public such as the Department of Inland Revenue, the Immigration Department, the Police Department, the Prison Department, the various ministries and so on.

Knowledge and awareness of these judgments would enhance the quality of services rendered by the members of the legal profession and the government agencies. For example, the private legal practitioners would be able to serve their clients better if they are aware of the latest legal development in the country. So would the courts be in carrying out their judicial duties if the presiding judge is aware of the latest decisions. The various government bodies would also be able to serve the public more efficiently if the laws and precedents in the country are made known to them.

In this respect, Laporan Mahkamah Agung has an important role to play in that judgments of the Supreme Court will be disseminated to the public and the private sector, accurately and speedily. I would also like to take this opportunity to congratulate the editor of the journal and his editorial advisory board

---

**At The Official Launching Of The Laporan Mahkamah Agung [1993] 1 LMA On 30th June, 1993 At The Dewan Raja Laut, 3rd Floor, Holiday Inn, City Centre, Kuala Lumpur.*

for all the efforts they have taken to publish the journal. We are all gathered together today to witness its launching.

With great pleasure, I now officially launch the Laporan Mahkamah Agung.

ROYAL SELANGOR GOLF CLUB CENTENARY BALL*

Mengadap Seri Paduka Baginda Yang di-Pertuan Agong Sultan Azlan Shah dan Seri Paduka Baginda Raja Permaisuri Agong Tuanku Bainun,
DYMM Raja Perlis dan Raja Perempuan Perlis,
DYMM Yang Dipertuan Besar Negeri Sembilan dan Tuanku Ampuan Besar Negeri Sembilan.
Ampun Tuanku,
Patik memohon ampun perkenan Duli-Duli Tuanku untuk menyampaikan sembah ucapan bagi pihak Kelab Golf Di-Raja Selangor dan Jawatankuasa Perayaan Seratus Tahun Kelab Golf Di-Raja Selangor.
Ampun Tuanku,
Alhamdulillah. Diizin Allah Subhanahu wataala dan dengan berkat dan rahmat Kebawah Duli-Duli Tuanku, maka Majlis pada malam ini dapat dilahirkan dan dapat kita semua berhimpun untuk tujuan yang tertentu.

Patik dengan segala hormat dan takzimnya merafak sembah menjunjung kasih yang tidak terhingga Kebawah Seri Paduka Baginda Yang di-Pertuan Agong dan Seri Paduka Baginda Raja Permaisuri Agong dan Duli-Duli Tuanku yang telah bermurah hati berkenan berangkat ke Majlis Makan Malam yang tidak sepertinya ini. Majlis Makan Malam ini adalah suatu acara kemuncak bagi perayaan yang patik sebutkan tadi. Di atas perkenan Duli-Duli Tuanku berangkat pada Malam ini, maka patik sekalian sungguh terharu dan terhutang budi yang tidak terhingga. Sehubungan ini maka tidak syak juga bahawa Keberangkatan Seri Paduka Baginda Yang di-Pertuan Agong dan Seri Paduka Baginda Raja Permaisuri Agong dan Duli-Duli Tuanku sesungguhnya menyerikan Majlis ini disamping itu memberi sesuatu kehormatan kepada Kelab Golf Di-Raja Selangor.

Di sini izinkan patik berucap sepatah dua kata kepada para hadirin.
Yang Berbahagia Gen.(B) Tan Sri Hashim Mohd. Ali, President RSGC,
Mr. Edward Soo, the Captain,
Past Presidents,
Honourable Ministers,

**At The Royal Selangor Golf Club Centenary Ball On 21st August 1993 At The Shangrila Hotel, Kuala Lumpur.*

Your Excellencies,
Ladies and Gentlemen,

We are indeed honoured that His Majesty the Yang di-Pertuan Agong Sultan Azlan Shah and Her Majesty Raja Permaisuri Agong Tuanku Bainun and Their Royal Highnesses Raja Perlis and Raja Perempuan Perlis and Yang Dipertuan Besar Negeri Sembilan and Tunku Ampuan Besar Negeri Sembilan have graciously consented to grace tonight's occasion.

Tonight's Centenary Dinner is the highlight of the Club's celebration marking exactly one hundred years today when the course of the Selangor Golf Club was opened, and 100 over years ago when an inaugural meeting was held on Saturday, 21st January at 6 p.m. at the Selangor Club to consider the formation of a golf club in Kuala Lumpur. When on 21st August 1893 the course was opened for play there were 30 founder members at which time the entrance fee was $5/-, with a monthly subscription of 50 cents. The first clubhouse, however, was completed in 1894. Incidentally golf was already played in Kuala Lumpur even before 21st August, 1893, in the Lake Gardens on a 5 hole course. As for the present site it was not until 1920 that work started there. Time marched on and much has happened since. War broke out and Malaya was invaded in 1941. During the Japanese Occupation the Club was taken over by occupying enemy forces, the golf courses were completely neglected and reverted, in places, to semi-jungle. However, after the war due to the efforts of so many people the Club steadily grew into a flourishing institution that it is today.

Royal Selangor Golf Club today as a meeting place not only for people of various races in Malaysia but also of various nationalities who are either residing temporarily on official assignments or on a short visit or for business purposes has indeed become truly international and therefore should play a role in projecting an image that we Malaysians are not only a peace loving and caring society but also a model for inter-racial harmony. On that note and to conclude may I, on behalf of everyone here convey our heartiest congratulations to the Royal Selangor Golf Club on its Centenary Celebrations.

This is intended to be kept as a record in a time capsule and shall be buried in front of the Club premise. God willing and barring any premature disposal by a developer it shall only be dug up 100 years hence by our great, great grand children. Finally I thank all of you for your presence here tonight.

Ampun Tuanku,

Sembah ucapan patik pohon diampun.

PENDIDIKAN SEIMBANG: PENGETAHUAN, KEMAHIRAN DAN SIKAP*

Saya bersyukur ke hadrat Allah Subhanahuwataala kerana dengan limpah dan hidayatnya dapat kita bersama-sama dalam satu upacara yang gilang-gemilang untuk merayakan kejayaan anak-anak kita yang baru menerima ijazah masing-masing sebentar tadi.

Saya mengambil kesempatan ini untuk mengucapkan setinggi-tinggi tahniah dan syabas kepada para siswazah serta kaum keluarga mereka atas kejayaan yang dicapai oleh siswazah sekalian hasil kegigihan mereka belajar dengan tekun dan tabah selama empat tahun yang lalu. Saya dapat merasakan betapa bangganya ibu-ibu, bapa-bapa serta waris-waris siswazah sekalian menyaksikan anak-anak naik ke pentas ini tadi dan menerima ijazah masing-masing.

Konvokesyen kali ini merupakan suatu yang istimewa kerana ia disertai dengan penganugerahan Ijazah Kehormat Doktor Falsafah kepada Yang Berbahagia The Rt. Hon. The Baroness Thatcher, Bekas Perdana Menteri Britain pada sebelah pagi tadi. Beliau adalah wanita pertama yang menjadi Perdana Menteri negara Inggeris. Walaupun kita tidak berpeluang bersama-sama beliau pada sessi petang ini saya berharap kehadirannya di kampus ini menjadi pencetus semangat kepada siswazah sekalian khususnya siswazah wanita untuk lebih giat dan berjuang dengan lebih gigih lagi untuk kecemerlangan negara.

Pada tahun ini sudah lebih sembilan tahun Universiti Utara Malaysia diasaskan. Jangka waktu sembilan tahun berlalu dengan begitu cepat sekali. Dalam masa sembilan tahun dari tempoh ia diwujudkan Universiti Utara Malaysia telah melalui perkembangan yang begitu pesat dalam berbagai-bagai aspek: pentadbiran, dan khidmat bakti kepada masyarakat.

Walaupun Universiti ini terletak di kawasan luar bandar, jauh dari pusat pemerintahan, perdagangan dan aktiviti ekonomi, seperti di bandaraya Kuala Lumpur, Ipoh dan Pulau Pinang, namun dengan adanya sistem komunikasi elektronik, Universiti Utara Malaysia berada dekat perkembangan terkini yang berlaku di seluruh dunia.

Dengan sistem perhubungan elektronik terkini dan canggih, Universiti Utara Malaysia boleh berkomunikasi secara 'online' dengan universiti-univer-

Di Upacara Konvokesyen Keenam Universiti Utara Malaysia Sesi Petang Pada 4hb September, 1993 Di Dewan Mu'adzam Shah, Universiti Utara Malaysia.

siti lain, baik di dalam negeri mahupun dengan universiti-universiti luar negara. Sistem JARING ataupun "Joint Academic And Research Integrated Networking" yang ada kini boleh disambungkan dengan pusat-pusat pengajian tinggi Amerika Syarikat, Britain dan Canada. Ini jelas menunjukkan Sintok adalah dekat dan senang dihubungi dari segi media.

Universiti-universiti terkemuka seperti University of Harvard dan University of Colarado dan universiti-universiti lain di Amerika Syarikat, Canada dan juga Britain dapat dirangkaikan dengan segera. Dengan adanya kemudahan komunikasi elektronik ini, saya yakin Universiti Utara Malaysia akan dapat bergerak maju jauh ke depan lagi dengan mewujudkan apa yang dipanggil "telelecture" atau kuliah jarak jauh di antara UUM dengan universiti-universiti di Barat.

Pendidikan di peringkat universiti dapat dibahagi kepada tiga aspek iaitu pengetahuan, kemahiran dan sikap. Dalam aspek pengetahuan atau 'knowledge' ia dibuat melalui kuliah, dan tutorial. Kemahiran pula, di peringkat awalnya diadakan oleh universiti manakala di peringkat amali disediakan melalui program praktikum ataupun latihan amali di beberapa syarikat, industri dan organisasi di seluruh negara. Oleh itu, setelah tamat pengajian di universiti, apabila siswazah memulakan kerjaya mereka, mereka telah pun bersedia untuk melaksanakan tugas masing-masing dengan penuh keyakinan kerana, di samping pengetahuan dan kemahiran, mereka juga mempunyai pengalaman.

Walau bagaimanapun, untuk bekerja, pengetahuan dan kemahiran sahaja tidak mencukupi. Seseorang itu perlu mempunyai sikap yang sesuai dengan kehendak masa dan tempat. Sikap yang berkait rapat dengan nilai adalah satu perkara yang rumit. Walaupun Universiti ini menawarkan etika pengurusan sebagai satu kursus, perkara ini melibatkan domain efektif. Dalam pendidikan, domain efektif merupakan satu aspek yang tidak mudah dilaksanakan kerana sikap dan nilai tidak boleh disampaikan secara langsung sama ada melalui kuliah, tutorial ataupun praktikum.

Sekarang ini negara kita berhadapan dengan gejala yang kurang sihat, iaitu jenayah kolar putih. Walaupun undang-undang dapat digubal untuk membanteras jenayah corak baru ini, undang-undang akan menghukum mereka yang didapati bersalah dengan sewajarnya. Undang-undang akan menjadi penghalang kepada mereka yang berniat melakukan kesalahan. Yang lebih mustahak ialah pendidikan dirancangkan sebegitu rupa supaya tiap-tiap orang siswazah dilengkapkan dengan sikap dan nilai yang dikehendaki.

Saya ingin tekankan di sini bahawa bukan hanya aspek persekolahan yang penting tetapi juga pendidikan. Ini mustahak untuk menyediakan bakal pentadbir, usahawan dan ahli profesional kita supaya menjadi insan yang beretika dan mempunyai kualiti yang tinggi serta menjadikan kecemerlangan sebagai matlamat.

Universiti Utara Malaysia adalah berbeza daripada universiti-universiti lain di negara kita. Ia merupakan sebuah universiti yang mengkhususkan kepada pengurusan. Falsafah UUM ialah berazam untuk membina kecemerlangan / keilmuan dan kecemerlangan prestasi dalam pengajaran, penyelidikan dan lain-lain. Saya harap, siswazah UUM pula akan menjadi insan yang seimbang dari segi keilmuan, kebudimanan, keimanan dengan mempunyai nilai-nilai lohor dan murni.

Satu lagi aspek penting dalam kehidupan kita ialah mengekal dan mempertingkatkan pencapaian ekonomi Negara Malaysia yang kita sayangi ini. Kerajaan sedang berusaha untuk mencari pasaran di rantau yang belum lagi diterokai selama ini. Ini memerlukan usahawan, pentadbir-pentadbir serta pegawai sokongan yang bukan sahaja mempunyai pengetahuan dan kemahiran dalam hal-hal perniagaan dan pentadbiran, tetapi pegawai-pegawai yang boleh berkomunikasi dan berinteraksi dengan baik menggunakan bahasa asing. Oleh itu kita memerlukan siswazah-siswazah yang bukan sahaja dapat memahami tetapi menguasai bahasa-bahasa terkemuka dunia, terutama Inggeris.

Sehubungan dengan ini saya mengucapkan tahniah kepada Universiti Utara Malaysia kerana mengorak langkah dengan menawarkan kursus Bahasa Sepanyol dan Bahasa Jerman selain Bahasa Malaysia sebagai Bahasa Kebangsaan dan Bahasa Inggeris sebagai bahasa kedua. Saya difahamkan UUM akan mula menawarkan Bahasa Perancis dan Jepun pada tahun hadapan.

Saya ingin mengingatkan para siswazah dan ibu bapa sekalian, tujuan kita mempelajari bahasa-bahasa selain daripada Bahsa Melayu adalah untuk menjadikan bahasa itu sebagai alat untuk mencapai tujuan. Semua bahasa adalah ciptaan Tuhan, dan kita semua tahu bahawa Tuhan tidak menjadikan sesuatu itu dengan sesia.

Saudara-saudari siswazah sekalian,

Saya berseru kepada saudara-saudari supaya berwaspada bahawa dengan memiliki ijazah bukanlah berakhir pembelajaran, tetapi bermakna titik permulaan kepada satu usaha berterusan hingga ke akhir hayat. Hari ini merupakan langkah pertama bagi perjalanan beribu batu panjangnya. Akhir sekali saya doakan agar Universiti Utara Malaysia akan bertambah maju dari semasa ke semasa menjadi Universiti yang akan disegani bukan sahaja di peringkat negara, bahkan diperingkat antarabangsa.

Sekian, wabillahi taufik walhidayah Wassalamualaikum Warahmatullahi Wabarakatuh.

SILVER JUBILEE LUNCH*

My wife and I are most grateful to all of you for the kind hospitality extended to us today and the generous tribute given to me. In all humility I feel that I hardly deserve such kind words. If at all I have achieved anything it is mainly due to the support I derive from my colleagues, members of the legal profession and the administration. In particular, I would like to mention my present Chief Justice Tan Sri Dato Gunn Chit Tuan and his predecessor Tan Sri Hashim Yeop Sani, who had to retire prematurely due to serious ill health. I thank God for giving me the courage of conviction to accept the responsibilities of the office of Lord President and continue with it despite the initial confrontation I faced from those whose support I was hoping for. My conviction that what I was doing was the right way to serve the public interest has enabled me to function effectively. The appointment was not sought by me but conferred on me by the Constitution. I feel that I am not important but what I stand for is. I also feel that in the short time that we are on earth we should make ourselves useful to our fellow men and country.

With regard to the function of lawyers, I can do no better than quote an Irish judge who said: "I would say to the Advocate upon this subject, let your zeal be as warm as your heart's blood, but let it be tampered with discretion and with self-respect. Let your independence be firm, uncompromising, but let it be chastened by personal humility; let your love of liberty amount to a passion, let it not appear to be a clock for maliciousness."

Leaving the law in the courts let me come to the law of life, to which I subscribe subject to human limitations, and that is "sincerity to God, sincerity to self, justice to all the people, service to elders, kindness to the young, generosity to the poor, good counsel to friends, forbearance with enemies, indifference to fools and respect to the learned".

In this regard I do ask that God grants me the serenity to accept things I cannot change, the courage to change things that I can and the wisdom to know the difference.

On my career as a lawyer and judge I believe it to be an accident for while in school I wanted to be a singer but as the saying goes–man proposes and God

---

**At His Lordship's Silver Jubilee Lunch Organized By The Legal Fraternity Of Malaysia, Held At The Lake Club, Kuala Lumpur, On Saturday, 18th September, 1993.*

disposes. In fact I find much happiness in sports, family life and social activities rather than in adjudication. In adjudication it is inevitable that someone has to lose and it is indeed very difficult to please both sides.

Before I conclude, may I take this opportunity to congratulate Yang Arif Datuk Wira L.C. Vohrah for the choice made by the United Nations for him to be on the International Tribunal to try war criminals of the former Yugoslavia. His election to the high office is a source of pride to the nation. This election is indeed an acknowledgement of the active role Malaysia is playing both in the legal and political field.

To conclude, my wife and I thank all those well wishers responsible for organizing this lunch.

LOVING AND CARING FAMILY FOR A DRUG FREE COMMUNITY*

Introduction

I thank the organizers for inviting me to deliver this keynote address. I am not an expert on the subject and I am sure that what I say will not be accepted as evidence in a court. I also have no medical training on drug or its abuse. Nevertheless, I venture to offer some comments on the useful role of the family in relation to this problem that the world now faces.

Apart from my limited judicial experience of slightly over 37 years in the legal and judicial service, I have been a citizen of Malaysia and, in general, of the world in a broad sense; married, also for approximately 37 years and am a father of two sons and two daughters. I have two daughters-in-law and two sons-in-law and nine grandchildren. My experience is not confined to my involvement in law alone but also extends to my interest in sports and voluntary service organizations like the Malaysian Red Crescent Society, the Spastics and the Leprosy Relief Associations.

I cherish being before you today to deliver this keynote address as this date has some significance in my life—being the 25th Anniversary of my tenure of office in the Superior Courts of Malaysia—having been elevated to the High Court Bench exactly 25 years ago today.

I have revealed all these to you with all humility merely to show that I have had the opportunity during the years I have spent on the Bench, to hear many drug cases both in the High Court, the Federal Court and now in the Supreme Court. This experience has enabled me to form some views on the drug menace.

Before I proceed to express my views I hasten to add that with regard to the objectives and achievements of this World Federation under the auspices of which we are meeting now, I need not waste your time to explain them as the details are well-known from the literature distributed and speeches you have already heard. The choice of this nation as the venue for this year's conference is very opportune as it gives us inspiration and encouragement to achieve our Vision 2020 whereby we expect to become an industrial yet caring nation among the third world countries.

**At The XVI World Conference Of Therapeutic Communities From 19-24th September, 1993 At The Nirwana Ballroom, Kuala Lumpur Hilton.*

Views only personal

Allow me to begin by stating that what I have to say today is strictly in my personal capacity with no official colour. In doing so, I shall focus mainly on the role of the family to diminish the drug menace particularly in the Malaysian context. I will touch on other aspects of the drug problem only insofar as they are relevant to demonstrate the linkage between the various issues.

Drug abuse is the most intractable and inexplicable social problem today perhaps next to that of refugees. Although I understand that numerous scientific papers have been published on this subject, approximately 1,000 on the hallucinogens alone in the last few decades, no ready made and simple solution seems to emerge in the horizon to solve the problem. As such, if my personal views occasionally and unavoidably overlap with those of others, it is only coincidental and supplementary. Anyway, as in the case of a family unit itself, there is no rigid ready made magical formulae that one can adopt to redeem a black-sheep in a caring and loving family. The effect of a recipe is dependent upon individual adaptations of certain basic principles stated here and elsewhere.

Gravity of the problem

The most striking citation on drug abuse which comes to my mind, among the multitude of available literature, is what a former Secretary General of the United Nations, Javier Perez de Cuellar, once stated, "Drug abuse is a time-bomb ticking in the heart of our civilisation. We must find measures to deal with it before it explodes and destroys us—the monetary value of drug trafficking has recently surpassed that of international trade in oil and is second to arms trade." In fact, the consequences of drug abuse may be worse than harm caused by misuse of arms. In the latter case, death is fast and the threat is hardly noticed. In the case of drug abuse, the latent disaster is voluntarily courted by the victims under the false illusion that it elevates them to an euphoria of bliss.

Definition of Drug Dependence

In order to better appreciate the problem it is necessary to understand the meaning of the phrase 'drug dependence'. 'Drug dependence' is defined as a state of periodic or persistent intoxication, detrimental to the individual, to society or both.

It is characterised by:

(a) a strong desire, need or compulsion to continue taking the drug;

(b) the development of tolerance with a tendency to increase the dose to produce the desired effects;

(c) physical and/or psychological dependence (craving).

The Dangerous Drugs Treatment and Rehabilitation Act 1983 of Malaysia defines a drug dependent as "a person who, through the use of any dangerous drug, undergoes a psychic and sometimes physical state which is characterised by behavioural and other responses, including the compulsion to take drugs on a continuous or periodic basis in order to experience its psychic effects and to avoid the discomfort of its absence". Incidentally a person may be dependent on more than one drug.

Local history of drugs

Malaysia and Singapore had a legacy of opium smoking from the days of the British Occupation. Following the banning of the opium trade its illegal use tended to be confined to elderly Chinese males who either ate or smoked opium in opium dens.

Ganja, the local name for marijuana (cannabis sativa) had been associated with the Indians and Pakistanis who brought over its traditional use from their motherlands.

By the end of the 1960's, a newer form of the opium menace appeared. This was the emergence of drug use among the young, particularly the use of pot (cannabis), MX pills ("mandrax" or methaqualone with diphenhydramine), speed (amphetamines) and later heroin. In Malaysia, heroin appeared sometime in 1970 and by early 1972 the government suspected that heroin was being manufactured locally. In October 1973, the first clandestine heroin factory was uncovered in Bukit Mertajam.

Punishment including death

At this juncture I wish to include another topic in my address although it is not strictly within the ostensible boundary of "loving and caring family for a drug free community". It is capital punishment and other preventive measures which Malaysia imposes on traffickers and others.

I touch on this topic in the beginning of my speech as some critics tend to question how the concept of capital punishment can be consistent with the idea of a loving and caring family.

Our mode of punishment has been thoughtlessly branded by overseas critics as cruel and barbaric. The question is—does our Government owe any apology at all in this respect to anyone? In this regard it should be stressed that drug addicts are not punishable with the capital penalty and that it is only confined to traffickers. Drug trafficking is an international criminal activity demanding maximum deterrence. The illegal production and illicit trafficking in drugs impede economic and social progress constituting a grave threat to humanity especially in developing countries. The eradication of trafficking in narcotic drugs is the collective responsibility of all states, especially those affected by problems relating to illicit production, trafficking or abuse. Therefore the beneficiaries of our stern deterrent measure include many of the European and overseas countries. Geographically, we are situated very vulnerably thus facilitating drug trafficking. This can be avoided if we close our doors to all international passengers but that is impossible for obvious reasons. I am sure you are aware of the "golden triangle" transit operations. Furthermore, our own people are not so literate and social oriented yet to withstand the temptations of drug consumption.

Newer methods of drug trafficking are emerging. It is worrying to note that women are being increasingly used as drug couriers. This is because the pushers behind the curtain believe that women could slip through the check point more easily or should they be caught they may escape harsh punishment. Some women apprehended at airports arrive with children or are at some stage of pregnancy. Some willingly swallow up to 100 (or even more) condoms filled with cocaine. Some insert packages into parts of their body where a search is unlikely for reasons of modesty. They travel thousands of kilometres away from their homes in developed countries because of the promise of financial reward. In such instances can there be any justification for them to be treated differently from men carrying out the same offence? In my view, any disparity shown in punishment will only aggravate skilful trafficking.

In these circumstances our Government, as well as that of neighbouring Singapore, clearly had no option but to impose the death penalty in the case of wilful trafficking. The theory of reformation and rehabilitation is hardly applicable to them as more than ample warnings of the death penalty are promulgated and emphasised at all entry points into the country. As head of the judiciary, I can assure you that a decision upon conviction to impose the death sentence is always taken with utmost pain. Every care is taken to ensure that the accused is given all possible benefit of the doubt. Decisions by trial judges are confirmed or reversed by the Supreme Court with utmost concern. Our judges and enforcement agencies are very religious by tradition and habit and they do not regard human life lightly. In deserving and exceptional circumstances the constitutional monarch exercises the prerogative of the privilege of pardon. However, when a trafficker wilfully causes the destruction of many other lives, we have to worry more about the human rights of innocent members of society and their families. Towards this aim, we must have laws to ensure that those who do traffick in drugs do not escape under legal disguises by presenting all types of rhetoric arguments. Our legislature has felt that having regard to the local conditions, to the disparity in literacy, the level of morality among our population and visitors, the culture in our heterogeneous society, and to the paramount need for maintaining law and order, this country cannot risk, at this stage, the abolishment of capital punishment for trafficking purely to satisfy human rights advocates in other countries who are not familiar with our risks. When the legislature so decides as a matter of policy there is no room for the judiciary to implement its own moral values. The right of the few to escape from death must be balanced with the rights of the majority for a remedy against social epidemics which kill many and cause many others to suffer.

The argument for abolishing the death penalty may be applicable in the case of other crimes arising from provocation, passion or other weaknesses. In the case of the drug trade, the offence is wilfully motivated purely by greed for money with no feeling for the right of others and their children to live. Those who are involved in trafficking should be treated like war criminals.

Apart from capital punishment Malaysia has also implemented other measures such as preventive detention and confiscation of property of convicted traffickers to control the drug trade. From experience our legislature has found that the conventional rules of evidence and penal laws are too outmoded and obsolete to deal with the syndicated international *modus operandi* of trafficking. This resulted in changes being made in the laws to deal with the problem. You will appreciate the gravity of the problem we are facing when you realise that even with our deterrent punishments and all other humanly possible preventive measures taken, the drug pedlars have just succeeded, as I was preparing my speech, to penetrate into our virgin farming village areas, called by us FELDA Areas, aimed at destroying our innocent youth living in a secluded and holy agricultural atmosphere.

Classifications of Drugs

The commonly-abused drugs are as follows:–

(1) Central Nervous System (C.N.S.) Depressants

(a) **Narcotics**
opiate group—opium, morphine, heroin
synthetic group—pethidine, methadone, codeine

(b) **Non-narcotics**
barbiturates e.g. phenobarbitone
non-barbiturates e.g. methaqualone, alcohol, benzodiazepines and hypnotics

(2) **Hallucinogens**

Includes cannabis (marijuana, ganja, hashish, pot, weed), LSD (lysergic acid diethylamide), mescaline (peyote, a Mexican cactus). phencylidine (pop, angel dust) and glue sniffing.

Effects

(1) **Depressants**

From the little that I know, all C.N.S. depressants reduce the activity of nerve cells, with a withdrawal syndrome. Tolerance develops rapidly with repeated use resulting in physical dependence. Depressants may also lead to psychological dependence and craving.

Narcotics produce sedation, analgesia, sleep and coma with slowing of respiration. A feeling of well-being and pleasurable sensation may produce a stage of excitement before the depressant effect.

Heroin may be smoked, or inhaled through a straw. "Chasing the dragon" consists of placing powdered heroin on a piece of metal foil, heating it with fire and inhaling the fumes through a straw. However, hard-core drug addicts (and in the West, where heroin is of low-grade) resort to "mainlining", i.e. by intravenous injections.

The classic symptoms of opiate overdose are pin-point pupils, severe breathing difficulties and coma. Early symptoms may be loss of appetite, constipation, nausea and retching.

Withdrawal symptoms are often dramatic with intense physical agony of successive feverishness and extreme cold, diarrhoea, vomiting, running nose, streaming eyes, muscle aches and insomnia.

(2) **Hallucinogens**

These do not cause physical or severe psychological dependency or craving. However, they produce hallucinations by distorting senses of perception such as sight, hearing, taste and sense of time which may have dangerous consequences. Accompanying effects on the mind result in fear, anxiety, impaired judgment and delusions and can precipitate a schizophrenic illness.

Physical effects are pupillary dilatation, nausea and abdominal cramps.

LSD is not a problem in Malaysia. The main culprit is still ganja (marijuana or cannabis). Cannabis preparations are usually smoked as cigarettes but may also be eaten in the form of sweets or cakes or drunk as "bhang". The active ingredient is tetra-hydrocannabinol (THC). The usual experiences include euphoria, an apparent slowing of time, enhancement and distortion of sensations and perceptions, and in appropriate circumstances, increased sexual arousal.

Cannabis users take the drug because of its pleasant effects, and on withdrawing, there is no craving for the drug and any psychological dependence is mild. Serious consumption of cannabis can result in paranoia, depression, dizziness, fatigue and visual impairment. There may be loss of control of behaviour, disturbances of memory and clouding of consciousness. More severe intoxication may result in delirium, extreme excitement and hallucinations. Physical effects include headache, gastrointestinal discomfort, dryness of throat, cough and bad taste in the mouth.

Of serious concern are reports of acute and chronic cannabis psychosis which produces a schizophrenic-like picture. Cannabis use also has a deleterious effect on memory, reaction time, concentration and personality. However, various studies produced conflicting reports of brain atrophy. The concept of "a motivational syndrome", characterised by apathy, inactivity and self-neglect suggest that heavy cannabis use can lead to social deterioration. Nevertheless, evidence pointing to this had been conflicting.

Health care and education

There are interrelated organs to combat the menace of drugs. Malaysia's communal attitude is embodied in the concept of community medicine which involves an integrated health service covering prevention, promotion, cure and rehabilitation. The first step in this concept is education. I believe this country has spent twenty percent of its total expenditure on health care in school education, the first in the ASEAN five to do so. Our Prime Minister has suggested that the next step should be to raise community awareness of health risks.

Cause of drug abuse

In my view, there is hardly any single reason that leads a person to drug abuse.

I shall now consider some of the causes—

(1) **Family Background and Childhood Environment**

This cause arises when there is a history of emotional deprivation in childhood, such as loss of one or both parents by death, or parental discord and separation. Overt or covert rejection where children are sent at a tender age to boarding school, or fostered or institutionalised surroundings is another contributory factor.

There are psychologists who maintain that the predisposition to delinquency is not a finished product at birth, but is determined by the emotional relationships. The delinquents are more often thwarted, rejected and disturbed at family or school level and find substitute satisfaction for their psychological needs leading to delinquency such as drug addiction. The non-delinquent are less often disturbed emotionally and express their needs in socially acceptable ways. Separation from parents, especially maternal deprivation is one of the undisputed causes of emotional disturbance of children leading them to anti-social development. Particular emphasis should be placed on adequate mothering focusing on a loving relationship, attachment, an unbroken relationship and a stimulating interaction in the child's own home. The role of the father is not less important although not so intimate. Desertion by a father creates general insecurity, tension and anxiety. An unhappy broken home creates in children a feeling of inadequacy making them vulnerable to all types of influences, whether good or bad.

Even if a family is not broken, it may be living in tension, discord and conflict which is as bad as a broken home, if not worse. Family tension manifested through hostility, hatred, resentment, nagging, bickering and psychomatic disorders retard children's development. It may be the discord and disharmony preceding the break rather than the break itself which lead the children to cultivate anti-social behaviour. When we discuss family discipline, it should be remembered that both extremely lax or extremely rigid control are unsound. Some critics tend to suggest that poor family discipline is more prevalent in socio-economic groups.

One problem which has caused me many sleepless nights is not the neglect of children but the stories of baby-battering and battered wife syndrome which constitute a form of criminal behaviour. These will have a detrimental effect on the development of the children.

(2) Unconscious Personality

Generally speaking most addicts' histories indicate pre-existing personality disorders, either inadequate or aggressive, sociopathic personality and the hedonistic ("thrill-seeking") personality.

(3) Psychological Precipitants

Anxiety and depression are frequently present just before the start of addiction. Addiction is usually precipitated by a stressful change in the lives of disturbed individuals, creating circumstances that thrust them into a new and more demanding role.

(4) Peer Group Influences and Surrounding Circumstances

Adolescence is the time when several adjustments have to be made, viz. break from childish dependency on parents, change to a more mature and responsible sexual activity and a search for a personal identity. This critical role transition from child to adult is often beset with anxieties of the conflicts generated. If the adolescent is unable to overcome his problem, he or she may get depressed and resort to drugs.

Adolescence is also a stage when teenagers rebel and reject parental values, seeking their own, instead, and acquiring them from their own age group. Adherence to a peer group that indulges in delinquency and drug abuse leads to emulation. Drug-taking may become a status symbol, a boasted sign of "adulthood". For lonely young people, of inadequate personality, the confidence induced by drugs enables them to meet strangers without embarrassment or anxiety. Young men may have difficulty in approaching girls without this form of self-boostering.

Other reasons may be the excitement of risk taking, of doing something wrong (anti-establishment), curiosity, the desire for new and pleasurable experiences, and the wish to be perceived as an "adult". The geographical area where one lives may also be a contributory factor to the drug problem.For example, I have observed that drug consumption and other acts of delinquency vary in different neighbourhoods. The rates of delinquency are generally highest in the low-rent areas near the centre of the city and decrease with the distance from the centre of the city. The areas with high rates of delinquency also have high rates of truancy from school and the areas with a high rate of delinquency for boys also have a similar high rate for girls. Another topic which we cannot ignore in this context is, in crude terms, the existence of petty gangs who tend to depend upon drugs as a stimulant. In every part of the world, not exempting this nation, we find certain characteristics of adolescent youths in gangs portrayed by a delinquent subculture whose features are the institutionalisation of promiscuity, violence, destructiveness and pointless anti-social behaviour as a kind of defiant reaction towards respectable middle class values which prevail in society at large. These youths find that growing up in a society which offers them little opportunity for success in terms of conventional goals of position and wealth is not fulfilling. By inverting social values and behaviour in a way demonstrating their contempt and rejection of accepted values the misled youths believe that they gain status and respect within their groups.

(5) **Psychosexual Problems**

Some people with problems such as impotence, rapid ejaculation, frigidity and other sexual neurosis may take drugs with a hope of overcoming their problem. Others may believe that drugs can enhance their sexual capacities.

(6) **Creativity**

Some artists, musicians, composers and poets do take drugs because they claim that their creativity is heightened. Psychedelic drugs, LSD and cannabis give them a different experience and different interpretation which they try to translate into art, music and poetry.

(7) **Summary**

In short, it cannot be disputed that individuals may become dependent on a wide variety of chemical substances covering the whole range of mental effects from stimulation to depression. All drugs are capable of creating a state of mind in some individuals which is termed psychic dependence. This drive requires periodic or chronic administration of drugs for pleasure or to avoid discomfort. It is not claimed that the measures suggested below are novel discoveries but are only humble suggestions arising from my own social and judicial experiences.

CONTROL OF ADDICTION

Proper use of leisure

In the first place, we should consider the effect of too much leisure available to the youth in affluent societies. Malaysia is one of them and the youth are found idling and aimlessly loitering in amusement parks, building complexes and the like. There is too much freedom to choose in secular philosophy. There is a tendency to regard anything good as good but anything evil as neutral. However, "freedom to choose" in Islam means freedom to pick only what is good while in the western concept it may mean freedom to choose anything whether it is good or bad. Such divergence creates food for thought as to whether the concept of freedom ought to be modified, at least in the case of relationships between parents and children, teachers and students. Coming back to idle leisure time, it seems necessary that instead of allowing youth to idle their time alternative programmes could be introduced for them including opportunities for them to spend time productively at recreational centres and libraries. I understand that the Malaysian Government has projects with a view to achieve such an object. I believe it would be shortly implemented.

Peculiar problems of undeveloped nations

There are many problems in the bringing up of children which undeveloped nations face in the mental development of children as they are exposed to the evils of modern civilisation including exposure by foul means to drug addiction. The recent killing of eight street children in Rio de Janerio by an "extermination squad" should make us wonder whether the global situation of human rights is illusory. Many youngsters may not be running away from their homes in developed nations but psychologically they are divorced from their parents. This behaviour in youngsters would appear to have been created by deeply hurt feelings in children, including grievances against the parents one way or the other. Although in Malaysia our children are not destitutes they may not be living in homes and surroundings that are endowed with love and care. In that event it may well be that some disappointed children partake in delinquent acts to hit back at their parents consciously or unconsciously by turning to drugs or other deadly sins.

Early detection and prevention

As the supply of drugs can never be totally eliminated education seems to be the best approach to diminish drug abuse. In my view, education programmes should attack the primary cause which is group pressure. Teachers should discreetly explore with students to find out what led them to drug abuse and encourage them to avoid such use. As teachers are readily accessible to students, their friendly suggestions could be more effective then casual visits and talks by experts. Teachers or school counsellors should play a one to one role in individual problems of all children especially in the age group of twelve or above. In any case, teachers and parents must keep a look out for symptoms.

Watching symptoms of dependency on drugs

Generally speaking, some of the relevant symptoms, according to medical opinion, are loss of interest in sports and daily routine, loss of appetite or weight, unsteady gait or clumsy movements or tremors, reddening and puffiness of eyes, unclear vision, slurring of speech, fresh or numerous injection sites on the body, blood stains on clothes, presence of needles, syringes or strange packets, etc. at home, nausea, vomiting and body pain, drowsiness or sleeplessness, lethargy and passivity, acute anxiety depression, profuse sweating, mood changes, temper tantrums, depersonalisation and emotional detachment, impaired memory and concentration, preference for solitude especially long hours in the toilet, disappearance of articles or money from home. The list is not comprehensive nor applicable in all cases. For example, it is not easy to diagnose a long standing heroin habit without clinical analysis of the urine or provoking a withdrawal. Apart from the need to inject the drug, there may be no outward signs of dependence at all. If the dose is nicely calculated to the addict's tolerance his behaviour is perfectly normal.

Role of family in cure of addicts

I am inclined to think that merely identifying drug dependants and lecturing to them on the evils of drugs will not improve the situation. It is like telling a man afflicted with infantile paralysis to run a 100 yards race.

Whether an addict remains off drugs after withdrawal depends on his morale and motivation. These depend entirely upon guidance and the relationship with his doctor, family members and even other well wishing leading members of society like social workers, etc. It is an unfortunate truth that in our mad rush to participate in this age of economic supremacy, the values that mould our ethics, politics and policies are those of competition, aggression, individualism and self glory and interest. All over the world, values like charity, compassion, care, truth and the common good seem to be diminishing.

I understand that there is a new programme in U.S.A. (N.A.P.)–a programme of complete abstinence from all dadah–introduced to kick dadah addition completely. The programme was introduced by a non-profit organization–expanded from the N.A. in California, United States in 1953. It is a worldwide programme and is involved in the caring of a few million recovering addicts.

General observations

The successful curer, whether a member of the family or not, has to combine the qualities ranging from those of gaoler and wild animal catcher to the gentleness and single mindedness of a devoted father or mother. Strictly his aim should be to correct as far as possible the personality difficulties of the addict. He should be given a sense of security, self reliance and self confidence and a sense of responsibility towards himself, his family and friends and towards the community. Primarily the remedy is to replace a sense of anxiety and insecurity with a sense of well being. Removed from the family unit and left alone children are exposed to opportunities to do what entices them and repetition of this point can never be superfluous.

An addict's life adds up to a self-enclosed system where he believes that he is able to provide his own pleasure. He isolates himself beyond the need for human help or satisfaction. His recurring periods of euphoria are balanced by the equally frequent periods of withdrawal. It has been wisely said by an expert that "The patient does not suffer from his illness, he enjoys it".

Those who have selected dependency on drugs have done so as a way of coping with their problems for reasons they are unaware of. Almost all accounts of people who are dependent on drugs have a very low opinion of themselves and their abilities. Anxiety is the mental mechanism that forces action to satisfy the basic drives to find food, shelter and a mate. Most of us cope with anxiety by altering the situation that causes it. In the case of an addict the drugs act on his central nervous system so that he feels he has eaten to his heart's content, experienced full sexual satisfaction and eliminated all his anxieties as well. The addict likes the image of himself because, in the main, one of his unconscious purposes in using drugs is to advertise himself in the most pitiful and hopeless light disguising the fact that he is the creator of his own future. He uses strong drugs to be seen as an irresistable enslavement because this exonerates him from responsibility. His family often shares the same view consoling themselves falsely with the notion that the son was a nice boy but he got hooked by the pushers. Society too prefers to think of addiction in terms of enslavement and inducement by pushers, giving excuses for not doing anything to self analyse and improve the quality of family life. Therefore any rehabilitation programme for a drug addict must make due allowance for the above abnormalities and eccentricities of the addict.

Religious upbringing

The role of religion is of utmost importance and should be encouraged but not thrust down the throats of addicts as it may evoke a hostile response from the young people resulting in rejection.

Every individual is equipped with a kind of sixth sense for religion no matter how irreligious he claims to be. This inborn religious inclination can be brought to blossom and flower or it can be destroyed depending on how one lives.

The modern life one is compelled to lead in the huge cities of industrial civilisation seems to wipe out the spiritual aspiration altogether. Some may say that city dwellers' existence ceases to have any real point or meaning at the moment. Therefore the importance of religion is very vital. It can play a very vital role in combating drug menace. There must therefore be some spiritual upliftment. Hence the addicts should be guided following one of the twelve principles laid out by N.A. to "seek through prayer and meditation, to improve conscious contact with God, to pray for knowledge of His will and power to carry that out".

Damaging social pressures

The person who is dependent on drugs, whether he is an addict or not, is the end result of many years of damaging pressures. He probably comes from an insensitive cold home, he has no self confidence, no belief in his own identity, no experience of normal living or normal satisfaction and lasting happiness. He has only the powerful impression of the hallucination and momentary pleasures to be got from drugs.

Rehabilitation

Drug addicts should preferably not be treated in mental institutions but should be sent to specially planned rehabilitation centres. If possible, rehabilitation programmes should be based on open air activities. Addicts should be encouraged to take part in work therapy, group discussions, counselling sessions and recreational activities. On discharge, it may be necessary to provide a protected environment for reformed addicts. The addict should be treated as a discharged patient and not as a wilful deviant. Human behaviour should be regarded not so much in terms of what it means to others and society in general but what it means to the actor. The way other people react or respond to one's behaviour powerfully influences our response and reaction. We all live in a world made up of our own perception of reality, which may or may not correspond with the truth and we act and interact in accordance with our reading of the situation which includes our perception of the way other people are reading it. In Malaysia, the Malaysian Anti-Narcotic Association (PEMADAM) is doing a very useful service but needs more public support. One of the problems to avoid after withdrawal is idleness on the part of the patients with no one to talk to. As a habit takes hold, other interests lose importance to the user. The addict himself often feels that he is leading a normal life and that drug is incidental. He does not realise that he is just going through the motions of recovery to normalcy. Therefore, once a person is addicted, the immediate family cannot afford to relax their vigilant eyes even for a short while and even after it is believed that he is cured in a rehabilitation centre or other institution. It has been stated on good authority that "the likelihood that significant abstinence would occur after prolonged involuntary supervision was fifteen times greater than after voluntary hospitalisation".

Treatment

I am sure that all of you are aware of detoxification and the method of treatment known as cold turkey. Within the limited time today, it will be superfluous for me to enlarge on this topic.

Resistance to psychotherapy

We should also appreciate that addicts are persistent in resisting ordinary psychotherapy. The success of any treatment depends upon communication with the patient and his acceptance of the therapist as a real human being who can have a real effect on him. But the addict's whole life is organized and oriented to remove any dependence on humanity. Given his drugs he thinks he is self sufficient, able to generate his own satisfaction and to live a supposed rich emotional life independent of the outside world. He therefore has no motives for communication when things are falsely believed to be going well. If and when he presents himself for treatment it is often not because he wants to be cured of addiction, but because his addiction is not working as it should be. All therapists including family members should not fail to realise these problems. To reach the addict the shell covering him should be cracked.

Views personal

Before I conclude there is one point which I wish to emphasise. I must make it clear to avoid being misunderstood or misquoted, that the views I have expressed are personal as stated in the beginning and I do not claim any infallibility. These ideas, perhaps in disjointed form for reason of time, should not be construed either as reflecting that of the Malaysian Government or the Malaysian Judiciary.

At this juncture, I feel that I have overstayed my hospitality. I conclude by wishing you all success and thank the organizers for giving me this marvellous opportunity to meet and address you. I will be monitoring your deliberations with keen interest hoping to share your expertise and wisdom. In any case, if you wish to study our ways of handling the problem you are welcome to visit our institutions and offer any advice and guidance that you may have to give.

SPEEDY DISPOSAL OF CASES*

Saya bersyukur ke hadrat Allah Subhanahu Wataala kerana dengan izinNya kita semua dapat berhimpun di sini pada pagi yang berbahagia ini.

Saya berasa sungguh bahagia kerana hari ini dengan berkat Allah Subhanahu Wataala maka beberapa orang pegawai tinggi Kerajaan dalam Jabatan Kehakiman dan Perundangan telah diperkenankan oleh SPB Yang di-Pertuan Agong untuk menyandang jawatan yang tinggi. Ini bermakna mereka diamanahkan untuk memikul lebih berat lagi tugas dan tanggungjawab. Saya percaya mereka yang telah diamanahkan dengan tanggungjawab yang berat ini akan berkhidmat dengan cemerlang, melahirkan penuh taat setia kepada negara.

Sebagai Pesuruhjaya-Pesuruhjaya Kehakiman yang baru maka mereka bukan sahaja perlu menjalankan tugas-tugas tadi dengan cekap dan beramanah bahkan juga mereka dikehendaki bertingkahlaku sesuai dengan jawatan tinggi yang mereka akan disandang. Khususnya mereka bukan sahaja perlu menjalankan tugas dengan adil dan saksama bahkan juga menyelesaikan sesuatu kes dengan seberapa segara untuk kepentingan keadilan.

Undue delay in the disposal of cases, either through a delay in giving the decision or in supplying the written decision where there is an appeal constitutes, in my view, a misconduct on the part of a judge in the discharge of his functions, judged in the context of how a judge is expected to carry out his duties to properly perform his function.

My advice to the new learned Judicial Commissioners is that in view of the high office that they hold and of its glory, they must not forget that they have to shoulder heavy responsibilities and have to perform that special kind of obligation expected of a person holding such an office. Therefore they must not conduct themselves in a manner that would tarnish the image of the judiciary.

As has been publicised recently there are many pending criminal cases involving civil servants which have not been disposed of speedily, the end result of which is that substantial government funds have been wasted. The Chief Justices of Malaya and Borneo and I have taken positive action to secure speedy

---

**At The Handing Over Ceremony Of Letters Of Appointment To Three Judicial Commissioners And The New Chief Registrar At The Supreme Court Annex On Friday, 31st December, 1993.*

disposal of these cases and for this purpose we considered it necessary to appoint a senior judge to monitor the disposal of these cases at all levels in the Subordinate Courts and in the High Courts. The total number of these cases pending in Malaya alone is approximately 750-800. We have received the facts and figures from the Subordinate Courts and High Courts in Malaya and it is expected that detailed information will soon be given by the Subordinate Courts and High Courts in Borneo.

A week ago I presided at a meeting of High Court Judges and Sesssions Court Judges from the States. The dialogue session was confined wholly to the question of speedy disposal of cases and the unanimous decision taken was that all these cases should be disposed of within the first six months of 1994. The other problem that has emerged is the non-hearing of appeals in 107 dangerous drug cases under S.39B for reasons I had already stated.. The Chief Justices and I have agreed to pursue an aggressive course of action to dispose of these cases hopefully within the first three months of 1994 and Yang Arif Dato' Mohtar Abdullah who will be functioning as the new Attorney-General from tomorrow has given his unqualified assurance to fully co-operate in our efforts to dispose of these cases speedily. Indeed, he has given the assurance that he will fully co-operate with the judiciary in all other matters requiring his co-operation and assistance to enhance the efficiency and effectiveness of the administration of justice in all courts in Malaysia.

There are many things I could speak on today about what we wish to do but it may not be fitting to do so here. However, I do feel that with the appointment of the new Attorney-General, much can be achieved if the Attorney-General's Office and the judiciary close ranks and put their heads together in administrative matters to secure excellence and it should be so not only in the interests of the judiciary and the legal department but also of our nation. A brief reference to the existing Rules is appropriate. Many of our Rules are outmoded. I am referring to the court rules such as the Supreme Court Rules, the High Court Rules and the Subordinate Courts Rules. With regard to the law relating to the administration of justice and the courts, I would say that some of the provisions are outmoded and need urgent amendments. We have discussed this problem briefly at the Rules Committee Meeting level and our decision was to set-up a sub-committee to be jointly chaired by the Chief Justice of Malaya and the Chief Justice of Borneo to review these Rules and other laws, such as the Courts of Judicature Act, the Subordinate Courts Act, the Evidence Act, the Criminal Procedure Code and the Penal Code and to submit proposals for consideration by the Rules Committee for submission to the Government. The object of these amendments is to secure a more effective machinery for the administration of justice by removing provisions that cause delay and introduce provisions that enhance speediness.

I hasten to add that when I speak of speed, it is not our intention that speed be achieved at the expense of justice. The sole object for speediness is to do justice for justice delayed is justice denied.

Lastly may I congratulate and welcome Dato Ghazali, Encik Hashim and Cik Zaleha to join "Yang Arif Sdn. Bhd."

PERANAN BADAN KEHAKIMAN*

Assalamualaikum dan Selamat Sejahtera,

Terlebih dahulu saya bersyukur kepada Allah SWT kerana dengan keizinan-Nya dapat saya bersama-sama dengan semua pegawai-pegawai kehakiman dari seluruh Malaysia ke Persidangan Pegawai-Pegawai Kehakiman Malaysia yang akan bermula pada hari ini sehingga 22 Januari 1994, setelah tidak diadakan selama tiga tahun berturut-turut.

Saya juga bersyukur kerana kita semua dapat berhimpun di sebuah Pulau yang sungguh permai ini.

Pulau Langkawi Pulau Mahsuri
Dayang Bunting nama tasiknya
Bertuah kita dapat kemari
Mengerat silaturrahim tujuannya.

Sebagaimana kita dapat melihat suasana di sekeliling Pulau Langkawi, dengan jelas menggambarkan kejayaan negara kita dalam bidang pembangunan ekonominya. Pada hemat saya, pulau ini adalah "showcase" yang mempamirkan kemantapan dan kepesatan pembangunan ekonomi yang mencerminkan kecekapan Kerajaan kita dalam bidang pentadbiran negara.

Apabila saya bercakap tentang Kerajaan, maka khususnya termasuk Badan Kehakiman dan peranannya kerana dalam kontek Kerajaan yang bercorak demokrasi berparlimen, maka Badan Kehakiman adalah salah satu daripada tiga anggotanya (one of the 3 organs of the Government). Oleh itu, pada hemat saya Badan Kehakiman sebagai salah satu anggota badan kerajaan perlu berusaha dengan gigihnya untuk mencapai tahap kejayaan dan kecekapan yang dapat di banggakan—satu kejayaan yang cemerlang untuk membantu menegakkan lagi "the stability of our Government".

Saya mempunyai penuh kepercayaan bahawa persidangan seperti ini bukan sahaja dapat mengeratkan lagi silaturrahim antara satu sama lain, bahkan juga dapat menjadi suatu forum dimana kita bersama mencari jalan yang paling baik dan sesuai untuk mengatasi masalah-masalah yang sering di hadapi dari masa ke semasa.

**Ucapan Perasmian Persidangan Pegawai-pegawai Kehakiman Malaysia, 1994 Di Berjaya Langkawi Beach Resort, Langkawi Pada 18-23hb Januari, 1994.*

Sebagai sebuah negara yang mengamalkan demokrasi berparlimen, sebagaimana yang saya sebutkan tadi, mandat yang diamanahkan kepada pegawai-pegawai kehakiman amatlah mencabar hasil daripada perubahan zaman. Ekoran daripada kestabilan politik dan perkembangan ekonomi negara yang pesat, citarasa manusia berasaskan kepada teknologi yang canggih menjadi semakin komplek. Namun begitu, kita mestilah menunaikan kewajipan kita dengan tabah dan penuh kesabaran, tetapi dengan secepat mungkin mengikut undang-undang dan peraturan-peraturan yang sedia ada dengan mengenepikan kepentingan sendiri. Hanya dengan berbuat sedemikian dapat Institusi Kehakiman menduduki dan menikmati mercu kegemilangan di bawah payong kedaulatan undang-undang negara.

Sebagaimana kita semua sedia maklum, mahkamah sentiasa dihujani dengan kes-kes yang kian bertambah yang menyebabkan kita sering mendengar rungutan daripada berbagai lapisan masyarakat dan media massa berkaitan dengan "backlog of cases". Di akhir-akhir ini, perkara tersebut menjadi semakin genting. Untuk mengatasi situasi sedemikian dan sejajar dengan hasrat Kerajaan yang bertema "Memimpin Melalui Teladan", saya berpendapat bahawa satu tatalaku, serupa dengan Perintah Am bagi kakitangan awam, hendaklah diadakan bagi Hakim Mahkamah Agung dan Mahkamah-Mahkamah Tinggi dengan secepat mungkin. Tujuan pokoknya ialah untuk memastikan bahawa semua Hakim-Hakim Mahkamah Agung dan Mahkamah-Mahkamah Tinggi terdiri daripada mereka yang benar-benar berkaliber dan berwibawa, InshaAllah.

Pada hemat saya, adalah perlu bagi Hakim-Hakim menyelesaikan kes-kes dengan secepat mungkin dan mengelakkan rungutan "justice delayed is justice denied". Oleh itu Pegawai-Pegawai Kehakiman yang hadir di persidangan perlu diingatkan bahawa tindakan akan diambil terhadap mereka yang sengaja melengah-lengahkan membuat keputusan sesuatu kes.

Sebagai tindakan susulan hasrat saya bagi mencapai "zero defect" dalam masalah tersebut, saya telah sendiri mengadakan dailog di Ipoh dan di Kuala Lumpur pada akhir tahun lepas dengan semua Hakim-Hakim Mahkamah-Mahkamah berkenaan. Ekoran daripada perbincangan tersebut, keputusan yang telah dibuat ialah bahawa semua kes-kes yang didaftarkan di semua mahkamah hendaklah diselesaikan dalam masa tempoh enam (6) bulan dari tarikh sesuatu kes tersebut didaftarkan di mahkamah berkenaan. Sehubungan dengan perkara yang sama, saya telah meminta Y.A. Tan Sri Dato' Mohd. Eusoff bin Chin, Hakim Mahkamah Agung, membuat lawatan ke beberapa buah negeri untuk memastikan arahan berkenaan dipatuhi sepenuhnya. Saya difahamkan bahawa beliau telah pun melakukannya. Di sini sukacita saya mengambil peluang untuk mengingatkan semua Pegawai-Pegawai Kehakiman supaya bersama-sama kita berusaha untuk membanteras masalah "backlog of cases" yang sepatutnya tidak harus berlaku.

Saya tahu bahawa pada keseluruhannya Pegawai-Pegawai Kehakiman yang hadir di persidangan ini berhemah tinggi, berwibawa dan bertanggungjawab. Dengan itu, suka saya sarankan di sini bahawa janganlah mana-mana Pegawai-Pegawai Kehakiman menilakan nama baik Institusi Kehakiman, kerana membuat sedemikian adalah seperti "menepuk air di dulang". Kita mestilah mengharamkan diri kita sendiri daripada diperintahi oleh gejala-gejala yang boleh menyebabkan orang awam mengatakan Institusi Kehakiman kita ini tidak mempunyai Pegawai-Pegawai Kehakiman yang berkaliber dan berwibawa. Hanya dengan menjalankan tanggungjawab dengan jujur dan ikhlas, barulah dapat kita menegakkan dan mempertahankan keadilan, dan sekali gus mendaulatkan undang-undang negara kita supaya dihormati oleh rakyat bukan sahaja di Malaysia tetapi juga oleh masyarakat dunia.

Selain daripada menyelesaikan masalah "backlog of cases", kita juga hendaklah mempertingkatkan lagi kebolehan dan prestasi kerja harian. Salah satu daripada cara yang baik untuk mencapai matlamat itu, ialah dengan mengadakan persidangan yang diaturkan dan disusun dengan teliti. Saya bergembira melihat dari aturcara persidangan ini, tajuk-tajuk ceramah yang dipilih ada mempunyai hubungkait yang rapat dengan apa yang saya utarakan di atas sebentar tadi.

Saya perhatikan bahawa tajuk "Penyelesaian Kes-Kes Perbicaraan" oleh Y.A. Tan Sri Dato' Mohd. Eusoff bin Chin, Hakim Mahkamah Agung, adalah tepat pada saranan hasrat saya untuk mengatasi keadaan "backlog of cases" pada masa ini. Kalaulah ada masalah tekanan kerja dalam menepuh cabaran tersebut, saya percaya ceramah yang akan disampaikan oleh Y. Bhg. Dato' Dr. Hj. Abdul Aziz Abdullah, Pakar Perunding Kanan, Jabatan Psikiatri, Hospital Kuala Lumpur dapat membantu keadaan sedemikian. Tajuk "Rasuah Dalam Perkhidmatan Dan Pencegahan" oleh Y. Bhg. Tan Sri Zulkifli Mahmod pada hemat saya, dapat membantu semua Pegawai-Pegawai Kehakiman memahami dengan lebih mendalam cara-cara mengelakkan daripada jatuh ke perangkap rasuah yang amat dikutuk oleh Allah dan masyarakat.

Pada tahun 1992 Kerajaan telah melaksanakan Sistem Saraan Baru. Dengan itu, ceramah yang akan disampaikan oleh Tuan Haji Luey bin Putih, sudah tentulah akan mendorongkan kita untuk mencapai tahap prestasi kerja yang lebih tinggi. Begitu juga dengan tajuk "Pembaruan dan Kemajuan Dalam Pentadbiran Awam" boleh menjadi petunjuk kepada kita sesuai dengan hasrat wawasan Kerajaan untuk mencapai pembangunan negara ke tahap yang boleh dibangga oleh semua rakyat Malaysia pada tahun 2020.

Sebagaimana yang kita semua maklum pada 31hb. Disember, 1993, Mahkamah Taiping mengalami kebakaran akibat salah satu daripada kelemahan sistem keselamatan. Oleh yang demikian ceramah berhubung dengan aspek keselamatan pejabat secara menyeluruh adalah pilihan yang arif dan tepat.

Akhir sekali, ceramah oleh Y.A. Tan Sri Harun Mahmud Hashim, Hakim Mahkamah Agung, berhubung dengan latihan Pegawai-Pegawai Kehakiman sudah pasti akan memberi perangsang kepada semua pegawai-pegawai yang hadir untuk berazam meningkatkan lagi kemajuan dalam kerjaya masing-masing.

Dengan adanya persidangan ini saya berharap pegawai-pegawai yang hadir dapat mengambil dan menimba seberapa banyak pelajaran yang boleh untuk mempertingkatkan lagi prestasi yang sedia ada dan jika perlu mengukir wawasan masing-masing.

Apabila perkataan "wawasan" disebut, apa yang terlintas di hati kecil saya ialah, wawasan 2020 yang mula diukir oleh Perdana Menteri kita, Y.A.B. Dato' Seri Dr. Mahathir Mohamad. Sehubungan dengan ini, saya melihatnya dari sudut peranan yang boleh dimainkan oleh Sistem Perundangan dan Kehakiman untuk mencapai sasaran wawasan itu. Ini adalah kerana undang-undang tidak boleh dipisahkan dari rukun undang-undang cara hidup rakyat sesebuah negara.

Untuk mencapai pendapatan sebanyak $26,100 per capita setahun dalam tahun 2020, ekonomi negara mestilah berkembang secara pro rata sebanyak 7% setahun. Jika Kerajaan mempunyai kemampuan sedemikian, masalah kemiskinan akan terhapus dan Malaysia akan menjadi sebuah negara yang maju dan disegani dunia, InshaAllah. Impian ini akan menjadi kenyataan, jika negara kita mempunyai, antara lain, kestabilan Sistem Perundangan dan Kehakiman yang kukuh. Oleh itu saya menyarankan di sini supaya bersama sama kita berusaha untuk mencari jalan yang boleh dipraktikkan ke arah mencipta sistem sedemikian.

Sebagai sebuah negara yang sudah lama merdeka tetapi masih lagi mempunyai beberapa undang-undang tertentu yang sudah ketinggalan zaman, sampailah masanya Malaysia mempunyai sebuah agensi untuk mengkaji semua undang-undang yang sedia ada secara menyeluruh, bukan secara ad hoc yang sedang diamalkan sekarang. Undang-undang yang ketinggalan zaman itu patut dikebumikan dan diganti dengan yang baru dan mudah difahami oleh semua rakyat, selari dengan perkembangan ekonomi dan politik negara.

Salah satu perkara yang menarik perhatian saya ialah, sama ada Sistem Perundangan dan Kehakiman Malaysia patut bergerak kearah menyelesaikan sesuatu kes secara pendamaian dan bertolak-ansur. Bagi diri saya, cara sedemikian hendaklah digalakkan dalam keadaan yang sesuai. Daripada pengalaman saya, dengan cara ini, seseorang litigan dapat menyelamatkan maruah diri dan keluarganya jika dibandingkan dengan cara yang ada sekarang ("adversarial system"). Presiden Abraham Lincoln berkata:

"Discourage litigation. Persuade your neighbours to compromise whenever you can. Point to them how the nominal winner is often a real loser in fees, expenses and waste of time."

Menyelesaikan pertikaian melalui Mahkamah Perusahaan patut juga digalakkan. Begitu juga melalui institusi-institusi timbangtara. Kedua-dua cara tersebut boleh menyelamatkan kos dan masa kerana prosidur yang digunapakai oleh institusi-institusi tersebut tidak begitu rumit seperti Mahkamah-Mahkamah Sivil.

Jika Malaysia mahu menarik lebih ramai lagi pelabur-pelabur asing, ia hendaklah mengadakan undang-undang yang boleh menyelesaikan kes-kes yang melibatkan pelabur-pelabur asing khasnya dan Malaysia amnya dengan cepat.

Selain daripada apa yang diperkatakan di atas, Badan Perundangan dan Kehakiman hendaklah juga dilengkapi dengan pegawai-pegawai yang mempunyai kepakaran tertentu untuk menyelesaikan kes-kes yang komplek, hasil dari perubahan masa. Kursus-kursus kehakiman bagi melengkapkan mereka untuk menghadapi berbagai-bagai cabaran semasa ekoran daripada perkembangan pesat ekonomi, politik dan sosial negara juga hendak di pertingkatkan. Bilangan Hakim-Hakim Mahkamah Agung, Tinggi dan Sesyen dan lain-lain Pegawai Kehakiman termasuk kakitangan sokongan hendaklah juga ditambah ekoran daripada pertambahan yang begitu ketara dalam bilangan kes-kes yang didaftarkan di mahkamah.

Beralih kepada penggunaan Bahasa Malaysia, saya berpendapat untuk tujuan mengintegrasikan rakyat Malaysia menuju ke arah wawasan 2020, penggunaan Bahasa Malaysia di semua peringkat pembicaraan telahpun dijadikan mandatori. Walau bagaimanapun, ini tidak bermakna kita akan mengorbankan keadilan dan kepentingan Bahasa Inggeris sebagai bahasa pengantaraan antara bangsa dan penuntutan ilmu.

Sebagaimana kita sedia maklum dengan mansuhnya rayuan ke Privy Council, Mahkamah Agung kini menjadi Badan Kehakiman Tertinggi di negara ini dan mempunyai bidangkuasa serupa seperti Privy Council di England. Dalam konteks ini, saya bersyukur kerana saya difahamkan bahawa konsep ke arah pengwujudan Mahkamah Rayuan telah direstui dan dipersetujui oleh Kerajaan, dan menunggu masa sahaja untuk menjadi kenyataan, InshaAllah.

Apa yang saya nyatakan sebentar tadi, adalah antara beberapa perkara yang menjadi darah daging wawasan saya untuk merealisasikan wawasan 2020; mungkin semua yang hadir di sini pada hari ini mempunyai pandangan yang berbeza. Samada pandangan saya itu serupa atau berbeza, para hadirin dan hadirat sekalian bolehlah berbincang antara satu sama lain semasa berada di Langkawi ini.

Akhir sekali dan dengan lafaz Bismillahhirrahmanirahim, saya merasmikan persidangan Pegawai-Pegawai Kehakiman Malaysia 1994, dan selamat bersidang; terima kasih.

MALAYSIAN CONSTITUTION: CURRENT AND FUTURE CHALLENGES*

It is a proud privilege for me to be invited to address you on the topic Malaysian Constitutional Development—Current and Future Challenges. At the outset, I must confess that it is impossible in this short lecture to do justice to the importance and breadth of the topic. Therefore, what I propose to do is to give you a very brief elementary outline of our Constitution and highlight only certain specific topics, that too inadequately for reasons of time.

This lecture is not to be taken as a forecast of what will be the Court's attitude if and when any constitutional dispute comes before it for adjudication. Every case depends upon the facts and circumstances of that particular case and a decision will be made after hearing the respective submissions of the parties concerned. I must make it clear that what I say today does not reflect my official or judicial stand. They are my personal views as I understand the law as it is today, and with all humility, I do not claim to be infallible.

Now let me introduce the subject. Since the dawn of civilisation, man has always grappled with the question of how society should be organized and governed. Out of this chain of thought arose the idea of constitutionalism and constitutional law. In simple terms the constitution embodies that body of doctrines and practices which form the basis for organizing a State.

On this occasion it is not opportune to discuss the history of our nation and constitutional development except for what has happened in this century, that too, to the extent of being relevant to the current and future events. Bearing in mind this limitation, let me start with the independence of this nation. As we are all aware an agreement was reached between the British Government, our then leaders and the rulers that Malaya should be fully self-governing by August 1957, if possible. Soon after the initial agreement a Constitutional Commission headed by Lord Reid, an English Law Lord was appointed with experts from some other Commonwealth countries as members to draft a constitution.

Their terms of reference were to examine the present constitutional arrangements throughout the Federation of Malaya, taking into account the positions and dignities of Her Majesty the Queen and of Their Highnesses the Rulers and to make recommendations for a federal form of constitution for the

---

**At The Universiti Teknologi Malaysia (Johore) On 29th January, 1994.*

whole country as a single, self-governing unit within the Commonwealth based on Parliamentary democracy with a bi-cameral legislature, which would include provisions for:

(i) the establishment of a strong Central Government with States and Settlements enjoying a measure of autonomy;

(ii) the safeguarding of the prestige and position of Their Highnesses as Constitutional Rulers of their respective States;

(iii) a Constitutional Yang di-Pertuan Agong (Head of State) for the Federation to be chosen from among Their Highnesses the Rulers;

(iv) a common nationality for the whole of the Federation;

(v) the safeguarding of the special position of the Malays and the legitimate interests of other communities.

The Report of the Commission was completed on 11th February 1957 which was subject to further study and changes in order to reach a consensus among the British Government, the Conference of Rulers and our then leaders. The Federal Constitution was thus created and as we all know, the Federation of Malaya was born as an independent nation on 31st August, 1957.

The modern state of Malaysia is a sequel to a merger of the Federation of Malaya, Sabah, Sarawak and Singapore in 1963. The original Constitution of the Federation of Malaya was amended to provide for this contingency but later Singapore left the Federation in 1965 voluntarily but with serious regrets by all parties concerned. This left thirteen states in the Federation. Subsequently, there have been no territorial changes except internal reconciliations of the carving of the federal territories of Kuala Lumpur and Labuan out of the States of Selangor and Sabah respectively.

In creating the Constitution our founding fathers had to accommodate modern institutions following the western style of democracy. These are in the main a Federal system with clear demarcation on the legislative authority between Federal and State legislatures, constitutional monarchy, parliamentary democracy with bi-cameral legislatures, separation of powers between the executive and an independent judiciary and demarcation of jurisdiction between Federal and State legislatures.

Apart from following modern nations of government and democracy, our founding fathers were anxious to incorporate in the Constitution certain entrenched provisions to protect the traditional rights and culture of original inhabitants. The framers of our Constitution must have thought, rightly so, that such entrenched provisions were absolutely essential for the stability and progress of a developing country. These are institutions of the Sultanate or Rulership, the Islamic religion, the Malay language and the Malay privileges. Some of these topics will be discussed later.

In this context, we should remember the need to amend the Constitution from time to time. We need not be alarmed at the need for amendments as the Constitution drafted in 1957 was only a foundation in creating a homogeneous nation embodying multi-racial, multi-religious and multi-cultural people under a common flag.

Proceeding upon such a foundation for more than four decades, we can be proud that today we are in the forefront rank of developing third world countries winning the admiration of the world's national leaders many of whom are anxious to follow our method of operation. This is by no means a small achievement and clearly it has been made possible by the flexibility of our Constitution which is a living organism. Amendments to the Constitution are not an isolated experience to us alone. According to Article 5 of the American Constitution, a resolution for amending the Constitution can be moved by at least a three-quarter majority of both legislative Houses at Federal level or on application of at least three quarters of the legislative bodies of the States.

In this regard, I am reminded of the writing of an American judge, Hamilton, who had this to say:

> "The people make the Constitution and the people can unmake it. It is the creation of their own will and lives only by their own will. Any Constitution should be flexible. It is all sail and no anchor. Yet, any bill amending constitutional provisions cannot be implemented at a thoughtless moment by invoking the simple majority of our representatives."

Under Article 159 of our Federal Constitution such a bill shall not be passed in either House of Parliament unless it has been supported on the second and third reading by the votes of not less than two-thirds of the total number of that House. The requirement is two-thirds of "the total numbers of that House" and not those present and voting. In making amendments we attempt to strike a balance between absolute rigidity and vulnerability to flexibility. A Constitution which is too rigid is likely to commend less legitimacy, obedience and respect a flexible one does i.e. a Constitution which may be amended from time to time to suit the changing aspirations of the people living under it.

Having given a brief outline of the basic features of the Constitution, let me divert at this stage to review fundamental liberties enshrined in our Constitution. In explaining them time permits me only to state the elementary fabric of the law. Article 5 by Clause (1) provides that no person may be deprived of his life or personal liberty save in accordance with law. Article 6 provides that no person may be held in slavery. All forms of forced labour are prohibited but Federal law may provide for compulsory national service. By Clause (1) of Article 7, it is provided that no person shall be punished for an act or omission which was not punishable by law when it was done or made and that no person shall suffer greater punishment for an offence than was prescribed by law at the time it was committed. Clause (2) of Article 7 provides that a person who has been acquitted or convicted of an offence shall not be tried again for the same offence except where the conviction or acquittal has been quashed and a retrial ordered by a superior court.

Clause (1) of Article 8 provides that all persons are equal before the law and entitled to equal protection. Literally it means that we should be treated equally under the law but this concept cannot be stretched too far to mean that all people should be treated alike. All that the law demands is that the persons in like circumstances should be treated alike. It is unthinkable that a child should be treated like an adult. From the practical point of view and bearing in mind the unequal nature of human beings from womb to tomb, the law has developed a classification under which, every person in a particular class should be treated alike, making it unlawful for any single person to be accorded discriminatory treatment.

Article 9 provides that no citizen shall be banished or excluded from the Federation. This absolute right is to be read with reference to Article 25 which permits the Federal Government to "deprive citizenship of any person who is a citizen by registration ... or a citizen by naturalisation under certain circumstances." Every citizen has the right to freedom of speech, peaceful assembly and association (and to disassociate) but Parliament may as it has done on occasions which time forbids me to elaborate, impose certain restrictions in the interests of security, public order or morality. Under this provision Parliament has amended the Sedition Act 1948 and made it an offence to question the sovereignty, powers and prerogatives of the Rulers, Malay as the national language, the special position of Malays and natives of Sabah and Sarawak and the legitimate interests of other communities. Every person has the right, under Article 11, to profess, practice and propagate his religion but laws may be made to control or restrict the propagation of any religion, doctrine or belief among Muslims. Islam is the religion of the Federation. Article 13 provides that no person shall be deprived of property save in accordance with law. No law may provide for the compulsory acquisition or use of property without adequate compensation.

While the above are the main fundamental rights of public interest, it is to be remembered that some of them may be overridden by Articles 149 and 150 of the Constitution. Article 149 empowers Parliament to make laws against subversive action prejudicial to public order etc., irrespective of whether an emergency is proclaimed. The Internal Security Act 1960 under which people of subversive tendencies can be detained without trial and the Public Order and Prevention of Crime Act and the Dangerous Drugs (Special Prevention) Act are examples of the powers of Parliament under Section 149. Article 150 deals with proclamation of emergency.

While concluding this topic, perhaps I am justified in entertaining some disappointment that the framers of our Constitution thought it fit to omit the duties of citizens to a State although these are impliedly understood. Consequently this omission may lead some people to think about only what the State and others owe to them ignoring the reciprocal duty owed by citizens to the State and others.

At this stage I must put a stop to the general analysis of the Constitution before I exhaust the limited time available as there are some specific topics of topical interest which I wish to highlight. By choosing them, it is not my intention to say that topics which I do not discuss are less important from an objective point of view but I have to make a choice from an individual point of view. Accordingly, I seek your indulgence to speak on Federal and State relationship, powers of the Yang di-Pertuan Agong and Rulers in the light of the recent amendment, powers of the executive vis-a-vis democracy, the structure and power of the judiciary and the division and synthesis of Common Law and Syariah Law and the use of the National Language.

A major feature of the Federal Constitution of Malaysia is its highly centralised form and the extensive powers it has to legislate over a wide variety of matters. In contrast the main exclusive state legislative powers of any real significance and consequence are those relating to land, forestry, agriculture, local government and the machinery of state government.

Accordingly let me deal with Federal and State relationship. Part V of the Constitution contains three Articles, i.e., Articles 70–73 which together with the eighth schedule relate to the States and their Constitutions. Each State has its own Constitution which is not otherwise part of the Federal documents. Article 70 provides for the precedence of State Rulers and Governors. Article 71 incorporates a federal guarantee of State Constitutions and essential provisions which must be contained in State Constitutions and Article 72 provides for privileges of State Legislative Assemblies. Although various parts of the Constitution relate to States, Part VI in particular, governs legislative and executive relations between the Federation and the States and Part VII governs the financial arrangements. In view of the vastness of the topic, even if one speaks for a whole day, he will not be able to do justice to the subject. Having already tested a good part of your patience I propose only to touch on certain other points. I now proceed to speak on the relations between the Federation and the States. In the light of various provisions in the Constitution, it seems clear that Malaysia has a strong Central Government with supervisory and controlling powers over States which are hostile or otherwise. All State Constitutions are required under Article 71(4) to have certain "essential provisions" set out in Part 1 of the Eighth Schedule or provisions substantially to the same effect. These deal with, among others the Ruler, the Governor, the Executive Council, the Legislative Assembly, financial provisions, impartial treatment of employees and amendments of State Constitutions. Article 71(4) empowers Parliament by law to make provisions for giving effect in any State for the "essential provisions". It may also remove inconsistent provisions. Conversely, Article 71(3) provides that if it appears to Parliament that in any State any provision of the Federal Constitution or the Constitution of the State is being habitually disregarded Parliament may, notwithstanding anything in the Constitution, by law make provision for securing compliance of those provisions.

States are not exempt from emergency powers of the Parliament. One such instance was the emergency declared in 1966 applicable only to Sarawak and intended to resolve the constitutional impasse arising from the purported dismissal of the Chief Minister.

Parliament may make laws for the whole or any part of the Federation including the States while a State legislature may make laws only for the whole or any part of the State. Article 75 provides that if any State law is inconsistent with a Federal law, the Federal law prevails and the State law is, to the extent of the inconsistency, void. One instance of such a situation is the case of *City Council of George Town and Another* v *The Government of the State of Penang* (1967) 1MLJ 169, where the then Federal Court held that the Municipal (Amendment) Penang Enactment 1966, enacted by the Penang legislature was inconsistent with the Local Government Elections Act 1960, a Federal law and therefore void to the extent of its inconsistency.

Article 76 provides that Parliament may make laws with respect to any matter enumerated in the State list but only

(a) for the purpose of implementing any treaty, agreement or convention between the Federation and any other country, or any decision of an international organization of which the Federation is a member or

(b) for the purpose of promoting uniformity between two or more States or

(c) if so requested by the legislative assembly of any State. The Land Conservation Act 1960 relating to the conservation of hill land and protection of soil from erosion and the inroad of silt was made under this provision.

Land and local government are two of the most important matters on the State List. With a view to ensuring uniformity Parliament may exercise great and perhaps full control over these matters in the States of West Malaysia. However, the rights of Sabah and Sarawak State Governments in these matters shall be viewed in the light of Article 95E of the Constitution (exclusion of States of Sabah and Sarawak for National Plan for land utilisation, local government, development, etc.).

Under Clause (4) of Article 76, Parliament may, for the purpose only of ensuring uniformity of laws and policy, make laws for West Malaysia (not East Malaysia) with respect to land tenure, diverse types of rights and interests over land, compulsory acquisition of land and so on subject to the approval of State Legislative Assemblies. An example is the Land Acquisition Act No.34 of 1960.

Article 76A empowers Parliament to authorise by Act a State legislature to make laws with respect to any matter enumerated in the Federal List.

In general, under Article 81, the executive authority of every State shall be exercised

(a) so as to ensure compliance with any Federal law applying to that State and

(b) so as not to impede or prejudice the exercise of the executive authority of the Federation;

With that note of conclusion, without covering certain other areas on this topic, let me now move on to the next topic.

Before I do so I should mention some features of the special relationship between the Federation and the states of Sabah and Sarawak. For this purpose, apart from the original Constitution, we have to study the Malaysia Act of 1963, designed to meet the requirements and safeguards demanded by these States. When these States joined Malaysia there was a degree of suspicion and fear in them that they would be exposed to the preponderance and exploitation of the more progressive, developed and sophisticated Malaysia and Singapore, which was then part of Malaysia. Therefore, safeguards for the special interests of the indigenous people of Sabah and Sarawak were raised at the negotiation table and were agreed to and assured. Accordingly, the important interests were spelt out in the Malaysia Act and the Constitution of Malaysia while other terms were left to be dealt with in legislation and in the exchange of letters between the governments concerned. These special matters cover such vital issues as religion, immigration, education, citizenship, distribution of legislative powers, land, the special position of the indigenous races, financial provisions, the judiciary, the national language, the public service and emergency powers. These undertakings were stipulated in the Report of the Inter-Governmental Committee. Where the details were not included in the Constitution and not communicated in letters as recommended by the Inter-Governmental Committee, they were preserved in the Report itself, apparently to be consulted and relied upon if the undertakings given were ignored, for the purpose of rectification of anything done contrary to or in breach of the undertakings.

The composition of the Inter-Governmental Committee marked a very major step in the formation of Malaysia. The Report, after being presented to and considered by Britain, Malaya, Sabah and Sarawak, was published for the general information of the public on 27 February 1963. The Report dealt with diverse topics like immigration, religion, education, citizenship, judiciary and so forth. In consequence, Sabah and Sarawak are in many respects in a different position when compared with the other States in Peninsular Malaysia. Even in the case of these two States their relationship with the Central Government is not the same as the other States in respect of all matters, although generally speaking they are identical (see Articles 95B).

As this is not the occasion to deal with both the States separately, let me give an outline of the special provisions for Sabah where national election is scheduled to take place shortly. Only selective items are chosen for interpretation. In the case of the State religion in Sabah, no law restricting the propagation of any religious belief shall be passed in the State without a two-thirds majority in the State Assembly, Federal funds will not be used in North Borneo for religious purposes and Sabah will be given an amount for welfare purposes corresponding to the amount of Federal funds spent in Malaysia for religious purposes. In the case of immigration Sabah will have control (a) subject to security control over immigration for State purposes from outside Malaysia into Sabah and within Malaysia, (b) subject to the right of the Federal Government to bring in government servants and people on a temporary purpose when required for Federal purposes. In the case of land development, no development can be put into operation in Sabah without the consent of the State. In the case of financial provisions Sabah will have a considerable measure of control. In the case of the judiciary, there will be a Supreme Court in the Federation and separate High Courts for Malaya and the Borneo States. Natives of Sabah will be placed in the same position as Malays in the Federation of Malaya. The form of special privileges in Sabah will be laid down after consultation with the Chief Minister. Provision will be made so that the special safeguards for the Borneo States cannot be amended or repealed without the consent of these States. The above examples are by way of illustration of the special position of Sabah and Sarawak. I do not propose to elaborate further and accordingly I now switch on to the next topic.

With regard to the recent amendment to the Constitution by Act A848 which revised the powers of the Yang di-Pertuan Agong and Rulers, it is not appropriate for me to comment on the political justification for these changes. Let me briefly deal with the changes introduced in simple terms without elaborate technicalities, so as to save time. For reasons well known and as published in the mass media, the Yang di-Pertuan Agong and Rulers do not enjoy any immunity from causing harm to others or from civil liability. Yet in line with our attitude of compromise and evolutionary progress, neither the Government nor any other sane citizen, in my view, has ever contemplated the total abolition of constitutional monarchy. The changes made are reflective of this attitude. For instance, while it is no longer an offence to criticise a Ruler, subject to traditional decorum and ordinary laws of sedition, it is still a serious offence to advocate the abolishment of the position of the Yang di-Pertuan Agong and Rulers. Loyalty and respect to Sultans is inherent in our blood for a variety of reasons. The constitutional amendments were intended to modify the role of Rulers with appropriate changes in order to bring the noble and time honoured institution in line with the concept of Parliamentary democracy and constitutional monarchy. In making such changes, a compromise had to be made so as not to rush into revolutionary reforms. Therefore, there could not have been any intention to humiliate or harass any Ruler which is against our traditions and concept of fairplay. For instance, the Rulers have not been deprived of their role in the Pardons Board, the only change being that those who themselves or their immediate family members are the convicted persons cannot sit in cases concerning them. It has to be decided by other Rulers or the Conference of Rulers. Similarly, regarding the trial of Rulers for any alleged offence, it is not fair to treat them as ordinary accused persons. It is to be remembered that it may happen that the allegations against a Ruler may be malicious or false. In such a case, if he is acquitted in accordance with law, he can continue his former dignified role as a Ruler. Therefore, the establishment of a special court was appropriate. No public interest would suffer thereby. Even in the constitution of the Special Court, the three topmost judicial personnel are permanent members of the panel while two other persons are appointees of the Conference of Rulers. The rules of procedure of the Special Court are awaiting approval of the Yang di-Pertuan Agong. For the sake of saving time, let me conclude this issue by repeating some of the comments made by foreign jurists on the role of the Yang di-Pertuan Agong, which are equally applicable to Rulers in their respective States. Professor Groves commented that the Yang di-Pertuan Agong is a symbol of unity in a remarkably diverse nation. Professor Trindale and Jayakumar say that the office of Yang di-Pertuan Agong has provided for the first time a living national symbol to a society whose people differ racially, culturally and linguistically.

I now move on to the issue of powers of the executive vis-a-vis democracy. As far as law is concerned, the judiciary acts as a watchdog to ensure that no executive exceeds the power entrusted to it. While on this topic, it is important that we distinguish between the Western concept of democracy and our Eastern values and religious sentiments. The West has a long tradition of free speech. In the West, administration is based on majority vote whereas in the East we care more for consensus. Unfettered democracy with full freedom of speech is conceivably based on overvalued intellectual discussion. In a full fledged democracy there is a need for individuals to be civic conscious, literate and educated and capable of debating public affairs vigorously without personal ill feelings. In the East the experience in Sri Lanka and our neighbouring countries except Singapore is ample proof that a responsible executive should have some power to restrain freedom of speech, assembly and other privileges if we are to avoid public disorder leading to assassination of political leaders, military rule, coup-de-tat and revolutions which are so common in African and some Asian countries. This is because of historical reasons where religious and racial sentiments have been allowed to overreach the needs for bread, butter and shelter. Even in the West, the situation cannot be said to be ideal. What about the Irish situation in England? In my personal view, during the transitional stages of any nation, it is necessary to have some restrain on freedom and operation of a full fledged democracy. In Malaysia, we are trying to build a consensus of values among people of a multi-religious, multi-racial and multi-cultural society, while at the same time maintain the essential and fundamental features of democracy. We have periodical free elections and our leaders are accountable to the public. We have attained economic freedom and are rising to the level of competing even with developed nations. Yet, we are accused of being non-democratic by critics. I can only conclude this issue by saying that it is easy to be critical. The taste of the pudding is in the eating and the label it carries. Whether our democracy is pure or diluted, the fact remains that ever since independence we have had a strong Central Government consisting of a coalition of parties with no shortlived merry go round circus like Parliament contributing to instability and economic ruin. I shall now proceed to discuss the next key topic which is the position of the National Language.

Role of the National Language

One topical problem that we are facing is the role of the National Language (Bahasa Malaysia) in national development. Incidentally, the language issue is very vulnerable for exploitation by politicians and when we deliberate the issue we must be rational and dispassionate. The legal position is clear but the problem we are facing is the implementation of the legislative policy on the national language with grace and accommodation perhaps to the extent of reviewing our concepts and values. When our Constitution was being drafted our founding fathers thought it fit that as an independent nation we could not continue to use English as an official language if we wanted to unite our people and create a homogeneous cultural society. Language is the best means of communication and of understanding each other. If people speak in different languages, it will be a barrier to create a consensus of values, an essential prerequisite to unity and development. Accordingly, it was agreed by all parties that it should be written into the Constitution that there must be a national language and that the language should be Malay or Bahasa Malaysia as it is now called. Article 152 provides that the national language is Malay and in a script prescribed by federal law. The Article does not prevent the right of the Federal Government or any State Government to preserve and sustain the use and study of the language of any community in Malaysia. After the promulgation of the Constitution, The Constitution (Amendment) Act 1971 has now provided that the national language shall be the Malay language with the right to use (except for official purposes) any other language. Ten years after Merdeka day, Parliament removed the temporary provisions relating to the National Language Act by introducing the National Language Act 1967, coming into force on 1 September 1967. The Act does not apply, however, to East Malaysia. The Act provides that on or after 1st September 1967, the National Language must be used for official purposes. Section 4 allows the Yang di-Pertuan Agong to permit the use of English for certain official purposes which power he has used in a number of instances to maintain the effectiveness of international relationship and the efficiency of our developing status. Time does not permit me further to make references to this Act. In short, the constitutional law now expects the National Language to be used for all official purposes, including its use in the courts. Having briefly outlined the legal position, let me express my personal views. Is it justified now to look back retrospectively and adopt a more tolerant policy in the use of other languages? From 1957 we have risen to be one of the most highly developing nations, hoping to reach the stature of a developed nation like the U.S.A. or any other high powered nation. We are no longer a voice in the wilderness in the regional and world arena and we are now a force to be reckoned with. Having reached this stature and to maintain our achievements in the technical and scientific field, we cannot exclusively depend upon our National Language alone for purposes of communication and acquisition of further expert knowledge in the technical world. Nobody would doubt that because of its structure and adaptability Malay is an easy language to learn. However, its popularity is confined only to this region for historical reasons. English has acquired a unique place in this world especially in relation to international commercial transactions and as a result of its achievements in medical, scientific, engineering and similar fields. When Britain was a Roman colony, Latin was the language of administration and of the law. The Roman administration began to diminish in AD350 and English became the language of the English nation. With the expansion of British colonialism English developed into a world language. It will be remembered that the U.S.A. was once an English colony. Although Britain lost most of its colonial possessions in the unavoidable cycle of events, the status of English remains appreciated and acknowledged by all nations for international communication. In short, we need not see English as the language of the foreigners but as a means of communication in the world. Therefore, the decision of the Government to allow English to be used for teaching tertiary science and engineering subjects is commendable, if we are to become this region's centre of "knowledge and excellence". At the same time the progress in the study of English should not be at the expense of our national unity and sovereignty.

Now let me deal with the use of Bahasa in the courts. In most of the developing countries, laws are written in the English Language and are not understood by the ordinary people. The greatest disparity existing in developing societies is the inequality between the English educated few and the multitude uneducated in English. In the field of law, great judicial principles have now become a part of human heritage. I and many of my brethren in the judiciary have studied in English and only look for foreign precedents in English which have persuasive value. Nevertheless, we in the legal circles have broken frontiers and there has been tremendous acceleration in the last few years in making Bahasa Malaysia almost mandatory in court proceedings. We felt that whatever be the virtue of English with its rich heritage, the continued use of it hampers original thinking among the masses and the growing generation. The continued use of English creates an unreal atmosphere and an unsuspecting readiness and conditioning of mind to rely on foreign values and cultures. If justice is a virtue which is to do good to the people it should be done in the language of the people. The principle is not so rigidly applicable in certain specialised fields like medicine, engineering and similar vocations. For instance, what matters to a patient is the best medicine and surgery in the world even if it has to come from a foreigner speaking a foreign language. Another illustration is the recent condominium disaster where we had to depend to some extent upon foreigners in the rescue operations. The same principle can be extended to other disciplines which are of universal application as distinguished from municipal law which is unique in our case for reason to be explained shortly. In so far as the courts are concerned, I am proud of the creditable progress made by the younger generation of non-Malay lawyers and the judiciary who are contributing to the ultimate elimination of English with replacement by Bahasa Malaysia. Meanwhile, during the transition period of the next few decades, it will be unfair and unjust to ban English totally as it will create a sense of injustice. The problem will be solved in due course of time, perhaps, by the year of Vision 2020 by which time all or most of our legal literature can be translated into Bahasa Malaysia and the new generation of the legal fraternity will be totally proficient in the National Language in Malaysia. The ideal course is for the people to be proficient both in English and Bahasa Malaysia. In fact, the more proficient one is in different languages the more chances one will have to be a better cultured person. Anyway, let me conclude by saying that the judiciary is fairly rigid in its implementation of the national policy and the only concession which we make is in the case of old and senior lawyers or judges whose expert knowledge or wisdom overweighs the advantages of them being compelled to speak in Bahasa Malaysia, they being unable to do so because of their age and real impossibility to study during the eleventh hour. Now, without exhausting your patience, let me jump into the final key topic, and that is, the role of the judiciary in the process of future development towards Vision 2020.

Role of the judiciary

Owing to lack of time I shall only be able to give a brief review of each matter that I have in mind, summing up my thoughts in a sentence or two. Whether my absolutely short analysis does justice to the relatively important issues may be in question. However, let me emphasise that there is no higher duty or more solemn responsibility upon the court than that of ensuring that protection given by the Constitution is used for the benefit of every citizen irrespective of race, creed or status. When I speak about improvements relating to the judiciary, I am not thinking about the immediate period ahead of us. It is my hope that when it is time for me to vacate, I leave the arena a better place than what I found it to be when I took over the responsibility entrusted upon me as head of the judiciary. At the outset I must state that the role of the judiciary in our country may be said to be somewhat different from that of a developed nation. In our case the survival of democracy and the rule of law cannot exist in abstract theory in a vacuum. They depend on access to economic development and growth of the society as much as the protection of individual rights. A problem faced by the judiciary in developing societies therefore is the need to harmonise and balance the difference between social control and social justice. For the successful implementation of social welfare programmes for the benefit of the hitherto underprivileged under foreign masters, the State generally assumes enormous powers for the regulation of economic and other activities of private individuals and groups in the name of collective interests of society. The vesting of vast discretionary powers in the executive may not be in the best traditions of what is known as democracy in the Western concept. The system may not be to the liking of judges trained in the Western school of thought but they must appreciate their limitation. They are only guardians of the Constitution in interpreting executive acts and the people are the masters of the Constitution.

Having said the above as the primary guideline, let me mention some of the improvements I visualise to enhance the effectiveness of the system. With the increasing commitments of the nation following economic input there has been a heavy need for more courts and judges and many new appointments of judges have to be made. Initially they serve as Judicial Commissioners and on gaining sufficient experience they are confirmed as judges. While the standard of ethics of judges is generally good, there is no uniform guidelines in the performance of their duties. To avoid confusion and to ensure efficiency, I have recommended that there be a code of conduct for all judges. Another suggestion is the periodic refresher courses to be held from time to time not only for all judicial officers but also for judges so as to promote uniformity of thought and to enable judges to keep abreast of the latest social and educational developments locally and abroad.

With the close co-operation of judges, the courts have managed to clear the backlog of cases. Delay by courts is a legacy of the past and hopefully we will achieve dynamic and accelerated speed in the disposal of cases. The remedy to the problem is not in the hands of the judiciary alone but also lies in the co-operation of prosecuting officers, the Attorney General's Chambers and the lawyers. Very often the court's time is wasted by unwarranted requests for postponements and too lengthy, verbose and repeated examination of witnesses and submission to the courts. Recently, I read in the newspaper that in other jurisdictions judges have openly rebuked lawyers who blatantly abuse the privilege and trust bestowed on them.

Another improvement that I would like to see is the standardisation of legal training and education as well as regulating the uncontrolled flow of lawyers. This needs a concerted effort by the Attorney-General's Chambers, the Bar Council as well as other agencies represented in the Qualifying Board.

Syariah Court

Initially, I thought that I will refer you to some of the important Supreme Court decisions on topics like religious freedom and interaction between the Syariah and Common Law but I leave the opportunity for another occasion. In so far as the co-ordination between the Syariah Law and Common Law is concerned, no system is superior to the other but both are esteemed in the eyes of the respective adherents.

The Constitution (Amendment) Act 1988 added a new clause to Article 121 which reads:

> "The Courts referred to in clause (1) shall have no jurisdiction in respect of any matter within the jurisdiction of Syariah Courts."

The effect of the new amendment is the removal of the Civil Court's jurisdiction over Muslim Law matters which have been conferred on Syariah Courts. The hierarchy of the Syariah Court is

(i) Syariah Subordinate Court with criminal and civil jurisdiction;

(ii) Syariah High Court with original and appellate jurisdiction;

(iii) Syariah Appeal Court.

The Syariah Courts possess civil jurisdiction in proceedings between parties who are Muslims and limited criminal jurisdiction involving offences by Muslims against the religion. Offences of a religious nature include, in the main, khalwat (sexual proximity), unlawful sex, incest, consumption of liquor, failure to fast during the month of Ramadan and non-payment of zakat and fitrah.

The civil jurisdiction of the Syariah Courts includes laws relating to marriage, divorce, property arising out of marriage, maintenance of dependents, legitimacy, guardianship and custody of infants, division *inter vivos* or *sepencarian* property and others conferred by diverse statutory provisions.

These two jurisdictions are like two independent streams flowing from different sources in their own course ending in the same ocean known as justice. In the case of secular courts, an intermediate appeal court between the High Court and the Supreme Court shall be established shortly after a constitutional amendment. As the arrangements are expected to be of an enduring nature, we do not wish to rush into the change especially in the selection of qualified and suitable persons to fill the posts. In the fusion of the two systems of law, Syariah and Secular, there is no real friction although there are bound to be teething problems in the transition stages which should be capable of amicable solution with mutual goodwill, accommodation and tolerance. There is no intention on the part of Government to enforce any system on any group by force. Although there is no competition between the two systems, the Supreme Court may be considered as the first among equals (*primus inter pares*) for the sake of administrative convenience at least. In the case of criminal law and civil law except where the personal laws of Muslims are concerned as stated earlier, the Civil Court should, in my humble opinion, take precedence subject to any future constitutional direction or endorsement by the Supreme Court when disputes arise.

Having already exhausted your patience it only remains for me to stop now. There are many other topics relating to the Constitution that I had to omit, not, of course, because they are not important but solely due to pressure of time. In saying goodbye may I now wish your Institution and each and everyone of you the best of luck and prosperity.

THE FUTURE OF THE LEGAL PROFESSION IN MALAYSIA*

Sebelum saya memulakan ucapan saya di Majlis ini, izinkan saya menzahirkan kesyukuran saya kepada Allah SWT kerana hanya dengan izin dan limpah kurniaNya dapat saya bersama-sama dengan hadirin dan para peserta-peserta sekalian. Izinkan juga saya mengucapkan setinggi-tinggi terima kasih saya kepada semua yang berkenaan kerana sudi menjemput saya ke Majlis ini yang bertema *The Future of the Legal Profession* in Malaysia.

Since Merdeka Day, the legal profession has always been able to command respect from the public and is considered to be one of the most noble professions in our country.

It is sad to say that in recent years, it has suffered a serious erosion of respect by our very own society due mainly to misconduct by some of the lawyers. Unless something is done to improve the present situation, I fear that there will be further erosion of respect and confidence by the Malaysian public in the practising lawyers and, generally, in the legal profession. Having said that I shall now advert briefly to some of the problems confronting the legal profession. Any suggestion that comes from me is personal in nature and should in no way be treated as having been made by the judiciary or the Lord President's office. I do believe that you have your own views to offer and conceivably this Convention is the appropriate platform for you to pool your resources together and address yourselves to these problems.

Malaysia is one of the fastest growing among developing countries in this region and much of the success is due to the economic and political stability of the country. To be able to sustain and improve further, Malaysia should also have lawyers equipped to handle cases in specialised areas such as the law dealing with international trade, banking and insurance, etc. It would, therefore, be necessary for local universities to provide courses to cater for this need. The object should be to secure exposure for law students in these specialised areas. By doing so, the chances are good that they will graduate to be better equipped lawyers.

**At The Opening Of The 2nd Malaysian Law Students Convention 1994 Held At Dewan Laksamana, Hotel NPC, Petaling Jaya On Friday, 4th February, 1994.*

With the present rapid development in Malaysia, more quality lawyers are required. Presently, our universities and I.T.M. can only offer limited places for students who are qualified to pursue law degrees. As a result a large number of Malaysians are compelled to pursue their legal studies in various private colleges, including Stamford College, with the view of securing an external LLB degree from British Universities. Students who obtain such degrees are required by the present law to take and pass the Certificate of Legal Practice (CLP) Examination before they can be considered for chambering and admission to the Malaysian Bar. In this respect, it would benefit these students greatly if private colleges in Malaysia incorporate in their curriculum local legal subjects such as Malaysian Legal System and Malaysian Constitutional Law alongside the usual LLB core subjects offered by the United Kingdom based universities.

Perhaps it is appropriate for me to touch on the issue of a common qualifying examination for lawyers. I understand that the Malaysian Government, in collaboration with relevant bodies such as the Malaysian Bar Council, is now considering the introduction of a common qualifying examination for all law graduates before they can go into private practice or be appointed as Magistrates or Deputy Public Prosecutors. Personally, I can foresee the immediate advantage of such a course and, indeed, I believe it will enhance the standard of the legal profession in the future.

Another matter that I believe is of some interest to the legal profession is refresher courses. For those in government service the decision by the Government to establish a Judicial and Legal Service Institute will certainly contribute to the enhancement of the standard of professionalism in such service. The Institute, I believe, will help those in the legal and judicial service to update their knowledge in the latest developments in relevant areas of the law and more importantly, in their respective functions. The Malaysian Bar should also consider such an institution for those in private practice.

Moving on to the use of Bahasa Malaysia, may I say that the use of Bahasa Malaysia for all official purposes will help greatly towards national integration.

I firmly believe that if justice is a virtue which is to do good to the people, it should be done in the language of the people without, however, ignoring English which is a language of universal use especially in the acquisition of technical and scientific knowledge and for more effective communication in international trade and commerce. Speaking of Bahasa Malaysia in the courts, I am amazed at the dedication and determination of the non-Malay graduates to be proficient in the use of our National Language in courts. This augurs well for the future.

I adverted earlier to the conduct of lawyers. One of the obvious causes of the loss of respect by the public towards lawyers and the legal profession is the conduct of lawyers themselves. As lawyers they are accountable to their clients. They must therefore carry out their duties honestly without fear or favour. Courts are anxious to speed up disposal of cases. Therefore lawyers must, and should not, take any case that they cannot actually handle. Honesty and integrity of lawyers are crucial to the relationship of counsel and client as lawyers invariably have to handle clients' money, in some cases running into millions of ringgit.

Finally, I wish to say that I am happy that the four topics selected for this Convention bear relevance to what I have just discussed. I hope this Convention will be a forum for all participants to actually discuss problems facing the legal profession. Besides interacting with one another, I am sure you will be able to come up with some practical ideas as to how to improve the legal profession in the future.

Your vision in this regard is important. As law students you are the future architects of how the legal profession in Malaysia should be moulded. What is suitable today may not be so in the future. So long as we lawyers are honest to our cause and design our profession in line with the country's needs and aspirations, I am positive that the legal profession in Malaysia will regain whatever it has lost. On that note I declare open this Convention and take this opportunity to wish you every success in your deliberations. May God bless you all, and thank you.

TOWARDS UNDERSTANDING SYARIAH*

I am indeed honoured to be present here this morning to officiate at the opening of the Law Students' Development Course entitled "Towards Understanding Syariah".

I would like to congratulate the Law Society of the International Islamic University, particularly the Organising Committee, for taking the initiative in organizing this Course. As this course on the understanding of Syariah is most relevant and timely to all students, I am happy to know that students, not only from the International Islamic University, but also from the other institutions of higher learning in the country are present here this morning.

A programme such as this is of utmost importance to expose the students to the experience and knowledge that they will be able to utilise once they venture into the outside world. This will later lead to the production of graduates who are able to adequately face the challenges of the future.

Exposure to intellectual discourses is important, so as to make students fully equipped in facing their future destiny—as leaders of tomorrow. Thus, a programme such as this will not only help to develop thinking but also streamline their vision in accordance with Vision 2020. It is my hope that this programme will not only provide the students with the opportunity to gain the required knowledge and experience but will also assist them to implement Syariah in the future.

Regardless of whether it is Common Law or Syariah, the nature of law is to educate a person against wrongdoings which could deprive others of their lives, property or off-spring. This is what law and order are all about. Once that is understood then there will be respect and obedience to law.

Every lawman must respect and obey the spirit and the rule of law. It is the duty of those with knowledge of the law to explain to those ignorant of it. It is the duty of each and everyone of the undergraduates to arm themselves with all the required knowledge and understand how the law works so that they would be able to appreciate the spirit of the rule of law in order to transform social intent into social reality.

**At The Opening Of The Law Students' Development Course Entitled Towards Understanding Syariah Held At Pusat Islam, Kuala Lumpur On 5th February, 1994.*

Law is never stagnant for it is an ever living and developing subject. Undergraduates must acquire the skills and knowledge of every discipline of the law and be critical as well as analytical in order to expand the law. If one is to limit the scope of law then one would see law as being outmoded and inadequate thus depriving it of the ability to keep pace with the changing times.

One of the objects of Vision 2020 as outlined by Y.A.B. the Prime Minister is the creation of a just and equitable society to share the wealth of the nation. Thus, rules need to be regulated towards a fairer distribution of the wealth of the nation so as not to deprive or to discriminate others. This is what that is being advocated by Islam and Syariah. In your discussión on the role to be played by the Syariah as instruments of law, I strongly urge you to deliberate on the question of Syariah as instruments of law to achieve a more equitable and just society.

Recent developments in the law of banking has seen the expansion of the Syariah into the daily banking transactions. Interest free banking or Islamic banking is a system where Syariah gives an alternative to the customary banking laws. All these, if I may say, owe much to the hard work of Professor Emeritus Tan Sri Datuk Ahmad Ibrahim and his colleagues, and I am pleased to know that Islamic banking and Insurance law is part of the discipline taught at the University. However I am certain that Syariah can also play an active role in the other fields of law.

A course of this nature ought to be organized to encompass the public at large in order to enlighten them on the wisdom of Syariah. I believe it will provide a platform for scholars to discuss and reach an agreement on the values, merits and principles of Syariah.

The importance of Syariah in Malaysia has grown in recent years. Whilst much research was previously conducted only in the areas of the Civil and Common Law, Syariah Law, which has been applicable in this country for a number of centuries, was often neglected. It was not until the establishment of the law schools in local universities, particularly the International Islamic University, that greater awareness has been placed on this branch of jurisprudence. Over the past few years local scholars like your Dean and Kulliyyah of Laws, Professor Tan Sri Datuk Ahmad Ibrahim have contributed much towards this development.

It is indeed encouraging to note that Syariah Law now plays a more important and meaningful role in our country. Syariah Courts have now been reorganized and suitably qualified persons, trained in Islamic law, are now appointed as judges. The recent amendments to the Federal Constitution relating to the jurisdiction of the courts, and the placing of greater importance on the Syariah Courts, is a clear manifestation of the Government's desire to give proper recognition to the Syariah. As most of you are aware, exclusive jurisdiction is now given to the Syariah Courts to determine all matters relating to Syariah Law.

There is no denying that whilst Syariah continues to develop, there has, at the same time, been much misunderstanding of the Syariah in this country. This is not only so amongst the non-Muslims but also amongst the Muslims themselves. I am given to understand that this Course which is organized by the law students has, as one of its objectives, the promotion of a proper understanding of the Syariah among Muslim students. It is my earnest hope that there would also be greater participation in the future by students who are non-Muslims, for without a proper understanding of the Syariah by them, misconceptions will continue to arise.

Students generally play an important role in nation building and I believe that law students have a greater role in the development of the Syariah in this country. Whilst most lawyers have only been trained under the Civil and Common Law systems, it is only recently that the graduates from the local universities have had the benefit of studying the Syariah Law in Malaysia. Law students are the future lawyers and some of them will be the future leaders of this country. I believe that with a proper understanding and a greater knowledge of the Syariah, they would be in a better position to lead the country towards achieving Vision 2020.

I notice that some interesting topics by some well-known speakers on Syariah law will be discussed over the next two days. I hope that all participants and speakers will have a meaningful session.

To the Law Society may I urge you to render your services for the benefit of the welfare of the public—true to the Roman maxim *Salus Populi est Suprema*–regard for the public welfare is the highest law.

Dengan kalimah Bismillahirrahmanirrahim it now gives me great pleasure to officially declare open the Law Students' Development Course: Towards Understanding Syariah.

EARLY LIFE*

First of all, may I say that I am very touched that you have made the efforts to attend the dinner tonight. I also feel greatly honoured that my well-wishers have taken the trouble to organize this function to celebrate my birthday as well.

When Mr. Sivaloganathan and Stanley Augustin saw me in my Chambers to express their intention to organize this dinner, I did not feel quite disposed to agree as I am not fond of celebrating my birthday. Each time you celebrate your birthday you are reminding yourself that you are one year older than the last year.

This celebration, if not for the extension of my service should indeed be a celebration of my retirement. For myself, I take it to be a celebration of the first day of my service as a re-employed pensioner.

May I say that it is my privilege to have all of you here tonight and I do hope that it is a pleasure for you to be at this dinner. I cannot, however, guarantee the pleasure of those who like to see me go. And to them I am sorry to say that they may have to put up with me for quite a while yet.

Speaking for myself, I am confident that whoever succeeds me to the office of Lord President will continue to be concerned with an efficient and effective administration of justice. I have said time and again that speedy disposal of cases in dispensing justice shall always be the order of the day. There is much to be done to clear the mounting litigation and work shall have to be done fast so as not to create a backlog of cases. There is also much to be done to implement the proposal for the establishment of the Court of Appeal when it becomes a reality. But God willing the judges will continue to strive hard to improve the judicial administration.

As an arm of the Government under a democratic system of government, judges would observe the working hours fixed by the Government as applicable to everyone in the public service. Courts will continue to commence chambers and open-court hearings at 9 a.m. using the time from 8 a.m. to 9 a.m. to study the cases. By and large it is the duty of all the judges to see that there is no

---

**At The Dinner Given By The Members Of The Bar At The Lake Club, Kuala Lumpur On 25th March, 1994.*

denial of justice on account of failure to give a decision or grounds of judgment on time when there is an appeal.

Perhaps I should at this point refrain from embarking on any serious topic. I, therefore, move on to something more personal. Your birthday boy was born in a small fishing village in the northernmost State in the Peninsula, very close to the Thai border exactly six and a half decades ago. Perlis is a small State, nonetheless, it now has a golf course quite close to the Thai border. The story goes that one golfer hit the ball so hard and sliced it so badly that it crossed the border into Thailand and, accordingly, he had to get a visa to retrieve the ball.

Perhaps I should also tell you why I grew up not so tall. I understand that when I was an infant I was fed mainly with *pisang lenyek*. *Pisang lenyek* is mashed banana. First the banana is grilled together with the skin. After the skin is removed you mash the banana. Hence *pisang lenyek*. Perhaps those who aspire to be Lord President should try it. My outlaw Tan Sri Majid had it too and he became the Director-General of the Ministry of Health.

My father was a school teacher and believe me, before I could walk I already found myself in school. As my father was transferred from one school to another I lost count of the number of schools I had attended as a boy and even when I went to the Sultan Abdul Hamid College in 1940 at the age of eleven—the Japanese saw it fit to interrupt my schooling following their invasion in December 1941.

Once again I had to change schools and this time it was from an English school to a Japanese school. Again, believe me, at the age of thirteen I could speak Japanese better than a Taiwanese.

On my return to Perlis, I applied for the job of a temporary clerk only to be told that the only post available was that of an orderly or a peon. I think it was a marvellous opportunity to be useful again and I grabbed it and served as a peon until the Japanese called it quits in 1945 and the British occupied Malaya. I was back to school again.

May I now move on to say that I am overwhelmed by your hospitality. I notice that there is a lot of Chivas flowing and waiting to be consumed. Speaking of Chivas, perhaps a word of caution is in order.

A lecturer in a teaching hospital was trying to demonstrate on the dangers of too much drink and to prove his point he placed a live worm in a glass of water and a live worm in a glass of Chivas. At the end of the lecture he turned to the two glasses. The worm in the water was wriggling about strongly but the worm in the Chivas was still—obviously dead. The lecturer turned to his audience of medical students and asked, "What is the lesson to be learnt from the demonstration?" A student from the back quickly replied, "If you do not want to get worms drink Chivas."

From what I can remember, as an infant, I was one of those who loved to drink cow's milk. Perhaps that accounts for my bad habit to bulldoze court proceedings.

Incidentally, the cows love open space, grass and greens and the same goes for me. Hence my addiction to golf. There are many stories you hear about golfers. One such story is about a golfer who was ambidextrous. Some days he would play right handed and some days left. One of his opponents asked him how he decided which hand he was going to play each time. "Oh! It's easy," he replied, "if, when I wake up, my wife is lying on her right side, I play right. If she is lying on the left, I play left." "Ah!" said the friend, "What if you wife is lying on her back?" "No problem. I ring up the club and say that I will be an hour late." So be it.

One other story concerns two dreamers. Jack and John were playing a round of golf together. Jack told John that he had a most beautiful dream—he played golf with Severino Ballesteros and what was so satisfying was that he played ten under (normally two or three under) beating Ballesteros. "Good for you," said John, "I too had a very beautiful dream. I was in bed when Marylin Monroe walked in wearing her negligee and she spent some time with me. By the time she left I was fully exhausted. No sooner after she left Elizabeth Taylor came in, also in her negligee, and by the time she left I knew I couldn't function any more (even with T.A.). Hardly a second later Jane Seymour came in, also dressed in a beautiful negligee. I had it. I couldn't do anything any more and I wish then I had a friend to help me out." "Gosh!" said Jack excitedly, "Why didn't you call me?" "I did," said John, "but your maid told me you were playing golf with Severino Ballesteros."

Jack and John are favourites in golf stories. They are neighbours. In another round of golf, Jack asked John whether he ever had a hole-in-one. "No", said John. "And you?" "No", said Jack, "but I'll scream if I ever get a hole-in-one." One night there was a loud scream in the middle of the night. John's wife asked him what that was. "Oh! It's in one."

This wife was telling her husband about her trip to the cinema. "I had to move my seat five times." "Why?" asked the husband. "Were you molested?" "Yes", she replied, "eventually."

Finally, before I adjourn these proceedings, I would like you to know that, as it should indeed be in life, a golfer has to be patient, contented, cannot be greedy and should not worry. If he is patient and contented, not greedy and does not worry, he can play good golf. Perhaps the same applies to life—philosophically speaking I am told that you live long if you do not worry. Balasingam from Ipoh reminded me that in Malaysia one should not worry because you either go to hell or to heaven. If you go to heaven there is nothing to worry.

If you should go to hell there is no time at all for you to worry as you will be busy shaking hands with all your friends there. I really must stop now.

Once again from the bottom of our hearts, my wife and I do thank all of you.

UNDANG-UNDANG PERDAGANGAN ANTARABANGSA: PERANAN DAN KEPENTINGANNYA DALAM MENUJU TAHUN 2020*

Bersyukur kita Kehadrat Illahi kerana dengan izin dan limpah kurniaNya, dapat kita bersama-sama sekali lagi meraikan bakal-bakal graduan undang-undang, Institut Teknoogi MARA di majlis yang indah permai ini.

Saya ingin mengucapkan syabas kepada kajian pentadbiran dan undang-undang ITM, kerana telah berjaya mengeluarkan graduan profesional bumiputra di bidang undang-undang dan justeru itu telah menyumbang dan memenuhi kehendak, hasrat dan cita-cita negara dalam mencapai objektif dasar ekonomi baru.

Saya telah difahamkan, setakat ini, kajian pentadbiran dan undang-undang ITM telah berjaya mengeluarkan seramai 411 graduan undang-undang bumiputra yang sedang menampuk kuasa berbagai jawatan di sektor swasta dan kerajaan. Saya juga difahamkan, pada tahun ini genaplah 10 tahun usia program diploma lanjutan undang-undang, Institut Teknologi MARA di mana graduan dari kursus ini adalah seramai 370 orang. Sementara graduan diploma undang-undang adalah seramai 731 graduan.

Adalah menjadi harapan saya, agar ITM terus melaksanakan amanah negara mencapai cita-cita dan hasrat negara dengan menambahkan bilangan bumiputra di sektor swasta. Walau bagaimanapun, pencapaian kejayaan bukanlah diukur dari segi kuantiti profesional bumiputra sahaja tetapi juga termasuk mutu graduan yang dikeluarkan oleh ITM.

ITM seharusnya mempunyai objektif utama untuk melahirkan graduan yang bermutu serta mempunyai kecekapan yang tinggi dan cemerlang.

Malaysia pada masa ini sedang melalui satu proses pembangunan ekonomi yang pesat. Adalah menjadi harapan pemimpin dan rakyat negara ini, bahawa tahun 2020 akan meletakkan Malaysia ke mercu kejayaan di bidang ekonomi. Tahun 2020 juga akan mengambarkan Malaysia sebagai sebuah negara maju bukanlah impian semata-mata. Berbagai strategi ekonomi telah dilaksanakan. Malahpun Malaysia telah dilihat oleh masyarakat dunia sebagai sebuah negara yang mampu bertanding dengan negara-negara maju yang lain.

**Di Majlis Makan Malam Pra Graduan Undang-undang, Kajian Pentadbiran Dan Undang-undang, Institut Teknologi Mara, Pada 27hb April, 1994, Di Hotel Istana, Kuala Lumpur.*

Diperingkat perdagangan antarabangsa pula, Malaysia telah memainkan peranan yang aktif. Cadangan untuk merealisasikan East Asia Economic Caucus, perundingan selatan-selatan, peningkatan perdagangan dikalangan negara Asean dengan temeterainya AFTA adalah di antara sumbangan-sumbangan utama Malaysia kepada masyarakat antarabangsa.

Sehubungan dengan ini, kepentingan peranan undang-undang tidak boleh diperkecilkan samada diperingkat dalam negeri maupun peringkat antarabangsa. Senario perubahan perdagangan antarabangsa kini setentunya akan membawa berbagai-bagai implikasi kepada Malaysia. Sekiranya kita tidak bersedia, maka Malaysia akan tenggelam di dalam arus perubahan ekonomi. Dari aspek profesion guaman, tidak syak lagi perubahan perdagangan antarabangsa akan memerlukan lebih ramai lagi peguam-peguam yang arif di bidang undang-undang perdagangan antarabangsa.

Oleh itu, sudah tiba masanya sekolah undang-undang di Malaysia mengorak langkah untuk memberi penekanan kepada kepentingan undang-undang perdagangan antarabangsa di dalam kurikulum mereka agar dapat menambah kehendak pasaran antarabangsa.

Saya suka mengingatkan kepada bakal-bakal peguam keluaran ITM, agar dapat menyahut seruan ini. Saudara dan saudari akan keluar dari kampus tidak lama lagi dan sudah tentu akan bersama-sama bersaing dengan graduan undang-undang lain. Dengan adanya persaingan, maka hanya yang terbaik sahaja akan berjaya. Oleh itu saudara dan saudari haruslah bersedia menghadapi cabaran-cabaran ini dan hendaklah sentiasa menjadikan 'merits' sebagai ukuran kejayaan saudara dan saudari.

Akhir kata saya ingin mengucapkan berbanyak-banyak terima kasih kepada dekan, kajian pentadbiran dan undang-undang kerana sudi menjemput saya dan isteri ke majlis yang indah ini. Saya juga ingin mengucapkan selamat maju jaya kepada bakal-bakal graduan undang-undang ITM. Semoga Allah memberkati usaha-usaha saudara dan saudari.

Sekian, wabillahi taufik.

THE BUILDING INDUSTRY AND THE ENVIRONMENT*

Izinkan saya terlebih dahulu mengucapkan ribuan terima kasih kepada penganjur Fakulti Alam Bina yang sudi menjemput saya dan juga isteri saya ke Majlis Watikah Perlantikan Profesor-Profesor Kehormat Fakulti Alam Bina, Universiti Teknologi Malaysia. I am particularly happy that the appointment of Profesor-Profesor Kehormat is being conferred by the Fakulti Alam Bina.

As we are all aware Malaysia is progressing rapidly. This growth is expected to accelerate over the next few years as we move towards Vision 2020. The construction of more residential houses, hotels, factories and office blocks will be undertaken by the building industry.

However, one aspect of the building industry which has now caused much concern has been the impact of the industry on the environment. Recent reports, both by the Government and the press, have highlighted the importance of maintaining a balance between progress and the environment. The recent collapse of the condominiums in Kuala Lumpur drew much attention, and highlighted the importance of the need for the construction industry to comply with the relevant laws, pertaining both to the engineering aspects of the construction industry and the environment.

It is sometimes said that the building industry has its own priorities, whilst the environmentalists have their own. Whatever it may be, it is important for both these groups of persons to work together to maintain the necessary balance. It is in this area that I feel that the Fakulti Alam Bina can play a more significant role in bridging the gap between these two interests.

I am happy to learn that the UTM will be establishing a Construction Law Centre soon. For the centre to achieve a degree of success, it is important that experts from the various disciplines—lawyers, engineers and environmentalists work closely together. There are now numerous laws pertaining to the construction industry and many changes are being made to the laws relating to the environment. Studies on the inter-relationship between these laws need to be undertaken.

**Di Majlis Watikah Perlantikan Profesor-Profesor Kehormat, Fakulti Alam Bina Universiti Teknologi Malaysia Pada 10hb Mei, 1994 Di Hotel Istana, Kuala Lumpur.*

I am glad that the Fakulti Alam Bina at the Universiti Teknologi Malaysia has taken the initiative to appoint Profesor-Profesor Kehormat. These Professors, with their wide practical experience and knowledge, will have much to contribute towards the success of some of the projects undertaken by not only the full-time members of the Fakulti but also the students of the University.

I do hope that these Professors will play a more active role in the Fakulti in other academic areas. Though they may not be full-time members of the Fakulti, their expertise and advice on the syllabus and curriculum for some of the courses to be run by the University would be most beneficial.

I congratulate Profesor-Profesor Kehormat who have been appointed and wish them, and the Fakulti Alam Bina, every success.

PERSEKITARAN BARU PERDAGANGAN ANTARABANGSA: IMPLIKASI PERUNDANGAN DAN EKONOMI KEPADA MALAYSIA*

Saya mengucapkan ribuan terima kasih kepada pihak Urusetia Seminar kerana sekali lagi menjemput saya untuk merasmikan seminar yang akan diadakan selama tiga hari bermula pada hari ini.

Saya juga ingin mengucapkan syabas dan tahniah kepada pihak Urusetia Seminar kerana telah terus berjaya menganjurkan Seminar Undang-Undang dan Masyarakat untuk kali ke VII. Sesungguhnya ketabahan dalam menganjurkan seminar ini haruslah diteruskan. Ini adalah perlu untuk memastikan graduan undang-undang yang bakal dilahirkan bersedia sepenuhnya untuk menghadapi cabaran apabila tamat pengajian kelak.

Dalam usaha kita untuk memastikan bahawa wawasan 2020 akan menjadi kenyataan, bakal-bakal pemimpin sepatutnya terlebih dahulu didedahkan kepada permasalahan dan pengetahuan mengenai hal ehwal antarabangsa. Oleh itu, pemilihan tema "Persekitaran Baru Perdagangan Antarabangsa : Implikasi Perundangan Dan Ekonomi Kepada Malaysia" adalah merupakan satu langkah yang tepat dan bijak memandangkan negara ini menghadapi dan menuju kearah era negara perindustrian. Sehubungan ini, pemerhatian dari segi perundangan dan ekonomi adalah elemen terpenting untuk memastikan perkembangan ekonomi terus dipertingkatkan dan kadar inflasi di Malaysia dapat dikawal.

Di samping itu kestabilan politik memainkan peranan penting untuk menjamin kejayaan Malaysia, yang secara tidak langsung mencerminkan kestabilan sistem perundangan dan ekonomi kita. Oleh yang demikian, persekitaran baru perdagangan antarabangsa sekarang ini, pasti memberikan implikasi kepada sistem perundangan dan ekonomi di Malaysia. Pada hemat saya, perbincangan ke arah menyediakan Malaysia kepada sebarang implikasi negatif perlulah diteliti secara serius. Perhatian terhadap GATT (General Agreement on Trade and Tariffs) yang diwujudkan pada tahun 1947 adalah salah satu faktor yang patut diberi perhatian.

**Di Seminar Undang-undang Dan Masyarakat VII, Universiti Kebangsaan Malaysia, Pada 10hb Mei, 1994 Di Pacific Ballroom, Pan Pacific Hotel, Kuala Lumpur.*

Sebagaimana yang kita sedia maklum, GATT beroperasi sebagai satu perjanjian yang menggariskan beberapa peraturan mengenai perdagangan dan perhubungan komersial. Di samping itu, GATT memberi satu forum untuk perundingan dan perbincangan (negotiations and consultation) bagi tujuan mengatasi masalah perdagangan.

Beralih kepada "Uruguay Round", maka pada pendapat saya adalah jelas kejayaannya memastikan kebolehramalan dan kemantapan pelaburan berorientasikan eksport (Export Oriented Investment), disamping membolehkan negara-negara membangun terus memberikan kerjasama. Hasilnya, satu reformasi polisi ekonomi yang menarik telah dilakukan oleh negara-negara membangun pada dekad 1980-an.

Kesedaran PERUNDANG dalam mencari satu penyelesaian dan persediaan untuk memastikan persekitaran baru perdagangan antarabangsa, khususnya memberikan satu implikasi positif terhadap perundangan dan ekonomi, haruslah dipuji.

Justeru itu, dalam dekad ini, Pemindahan Teknologi (Transfer of Technology) memainkan peranan penting dalam perkembangan ekonomi negara membangun. Ia biasanya dilakukan dengan merujuk kepada negara yang telah maju dalam bidang yang berkenaan. Contoh yang paling mudah untuk diperhatikan ialah pertukaran teknologi automobil di mana PROTON telah mengambil dan menggunakan teknologi syarikat Mitsubishi dalam pembuatan kereta nasional. Pertukaran teknologi ini sedikit sebanyak membantu menambahkan pengetahuan teknologi kepada sektor perindustrian di Malaysia. Seterusnya, ini pasti akan membantu kepada era penciptaan yang lebih moden. Sehubungan itu, sistem perundangan yang sistematik yang bakal menjamin kemampuan dan kekuatan teknologi dalam era negara perindustrian adalah amat perlu diwujudkan dan dikongsi bersama sama dengan negara-negara lain di Asia Pasifik, Eropah dan Latin Amerika.

Di sini perlu saya menyentuh tentang peranan institusi kewangan. Institusi kewangan di Malaysia juga perlu berusaha lebih gigih di peringkat antarabangsa untuk mencari pelabur dan pembeli baru. Penubuhan Suruhanjaya Sekuriti pada 1 Mac 1993 adalah wajar untuk memastikan kemantapan pasaran sekuriti negara dengan perkembangan yang teratur dan stabil. Ia juga adalah untuk memastikan keberkesanannya dalam pasaran hadapan, selaras dengan objektif pembangunan ekonomi negara. Pada hemat saya, Akta Suruhanjaya Sekuriti 1993 ini adalah juga merupakan suatu peraturan statut yang membantu ke arah perlaksanaannya dan seterusnya berfungsi sebagai penasihat dan penyiasat bila diperlukan.

Peranan utama para usahawan, cendekiawan, pengamal undang-undang serta pemimpin-pemimpin ialah untuk mengenalpasti peluang-peluang pelaburan yang ada di peringkat antarabangsa. Keupayaan sesebuah negara sedang membangun seperti Malaysia akan sentiasa menjadi perhatian dunia. Oleh itu, sistem perundangan dan ekonominya perlulah bergerak selari dengan dasar politik luar Malaysia. Sikap irihati negara-negara lain pula janganlah dipandang ringan kerana ini boleh membawa kesan buruk kepada negara.

Keupayaan Malaysia dalam bidang ekonomi amatlah memuaskan dan kita patut berbangga dengan kejayaan ini. Namun demikian, usaha berkaitan dengan pembangunan bidang ekonomi ini haruslah terus dipertingkatkan.

Di peringkat ASEAN pula, Malaysia di samping Indonesia, Filipina, Singapura, Brunei dan Thailand, perlulah berganding bahu dalam menyediakan satu jaluran ekonomi dan perundangan yang kuat kerana usaha atau kerjasama berorientasikan ASEAN akan dapat mengawal negara-negara ASEAN dari sebarang gangguan kuasa-kuasa besar. Perundangan yang sesuai juga membolehkan usaha untuk membuka sistem perdagangan Malaysia ke peringkat yang lebih luas.

Seminar Undang-Undang dan Masyarakat selama tiga hari ini hendaklah dimanfaatkan dengan sebaik-baiknya. Penyertaan dari hadirin dan hadirat sekelian merupakan komitmen yang baik dan membuktikan usaha gigih semua pihak untuk mencapai kekuatan perundangan dan ekonomi Malaysia.

Akhirkata, dengan lafaz Bismillahirrahmanirrahim, saya dengan ini merasmikan Seminar Undang-Undang dan Masyarakat VII.

MALAYSIAN RED CRESCENT SOCIETY*

Saya bersyukur ke hadrat Allah SWT kerana dengan berkat dan hidayahNya kita semua dapat berhimpun bersama bermesyuarat bertukar fikiran untuk mencari jalan menegak dan meningkatkan lagi mutu dan khidmat bakti kita kepada masyarakat.

Pada hari yang sungguh bahagia ini, saya berasa sangat terharu di atas kesudian tuan-tuan menerima pencalonan Y.A.M. Tunku bagi saya mengganti beliau sebagai Pengerusi Persatuan Bulan Sabit Merah Malaysia. Saya juga sangat terharu kerana pada hemat saya pencalonan ini membayangkan kepercayaan Tunku pada saya untuk meneruskan tugas dan tanggungjawab yang beliau telah laksanakan sekian lama dengan sempurna dan cemerlang. Sehubungan ini saya juga menganggapkan penerimaan oleh ahli-ahli Majlis cadangan Tunku sebagai kepercayaan tuan-tuan dan puan-puan kepada saya. Bagi diri saya perlantikan ini adalah sesuatunya kehormatan yang saya sanjung tinggi.

It is with all humility I say that I am overwhelmingly touched by Y.A.M. Tunku's nomination that I take over his duties and responsibilities as Chairman of the Malaysian Red Crescent Society. I am equally touched by the favourable response from all of you to the nomination as reflected by your unanimous decision that I be entrusted with the duties and responsibilities that Tunku has discharged for so long with distinction.

On my part, I say with all sincerity that no one can really replace Tunku as he stands at a level not many can achieve in view of his absolute dedication and selfless service to the cause of humanity.

For myself, I find that Tunku has been and is always a gentleman. His gentleness and consideration has been a great source of inspiration to all of us. It is indeed so to me personally during the few years that I have been privileged to serve the Society. Under the circumstances, it is appropriate for me to express our gratitude to Tunku and Tunku Puan Sri Azizah both of whom possess all the qualities of fine Red Cross and Red Crescent membership—dedicated vol-

---

**At The 29th Annual General Meeting Of The Council Of The Malaysian Red Crescent Society On 31st July, 1994 At The MRCS National Headquarters, No:32, Jalan Nipah, Off Jalan Ampang, Kuala Lumpur.*

unteers who strictly adhere to the fundamental principles of Red Cross & Red Crescent.

On the agenda for today, I am supposed to address the Council on the future direction of the Society. Be that as it may, I ask for your indulgence to say, instead, something quite pertinent to the future direction of this Society. I am convinced that much can be learnt from Tunku. His very fine leadership all these years has, I think, firmly established the direction the Society should follow:

1. **Tunku's humility:** In the discharge of our duties and responsibilities Tunku's humility teaches us not to be a hindrance to others in the Society. By the same token it has taught us not to be suspicious amongst ourselves.

2. **Tunku's impartiality:** It teaches us not to be intolerant or in any manner indifferent especially in areas of sensitivity. I believe this is crucial to the well-being of the Society. Conceivably impartiality will help much in the promotion of understanding amongst members of the Society.

3. **Tunku's neutral approach:** It teaches us not to be *non compos mantis*. Pardon me for using the Latin term which means "not the master of one's mind". I firmly believe that fundamentally one cannot be neutral if one chooses not to be balanced in one's thinking.

4. **Tunku's independence:** It teaches us not to be indisciplined and not to have indisposition, indiscretion and indecisiveness.

5. **Tunku's absolute dedication:** In rendering voluntary service what is most significant is that one should not be void or hollow in rendering service and above all one should not be vociferous and volatile.

6. **Tunku's strong adherence:** To achieve unity it teaches us not to be uncooperative, uncompromising and unbending and

7. last but not least **Tunku's implicit subscription:** To the fundamental principle of universality it teaches us not to be umbrageous, uncouth and unfriendly.

I have elected to express my feelings at this juncture in this fashion to make a point that Tunku's humane perception is not to be taken for granted. Very often one fails to see the obvious even if it is not right before one's own eyes. Therefore, I take this liberty and I am sure all of you share my feeling to express on behalf of all of us, our sincere admiration and gratitude for the contribution Tunku has made to the Society.

May I move this assembly to give its unanimous and unequivocal support for a vote of thanks and sincere gratitude to Y.A.M. Tunku for the dedicated service that he has rendered to the Society, in particular as Chairman of Malaysian Red Crescent as well as for the role he has played in the Red Cross and Red Crescent Movement internationally. By the same token I also move that this assembly records its sincere thanks and gratitude to Y.A.M. Tunku Puan Sri Azizah who has equally shown absolute dedication to the service of MRCS. There is no doubt whatsoever that Y.A.M. Tunku Puan Sri has done much to provide strength and resolution to Y.A.M. Tunku Tan Sri Mohamed bin Tunku Besar Burhanuddin.

In conclusion I take this opportunity to ask all of you to give me the trust and confidence that you have given Tunku for I believe that only by you so doing that I can discharge the onerous responsibilities. I too need your close cooperation and loyalty. Together we will chart the Society's future destiny. To attain this objective it is important that we act in a manner consistent with the principles of the Red Cross and Red Crescent Society.

May I, at this point invite your attention to the lyrics of the Red Crescent Song, *Bulan Sabit Merah Malaysia*

> Bulan Sabit Merah di Malaysia
>
> Giat berjasa untuk negara
>
> Tanpa kaum puak dan agama
>
> Waktu aman atau bahaya.

Tunku, thank you once again for all your services rendered in the cause of humanity.

KEPEKAAN SISTEM PENDIDIKAN TERHADAP PERKEMBANGAN DAN KEPERLUAN SEMASA*

Saya bersyukur ke hadrat Allah Subhanahu Wata'alah kerana dengan limpah rahmat dan hidayatNya dapat kita bersama-sama dalam satu upacara yang gilang gemilang untuk merayakan kejayaan anak-anak kita yang baru menerima ijazah masing-masing sebentar tadi.

Saya mengambil kesempatan ini untuk mengucapkan tahniah dan syabas kepada para siswazah serta kaum keluarga mereka atas kejayaan yang dicapai oleh siswazah sekalian hasil kegigihan, ketekunan dan ketabahan selama empat tahun. Saya dapat merasakan betapa bangganya ibu-ibu, bapa-bapa serta waris-waris siswazah sekalian menyaksikan anak-nak naik ke pentas dan menerima ijazah masing-masing.

Konvokesyen kali ini adalah istimewa. Ini adalah kerana pada tahun ini Universiti Utara Malaysia melangkah masuk ke dekad keduanya setelah sapuluh tahun menempuh cabaran dan pencapaian sejak penubuhan rasminya pada 16 Februari, 1984. Selepas sapuluh tahun penubuhannya, Universiti Utara Malaysia terus menampakkan kecemerlangan dari segi sumbangannya dalam bidang yang berteraskan pengurusan. Bidang ini akan terus menjadi tonggak kepada perkembangan Universiti Utara Malaysia. Dengan adanya rangkaian dan sistem komunikasi yang canggih, Universiti Utara Malaysia mampu berkomunikasi secara elektronik dengan universiti-universiti lain di seluruh dunia. Sehubungan itu, saya yakin UUM dapat bergerak maju ke depan dengan mewujudkan apa yang dipanggil sistem pembelajaran jarak jauh atau "distant learning" antara UUM dengan masyarakat luar.

Ini adalah satu usaha baru dalam pengembangan pendidikan pengurusan yang sudah pasti lebih mencabar. Saya juga bangga dengan peranan Universiti Utara Malaysia yang dapat menyediakan peluang latihan jangka pendek untuk para golongan usahawan dan khidmat perundingan dalam bidang pengurusan khususnya di kawasan utara ini. Saya percaya ini akan meningkatkan imej UUM sebagai pusat kecemerlangan dalam bidang pengurusan.

Sejajar dengan Falsafah dan Objektifnya, Universiti Utara Malaysia menggalakkan kakitangan akademiknya menjalankan penyelidikan—asas dan lan-

---

**Di Upacara Konvokesyen Ke-tujuh, Universiti Utara Malaysia Pada Sesi Petang Pada 7hb Ogos, 1994 Di Dewan Mu'adzam Shah, UUM.*

jutan, secara aktif dengan memberi penekanan kepada bidang-bidang yang berteraskan pengurusan menerusi program penyelidikan dan pembangunan (R & D). Saya bangga kerana Universiti Utara Malaysia menggalakkan ahli akademiknya menjalankan kegiatan perundingan sebagai salah satu tugas dalam bidang akademik. Dengan cara ini ahli akademik dapat meningkatkan profesionalisme dan berpengalaman dalam kegiatan perundingan serta penyelidikan. Kepakaran mereka akan bertambah dari segi teori dan penyelidikan.

Sejajar dengan perkembangan pesat negara menuju era perindustrian, Universiti ini telah membuat perancangan untuk bergerak ke arah yang sama bagi membantu negara dalam usaha mencapai tahap negara maju menjelang tahun 2020. Untuk tujuan ini, Universiti ini sentiasa bersedia menangani perkembangan mutahir teknologi dan berupaya mencara paradigma baru dengan mewujudkan kursus yang sesuai untuk keperluan industri. Melalui kerjasama di antara Universiti dengan industri, saya percaya kepakaran dan kemudahan yang ada di Universiti dapat digemblengkan dengan pengalaman industri untuk menghasilkan penemuan teknologi baru serta tenaga mahir yang sesuai dengan keperluan industri maju. Saya bangga kerana Universiti Utara Malaysia peka dalam hal ini dengan menempatkan pelajar-pelajarnya menjalani prakitkum di lebih 1000 buah organisasi di seluruh Malaysia dan juga luar negeri setiap tahun.

Pendidikan adalah penting dalam menerajui sesuatu perubahan dan pembangunan sesebuah negara. Sejarah membuktikan bahawa hanya negara yang menitikberatkan budaya ilmu sahaja yang mampu bersaing.

Dengan itu, untuk merealisasikan Wawasan 2020 adalah menjadi tanggungjawab semua pihak, mewujudkan sistem pendidikan yang terbaik untuk menghasilkan insan yang mempunyai daya ketahanan tinggi bagi memenuhi aspirasi negara. Sejajar dengan ini, sistem pendidikan negara kita mampu mewujudkan insan-insan kreatif ke arah melahirkan bangsa Malaysia yang berjiwa besar, inovatif, futuristik dan progresif. Sistem pendidikan kita menitikberatkan pemupukan bakat kreatif dan kecenderungan terhadap sesuatu bidang yang diminati oleh para pelajar sejak diperingkat awal lagi. Justeru itu, sistem pendidikan kita juga memberi insentif dan penilaian yang lebih kepada pelajar yang kreatif, inovatif dan berupaya mencabar idea lama. Saya yakin bahawa sistem pendidikan masa kini, sama ada diperingkat sekolah mahupun universiti mampu mencetuskan budaya positif dan melahirkan para pelajar yang aktif dan berwibawa.

Dengan perkembangan sains dan teknologi dan bermulanya era baru yang dikatakan sebagai pertembungan antara budaya, kita dikejutkan dengan kejatuhan nilai moral manusia, keruntuhan institusi keluarga dan pencabulan hak asasi. Di Malaysia juga telah dapat dilihat adanya perkembangan tidak menyenangkan yang mungkin berpunca daripada kecenderungan mencontohi dan meniru keadaan di negara-negara barat.

Dalam menghadapi cabaran ini, rakyat Malaysia seharusnya mempunyai keperibadian tersendiri. "Di mana bumi dipijak disitu langit dijunjung" adalah perumpamaan paling tepat yang patut menjadi pegangan semua orang di negara ini, tidak kira apa keturunan dan pegangan agama mereka. Masyarakat Malaysia tidak seharusnya cuba meniru apa yang menjadi amalan masyarakat di negara-negara maju, terutama di barat, dalam usaha mengejar kemajuan ke arah menjadikan negara ini setanding dengan negara maju yang lain. Ini bermakna Universiti harus berperanan untuk menangan bukan sahaja cabaran moral ini, tapi yang lebih besar isu cara gaya kehidupan yang semakin bersenang-senang (complacent). Cara gaya hidup yang terlalu mewah sehingga melupakan tanggungjawab membina tamadun dan kehidupan untuk dunia dan akhirat harus dielakkan.

Saya ingin mengingatkan kepada saudara-saudari bahawa dengan memiliki ijazah bukanlah bermakna berakhir pembelajaran, tetapi ianya adalah titik permulaan kepada satu proses yang berterusan hingga ke akhir hayat. Hari ini merupakan langkah pertama bagi perjalanan beribu batu jauhnya di hadapan. Adalah menjadi harapan saya agar perjalanan itu direstui dengan kejayaan.

Akhir sekali saya berdoa kepada Allah Subhanahu Wata'ala untuk memberikan taufik dan hidayatNya kepada semua anggota masyarakat Universiti Utara Malaysia, moga-moga mereka dapat berusaha bersama-sama bagi mencapai tujuan murni Universiti ini selama-lamanya.

CEMERLANG BAHASA GEMILANG KEADILAN*

Saya bersyukur ke hadrat Allah SWT kerana dengan berkat dan izinNya kita dapat berhimpun bersama di Majlis yang berbahagia ini.

Terlebih dahulu saya ingin merakamkan ucapan tahniah kepada pihak ahli jawatankuasa dan Persatuan Undang-Undang, Universiti Islam Antarabangsa Malaysia di atas inisiatif menganjurkan program "Minggu Bahasa Malaysia : Cemerlang Bahasa Gemilang Keadilan."

Saya juga ingin melahirkan rasa bangga di atas usaha pihak Persatuan Undang-Undang, Universiti Islam Antarabangsa Malaysia kerana mengketengahkan Bahasa Malaysia sebagai pengantar bahasa keadilan. Ini secara tidak langsung menyokong hasrat murni kerajaan untuk mendaulatkan Bahasa Malaysia serta memantapkan penggunaannya di kalangan para pelajar dan pengamal undang-undang, khasnya dan seluruh penduduk Malaysia amnya. Maka dengan ini ia akan dapat menghapuskan keraguan dan rasa sangsi orang ramai terhadap kemampuan Bahasa Malaysia itu sendiri.

Cadangan menjadikan Bahasa Malaysia sebagai bahasa penghantar di mahkamah banyak menimbulkan pro dan kontra daripada pelbagai pihak. Ada sesetengah golongan yang berpendapat bahawa sudah sampailah waktunya Bahasa Malaysia sebagai bahasa kebangsaan diketengahkan ke peringkat yang lebih mencabar. Namun demikian, terdapat juga suara-suara yang meragui kemampuannya sebagai bahasa di mahkamah. Antara hujah yang diutarakan ialah sistem keadilan itu sendiri akan terjejas jika Bahasa Malaysia digunakan.

Sehubungan dengan penggunaan Bahasa Kebangsaan dalam sistem perundangan, saya telah memberi ceramah dalam satu Majlis Makan Malam Tahunan Pelajar Undang-Undang ITM Shah Alam pada 13hb April, 1988 : dimana saya berkata bahawa permulaan kerjaya mereka disaingi dengan perjuangan untuk melaksanakan penggunaan Bahasa Malaysia di bidang perundangan dan mereka perlu berusaha bersungguh-sungguh ke arah ini.

Dalam Majlis Jamuan Makan Malam Persatuan Peguam-Peguam Islam Malaysia di Dewan Tun Dr. Ismail, Pusat Dagangan Putra pada 12hb Februari, 1988 saya juga berkata:

**Di Majlis Perasmian Minggu Undang-Undang Dan Minggu Bahasa Malaysia 1994: Cemerlang Bahasa Gemilang Keadilan Pada 15hb Ogos, 1994 Di Dewan Al-Malik Faisal, Universiti Islam Antarabangsa Malaysia.*

"Wajar kita bertanya sama ada kita masih mampu meneruskan kudrat diri kita untuk mempergiatkan lagi penggunaan Bahasa Kebangsaan di bidang kehakiman mahu pun perundangan. Badan Perundangan berkebolehan pula merangkakan dan menulis undang-undang dalam Bahasa Kebangsaan. Tambahan pula dengan pengiktirafan beberapa institusi pengajian tinggi tempatan, ramai siswazah undang-undang yang telah lulus setelah mendapat didikan dengan menggunakan Bahasa Kebangsaan sebagai bahasa pengantar."

Dalam Kenyataan Rasmi saya menjelang pelaksanaan penggunaan Bahasa Malaysia di Mahkamah pada 31.5.90, saya menekankan bahawa pelaksanaan penggunaan Bahasa Malaysia sepenuhnya di Mahkamah bolehlah dianggap sebagai usaha kemuncak dalam mendaulatkan Bahasa Malaysia di negara kita, memandangkan bidang perundangan dan kehakiman adalah benteng yang terkuat bagi penggunaan Bahasa Inggeris. Mungkin tidak berapa lama dahulu ramai di kalangan kita kurang yakin dengan kemampuan Bahasa Malaysia untuk mengambil alih peranan Bahasa Inggeris sebagai Bahasa Mahkamah. Akan tetapi kesungguhan dari semua pihak yang berusaha dengan ikhlas dan bersungguh-sungguh membuktikan keraguan tersebut ternyata tidak tepat.

Jika dilihat dari sudut sejarah, masyarakat kita telah disemaikan dengan perasaan cinta dan bangga terhadap Bahasa Inggeris itu sendiri. Sebagai contoh, sistem pendidikan kita sebelum merdeka adalah berdasarkan sistem pendidikan Inggeris di mana Bahasa Inggeris menjadi bahasa perantaraan di sekolah dan merupakan matapelajaran utama untuk lulus sebelum melanjutkan pelajaran ke peringkat yang lebih tinggi serta untuk mendapatkan pekerjaan.

Selepas negara mencapai kemerdekaan dalam tahun 1957 dengan kesedaran dan keinsafan di hati para pemimpin yang pada ketika itu yang melihat Bahasa Malaysia ketinggalan di belakang, maka pihak kerajaan telah berusaha menaikkan semula taraf Bahasa Malaysia dengan menjadikan Bahasa Malaysia sebagai bahasa rasmi di negara kita. Ini telah termaktub di dalam Artikel 152 Perlembagaan Persekutuan iaitu Bahasa Malaysia merupakan bahasa kebangsaan.

Di dalam usaha menaikkan taraf Bahasa Malaysia, kita harus sedar bahawa ianya memerlukan tanggungjawab dan peranan semua pihak, di mana pihak media-massa dan masyarakat seluruhnya harus menyokong perjuangan untuk mendaulatkan bahasa ibunda kita. Di antara langkah yang perlu diambil ialah semua pihak harus berusaha menjadikan Bahasa Malaysia sebagai bahasa perpaduan kerana "Bahasa Menyatukan Bangsa".

Manakala di dalam sistem pendidikan Malaysia, pihak Kementerian Pendidikan telah meletakkan garis panduan dan peraturan di mana setiap pelajar diwajibkan lulus di dalam mata pelajaran Bahasa Malaysia sebelum melanjutkan pelajaran ke peringkat yang lebih tinggi.

Kini penggunaan Bahasa Malaysia telah dilaksanakan di dalam sistem perundangan Malaysia di mana Bahasa Malaysia menjadi medium keadilan. Ini merupakan satu langkah yang amat positif dan membuktikan bahawa Bahasa Malaysia menjadi bahasa ilmu dan perundangan. Keunggulan Bahasa Malaysia sememangnya tidak dapat kita nafikan kerana sebelum kedatangan Inggeris ia merupakan 'lingua franca' di nusantara.

Justeru itu kita sebagai generasi baru tentulah tidak ingin melihat bahasa ibunda kita diperkotak-katikkan di tanahair sendiri. Adalah menjadi hasrat kerajaan dan harapan masyarakat Malaysia untuk melihat semula kegemilangan Bahasa Malaysia, bersesuaian dengan tema yang telah dipilih pada tahun ini: "Cemerlang Bahasa Gemilang Keadilan". Sekali lagi sekalung tahniah saya berikan kepada pihak penganjur, Universiti Islam Antarabangsa Malaysia dan juga Dewan Bahasa dan Pustaka di atas usaha yang dilakukan. Sehubungan dengan itu, adalah diharapkan agar program ini dapat mencari formula bagi menangani masalah-masalah yang timbul.

Maka dengan lafaz.

OPENING CEREMONY OF THE COURT OF APPEAL*

Mengadap Seri Paduka Baginda Yang di-Pertuan Agong, Tuanku Ja'afar ibni Almarhum Tuanku Abdul Rahman.
Ampun Tuanku beribu-ribu ampun, sembah patik harap diampun.
Syukur ke hadrat Allah SWT kerana dengan berkat dan izinNya dapat kita semua berhimpun bersama-sama pada hari yang sungguh bahagia ini.

Dengan perkenan Tuanku jua patik bagi pihak semua jemaah hakim bersyukur dan merafak sembah menjunjung setinggi-tinggi kasih di atas limpah perkenan Duli Tuanku berangkat mencemar Duli ke Majlis Perasmian penubuhan Mahkamah Rayuan negara.

Tidak syak lagi keberangkatan Duli Tuanku bukan sahaja menyerikan perasmian ini bahkan juga melambangkan kedaulatan undang-undang.

Di sini patik pohon izin untuk berucap sepatah dua kata pada para hadirin sekalian.

The Honourable President of the Senate, the Speaker of the Dewan Rakyat, the Minister of Law, the Chief Judges of the High Courts, the Attorney-General Malaysia, Ladies and Gentlemen.

Today is indeed a very special day for the judiciary.

Firstly, the judiciary is greatly honoured by the gracious presence of Seri Paduka Baginda Yang di-Pertuan Agong, Tuanku Ja'afar ibni Almarhum Tuanku Abdul Rahman this morning. We are particularly proud of His Majesty's presence in the courts this morning. His Majesty Tuanku Ja'afar is himself a lawyer and has had a distinguished career in the Malaysian diplomatic service.

Secondly, His Majesty's visit to the courts this morning is also significant in one other aspect: today marks another milestone in the evolution of the judiciary in the country—the official opening of the newly established Court of Appeal.

Since the abolition of appeals to the Privy Council in 1985 and the establishment of the then Supreme Court as the highest court of appeal there has been no intermediate court in the Malaysian legal system. The need for such a court has been long felt, and I am happy to note that the Government has ac-

---

**At The Opening Ceremony Of The Court Of Appeal On 17th September, 1994.*

cepted the recommendation of the judiciary to set up this new Court of Appeal.

With the establishment of the Court of Appeal, the Federal Court will now play an even more important role. Being the final court of appeal, a greater responsibility is now placed on the judges of the Federal Court to further develop the laws of the country to suit the nation's needs. As the nation marches towards achieving developed nation status by the year 2020, and after 37 years of independence, it is timely that the judicial system in the country be now firmly established. It can now be said that with the abolition of appeals to the Judicial Committee of the Privy Council followed by the establishment of an intermediate court, the Court of Appeal, the Malaysian judiciary has truly matured.

The newly established Court of Appeal, besides providing a litigant with a further right of appeal, will also filter the number of appeals from the High Court going up to the Federal Court. This will of course necessarily mean that there would be an even faster disposal of appeals so that justice is not seen to be delayed, and hence denied. I am confident that members of the Court of Appeal will fulfil their obligations and responsibilities as expected of them.

At this juncture, may I also take this opportunity to say a few words on the need for all persons to respect our laws, particularly the supreme law of the country, namely the Constitution. As we all know the Constitution sets out the machinery of the three organs of Government, the judiciary being one. At the same time, the Constitution also provides for the fundamental rights of all citizens. It is indeed the most sacred document of the nation and accordingly it should be respected by one and all. Where there is a transgression of any provision of the Constitution, the courts, as the guardians of the Constitution, provide the necessary remedy. Therefore, until then, any act done, or any function performed, or any appointment made thereunder, pursuant to, and strictly in accordance with the provisions of the Constitution, must be respected by all. No one, therefore, is in a position to question or disobey any such act or appointment, unless it has been challenged and subsequently declared to be unconstitutional by the courts. In other words, no person or body of persons can take it upon himself or itself to disregard any constitutional act or appointment. To do so would be tantamount to showing disrespect to the Constitution. As the Federal Court had the occasion once to observe, "The Constitution ... is the supreme law of the land ... and we are a Government of laws and not of men."

Ampun Tuanku, patik sekali lagi merafakkan sembah menjunjung kasih ke bawah Duli Tuanku. Ampun Tuanku. Sekian, wabillahi taufik walhidayah, wassalamu alaikum wabarakatuh.

THE ROLE OF COMMISSIONERS FOR OATHS*

Saya bersyukur ke hadrat Allah SWT kerana dengan berkat dan izinNya kita dapat berkumpul bersama-sama di malam yang bahagia ini.

Permit me to thank the organizers of this function for their kind invitation for me to be present at this dinner and to say a few words. I would therefore, first of all, express my appreciation to the organizers for the honour and privilege extended to me.

This dinner, I am told, is an occasion to mark the formation of the Association of Commissioners for Oaths. I suppose it is an association that is formed with objectives similar to that of the Association for Justices of the Peace and other associations. The main objective will be, generally, to look after the welfare of the Commissioners for Oaths.

Apart from the Commissioners for Oaths who are practising advocates and solicitors, the majority of the serving Commissioners for Oaths are those, who had served either as police officers, civil service officers or who had at one time or another served in the Judicial or Legal Department. Accordingly the majority now serving as Commissioners for Oaths fully understand the rules pertaining to their office. In view of this I would expect the members of the Association to shoulder their responsibilities well, in particular, to ensure that they do not abuse their positions or, in any way deviate from the appropriate legal directions that they are subjected to in the performance of their duties.

Courts take a serious view of documents supposedly to be attested in the presence of Commissioners for Oaths but are not otherwise done in the manner prescribed by law. Should that occur, I believe the appointing authority would view the matter seriously and conceivably a contravention of the legal direction by a Commissioner for Oaths may, most probably, result in his appointment being cancelled and services terminated.

I would urge all Commissioners for Oaths to know the new stringent rules well to avoid breaching them. By maintaining the proper register as required by the rules you are protected, for example, from any allegation of non-execution of any document by any person.

**At The Dinner Of The Association Of Commissioners For Oaths, Wilayah Persekutuan And Selangor Darul Ehsan, At Kelab Darul Ehsan, Ampang On 18th September, 1994.*

At the present time, there are some 448 Commissioners for Oaths throughout Malaysia. The number is growing. The appointments are not automatic or for life. The appointing authority is of the view that those appointed should not only comply with the rules governing them but should also not abuse their position. It is important that all appointed commissioners should exercise the authority given to them by law in accordance with established principles and professional ethics. The Association is at liberty to forward constructive suggestions on matters relating to their duties and functions with a view to effect improvement.

I wish the Association well and it is also my wish to see that all members co-operate with the Association's office-bearers in their efforts to achieve success.

INDEX